READING MEDIA

CRITICAL CULTURAL COMMUNICATION SERIES
General Editors: Jonathan Gray, Aswin Punathambekar, and Adrienne Shaw
Founding Editors: Sarah Banet-Weiser and Kent A. Ono

Dangerous Curves: Latina Bodies in the Media
Isabel Molina-Guzmán

The Net Effect: Romanticism, Capitalism, and the Internet
Thomas Streeter

Our Biometric Future: Facial Recognition Technology and the Culture of Surveillance
Kelly A. Gates

Critical Rhetorics of Race
Edited by Michael G. Lacy and Kent A. Ono

Circuits of Visibility: Gender and Transnational Media Cultures
Edited by Radha S. Hegde

Commodity Activism: Cultural Resistance in Neoliberal Times
Edited by Roopali Mukherjee and Sarah Banet-Weiser

Arabs and Muslims in the Media: Race and Representation after 9/11
Evelyn Alsultany

Visualizing Atrocity: Arendt, Evil, and the Optics of Thoughtlessness
Valerie Hartouni

Authentic™: The Politics of Ambivalence in a Brand Culture
Sarah Banet-Weiser

The Makeover: Reality Television and Reflexive Audiences
Katherine Sender

Love and Money: Queers, Class, and Cultural Production
Lisa Henderson

Cached: Decoding the Internet in Global Popular Culture
Stephanie Ricker Schulte

Black Television Travels: African American Media around the Globe
Timothy Havens

Citizenship Excess: Latino/as, Media, and the Nation
Hector Amaya

Feeling Mediated: A History of Media Technology and Emotion in America
Brenton J. Malin

The Post-Racial Mystique: Media and Race in the Twenty-First Century
Catherine R. Squires

Making Media Work: Cultures of Management in the Entertainment Industries
Edited by Derek Johnson, Derek Kompare, and Avi Santo

Sounds of Belonging: U.S. Spanish-language Radio and Public Advocacy
Dolores Inés Casillas

Technomobility in China: Young Migrant Women and Mobile Phones
Cara Wallis

Orienting Hollywood: A Century of Film Culture between Los Angeles and Bombay
Nitin Govil

Asian American Media Activism: Fighting for Cultural Citizenship
Lori Kido Lopez

Struggling for Ordinary: Media and Transgender Belonging in Everyday Life
Andre Cavalcante

Homegrown: Identity and Difference in the American War on Terror
Piotr M. Szpunar

Dot-Com Design: The Rise of a Useable, Social, Commercial Web
Megan Sapnar Ankerson

Postracial Resistance: Black Women, Media, and the Uses of Strategic Ambiguity
Ralina L. Joseph

Netflix Nations: The Geography of Digital Distribution
Ramon Lobato

Celebrity: A History of Fame
Susan J. Douglas and Andrea McDonnell

Fake Geek Girls: Fandom, Gender, and the Convergence Culture Industry
Suzanne Scott

Locked Out: Regional Restrictions in Digital Entertainment Culture
Evan Elkins

Beyond Hashtags: Racial Politics and Black Digital Networks
Sarah Florini

The Digital City: Media and the Social Production of Place
Germaine R. Halegoua

Distributed Blackness: African American Cybercultures
André Brock, Jr.

Wife, Inc.: The Business of Marriage in the Twenty-First Century
Suzanne Leonard

Race and Media: Critical Approaches
Edited by Lori Kido Lopez

Border Optics: Surveillance Cultures on the US-Mexico Frontier
Camilla Fojas

Dislike-Minded: Media, Audiences, and the Dynamics of Taste
Jonathan Gray

Digital Media Distribution: Portals, Platforms, Pipelines
Edited by Paul McDonald, Courtney Brannon Donoghue, and Timothy Havens

Digital Black Feminism
Catherine Knight Steele

The Identity Trade: Selling Privacy and Reputation Online
Nora A. Draper

Latino TV: A History
Mary Beltrán

The Digital Border: Migration, Technology, Power
Lilie Chouliaraki and Myria Georgiou

Digital Unsettling: Decoloniality and Dispossession in the Age of Social Media
Sahana Udupa and Ethiraj Gabriel Dattatreyan

Streaming Video: Storytelling Across Borders
Edited by Amanda D. Lotz and Ramon Lobato

Chinese Creator Economies: Labor and Bilateral Creative Workers
Jian Lin

Fandom Is Ugly: Networked Harassment in Participatory Culture
Mel Stanfill

Projecting Desire: Media Architectures and Moviegoing in Urban India
Tupur Chatterjee

After Mass Media: Storytelling for Microaudiences in the Twenty-First Century
Amanda D. Lotz

Social Media and Ordinary Life: Affect, Ethics, and Aspiration in Contemporary China
Cara Wallis

Targeted: Corporations and the Police Surveillance Economy
Kelly A. Gates

Reading Media: How to Do Textual Analysis
Edited by Jonathan Gray and Daphne Gershon

Rebooting Inequality: Critical Takes on Film and Television Remakes
Edited by Isabel Molina-Guzmán and Angharad N. Valdivia

Reading Media

How to Do Textual Analysis

Edited by Jonathan Gray and Daphne Gershon

New York University Press
New York

NEW YORK UNIVERSITY PRESS
New York
www.nyupress.org

© 2026 by New York University
All rights reserved

Please contact the Library of Congress for Cataloging-in-Publication data.
ISBN: 9781479830299 (hardback)
ISBN: 9781479830305 (paperback)
ISBN: 9781479830336 (library ebook)
ISBN: 9781479830312 (consumer ebook)

This book is printed on acid-free paper, and its binding materials are chosen for strength and durability. We strive to use environmentally responsible suppliers and materials to the greatest extent possible in publishing our books.

The manufacturer's authorized representative in the EU for product safety is Mare Nostrum Group B.V., Mauritskade 21D, 1091 GC Amsterdam, The Netherlands. Email: gpsr@mare-nostrum.co.uk.

Manufactured in the United States of America

10 9 8 7 6 5 4 3 2 1

Also available as an ebook

CONTENTS

PART I: INTRODUCTION TO TEXTUAL ANALYSIS

1. Welcome to the Text 3
   Jonathan Gray and Daphne Gershon

2. Textual Analysis: The Foundational Method 23
   Susan J. Douglas

3. Producing Meaningful Analyses of Racial Representations 38
   Lori Kido Lopez

PART II: CANONICAL APPROACHES AND THEORIES REVISED

Introduction 53

4. The Upside-Down Comic Book: A Narratological Analysis of M. Night Shyamalan's *Unbreakable* 55
   Patrick Keating

5. At the First Sign: Analyzing Television Posters with Semiotics 68
   Jonathan Gray

6. Fragmented, Playful, Uncomfortable: The Textual Analysis of Digital Games 81
   Diane Carr

7. Historical Poetics and TikTok 96
   Meg L. Thomas and Ted Nannicelli

8. Reading Gender Relations in an Afrobeats Music Video: A Multimodal Textual Analysis 110
   Simphiwe Rens

9. How to Read a Colony on a Game Board: *Settlers of Catan* and Postcolonial Thinking 123
   Souvik Mukherjee

10. An Autotheory for Game Studies: *Shadow of the Colossus* 137
    Soraya Murray

11. Is There an Argument about This Text? Textual Analysis as Collaborative Disputation 151
    Paul Frosh and Lillian Boxman-Shabtai

    PART III: NEW AND UNDEREXPLORED OBJECTS FOR TEXTUAL ANALYSIS

    Introduction 169

12. What Could Rubbish Say? On the Textual Politics of Plastic Waste 171
    Mehita Iqani

13. "That's What We Storytellers Do. We Restore Order with Imagination": Analyzing Decoration and Plot in Walt Disney World Resort's Pandora: The Valley of Mo'ara 184
    Colin Burnett

14. Images on the Move: Close Reading Migrant- and Refugee-Authored Media Online 199
    Eszter Zimanyi

15. Reading the Effects Program: The *Mission: Impossible* Series and Special/Visual Effects Discourse 213
    Julie Turnock

    PART IV: TEXTUAL ANALYSIS ACROSS TEXTS

    Introduction 229

16. "Such Amaze, Much Wow" (Or How to Read a Meme) 231
    Anirban K. Baishya

17. A Textual Analysis of #RIPTwitter 246
    Raven Maragh-Lloyd

18. The *Dateline* Formula: True Crime, Genre, and Citizenship 259
    Laurie Ouellette

19. Playing with Patterns: An Approach to Analyzing
    Children's Television Texts   273
    Kyra Hunting

20. A New Situation: Textual Analysis Across TV Texts   286
    Daphne Gershon

21. Transmedia Tarantino: Reading the Many Texts of
    Once Upon a Time in Hollywood   300
    Henry Jenkins

    PART V: COMBINING TEXTUAL ANALYSIS
    WITH OTHER METHODS

    Introduction   317

22. Exploring Soundwork: Texts, Technologies, and
    Cultural Form   318
    Michele Hilmes

23. Patterns and Categories: Connecting Textual Features
    and Industrial Conditions   330
    Amanda D. Lotz

24. Audience-Led Textual Analysis: The Case of *Bridgerton*'s
    Daphne Raping the Duke   342
    Joke Hermes

25. Analyzing Texts Using Sounds and Images: Making
    Video Essays as Critical Practice   354
    Jason Mittell

26. Getting Critical: How NPR's TV Critic Analyzes Media
    for a Mass Audience   365
    Eric Deggans

    About the Contributors   379

    Index   385

PART I

Introduction to Textual Analysis

1

Welcome to the Text

JONATHAN GRAY AND DAPHNE GERSHON

Introducing the book, Gray and Gershon first offer working definitions of what constitutes a text and how we might study it through textual analysis. They then consider the state of textual analysis in the 2020s and its need for reinvigoration and rejuvenation.

Ours is truly a world full of media. Recent decades have given us not just more media, but exponentially more than previously produced, in a staggering abundance and variety: more television shows on more platforms, more podcasts, more films, more video games, more radio, more comics, more books, more music, more photos, and many more short videos. All these media have things to say, things they want us to think, feel, or better understand. As Paul Frosh writes, media are "generators for constructing and revealing worlds—including the 'actual' world that we imagine we live in and possible worlds that we propose as alternatives or refuges."[1] But what are these different texts saying, what are they generating, and how are they doing so? How do they work? Traditionally, textual analysis has been the preeminent method for answering such questions.

Yet, while textual analysis has been a tried-and-true method, in recent years, it has also been viewed as a lackluster, unremarkable, and even outmoded form of analysis, rarely approached with as much enthusiasm and intellectual curiosity as other, newer methodological approaches within the field. As a result, the method of textual analysis has fallen out of fashion for many within media, communication, and cultural studies, thereby resulting in fewer textual analyses at a time when more thoughtful, close, and inventive analysis is especially needed. This book aims to address this gap between textuality and the study of texts, by calling for a revitalization of textual analysis as method. Across its pages and chapters, our authors offer a diverse toolkit for conducting high-quality, probing, and innovative textual analysis, and we hope they will inspire more textual analysis, not only by showcasing the continued value of this method, but also by pointing to new and underexplored directions, approaches, and cultural objects.

From the outset, let us be clear that we are not methodological zealots, calling for only textual analysis. A full and rich understanding of media's roles, places, and functions in society requires exacting analysis of production, reception, technology, history, and context too. But studying those parts of the picture is not enough, and thus, we also want to see more and better textual analysis. And by "better," we mean textual analysis with method and direction, elements that we view as especially vital for a method that for too long has been misunderstood as intuitive or self-explanatory. We also want textual analysis to grow alongside the media environment: a method designed for literary analysis, and adapted for television and film, needs yet more adaptation to work better on texts of the digital era, including memes, TikToks, and more.

We want more and better textual analysis for the academy, yes, and especially for media, communication, and cultural studies, but we also want more and better textual analysis in everyday life. One of the key reasons textual analysis is so consequential, yet also trivialized and dismissed, is that it is—or at least *should be*—not solely the domain of skilled researchers, but a practice most people engage in on a daily basis. When people ask, for example, What did you think of last night's episode? What does that review of this movie get wrong? What does your favorite book do or say that nothing else does or says as well? Why do you think kids should or should not have access to that webpage? Why does it excite or anger you that this comic book character was cast this way in the adaptation? they take part in conversations that revolve around and could benefit from textual analysis. Moreover, social discourse and media coverage frequently invoke textual analysis in calling for greater "media literacy," or in using phrases such as "representation matters." These private and public conversations, however, too rarely engage with the complexity of texts and the methodical ways in which we can interrogate their meanings. Our hope is that shedding light on the specific tools and procedures that textual analysis entails will encourage those within and outside of academia to engage in a more careful and methodical analysis of the messages, operations, mechanics, meanings, and resonances of relevant texts.

Before we journey onwards, though, and before we elaborate further upon the waning of textual analysis in the twenty-first century, we should clear up, first, what we even mean by texts and textual analysis and, second, on what basis we opine that there is not enough textual analysis, or that it could be better. Let us take each in turn.

Of Meanings and Definitions: What Is a Text?

Not everyone agrees on exact definitions of texts, textual analysis, or what they should entail. Broadly speaking, though, we consider a text to be (1) a relatively discrete unit (2) of meaning for analysis, interpretation, and understanding, (3) almost definitely created or devised by a specific person or people working together. A song is a text, for instance, as is a television show, a podcast, a film, a video game, or a newspaper article, since all are relatively discrete units of meaning for analysis, interpretation, and understanding, created by specific people.

That might seem like a simple enough definition for a second or three, but all sorts of tricky cases present themselves thereafter. What counts as *a discrete unit*, for instance? If a song is a text, is an album also a text? How about the entire collection of a given artist's songs? Here, the answer is determined by social practice, so we ask first whether the album or collection is *treated* as discrete and unified in some way, and second—even if it currently is not—whether that argument could be made. Taking Taylor Swift's music as an example, Swiftie fan discourse recasts each album as its own "era," with fans debating which era is best. That debate treats each album as a relatively discrete unit of meaning—*Folklore* is saying and doing at least some things that *1989* is not. Or, stepping back further, fans and nonfans alike regularly see specific meanings, styles, tones, themes, or resonances in Swift's music that they see as distinct (for better or worse) from the work of others, in ways that rely upon notions of distinction and coherency. And so, we could say that there is a text of Swift's music, or indeed layers of text—song, album, entire work. By contrast, treating a single verse of a song as its own text is more dubious, though possible if for instance it travels—through regular quoting—by itself. Other media texts may more naturally seem to break off into more obviously text-like smaller parts: television shows or podcasts come in discrete episodes, for instance, and a single book of poetry may contain discrete, separate poems. As for series of texts also being texts, if they are not generally treated as connected, as clearly different from others, they should not count as texts.

Why is a text only "relatively" discrete, not fully so? Because language ensures that no meaning is ever wholly discrete, or in the words of Julia Kristeva, "Any text is constructed as a mosaic of quotations; any text is the absorption and transformation of another."[2] We only understand any word, image, or symbol because we have a textual history with it, and indeed any textual creator launches it into a specific moment in textual history, for as Mikhail Bakhtin writes, "Any speaker is himself a respondent to a greater or lesser degree. He is not, after all, the first speaker, the one who disturbs the eternal silence of the universe."[3] Everything that was part of that textual history is invited into the process of meaning-making, through what is called intertextuality.[4] Intertexts are most obvious when they allude to specific texts—if we encounter a character called Mr. Macbeth, we're invited intertextually to "import" meaning from *Macbeth* to frame and inform our understanding of him. Sequels or prequels also piggyback meaning on other texts, while reboots and remakes may rely heavily on us seeing differences from past versions of a character or scene to appreciate the current version. But in truth, all texts are brimming with intertextual meaning that may unpredictably connect to all sorts of other texts: a flower may have particular meaning for some viewers who've seen a prominent use of it in another text, an actor's presence may invite us to read in elements of other characters they've played, a song's use might invoke other uses elsewhere. No text, in short, is wholly discrete, but for analytical purposes we can view most texts as *relatively* discrete.

Our second stipulation is that a text must be a unit *of meaning for analysis, interpretation, and understanding*. While many of the objects of textual analysis may not even include any written words, consisting mainly of audio or visual language, these cultural objects are nevertheless referred to as "texts," in order to signal that they too, like any traditional written text, employ, as Stuart Hall notes, "symbolic means, shaped by rules, conventions and traditions intrinsic to the use of language," thereby making them structures of meaning.[5] Just as the meanings of a book are created through its various chapters, sentences, and words, in the ways they are arranged, television shows, films, podcasts, and TikToks similarly possess different sections and components that together produce meaning. First, "meaning" need not take the form of a "message" per se, as feelings and resonances are literally meaning-ful too. Some meanings are more tonal, less enunciative. For example, in describing how analysts identify the underlying meanings of texts and their recurring themes, Hall notes that "position, placing, treatment, tone, stylistic intensification, striking imagery, etc., are all ways of registering emphasis."[6] Second, meaning need not be intentional, and instead, the question for textuality should be simpler: did meaning occur? As above, this veers us back to social practice, and even to relativity, allowing that some things are meaningful to some people, meaningless to others. And thus, third, meaning may be additive, created and built upon over time.[7]

This opens the door wide to a fourth point, namely that meaning needn't be singular. A song, for example, may mean one thing to one group, another to others. The recognition of the many meanings of a single text also distinguishes textual analysis from content analysis. Content analysis strives to reach a state of reliability in which different researchers agree on the meaning and categorization of a text. Rather than attempt to eliminate or ignore polysemy and the power of interpretation, though, good textual analysis will acknowledge and even embrace these complexities.[8]

Still, the awareness of multiple interpretations has also risked surrendering the text entirely to the user's whims. Indeed, some theorists of textuality have insisted that any text can mean anything, most famously Stanley Fish, with his declaration that "the reader's response is not *to* the meaning; it *is* the meaning."[9] And it is not just theorists who might make this move: Cornel Sandvoss has expressed concern that some fans have rendered their beloved objects not just "polysemic" (having multiple meanings) but "neutrosemic," open to meaning anything whatsoever.[10] Recognition of the multiplicity and mutability of meaning has certainly lead some scholars to abandon textual analysis and lose faith in its utility. Yet, we encourage our readers not to view the existence of polysemy as a deterrence, but instead to let it instead encourage us to develop more sophisticated analyses, grounded in an understanding of broader social norms and ideologies, cultural contexts, industrial contexts, media, authorship, paratexts, and genres, in order to contextualize the possible interpretations of the text and help identify its dominant reading. Such a move would turn what might be perceived as a methodological weakness into a methodological strength.

Our final stipulation, that a text is *almost definitely created or devised by a specific person or people working together*, requires further elucidation too.[11] Collaboration should not mean something as broad as working on something vaguely similar in a different time and place, as is the case with genre, for example, but thereafter, we should still regard collaboration, creation, and authorship somewhat capaciously. Some texts absolutely and easily have a singular author figure, but many have a team of creators working on them. This fact may itself contribute to a multiplicity of meanings—maybe the artist and the writer of a comic book, for example, weren't entirely in sync with each other (not necessarily a bad thing, as we should expect and hope for creative people to have different ideas). In many cases, we can squabble over exactly who should be accorded authorial/creative credit, or how much, and who should not, while still acknowledging the presence of a text. But for the sake of our definition of a text, we note some special cases.

One comes in the form of a franchise. Consider the Marvel Cinematic Universe (MCU), for instance, where most films have a different director and writer(s), and may have mostly or completely different crew, and furthermore may be based on stories by a range of different comic book writers. However franchises typically have overseers, whose job is to ensure a certain level of coherence. Sometimes these are specific people (Kevin Feige has been one of the key people to play this role for the MCU, for instance), sometimes a corporation (Marvel or Disney). Or it might work as a baton that is passed from one creative team to another, so that even reboots with entirely new creators regularly use interviews and such to actively create some form of connection to the original material, in ways that encourage and allow us still to talk about, for instance, the *text* of Batman, James Bond, or Mad Max.[12]

Another special case comes in the form of paratexts, a term offered by Gerard Genette, referring to all those things that surround a text that may not be considered a proper part of it, yet that constantly refer to it and create meaning for it nonetheless.[13] Writing of books, for instance, Genette saw the cover, preface, typeface, and page quality as paratextual, but also interviews with authors, ads for the book, and other paratexts not physically appended to the work. Following Genette, elsewhere Jonathan Gray has argued for the utter importance of paratexts to the creation of meaning: "Paratexts are not simply add-ons, spinoffs, and also-rans: they create texts, they manage them, and they fill them with many of the meanings that we associate with them."[14] Paratexts necessarily expand our understanding of specific people working together, since the various acts of creation may be separated entirely from each other: someone designing a book cover in 2024 for Jane Austen's *Sense and Sensibility* is obviously not "working together" with Austen, but so too are advertising teams regularly divorced from primary creators, and so forth. And thus, some analysts will see the paratext as separate and distinct from the text, though we ourselves follow Gray's earlier insistence that it is only separate from the "work," but very much a part of the overall text as the relatively discrete unit of meaning for interpretation and understanding.[15]

Texting in Class: What Is Textual Analysis?

Armed with a working definition of the text, and since questions of practice are now upon us, let us now turn to the question of what constitutes textual analysis. Ultimately, we defer to the rest of the book's contributors, as we are less interested in strict boundary maintenance than in a big tent approach that sees textual analysis happening between and among many practitioners, not as a singular act with set rules. If textual analysis has lost practitioners along the way, that result may in part have followed from too many overzealous commentators planting flags and demanding that it *must* be done this or that way. Each of these commentators has had their reasons, concerned about what is lost or gained by, for instance, caring about aesthetics (or caring about them in certain ways), moving beyond analysis to interpretation, or not attending to audience and production realities while doing so.[16] Our interests, however, lie in offering various ways forward, some of which may serve one political or aesthetic project, some of which may serve another. Indeed, this is why this book is an edited collection, the product of many voices, not a monograph entailing only our own. But if that seems a cop-out, let us sketch out a few propositions here.

First, we return to our own earlier, troubling suggestion that texts can mean anything. If that's true, why bother with textual analysis? Why not go straight to the audience? Certainly, we see great importance in audience research. But as Fish himself noted in response to concerns that he was making the study of meaning entirely relativist, just because a text can, *in theory*, mean absolutely anything doesn't mean that it will, *in practice*, have limitless meanings. Fish attributed that to "interpretive communities," arguing that meaning will be produced not just individually, and that certain interpretive communities are more or less powerful, thereby exerting more or less power over what is publicly seen as an acceptable meaning.[17] That response fairly encourages us to think about meaning as socially, not textually, constructed, but we personally still see texts as anchoring a great deal. "Bad" readings or "mis-readings," as Umberto Eco noted, struggle with finding coherence across the text—we might see one line that encourages a particular reading, for instance, but does the rest of the text support or dismiss that reading?[18] Readings are also sometimes unpredictable and hence not worth studying: sure, we could say that *Star Wars* is about how great cheese is, but such a reading has no defensible mooring in the text, and even the dairy lobby is not powerful enough to constitute an "interpretive community" that is likely enough to encourage others to read such a meaning into *Star Wars*, so no self-respecting academic should care about that reading (unless they are explicitly interested in bizarre audience readings). However, everything in a text establishes points that each audience member should consider as they make sense of it. Textual analysis is the act of drawing connections between those points, connections that are salient enough that we can and should expect many others to connect them similarly. And thus, textual analysis is about working out our best hypotheses for which paths most audiences will follow, based on what we see before us. As Hall explains, it is this process that also demonstrates the rigor and empiricism of textual analysis. He writes:

> The error is to assume that . . . because literary/linguistic analysis steers clear of code-building it is merely intuitive and unreliable. Literary/linguistic types of analysis also employ evidence: they point, in detail, to the text on which an interpretation of latent meaning is based; they indicate more briefly the fuller supporting or contextual evidence which lies to

hand; they take into account material which modifies or disproves the hypotheses which are emerging; and they *should* (they do not always) indicate in detail why one rather than another reading of the material seems to the analyst the most plausible way of understanding it.[19]

Moreover, even if we wanted to eschew textual analysis completely, after all, and enter a world of only audience research, audiences are hard or even impossible, and often very expensive, to study. Practically, therefore, with *some* research questions, we are far more likely to get further with good textual analysis than with really bad audience research. Or, better yet, we will likely get further with both textual analysis and audience research (ideally when both are good!). Furthermore, the issue of the multiplicity of meaning can still be found within audience studies, for just as media texts can be interpreted in different ways, so too can audiences' interpretations of texts.

Our discussion of texts above, though, also raises questions about what we analyze. We have noted the disagreements that some have over whether to study paratexts, for instance. Other disagreements may be caused by intertextuality, as some may see the textual analyst's job as requiring an excavation of all known intertexts, while others may not. And as the textual world fills with ever more remakes, reboots, sequels, franchises, and other textual continuations, perhaps some texts force our hand more than others. In a new iteration of Batman, for instance, *can* we analyze various elements that exist across multiple past Batmans— Commissioner Gordon, the Batmobile, the killing of Batman's parents, the character of Gotham City, Batman's vigilantism and view of criminal justice institutions—without reference to those past meanings and texts? Or even if new elements exist, how can we not see them in relation to their previous nonexistence? And yet, even as some intertexts cry out for consideration, again, we offer no prescription for what *all* analysts *must* do; we only insist that *across* analysis, the doors opened by intertextuality not be foolishly closed simply to create tidier analysis.

In general, as befits the structure of this book, what we call for is not more of a specific type of textual analysis, but a flourishing of types. Greedily, we want some more of already-established types, and more experimentation with new ways to do textual analysis; more of media already examined, more of media not sufficiently examined; more in a familiar format, more in a novel format. But before we get there, we now ask where textual analysis finds itself in media, communication, and cultural studies in the mid-2020s.[20]

The Current State of Textual Analysis in Media, Communication, and Cultural Studies

Textual analysis may seem deceptively familiar to most university students. After all, it is one of the few methods of media analysis taught in primary and secondary schools. Most of us arrive at a university untrained in content analysis, critical media industry studies, ethnography, archival work, interface analysis, walk-through methods, audience research, and most of the other methods we might eventually use in media studies, yet surely we have all written book reports and analyses of novels and/or plays before we arrive. Some may therefore understandably believe that textual analysis is already in our tool kit. Even if we didn't study film, television, video games, or other nonprint media in our high schools, we might think, "How hard can it be to apply the same tools we applied to *Macbeth*, *To Kill a Mockingbird*, *Lord of the Flies*, *Animal Farm*, or *The Giver* to a different medium?" And if students are thinking that, instructors might be thinking it too, hoping students already know how to analyze texts, thereby allowing said instructors to focus their efforts on other methods, theories, and content.

Textual analysis, then, may never truly be a new method, but one that nevertheless should be honed, developed, and advanced, in order to attend to and account for the specifics and new characteristics of each form. Still, not all skills need or deserve universal practice, so why *should* we work on our skills of textual analysis? Because texts are everywhere, and indeed it is their ubiquity that makes media studies exciting and vital for many. Our primary and secondary school teachers taught us well that books, plays, short stories, and poems are texts we can analyze, yes; but so are songs, films, television shows, video games, social media reels and shorts, tweets, podcasts, comic books, photos, posters and billboards, webpages, magazines and newspapers, and interfaces; and even many everyday objects become texts, from architecture to clothing, vehicles to collectibles and onwards. We interact with texts constantly. Admittedly, many are simple or shallow, requiring little analysis or interpretation. But many others are dense and rich with meanings and resonances that cannot easily be gleaned from a quick glance at their surface (or a quick listen, if they are sonic). No matter what other questions we might ask of media, being able to read them and make sense of them as texts matters. Even media and cultural studies methods that seem decidedly separate from textual analysis rely on presumptions of what texts are doing or saying, and/or require us to create other texts to be read (the text of an interview with a producer or audience member, for instance). Textual analysis is an ur-method, therefore, one we all use as citizens and consumers, one that all media scholars and students must use, and hence one we should all develop. This is why we worry about media, communication, and cultural studies' dwindling focus on and care for textual analysis, and why this book aims to encourage more and better textual analysis.

An obvious exception to media, communication, and cultural studies' ambivalence toward texts and textual analysis is film studies. No fair observer could accuse film studies of dropping the ball on teaching textual analysis. Certainly, almost all of the major competing textbooks for film studies are books about textual analysis, teaching their readers how to parse various shot compositions, styles of editing, and more. On the one hand, then, if one's introduction to media, communication, and cultural studies comes in a department or program featuring film studies, one is sure to be introduced to a vast vocabulary and toolset for appreciating the form and composition of visual texts.

On the other hand, many media, communication, and cultural studies programs are not based in film studies. Some began from within the social sciences, and hence a humanistic approach like film studies was never in the cards, but it should be noted that many other media, communication, and cultural studies programs were developed in tension with (a certain version of) film studies. Film studies' focus on form appeared myopic to some, ignoring the text as social and cultural actor, veering too concertedly away from issues such as representation, social power, ideology, and identity. For its part, this "neoformalist" vein of film studies, often associated most with David Bordwell and Kristin Thompson, saw itself as focusing on aspects of the text that were too often forgotten in a headlong race to determine message and ideology.[21] Moreover, it saw the act of interpretation as too often predetermined, guaranteeing its own outcome from the outset, and as categorically unable to appreciate art—and the *experience* of art—as more than just a slew of messages.

It is our contention that this battle between film studies and cultural and communication studies hobbled the prospects for textual analysis to flourish. In the acrimonious divorce between scholarly disciplines that occurred in some programs, one side walked away caring about a close, exacting, and rigorous method of analyzing form, yet variously suspicious of or simply uninterested in "interpretive" acts, while the other cared deeply about ideological messages and representation, yet had too little method for excavating such messages, and simplistically regarded form and aesthetics as irrelevant. Both endeavors produced some superb scholarship, for sure, and we are sympathetic to each side's concerns. But if disciplinary history has often asked students to sign up for Team Form or Team Content, we propose Team Both. Bordwell and Thompson productively insisted that, as Michael Z. Newman notes, form and content "tend to blend together inseparably [so that] the meanings of the text can be hard to grasp without understanding form and content as one," and though some used that observation to retreat into one or the other, let us instead give new life to textual analysis by caring deeply about form *and* content, style *and* message.[22] For one, disciplinary wars can be tedious, and we don't doubt that these wars lost textual analysis potential practitioners along the way. Part of our call to move beyond these disciplinary scars is a call for a reinvigorated textual analysis that both learns from the techniques of formal analysis that film studies developed *and* engages and systematizes analyses of representation, social power, ideology, and identity. Some programs and scholars have integrated this approach all along, of course (hence our inviting several of them to contribute to this present collection), but we would love to see a media, communication, and cultural studies that cares as deeply about textual analysis as film studies has classically, *and* as deeply about texts as cultural actors as cultural studies has classically.

But if many analysts have eschewed textual analysis and moved to supposedly more exciting methods, finding them more vibrant and/or relevant, we cannot or should not blame interarea squabbles and positionings alone. Another key challenge that exists for a would-be textual analyst who cares about texts as cultural actors is that the rationale behind such textual analysis has arguably eroded in the last few decades. A key reason why texts have been analyzed throughout media, communication, and cultural studies' history is because of their perceived cultural and political power, which has stemmed from their wide-ranging reach as mass media. To take a stark example, when in January 1953 71.7 percent of television sets in the USA were tuned to CBS to watch "Lucy Goes to Hospital," an episode of *I Love Lucy* (CBS, 1951–57) where Lucy gives birth to Little Ricky, of course this episode matters for media representations of pregnancy and mothering. Of course it should be studied and analyzed. And though few texts in world history have commanded as large a portion of their potential audience as did that episode in the US, media, communication, and cultural studies' early years were also years in which hit television programs could pull in forty million viewers (in the US), and between a third and a half of all people watching at that moment. Then came cable and satellite TV, the rise of video games, the Internet, mobile and social media, and podcasting, splitting the audience among so many more venues and sites. First VHS, then DVD and Blu-ray, then ultimately streaming technologies also ruptured the synchronicity of much earlier mass media within each nation, though of course staggered release windows had meant that mass media were always asynchronous in *global* terms. Today, then, texts struggle to command either the same viewer numbers or the same levels of press amplification. Prominent exceptions exist: films from big franchises like Marvel, Star Wars, or Harry Potter; musicians like BTS, Taylor Swift, or Beyoncé; and some sports broadcasts. But as Amanda Lotz argues, we would be wise to accept that the era of truly massive mass media was a historical blip, as most texts must now aspire—as they did for most of human history—to reach a much smaller audience.[23]

As mass audiences dwindle, though, so too might the obvious rationale for studying many texts. If a television show or video game reaches "only" one million people, if a popular board game or podcast reaches "only" three hundred thousand people, can or should we muster the same drive to study what textual messages it is offering those people? Or does textual analysis risk becoming an arcane act of studying the tree that fell in the forest with very few people hearing? Such an act might seem to produce little more than a catalog of thumbs-up or thumbs-down verdicts on yet more already-canceled, largely unconsumed texts.

We have also seen textual analysis become a wing of fan studies, perhaps producing superb readings, but ones that are designed for other fans alone, leaving the broader significance, interest in theory-building, and hence relevance to the field aside. We do not mean to censure such readings, but they still leave us asking what roles remain for textual analysis *for the field*, not just for any particular fandom. As fans, we might care deeply about the meaning of this or that scene, character, relationship, or plot development, but the challenge for media, communication, and cultural studies analysis has always been and should remain, when textual analysis is offered to a broader community, why does it matter, and what does it have to tell us about the grander workings of texts, identity, aesthetics, industries, representation, power, language, audiences, technology, our moment in history, or so forth? Textual analysis has always existed in part for fans, and we hope it always will, but what purposes should or *must* it serve for the field at large? We posit that currently there is no clear answer.

And thus we call not just for a resurfacing of textual analysis as method, but for a reinvention and reinvigoration, redesigning it for the current era. "Standard rules" may apply for the megahits—what *do* Taylor Swift's songs say about gender, for instance, to the many millions who hear them? Or what does the Marvel Cinematic Universe say about heroism, nation, race, dis/ability, or more?—but are there other rationales for performing textual analysis that we can develop for lesser-consumed texts? And are there new forms and practices of textual analysis that could better account for our current media era? We do not attempt to answer this question here in our Introduction, but note that many of this collection's authors provide strong answers.

Meanwhile, as the media environment has shifted, many "new" objects have come into existence, objects that may need new methods for studying. If we have all learned some form of textual analysis in our primary and secondary schools, usually applying it to novels, plays, short stories, and poems, that form of analysis may help us to make sense of narratives and dialogue across various audiovisual media, such as television shows, films, and video games. But part of film studies' labor has involved developing a large host of techniques for studying visual texts and moving images. Sound studies scholars, meanwhile, have worked against a general privileging of the visual to offer ways in which sound can and should be analyzed. But even more updating is required. How do we study a brief video on social media, for instance? Or a video game whose play is as or more important than its plot or dialogue? Or a meme, a hashtag, a selfie, or a social media challenge? As texts proliferate across media, how do we study these various instantiations, such as merchandise, advertising, theme park rides, or websites? Again, many of this collection's authors provide answers, thereby making textual analysis as useful and as vital a method for analyzing the media artifacts that surround us in the 2020s as it once was for media objects from decades past.

Importantly, then, this edited collection not only explains why we should still care about textual analysis, but also demonstrates how to *do* textual analysis, offering a concrete step-by-step manual. There are some books about methodology that focus mainly on the theoretical reasoning behind the method, its history, the ethical concerns it may entail, or the reasons why this method is so valuable. Though this book at times touches on these issues, at its core it is about the practice of textual analysis and the ways of operationalizing method. This is especially important when it comes to textual analysis because, as we have mentioned previously, the actual steps and procedures of textual analysis are rarely acknowledged and discussed. As Glen Creeber notes, "Textual analysis has sometimes been shockingly poor at explaining and accounting for itself," with practitioners showing insufficient awareness and reflexivity of its various processes.[24] To help remedy this, almost all of the chapters in this book are divided into two parts. The first part includes a more general description of an approach to textual analysis, while the second part includes a detailed example of this analysis in action, with our contributors walking readers through a step-by-step account of their analysis. In the process, this instructional guide offers a transparency that we believe has been sorely needed. Rosalind Gill, in describing the method of discourse analysis, notes that just because its skills "do not lend themselves to procedural description" and can be seen as "elusive," "there is no need for them to be deliberately mystified and placed beyond the reach of all but the cognoscenti."[25] Similarly, we too seek to demystify and outline the very procedures of textual analysis that may have been deemed by others as either too intuitive or too slippery to explain. The authors in this collection address how we might decide which texts to examine, how to find and gather relevant texts, how to break texts down and decide which questions to ask, what features to pay attention to, how to take notes, how to contextualize our analyses, and how to organize information and to present our findings. Through these inventive analyses that offer clarity, transparency, and rigor, our authors provide resources and tools for both novice students and experienced researchers. This instructional book serves as a guide for those who wish to learn more about textual analysis, who are curious as to how to deconstruct new or unfamiliar texts, and who wish to view textual analysis through new perspectives.

We could not include every approach or possible object of analysis. Rhetorical analysis is absent as an approach, for instance, as is journalism as an object of analysis. We privileged those approaches and objects more likely to appear in a media studies classroom (where, for instance, rhetorical studies and journalism studies often command separate classes). But in general we encourage readers to treat the book as a trampoline or launch pad, not as a destination: please use these techniques to launch yourself freely into other realms, to consider other objects, or even to innovate other approaches.

The Book Ahead

Our challenge to almost all of our contributors in this collection was to tell readers how or why to perform textual analysis in a certain way, and then to actually do it. Therefore, after our three introductory essays, every chapter not only makes the case for or explicates a specific method, but also includes at least one extended example that shows how this method works in action. We asked some of our contributors to revisit key approaches to textual analysis, so that the book doesn't just look forward to new approaches, but also looks back and considers already extant approaches. Other contributors were tasked specifically with the act of innovation, asked to develop new approaches. At times that innovation was required by the nature of the object: selfies (Zimanyi), hashtags (Maragh-Lloyd), or memes (Baishya), for instance, might all require new practices. At times the innovation stems from applying an extant approach to a nontraditional object, as with, for example, Colin Burnett's "plot analysis" of a theme park ride, or Souvik

Mukherjee's postcolonial critique of a board game. We also tasked three of our authors to discuss how audience research (Hermes), production analysis (Lotz), and both technological and historical analysis (Hilmes) might intersect and interact with textual analysis. And the book closes with Jason Mittell's argument for textual analysis in video form and Eric Deggans's discussion of popular criticism outside the academy, as they and we aim to challenge the boundaries of how and where textual analysis occurs.

We offer separate section introductions and abstracts at the top of each chapter so that readers may work out their own, alternate paths through the book. But our own loose structuring method somewhat follows some of the above striations.

Part I offers three chapters (including the one you're currently reading) that together aim to situate textual analysis at this current conjunctural moment, considering the method's past, present, and possible futures in media studies.

Part II then offers a series of approaches to textual analysis, in order: narratology, semiotics and paratextual analysis, fragmentary/lexial analysis, historical poetics, feminist content analysis and multimodal analysis, postcolonial critique, autotheory, and collaborative disputation. The opening chapters consider some "greatest hits" of textual analysis approaches, before the final two chapters offer "fresh cuts," proposing newer ways to engage the text.

Continuing with novel approaches, Part III offers four provocations for analysis of particular types of objects either not usually considered by textual analysts, or not considered in the careful ways of their authors—trash/rubbish, theme parks and experiences, refugee and migrant selfies, and special effects and effects discourse.

In Part IV, the texts become explicitly plural, the approaches now designed to consider movement across and between them. This tension is operative in other parts of the book, but is more focal in this part, which offers approaches to textual meanings that don't inhabit singular textual bodies, considering, in turn, memes, hashtags, genres, patterns, situations, and transmedia.

Part V then closes with various extensions. Its first three chapters each model textual analysis used in conjunction with other methods—namely, historical and technological analysis, industrial analysis, and audience analysis—while the last two discuss and model how textual analysis can work, respectively, in videographic form, and when written for the popular nonacademic audience.

We close with NPR television critic Eric Deggans to underline that textual analysis needn't exist "only" in and for academia. We are surrounded by media. Many of us spend substantial portions of our waking hours engaging—whether actively and intentionally, or passively and accidentally—with so very much media. Textual analysis helps us make better sense of these media, allowing us to see deeper structures and meanings, to appreciate deeper resonances both of the media in question and across other media. We intend this book, therefore, to help readers hone those skills, whether with the ultimate aim of becoming a full-time, paid textual analyst; a dabbler in the art; or "just" a media-literate, savvy reader, user, viewer, listener, player, and contemplator of media.

We extend our sincere thanks to this book's contributors for helping us assemble this diverse, comprehensive, and detailed guide. We would also like to thank our anonymous reviewers for their thoughtful feedback; Lesley Stevenson, for her assistance in formatting and editing; the Critical Cultural Communication series' editors Aswin Punathambekar and Adrienne Shaw; and NYU Press's superb Eric Zinner and Furqan Sayeed for their continued support and expert shepherding of this project. Jonathan also wishes to acknowledge and thank George and Pamela Hamel for their continuing, gracious support.

Notes

1 Paul Frosh, *The Poetics of Digital Media* (London: Polity, 2019), xix.
2 Julia Kristeva, "Word, Dialogue, and Novel," in *Desire in Language: A Semiotic Approach*, translated by Thomas Gora, Alice Jardine, and Leon S. Roudiez (Oxford: Basil Blackwell, 1980), 66.
3 Mikhail Bakhtin, *Speech Genres and Other Late Essays*, translated by Vern W. McGee (Austin: University of Texas Press, 1986), 69.
4 See Kristeva, "Word, Dialogue, and Novel"; Bakhtin, *Speech Genres*; Valentin Volosinov, *Marxism and the Philosophy of Language*, translated by Ladislav Matejka and I. R. Titunik (London: Seminar Press, 1973).
5 Stuart Hall, "Introduction," in *Paper Voices: The Popular Press and Social Change, 1935–1965*, edited by Anthony C. H. Smith, Elizabeth Immirzi, and Trevor Blackwell (London: Chatto & Windus, 1975), 17.

6   Hall, "Introduction," 15.
7   Jonathan Gray, "When Is the Author?," in *A Companion to Media Authorship*, edited by Jonathan Gray and Derek Johnson (Malden, MA: Wiley-Blackwell, 2013), 88–111.
8   For more on the limitations of content analysis versus textual analysis, see Siegfried Kracauer, "The Challenge of Qualitative Content Analysis," *Public Opinion Quarterly* 16, no. 4 (1952–53): 631–42.
9   Stanley Fish, *Is There a Text in This Class? The Authority of Interpretive Communities* (London: Harvard University Press, 1980), 3.
10 Cornel Sandvoss, "One-Dimensional Fan: Toward an Aesthetic of Fan Texts," *American Behavioral Scientist* 48, no. 7 (2005): 822–39.
11 While some might argue that nonhuman actors including AI are creating texts, the existence of such texts still relies on human thought, programming, creativity, and production. Therefore, we see these texts, too, as primarily (even if tangentially) human creations.
12 See Roberta E. Pearson and William Uricchio, eds., *The Many Lives of the Batman: Critical Approaches to a Superhero and His Media* (London: BFI, 1991); Tony Bennett and Janet Woollacott, *Bond and Beyond: The Political Career of a Popular Hero* (London: MacMillan, 1987); Colin Burnett, "A Poetics of the Popular Film Series: How the James Bond Films Tell Continuing Stories Differently," *Journal of Narrative Theory* 54, no. 1 (2024).
13 Gerard Genette, *Paratexts: Thresholds of Interpretation*, translated by Jane E. Lewin (Cambridge: Cambridge University Press, 1997).
14 Jonathan Gray, *Show Sold Separately: Promos, Spoilers, and Other Media Paratexts* (New York: New York University Press, 2010), 6.
15 For more on this distinction between "work" and "text," see Roland Barthes, "From Work to Text," in *Image—Music—Text*, translated by Stephen Heath (Glasgow: Fontana/Collins, 1977).
16 For aesthetics, see, for instance, Jason Jacobs, "Television Aesthetics: An Infantile Disorder," *Journal of British Cinema and Television* 3, no. 1 (2006): 19–33; and Matt Hills, "Television Aesthetics: A Pre-Structuralist Danger?," *Journal of British Cinema and Television* 8, no. 1 (2011): 99–117; for interpretation, see especially Susan Sontag, "Against Interpretation," in *Against Interpretation and Other Essays* (New York: Picador, 2001[1961]), 3–14; and for audience and production realities, see, respectively, David Morley, *Television, Audiences and Cultural Studies* (London: Routledge, 1992); and James Curran, "Rethinking Mass Communications," in *Cultural Studies and Communications*, edited by James Curran, David Morley, and Valerie Walkerdine (London: Arnold, 1996), 134–36.
17 Fish, *Is There a Text in This Class?*
18 Umberto Eco, "Overinterpreting Texts," in *Interpretation and Overinterpretation* (Cambridge: Cambridge University Press, 1992).
19 Hall, *Introduction*, 15.

20 It is beyond our capacity to offer here a full account of textual analysis's rich history, or of its interactions with and travels within other academic fields such as literary studies, rhetoric, and more. See Susan Douglas's chapter in this collection for a superb account of media studies' early days, and indeed its early reliance on textual analysis.
21 For clear articulations of this approach, see David Bordwell, *Narration in the Fiction Film* (Madison: University of Wisconsin Press, 1985); and Kristin Thompson, *Breaking the Glass Armor: Neoformalist Film Analysis* (Princeton, NJ: Princeton University Press, 2020).
22 Michael Z. Newman, *The Media Studies Toolkit* (New York: Routledge, 2022), 39.
23 Amanda Lotz, *After Mass Media: Storytelling for Microaudiences in the Twenty-First Century* (New York: New York University Press, 2025).
24 Glen Creeber, "The Joy of Text? Television and Textual Analysis," *Critical Studies in Television* 1, no. 1 (2006): 85–86.
25 Rosalind Gill, "Discourse Analysis in Media and Communications Research," in *The Craft of Criticism: Critical Media Studies in Practice*, edited by Michael Kackman and Mary Celeste Kearney (New York: Routledge, 2018), 29.

2

Textual Analysis

The Foundational Method

SUSAN J. DOUGLAS

In this chapter, Douglas provides a history of the essential role that textual analysis played in media studies' development as a discipline from the late 1950s through the 1970s, asserting that textual analysis is indeed media studies' "foundational method." She documents how a new wave of scholars looked past models of communication that posited popular texts as mere inputs, instead probing them for the complexity of their messages.

Let's begin with first principles: the field of media studies was founded on textual analysis. Beginning in the late 1950s and early 1960s, this method produced the pioneering texts in our field that opened up a whole new way to unpack the values, attitudes, and norms embedded in media fare. With textual analysis periodically dismissed as being overly subjective, and allegedly producing work that is nonverifiable, not reliable, and nongeneralizable, it is time to remind ourselves of the origins and evolution of this method, why it matters, and the compelling and persuasive work it has produced.

In the 1950s and early 1960s, in the United States and Britain, media studies—the humanities-based analysis of media content, audiences, institutions, and history—did not exist. There was what was commonly called mass communications research in the US, pioneered in the 1930s in response to the rapid and widespread adoption of radio. This work relied primarily on statistical methods, especially surveys of how certain media fare affected people's behaviors—did X media message produce Y behavior?—but also included controlled experiments and quantitative content analysis, counting how many times a word or phrase appeared in a media text. It did not delve into the values, attitudes, and beliefs embedded in the media, and the bulk of this work maintained that the media had only limited effects.

Meanwhile, among humanities scholars and public intellectuals, the concept of studying the media was beneath contempt. In a 1957 collection of essays, *Mass Culture: The Popular Arts in America*, Bernard Rosenberg, one of the editors, laid out the anti–mass culture manifesto: "Mass-circulation magazines, 'comic' books, detective fiction, movies, radio, television . . . present a major threat to man's autonomy." Mass culture is "vulgar and exploitative" and homogenizes everything into a "single slushy compost . . . nothing remains untouched."[1] Graeme Turner, the Australian scholar, affirms that popular culture was seen by academic elites as no less than "a threat to the moral and cultural standards of modern civilization."[2]

However, with the explosive growth of the media, and especially television's rapid conquest of people's living rooms and their culture in the 1950s, scholars in Britain and the US felt TV was launching a major transformation in people's lives. It was exactly because of the media's ubiquity, its consumption by millions, *and* its banality that the values the media were emitting into the cultural ether called out to be analyzed. But how to begin? Where to start, given the absence of tradition, theory, or method, not to mention the scorn heaped on even doing such work?

The answer was textual analysis, pioneered in the late 1950s and early 1960s by the British scholars Richard Hoggart, Raymond Williams, Stuart Hall, and Paddy Whannel, and in the US by John Cawelti, Horace Newcomb, and the early work of George Gerbner. These scholars had absolutely no use for what Hall dismissed as the social science "transmission" model of the media; as he put it, "We know the television programme is not a behavioral input, like a tap on the knee-cap."[3] As Gerbner wrote somewhat damningly in 1966, "The excessive concern with usually short-term, private, and personal effects, conceived as behavior change . . . the gaining of a vote, the sale of a new product . . . has obscured not only the concept of communication as a special type of social interaction, but also the meaning of effect."[4] Such narrow, sclerotic research simply failed to consider the powerful, constantly reinforced norms embedded in magazines, advertising, television shows, and films.

It was this behaviorist, limited-effects model of the media that textual analysis sought to challenge.

Today, we utterly take for granted that most media fare in the 1950s and 1960s was racist, sexist, class biased, and exclusionary. Black folks could only get on variety shows as singers and dancers; women were either sex objects or confined to the domestic sphere; most sitcoms, dramatic programs, and soap operas featured aspirational, upper-middle-class homes and settings; and gay people were either invisible or pathologized. The values and norms disseminated were those buttressing white patriarchy. But how did we learn all this; how was this exposed, and then attacked? Through textual analysis: examining the language, structures, metaphors, characters, settings, and more, in media fare and laying out what their dominant meanings seemed to be.[5]

The initial, groundbreaking work was Richard Hoggart's *The Uses of Literacy* (1957). Born to an impoverished working-class family and orphaned by the time he was eight years old, Hoggart won a scholarship to study English at the University of Leeds in 1936. Towering over the study of English at British universities then were F. R. Leavis and his wife, Queenie. Leavis became a Cambridge institution, producing both devoted acolytes and repelled detractors. His work had a profound influence on Hoggart (as well as Williams and Hall) and, ironically, planted the seeds of media studies. Leavis, a passionate defender of high culture, insisted on the sacrosanct nature of certain English literature—Jane Austen but not Charles Dickens, Joseph Conrad but not Thomas Hardy—and railed against what he saw as the predations of the media. The Leavises became, as the media historian Paddy Scannell put it, "the most outspoken critics of the new mass culture."[6] For them, the media were "dooming us to moral depravity." But, methodologically, they emphasized that the close analysis of texts mattered to understanding how those texts expressed and also acted upon cultural values. So, if analyzing, say, the books of George Eliot for their meanings, cultural values, and attitudes was important to understanding British culture, why not apply the same techniques to popular literature, the press, and advertising on offer in the 1950s to multitudes?

Hoggart spent the early years of his career not as a black-robed professor at a university, but teaching adult education classes in what were referred to as "extramural" departments. Thus, he was in an educational tradition "entirely marginal to the centers of English academic life."[7] This outside-looking-in stance enhanced his ability to see the prevailing, hidebound notions of culture as strange, and as amputated from most people's lives. Given his working-class background and the students he was now teaching, why should he concentrate on teaching James Joyce or Jane Austen to working people when, as Hoggart recalled, "they lived in another world . . . the world of newspapers and magazines and radio (not television at the time) and pop song"?[8] How could one help them make sense of *that* culture?

Too few people today appreciate how this brilliant scholar launched what is now a major field of teaching and research. *The Uses of Literacy* was field exploding. The first half of the book was about a working-class life and culture that he felt was slowly being diluted, fragmented, eroded. The second half was about what he was initially going to call "the misuses of literacy," how the new mass culture was promoting "a soft mass-hedonism," "invitations to self-indulgence," and a phony, conformist notion of "the common man."[9] The increased onslaught of Tin Pan Alley songs, cheap detective novels, and American television was becoming a "sprayed-on varnish stain veneer" occluding traditional working-class practices and values.[10]

Hoggart brought the skills he had learned in literary studies to bear on the media through detailed (and unsparing) analyses of media texts. He looked for common and repeated appeals, modes of address, and language—the principles embedded in rhetorical patterns. So, what new attitudes and values were being sold? Twenty-first-century readers will find these so familiar they seem clichéd. But they were new in Britain at the time, and no one had called them out before.

Instant gratification, materialism, competitive individualism (corroding the communal values of yore), and a reworked, consumption-based notion of progress based on cool new products (antithetical to a notion of progress based on increased rights and social justice)—that's what was on offer. All this was pushed by publications and ads that promised vast and exciting-sounding "horizons, new dawns, broad highways, forward movements" that were superior to older, old-fashioned outlooks.[11] "It's new, it's different," he mimicked, so it must be better, while "the past becomes laughable and odd." There was great pressure on "outdoing all others" yet within a highly conformist, faux-consensus construction of society: the ever-familiar bandwagon approach, with slogans such as "Everybody's doing it" and "Ten million people can't be wrong." This new gleaming world was democratic because allegedly there was a democracy of goods for everyone. All these popular entertainments legitimated this new status quo they were seeking to promote and profit from; people were subjected to "a bombardment of invitations to assume that whatever is right, is right, so long as it is widely accepted." So above all, under the sparkling sheen of newness, modernity, and the idea of being "with it," what was being promoted were "conservatism and conformity." The "mass arts," as he sometimes called them, wanted "irresponsible obedients.... 'Only conform' whispers the prevailing wind today."[12]

The overall message from so many of the ads and publications was "the urge for gaiety and slickness at all costs... the constant pressure to be 'bright' at the expense of more sober qualities." One way this was achieved was through rhetorical ploys that especially peeved and grated on Hoggart: overly simple language and a chummy, often quasi-working-class accent and mode of address that sought to create a fake intimacy with audiences. If a word of more than three syllables had to be used in an article, he noted, it would be marked by an asterisk "with a 'pally up' explanation," which typically went "'that means ... to us, fellers.'" Hoggart's analysis of how this mode of address simultaneously hailed people as distinct individuals yet part of a convivial, like-minded group was astute. "The 'you' who is cajoled, invited to laugh, flattered, is not simply the individual 'you,' but a great composite 'you' of the unexceptional ordinary folk; minnows in a heated pool."[13] At the same time, Hoggart wanted to debunk the notion that the working classes were the willing dupes of mass culture, accepting its blandishments uncritically. People knew that advertising was "a commercial racket," that most of what they read in the papers was phony, that they were being "got at." So, they did develop "a strong patina of resistance."[14]

The Uses of Literacy was an instant sensation; as Hall noted, "everybody read it," and more scholars began putting the media in their crosshairs.[15] The book showed convincingly how textual analysis could be deployed to expose the prevailing, insinuating ideological frameworks embedded in the media. In a 1961 edition of the *New Left Review*, edited by Hall, an article co-authored by Williams, Paddy Whannel, and others offered an analysis of commercial television's "positively harmful" fare (much of it American) being pumped out by the industry's "gimmick-mongers." Some of these shows were "bristling with moral dilemmas," such as the American import *Beat the Clock* (ITV 1955–67), requiring quiz show contestants "to do tricks like animals at the circus." This show often featured a husband-and-wife team—cooperating yet pitted against each other—one of whom had to, say, carry an orange tucked under their chin and successfully transfer it to their spouse, also under their chin, without using their hands. If they succeeded, they could win a motor scooter or new Naugahyde furniture. The authors found this utterly demeaning.[16]

At the end of the article, they argued for what would come to be called the teaching of "media literacy," to help audiences "become more discriminating over the whole field of television output." They recommended that "courses in critical appreciation of the mass media . . . be established," especially in secondary schools, and that textbooks be produced to help with such instruction.[17] This is where Hall and Whannel came in: they pushed media studies even further in Britain. How to teach such media literacy? Deconstruct media texts. And show how they sustained unequal power relations in society.

By the mid-1960s, Hall was teaching young people at the Chelsea College of Arts and collaborating with Whannel, then working for the British Film Institute as an education officer lecturing around the country about the importance of taking the study of cinema seriously. The mission of their trailblazing *The Popular Arts: A Critical Guide to the Mass Media* (1964) was to address the failure of schools to come to terms with how deeply and enthusiastically their students were engaged with popular culture. "The world of mass communication and popular entertainment represents the most important environmental factor with which teachers have to cope," they observed.[18] Hall recalled, "We wanted to know, what was the dream life of the masses?" When he asked his students what they thought of *Rock Around the Clock* (dir. Fred F. Sears, 1956), which nearly all of them had seen, or skiffle music and the "king of skiffle" Lonnie Donegan, they'd say: "Think about it? You move your body to it. You don't think about it."[19] There was the challenge.

Hall had just a one-room flat in London, so on the weekends he would go to Paddy and Kay Whannel's home in Putney, in the southwestern part of London, to conduct research for their book. Their goal was not to trash all of the popular arts but to help students put media texts under an analytical microscope and parse out the great from the awful. And remember, they did this years before researchers had access to VCRs or boxed sets of DVDs; they had to take notes in real time. "We would just watch television, play records, argue about them, look at advertisements, eat, come back and watch more television, listen to Billie Holiday . . . we [were] just saturated weekend after weekend after weekend" from "first thing Saturday morning until late on Sunday night," Hall recollected.[20] They "watched more bad TV programmes, suffered more noisy records, and sat through more bad films than even the most dedicated critics ought to expect."[21] Drawing from their training in literature and the arts, and emphasizing that their debt to Williams and Hoggart was "immense," they conducted textual and visual analyses of all sorts of media fare to lay out the values and attitudes being conveyed, reinforced, or corrupted. And, extending Hoggart's work, they emphasized how camera angles, long shots or close-ups, and editing techniques all played a role in conveying the meaning of a media text as well. And this was the method they urged teachers to impart to their students.

The Popular Arts was "defined as a handbook for that moment in education," Hall recalled, because they saw the media playing its own educational role with young people. Hall and Whannel focused on various media genres: the Western, detective shows, crime novels, teen girls' and women's magazines, comics, romantic comedies, the press, popular music, television journalism, media geared specifically to the young, and advertising. What messages, norms, and dreams did these various genres impart to those who gobbled them up? As men ahead of their time, they paid considerable attention to gender. Westerns and detective shows were very much a man's world filled with fistfights and gunplay. Of particular danger here was that "we gradually become habituated" to think that violence "is the 'natural' solution to difficult social problems."[22] One noxious celebration of violence was featured in hugely popular crime novels, notably those of the American writer Mickey Spillane and the British writer Ian Fleming. Particularly repellant (and concerning) were the ruthless objectification of women and the enjoyment of sexual violence against them, which Hall and Whannel illustrated with direct quotes from both authors.

What about the representation of women in women's magazines or love comics? For the female protagonist, "the ultimate reward is 'marriage'" and thus a girl or woman's main goal was to "capture the boy," but of course, "never yield." If they did, they were severely punished reputationally, even if they didn't get pregnant. As in their concern about the enforcement of the double standard in love stories geared to girls, Hall and Whannel criticized the "moony," "magic of love" set patterns of pop song lyrics that, with few exceptions, didn't dare tiptoe anywhere near sexual desire.[23] Hall and Whannel could make no claims about the effects of such romantic fantasy rubbish or media violence on media audiences, as there was simply no funding for audience research. However, as textual analysis of the media took hold in the 1970s and beyond, many scholars would come to insist that when multiple media texts repeat the same stories, and reinforce the same values and attitudes, over and over, it's hardly a stretch to conclude that such values might be imbibed by those who consume them.

In "The Big Bazaar," Hall and Whannel turned to advertising, the bête noire of Williams, Hoggart, and themselves. Deploying scalpel-like derision, they quoted the language and appeals used in ads but also emphasized how imagery was now the crucial hook. Together, image and text produced an argument directed personally to you on behalf of the product, in an I-you mode of address. They included an illustration for an ad for Vaseline shampoo in which we see only the back of a woman's head, with a man's hands caressing each side of it. "How Long Since This Happened to You?" the copy demanded. "Too long?" the ad goaded. "Then look to your hair." So, concluded Hall and Whannel, if you want to be loved and caressed, you must have beautiful hair, which you can only get with this product. Only then will you be truly loved. In some ads, preposterous words were made up, such as "teenfresh" or "foot-fabulous." Hall and Whannel categorized ads into three major groups: appeals to status and social climbing ("when only the best will do"), appeals to glamour and luxury ("communicated directly by the cold, haughty expression on the model's face"), and appeals associated with dreaming and fantasy ("the Dream you can afford").[24]

What especially broke new ground in *The Popular Arts* was that, at the end of the book, Hall and Whannel proposed a series of activities for teachers to assign designed specifically to promote media literacy among their students. In one such exercise, students were asked to describe who is a hero, and then who is a hero in the media. "Can a girl be heroic?" was one question the students had to discuss. Students would watch film clips, TV shows, and read excerpts from mass market books and then learn how to analyze media texts and the beliefs, attitudes, and behaviors they reinforced or diminished.

Richard Hoggart was so dedicated to the importance of exposing the impact of commercial media on culture that he founded the Centre for Contemporary Cultural Studies at the University of Birmingham in 1964. His first hire was Stuart Hall, and their textual analysis was a political project, unmasking the ideological messages curled up in what was dismissed as "just entertainment."

What about parallel developments in the US? George Gerbner, who as Dean of the Annenberg School at the University of Pennsylvania became most widely known for his "cultural indicators" project that used content analysis, interviews, and other methods to examine media content (especially media violence), also did textual analysis at the beginning of his career. In summer 1960, Gerbner published "The Individual in a Mass Culture" in the *Saturday Review*. Had Gerbner, by 1960, read Hoggart or Williams? We don't know. His colleague Larry Gross doubted it.[25] But Gerbner's concerns and theirs were strikingly similar; some of the language was nearly identical. In the media texts he reviewed, this marketing system was urging people to embrace and indulge in "immediate self-gratification," and to celebrate a new human right being sold to them, "the right to be constantly entertained." It peddled "privatism" and urged people to focus on themselves and ignore broader social issues. Like Hoggart, Gerbner reviled the "soothing voice" of marketers who sought to sell commodities by assuring the viewer they "were on his side." With the newly intensified focus on the youth market, he wrote, the media wormed their way into adolescents' desire by assuming the persona of "the roguish, indulgent uncle," not some squares like their parents or teachers. Despite such feints at being modern and trendy, "the dominant market-orientation of mass culture limits its major functions to cashing in on the *status quo*."[26]

One early piece of textual analysis Gerbner did was about magazines such as *True Confessions* and *True Love Stories*, and another was about how the media portrayed schoolteachers. In the former, Gerbner sought to analyze the incongruity between the magazines' blaring first-person headlines such as "The Most Shameful Night of My Life" and the smiling, wholesome, fresh-faced, happy young cover girls. In a 1963 article titled "Smaller Than Life," Gerbner and his research team reported that in movies and popular magazines, teachers were portrayed as in "material and financial difficulty," and the best fix to this typically was to quit the profession. In movies, teachers (especially women) were losers at love, with the majority unmarried at the beginning and the end of the film. Again, the main solution to being a failure at love was to leave teaching altogether. So, basically, teachers were flops.[27]

John Cawelti was another pioneer in textual analysis, although his focus was on the formulas the media repeatedly reproduced. In his pathbreaking study of Westerns, *The Six Gun Mystique* (1970), he wondered "why I and so many other people drew such pleasure and gratification from literary works [such as Westerns or detective novels] which many of the most respected critics dismissed as contemptible trash."[28] In 1959, he noted, a staggering eight of the top ten TV shows were Westerns and thirty of the prime-time shows were "horse operas." The Western thus deserved to be studied, the formulas they promulgated revealed. To do so, one had to analyze Westerns as texts.

Cawelti sought to consider the ideologies that Westerns reaffirmed and question how "conventionalized narrative types . . . enable people to reenact and temporarily resolve widely shared psychic conflicts."[29] That certain programs or genres could become popular precisely because they managed, however metaphorically, prevailing cultural anxieties was a crucial and prescient point, later taken up by others. It is not known for certain whether Cawelti read Hall and Whannel's *The Popular Arts*, but there were important similarities in their readings of the genre. The Western was, not surprisingly, a "vanishing symbol of individualism in an era of conformity" like the 1950s. And its main focus was the "justification of acts of violent aggression," so villains had to be depicted such that "the hero is both intellectually and emotionally justified in destroying them."[30]

In most Westerns, the everyday pioneers and settlers were "virtuous and honorable," valuing hard work and mutual loyalty, but they typically lacked the individual hero's ability to "cope with savagery," either from Native Americans or white villains. Cawelti was especially fascinated by the gunfighter heroes and the repeated ritual of "the draw," which had become a de rigueur moment in so many Westerns. The gunfighter hero, he argued, addressed anxieties about "the sense of decaying masculine potency which has long afflicted American culture," especially in the *Organization Man* you-must-fit-in 1950s. This potency was, obviously, represented by the phallic symbol of the gun.[31]

With the gun duel at a distance, the hero was often reluctant to participate; he killed cleanly and imposed an "aesthetic order" on the draw. Thus the cowboy/hero symbolically resolved America's ambiguous attitudes toward violence and power by imbuing violence with a sense of order and moral significance.[32] He also, multiple times a week in the 1950s and '60s, assured America that men were still men, whatever suits or uniforms they had to don and whatever obeisance they had to pay to others at work.

Cawelti had an enormous influence on Horace Newcomb, the founder of television studies in the US. With the publication of *TV: The Most Popular Art* (1974), Newcomb took aim at the academic elitism that dismissed studying something like television, pointing to the "social stigma" attached to TV by cultural elites. Like Cawelti, Newcomb wanted to examine television formulas, which were just taken for granted, and unpack their elements and their implications. And while the book covered the major genres—Westerns, detective shows, sitcoms—Newcomb came to emphasize a truly essential, fundamental point. Despite their significant differences, most genres emphasized the importance of white, almost always wise, male authority and offered fantasies of simple solutions to complex problems. Women were routinely stereotyped as passive, nurturing helpmates. TV was a white, upper-middle-class world. Newcomb did not use the word "patriarchy," but that's what his analysis found: television's consecration of white patriarchy. But Newcomb also noted that certain episodes of shows—*Gunsmoke* (CBS, 1955–75), *The Defenders* (CBS, 1961–65), and *Dr. Kildare* (NBC, 1961–66), for instance—also challenged bigotry, homophobia, racism, and sexism.

Newcomb's most iconoclastic move in *The Most Popular Art* was his defense of easily the most reviled genre on television, the soap opera. Notoriously exaggerated or melodramatic, soaps were popular because the dilemmas were "far more closely related to the problems of the audience than the continued diet of spectacular murder solved by the spectacular detective." Audiences were bound not by the chains of hero worship but by the easily recognized bonds of "human frailty and human valor."[33] However preposterous some of their story lines were, soaps mattered, Newcomb insisted, because they offered less of a fantasy world, with its idealized solutions to complex problems, than most prime-time TV. Also, as a male writer and critic, he took the mostly female audience's connection to soaps seriously. Soaps had been so put down (like other "feminized" pop culture forms) because they were geared to and embraced by girls and women. So Newcomb helped pave the way for subsequent feminist media studies scholars to redeem such "feminized" media texts and explore how they spoke to women living in a male-dominated society.

These studies, and especially those pioneered at the Centre for Contemporary Cultural Studies at the University of Birmingham in the early 1970s and beyond, provided tutorials on how textual analysis could reveal the ideological work media texts perform. For example, in "The Determinations of New Photographs," Stuart Hall showed how textual and visual analysis could be paired to expose the values news photographs conveyed that typically reaffirmed dominant belief systems and values.[34] Journalists, Hall noted dryly, "speak of the 'the news' as if events select themselves" and that what became top stories was somehow "divinely inspired." But news photographs could rarely produce meaning on their own, so here Hall deployed a concept from the French semiotician Roland Barthes, "anchorage." News photos almost always have a caption, which "anchors" the meaning of the picture and tells you how to read it, what you should feel about it.

Hall illustrated this using four very similar, emotionless (think resting face) headshots of a Conservative home secretary forced to resign amid a bribery scandal. One paper captioned the face as "angry," even though, as Hall pointed out, equally plausible captions could have been "thoughtful" or "listening patiently." Another paper captioned the headshot by referring to "the tragedy" surrounding the politician. Yet another cast his forced resignation as "a sacrifice" while a fourth cited his "look of resignation." "Since this photo is generalized enough to be linked to a vast range of expressions, it requires . . . an extra linguistic anchor which the caption supplies," Hall emphasized. "It is a very common practice for the captions to news photographs to tell us, in words, exactly how the subject's expression *ought to be read*." Thus, anchoring guides the reader "towards a meaning that has been chosen in advance," depending on the politics of the newspaper.[35]

Hall continued his focus on the texts of captions to conduct an ideological analysis of the most infamous news photograph taken at the 1968 anti–Vietnam War demonstration in London, the "kick photo." Capturing a clash between a small group of demonstrators and police, the photograph showed the foot of a protestor hitting the head of a policeman. Captions included "What the Bobbies Faced," "And They Talk about PROVOCATION," and "Victory for the Police." The photo and its varying captions reinforced a common press trope that this demonstration (allegedly like others) would be and was violent, and they signified the police as the "center" and heroes of the story. As Hall summed it up, the denoted message—"'a man in a crowded scene is kicking a policeman'"—is ideologically "read" as "'extremists threaten law-and-order by violent acts'" or, similarly, "'anti-war demonstrators are violent people who threaten the state and assault policemen unfairly.'" Headlines like "Fringe Fanatics Foiled at Big Demonstration" and "The Day the Police Were Wonderful" cemented the ideological theme and message. What national mythic theme did this reinforce? That the British police are "wonderful," contrary to what many actually experienced.[36]

Another study at the Centre, "Images of Women in the Media," a textual analysis of one week of various British print media in October of 1974, documented the taken-for-granted representations of women that were, not surprisingly, sexist.[37] The data such work relied on (and it *was* data)—inveigling language, direct address to consumers often filled with prescriptive norms or exhortations, didactic narrative structures with clear heroes and villains, patterned formulas, value-laden metaphors, the pairing of images and text—especially through captions—to powerful effect—provided conclusive and persuasive evidence of the gendered, raced, and class-bound worldview that sought to shore up the status quo. Textual analysis was hardly some self-indulgent, fan-based take; it was a deeply political method and project.

At the same time, textual analysis could also reveal the contradictions and even critiques curled inside certain media fare. Other modes of analysis emerged in the 1970s—psychoanalytical theory in film studies (what does it mean to be in a darkened movie theater staring up at those larger-than-life figures?), semiotics in advertising (what and how do images and words signify?), and audience ethnographies—for which textual analysis was a springboard, whether built upon or even rejected.

So many important works followed and exposed much about the interpretive frameworks the media were seeking to fold us into, consciously or not. These included, to name just a few, David Morley and Charlotte Brunsdon's reading of the British newsmagazine, *Nationwide* (1978); Todd Gitlin's exposé of how the news media covered the antiwar movement, *The Whole World Is Watching* (1980); Janice Radway's *Reading the Romance* (1984); and Herman Gray's *Watching Race* (1995); the list is too long to include here. But many of us, when we aspired to do this kind of work, remember that moment, in a library, a bookstore, a class, when we discovered *The Uses of Literacy*, or *The Popular Arts*, or Horace Newcomb and said "Amen" and "Thank you" and then got very busy.

Notes

1 Bernard Rosenberg, "Mass Culture in America," in *Mass Culture: The Popular Arts in America*, edited by Bernard Rosenberg and David Manning White (New York: The Free Press, 1957), 3–9.
2 Graeme Turner, *British Cultural Studies: An Introduction* (Cambridge, MA: Unwin Hyman, 1990), 2.
3 Stuart Hall, "Encoding and Decoding in the Television Discourse," paper presented at the Centre for Mass Communication Research, September 1973, in Cadbury Collection, University of Birmingham, 5–6.
4 George Gerbner, "On Defining Communication: Still Another View," *Journal of Communication* 16, no. 2 (June 1966): 101–2.
5 To be fair, especially in the wake of the women's movement, there was also content analysis done in the early and mid-1970s documenting the stereotyping of women in television and advertising.
6 Paddy Scannell, *Media and Communication* (London: Sage Publications, 2007), 99.
7 Stuart Hall, "The Emergence of Cultural Studies and the Crisis of the Humanities," *October* 53 (Summer 1990): 11–23, https://doi.org/10.2307/778912.
8 Richard Hoggart, *The Uses of Literacy* (New Brunswick, NJ: Transaction Publishers, 2008; originally published in 1957 by Essential Books), 271.
9 Hoggart, *The Uses of Literacy*, 128.
10 Paul Vitello, "Richard H. Hoggart, 'Lady Chatterley's' Savior, Dies at 95," *New York Times*, April 23, 2014, www.nytimes.com/2014/04/24/books/richard-h-hoggart-lady-chatterleys-savior-dies-at-95.html.

11 Hoggart, *The Uses of Literacy*, 130.
12 Hoggart, *The Uses of Literacy*, 135, 143, 145–46, 148, 182.
13 Hoggart, *The Uses of Literacy*, 143, 150, 154, 184, 186.
14 Hoggart, *The Uses of Literacy*, 183–84, 213, 252.
15 Author interview with Stuart Hall, July 21, 2011.
16 Kit Coppard, Tony Higgins, Paddy Whannel, and Raymond Williams, "Television Supplement," *New Left Review* 1 (January/February 1961), https://newleftreview-org.proxy.lib.umich.edu/issues/i7/articles/kit-coppard-paddy-whannel-raymond-williams-tony-higgins-television-supplement.
17 Coppard et al., "Television Supplement."
18 Stuart Hall and Paddy Whannel, *The Popular Arts: A Critical Guide to the Mass Media* (Boston: Beacon Press, 1967; first published in 1964), 387.
19 Author interview with Stuart Hall.
20 Author interview with Stuart Hall.
21 Hall and Whannel, *The Popular Arts*, 16.
22 Hall and Whannel, *The Popular Arts*, 112.
23 Hall and Whannel, *The Popular Arts*, 279, 281, 289–91.
24 Hall and Whannel, *The Popular Arts*, 324–26, 329–34, 337.
25 Author interview with Larry Gross, February 22, 2022.
26 George Gerbner, "The Individual in a Mass Culture," *Saturday Review*, June 18, 1960, 11–13, 36–37. This was based on a scholarly article in a journal with a much more restricted circulation: George Gerbner, "Education and the Challenge of Mass Culture," *AV Communication Review* 7, no. 4 (Fall 1959): 264–78.
27 George Gerbner, "Smaller Than Life: Teachers and Schools in the Mass Media," *Phi Delta Kappan* 44, no. 5 (February 1963): 202–5.
28 John Cawelti, *The Six Gun Mystique* (Bowling Green, KY: Bowling Green University Press, 1970), ix.
29 Cawelti, *The Six Gun Mystique*, 7–12.
30 Cawelti, *The Six Gun Mystique*, 4, 14.
31 Cawelti, *The Six Gun Mystique*, 59–61; William H. White, *The Organization Man* (New York: Simon & Schuster, 1956).
32 Cawelti, *The Six Gun Mystique*, 58–61.
33 Horace Newcomb, *TV: The Most Popular Art* (New York: Anchor Books, 1974), 174–81.
34 Stuart Hall, "Determinations of News Photographs," reprinted in *Writings on Media: Stuart Hall*, edited by Charlotte Brunsdon (Durham, NC: Duke University Press, 2021), 54–55.
35 Stuart Hall, "Determinations," 55, 62.
36 Stuart Hall, "Determinations," 66–67, 72–74.
37 Helen Butcher et al., "Images of Women in the Media," stenciled paper, Women's Studies Group and the Centre for Contemporary Cultural Studies, Birmingham, November 1974, 3.

3

Producing Meaningful Analyses of Racial Representations

LORI KIDO LOPEZ

In this chapter, Lopez discusses the challenges facing textual analysts to come up with novel insights, especially in relation to the subject of racial representation. Lopez suggests ways we can move beyond the reproduction or subversion of existing stereotypes, thereby giving textual analysis greater purpose and relevance. In doing so, she considers textual analysis's possible futures.

Introduction

Across methods, media studies scholars have been successful in helping us to better understand the ways that race and ethnicity are represented in mainstream media narratives. One of their central tenets is that such images serve to marginalize communities of color in multiple ways due to the overwhelming whiteness of mainstream U.S. media industries in terms of general employment, executive leadership, and prioritized consumers. People of color are underrepresented relative to the growing number of racial minorities in the regions being depicted, and they wield limited creative control over how their own stories are told. As a result, they suffer the indignity of misrepresentation in many different forms. There are a plenitude of studies outlining the different ways that people of color have been harmed by histories of repeated patterns, and textual analysis has been the dominant methodology for producing such work.[1]

Due to the rich body of literature that already exists on how race is represented, however, it can be difficult for scholars to produce textual analyses of racial representations that contribute something new and meaningful to the scholarly record. In many ways, the standard ways we have done textual analysis of racial representation have run their course, and if scholars continue in this same vein, their work risks becoming grievously narrow and stale. This chapter will explore two aspects of this challenge—struggles for novelty and originality, and struggles for significance. How does one avoid performing a textual analysis that simply catalogs whether a certain text is harmful, and what other questions can or should we be asking? Indeed, scholars might be able to perform a representational analysis of previously unstudied texts and answer questions about whether they affirm or resist known patterns. But it is hard to say that such analyses contribute to new understandings of racial representation. One might also be able to generate questions about racial representation that sidestep the basic question—"Is it racist or not racist?"—and instead turn to more unpredictable or unusual inquiries. But this raises questions about why readers should care about what is learned from such studies. The investigation of racial imagery without foregrounding considerations of systemic racism or the potential for antiracism seems inadvisable, and possibly dangerous, to communities of color. This chapter helps identify some of the perils of racial representation analysis by considering how we have arrived at this dilemma and provides some questions for today's scholars to ask themselves as they work toward producing textual analyses of racial representation that are both new and meaningful.

Identifying Racial Stereotypes

One of the most clearly defined analytical frameworks for understanding the harms done to people of color through media is the stereotype. Stereotypes are the limited and rigidly defined set of characteristics attributed to a certain identity or thing. Our brains are naturally inclined to categorize and recognize patterns, and stereotypes help to create order out of an overwhelmingly chaotic and multifaceted world. Yet they are also clearly limiting, since they contribute to processes of reducing a complex human being into a tightly fitting mold that may be inaccurate, and they are often connected to histories of oppression. Disempowered racial minorities have always been understood through an offensively narrow set of stereotypical characteristics that serve to reinforce the superiority of whiteness, to mock or denigrate that identity, or to contribute to the subordination of another marginalized group.

For instance, African American women are often portrayed as the stereotypical "Angry Black Woman." Characters who fit into this stereotype are portrayed as overly aggressive and quick to lash out with verbal insults and physical violence. Their families are assumed to suffer because they are cruel mothers and emasculating wives, incapable of providing proper support. In addition to being stereotypical, portrayals that fit into this category have been theorized by Patricia Hill Collins as "controlling images."[2] By this she means that such harmful depictions end up providing justification for continued oppression; in this example, Black women are depicted so negatively that it seems like they are the cause of their own social struggles and disadvantages. If Black women have done this to themselves, then it becomes easier to restrict social support such as food stamps or stymie efforts for structural change. Controlling images are designed to place the blame on individual choices, rather than on the root causes of injustice such as underfunded schools, discriminatory hiring practices, or other forms of institutionalized racism.

There are many other well-trodden stereotypes that end up reinforcing a similar mentality that denies the actual impacts of historical racism. These include stereotypes of Indigenous peoples as primitive savages or lazy alcoholics, which overlooks the histories of genocide and settler colonization that forcibly removed native communities from their lands and deprived them of opportunities for sovereignty and community support. Mexican Americans are consistently reduced to the stereotype of the illegal alien who doesn't belong in the US, which denies the structuring forces of racist immigration and labor policies that bring workers into the country while denying them a path to citizenship.

In addition to the many stereotypes such as these that are easily identifiable by name, there are also many other analytical frameworks outside of stereotypes that we can use to similarly identify common thematics in the representation of people of color. This includes the identification of racial scripts, tropes, archetypes, frames, and other ways of describing and categorizing representational patterns.[3] In each of these cases, scholars have clearly helped us to see the harms that have come from histories of repeated images. They help us understand why the communities being represented might feel uncomfortable, frustrated, or offended when they see those same old patterns over and over. Media stereotypes clearly connect to histories of institutional oppression and serve to reinforce their familiar power dynamics.

Identifying Challenges to Stereotypes

Media studies scholarship has also taught us about the alternatives to racial stereotypes. While stereotypes are defined by their resilience and persistence, there are always opportunities to challenge their impacts. As Charles Ramirez Berg has outlined, the existence of many forms of counterstereotypes reminds us that "Hollywood cinema is not as simple, static, or ideologically one-sided as *that*."[4] Indeed, it is also possible to use textual analysis to identify moments where stereotypes are reversed and subverted. This can happen through the role itself being one that opposes stereotypical norms—such as *Awkwafina Is Nora from Queens* (Comedy Central, 2020–) countering the stereotype of Asian Americans as the "model minority" by depicting an Asian American twentysomething who lives at home while she smokes weed, struggles to find employment, and is largely directionless and unmotivated for improvement.

Beyond roles themselves serving to counter long-standing stereotypes, there are numerous other ways to resist their negative impacts. Actors can subvert stereotypes through subtle choices in their performance that call winking attention to the stereotype itself. Or the stereotype can be depicted in such a laughable or cruel way that it becomes clear to the viewer that the stereotype itself is being criticized and shown to be misguided or harmful. Another way of countering stereotypes would be for a character who is initially represented as stereotypical to later evolve as their portrayal becomes more nuanced and complex.

Some textual analyses argue that such interventions are effective in challenging the harms of stereotypes. For instance, Isabel Molina-Guzmán investigates contemporary portrayals of Latinas in television comedy. She argues a character like April, portrayed by Aubrey Plaza in *Parks and Recreation* (NBC, 2009–15), "as an awkward, shy, underachieving tomboy ... eschews the standard expectations of Latina heterosexuality and white femininity."[5] She offers this reading of what she calls "the antiexotic Latina" as a way of disrupting stereotypic assumptions and adding nuance and complexity to understandings of U.S. Latinas.

Yet other analyses suggest that such efforts to undermine stereotypes through alternative representations can also unwittingly contribute to support for troubling media narratives. In her investigations of how

Arab and Muslim Americans are depicted in post-9/11 narratives, Evelyn Alsultany identifies multiple attempts to challenge portrayals of "bad" Muslims with "positive" and "good" portrayals. Yet she restates the familiar warnings of Stuart Hall, who claims that "writers and producers who seek to subvert racial hierarchies can inadvertently participate in inferential racism," or a kind of racism that is simply more covert and reliant on unstated assumptions.[6] For instance, we may see stories about Arabs and Muslims who work in counterterrorism units or are patriotic Americans also victimized by terrorism as an attempt to challenge the stereotype of Arabs and Muslims as hateful terrorists. As Alsultany points out, though, such plots reinforce the assumption that we can only understand Arabs and Muslims through their relationship in one way or another to terrorism.

All of the arguments described here fall under the umbrella of stereotype analysis. When scholars are assessing the persistence of stereotypical representations or the opportunities for counterstereotypes to offer (successful or unsuccessful) moments of resistance, they are all analyzing stereotypes through this well-established scholarly framework.

Difficulties in Producing New Stereotype Analyses

As new media texts are being produced every day, we might benefit from the continual production of textual analyses in order to refresh the data. New studies can ask if we still see the same patterns being repeated, or if modern formations have emerged to contest previous patterns. In addition to studying emerging images in commonly studied platforms like movies and television shows, we might also look at how racial identities are represented in new media platforms and digital spaces, including examinations of racial representations in social media platforms like TikTok, virtual reality narratives and experiences, or video gaming communities like Twitch and Twine. Different platforms may have the potential to inspire shifts in representational norms, or they may resort to the same old problems.

Yet there is always a limiting factor to such modes of inquiry, which is that processes of racialization are incredibly well established and deeply entrenched. One of the fundamental reasons to study race in the first place is to better understand how white supremacy and racism have become hegemonic, or socially dominant. The concept of hegemony is based on the fact that social power structures are institutionally upheld and reinforced. Those who already wield social power are protected through legal, educational, political, economic, and other institutions that work together to strengthen their position and make it nearly impossible to meaningfully disrupt or dismantle it. While the power of racism has been challenged with antiracism and other forms of activism, the status quo of white supremacy remains dominant and requires very minimal modifications to do so.[7]

The example of blackface and how its harms have been systematically absorbed across generations can help to illustrate the way this works. African Americans have long called attention to the problems of blackface, or white actors donning garish black face paint and acting like buffoons in an offensive mockery of real African Americans. This practice originated during the era of legal slavery in the US, when enslaved people were not allowed to perform in theaters that were owned and controlled by whites and that served white patrons. Blackface minstrelsy was a way for white people to maintain superiority and justify the dehumanizing practice of enslavement by portraying African Americans as dumb, childish, lazy, and a host of other negative characteristics.[8] Blackface also denied African Americans the right to self-representation, implicitly suggesting that white people were more talented and better suited to portray blackness than actual Black performers. We can see through this narrative that multiple forms of oppression are interlocked through this practice—the institution of slavery is defended, the economic potential and creative freedoms of African Americans are curtailed, and harmful ideologies about the existing racial order are maintained.

These same intentions and impacts continue generation after generation, upheld through the practices of white actors playing roles of all racial backgrounds while denying actors of color the opportunity to participate or tell their own stories. The beliefs that African American men are unintelligent and unfit for advanced education, that they are solely prized for their physical stature and athletic prowess, that they are a sexual threat to white women, and that they exist for the comedic entertainment of white audiences continue to be upheld throughout contemporary media practices. Even if slight improvements or shifts occur, this system of ideologies has been so thoroughly affirmed and rigorously upheld that this history can never be completely erased or overlooked. Indeed, even after an African American man rose to the powerful office of the president of the US, the resilience of these histories and narratives cannot be denied.

Hopefully, this example helps to reveal how hegemonic ideologies about race are by definition resilient and somewhat impervious to change. Since racist stereotypes are institutionally supported and reinforced across generations, it can be difficult to conceive of a textual analysis project that contributes something new to our understanding of race and representation. We can certainly ask whether a stereotype is still present, but it is a foregone conclusion to find out that a known stereotype continues to persist. Even when looking for challenges to stereotypes, it can be easy simply to locate new data that ultimately repeats previous understandings that all stereotypes can be disrupted to some degree—but not completely.

Opportunities for New Stereotype Analyses

While this chapter has explored what makes new forms of stereotype analysis difficult, this does not mean that such an endeavor is impossible or futile. In undertaking a new analysis of racial representations, it is simply important to ask these questions:

- Does this study acknowledge the significant amounts of research that have already established a baseline of understanding for how racial stereotypes operate?
- Does this study go beyond simply concluding that known racial stereotypes persist or that media representations can engage in the practice of counterstereotypes?
- Does this study put forward an important new analytic or framework for making sense of racial representations?

In pushing scholarship to answer these questions, we can start to develop a rubric for assessing the value of textual analyses of race. This is particularly important when thinking about publishing new research for a wider academic audience, but even scholars who are engaging in textual analysis with no expectations of scholarly publication can still strive to build from previous understandings of how media have propagated racism. One way to build these skills is to look at some examples of media studies research that use textual analysis to build from understandings of stereotypes but answer these questions affirmatively.

For instance, Melissa Phruksachart's study of *Breakfast at Tiffany's* (dir. Blake Edwards, 1961) begins with the fact that the Japanese character Mr. Yunioshi is an explicitly racist caricature.[9] She acknowledges that his role as a pesky and lascivious neighbor to Audrey Hepburn's pretty white heroine Holly Golightly aligns with anti-Asian tropes of being out of place and socially improper. Additionally, the white actor Mickey Rooney plays the role in yellowface by relying on offensive makeup, prosthetics, and dialect. But rather than stop there, Phruksachart further reads the character of Mr. Yunioshi as a foil for the evolution of Holly, whose journey throughout the film is about transforming from an independent and kooky call girl into the picture of white femininity and heteronormativity. In doing so, Phruksachart forwards the concept of "buzz" as a framework for understanding how the racial anxieties of yellowface and the queerness of Asian masculinity serve as constitutive foils of modern white womanhood. Such work clearly builds from classic understandings of stereotypes (and even returns to an oft-studied classic text) without falling into the trap of merely repeating previous knowledge.

Difficulties in Moving Beyond Racism

One of the most important ways to continue expanding understandings of race and representation through textual analysis is of course to move beyond stereotype analysis itself and generate new research questions altogether. Indeed, not all textual analyses of racial representations have to merely ask the question "Is this text racist or not racist?" While studies of stereotypes are never this simple, the profound connection between stereotypes and racism does somewhat shape the ultimate contributions of many textual analyses that center stereotype analysis. Clearly, stereotype analysis is valuable because it helps us understand more broadly just how media texts have contributed to harming people of color or to offering opportunities for resistance and empowerment.

Yet this deeply rooted focus can also lead toward a path of scholarly repetition and reinforcement rather than advancement. Charlotte

Brunsdon has elaborated upon the "Ur feminist article that feminist scholars in textual studies have been writing for some time," which aims to recuperate problematic depictions of women through performing feminist textual readings.[10] Similarly, there is what we might call an "ur-racial stereotype analysis" that media studies scholars have been writing for some time. It is oriented in one of two ways: 1) a text about racial minorities can be redeemed because there are moments of resistance in its representations, or 2) a text about racial minorities must be read more carefully to understand how it still upholds institutionalized racism. But how can researchers step outside of this binary and move beyond questions centered around identifying racism in media texts?

Indeed, it is certainly possible to imagine any number of textual approaches to communities of color that have not yet been investigated and that would help to flesh out a richer understanding of racial representations. For instance, a researcher setting out to perform a textual analysis might ask, How do African American media narratives deal with grief? How have Asian American food cultures been imagined through media? What kinds of relationships do we see represented between Indigenous communities and sports? Do media depictions of Latinx families represent conflict as productive? Such questions could certainly produce valid and novel research findings that would contribute to knowledge about media and communities of color.

However, within a critical/cultural studies framework, it is important to center research inquiries that help us to better understand power dynamics and institutional oppression. While these alternative inquiries offer endless possibilities for producing new textual analyses, it is helpful to push beyond mere description of textual occurrences to also gesture toward larger analytical significance, particularly now that the burden of representation may finally be starting to lift. Representations of minority communities still face additional expectations due to histories of marginalization, but an ever-expanding and fragmenting media landscape may be alleviating pressure for any one text to accomplish everything on its own. We must always answer the "Who cares?" and "So what?" questions, conducting research that moves beyond exposition of a single example to forwarding understandings of socially significant phenomena.

There are many ways that this can be accomplished. For instance, if we are interested in institutionalized power structures and hierarchies, there are many other systems of power that can be brought into our textual analyses beyond just racism. Indeed, scholars of racism have productively engaged with intersectional axes of identity such as sexism, ableism, classism, heterosexism, nationalism, and others. Scholars have also used broader political frameworks such as neoliberalism, capitalism, and colonialism to make sense of the meaning of racial representations. There are also productive frameworks around activism and the backlash to activist movements that can add nuance and dimension to our understandings of power—for instance, feminism and postfeminism, antiracism and postracialism. Engagements with the complexities of these theories can propel studies of racial representation into important new areas of inquiry by meaningfully connecting questions about texts to discussions of larger institutional systems that resist overly simplified or binary conclusions.

Opportunities for Moving beyond Racism

Despite the challenges that researchers may face in generating new research inquiries that use textual analysis to investigate racial imagery, we can remain optimistic that valuable and important research in the area of race and representation can be produced. In this spirit, here is another set of questions for researchers to ask themselves when taking on textual analyses of racial representations:

- Does this study acknowledge the important role of institutionalized racism in its understanding of racial imagery while also moving beyond simply asking if a media text helps or harms communities of color?
- Does this study go beyond merely describing a textual phenomenon to also help us better understand the role of media within larger interconnected systems of oppression?
- And, yet again, does this study put forward an important new analytic or framework for making sense of racial representations?

There are many spectacular examples that do all of these things and can serve as inspiration for future scholarship. LeiLani Nishime's *Undercover Asian: Multiracial Asian Americans in Visual Culture* closely reads texts starring mixed-race Asian American performers in order to reflect on the racialized consequences of visibility versus invisibility.[11] In her analysis of texts like the television show *Battlestar Galactica* (Sci-Fi, 2004–9), the films of Keanu Reeves, and the artwork of Kip Fulbeck, she reveals the different ways that representations of mixed-race Asian Americans both support and challenge racial categorization itself. Another exciting example can be seen in Mila Zuo's analysis of the images of Chinese and Chinese American women such as Joan Chen's performance in *Twin Peaks* (ABC, 1990–91) and Ali Wong's standup comedy. In *Vulgar Beauty: Acting Chinese in the Global Sensorium*, Zuo argues that their mediated beauty must be understood through the lens of vulgarity. Moreover, she produces a new framework for interpreting such representations based on the five Chinese medicinal flavors of bitter, salty, pungent, sweet, and sour—offering a reconceptualizing of Chinese female beauty as something that is tasted, consumed, and digested.[12]

This advice about how to advance the field of racial representation has focused on what can be accomplished through textual analysis alone. Indeed, the works showcased here have been able to provide new theorizations of race and representation through simply performing close critical readings of texts. But it is important to note that textual analysis can always be taken up along with other methods and modes—for instance, participant observation of media production, industry analysis of what was going on behind the scenes, production analysis of how a text was created, and interviews with audience members or media producers. Using such modes of analysis can expand textual analysis beyond its usual suspects and continue to extend our field into new areas of scholarly inquiry.

Notes

1. John Downing and Charles Husband, *Representing "Race": Racisms, Ethnicity and the Media* (London: Sage, 2005); Lori Kido Lopez, ed. *Race and Media: Critical Approaches* (New York: New York University Press, 2020).
2. Patricia Hill Collins, *Black Feminist Thought: Knowledge, Consciousness, and the Politics of Empowerment* (New York: Routledge, 2000).
3. Ronald L. Jackson, *Scripting the Black Masculine Body: Identity, Discourse, and Racial Politics in Popular Media* (New York: SUNY Press, 2006); Jonathan Branfman, "'Plow Him Like a Queen!': Jewish Female Masculinity, Queer Glamor, and Racial Commentary in Broad City," *Television & New Media* 21, no. 8 (2020): 842–60.

4   Charles Ramirez Berg, *Latino Images in Film: Stereotypes, Subversion, and Resistance* (Austin: University of Texas Press, 2002), 78.
5   Isabel Molina-Guzmán, *Latinas and Latinos on TV: Colorblind Comedy in the Post-Racial Network Era* (Tempe: University of Arizona Press, 2018), 84.
6   Evelyn Alsultany, "Representations of Arabs and Muslims in Post-9/11 Television Dramas," in *The Colorblind Screen: Television in Post-Racial America*, ed. Sarah Nilsen and Sarah E. Turner (New York: New York University Press, 2014), 140–66, www.jstor.org/stable/j.ctt9qg55f.9.
7   Michael Omi and Howard Winant, *Racial Formation in the United States*, 3rd ed. (New York: Routledge, 2015).
8   Yuval Taylor and Jake Austen, *Darkest America: Black Minstrelsy from Slavery to Hip-hop* (New York: Norton, 2012).
9   Melissa Phruksachart, "The Many Lives of Mr. Yunioshi: Yellowface and the Queer Buzz of *Breakfast at Tiffany's*," *Camera Obscura: Feminism, Culture, and Media Studies* 32, no. 3 (2017): 93–119, https://doi.org/10.1215/02705346-4205088.
10 Charlotte Brunsdon, "Feminism, Postfeminism, Martha, Martha, and Nigella," *Cinema Journal* 44, no. 2 (2005): 110–16, www.jstor.org/stable/3661098.
11 LeiLani Nishime, *Undercover Asian: Multiracial Asian Americans in Visual Culture* (Champaign: University of Illinois Press, 2014).
12 Mila Zuo, *Vulgar Beauty: Acting Chinese in the Global Sensorium* (Durham, NC: Duke University Press, 2022).

PART II

Canonical Approaches and Theories Revised

Introduction

Whereas many methods employed in media, communication, and cultural studies have a short history, textual analysis has existed in one form or another for as long as people have discussed what they think about a work of art. As should be expected from such a mature method, multiple approaches to textual analysis have thus become canonical, found in dozens if not hundreds of published books and articles about media.

Part II offers a textual analysis "starter kit" of several such approaches. The book aims to move textual analysis into exciting new realms, and to innovate and further develop it, but not simply by ignoring or abandoning approaches that have stood a test of time. Each of the approaches covered in this section is, therefore, still a handy tool for the textual analyst to have in their belt. Indeed, each is well suited to application across a wide variety of texts from a wide range of media.

The first six chapters introduce and utilize classic approaches to textual analysis: narratological, semiotic, historical poetic, feminist, and postcolonial, with Jonathan Gray, Diane Carr, Simphiwe Rens, and Souvik Mukherjee also engaging in ideological analysis along the way. Gray combines his approach with paratextual analysis (also practiced by Julie Turnock later in this collection), while Rens incorporates humanistic content analysis and multimodal analysis to his approach.

However, we offer these approaches not "just" to provide a starter kit, but to showcase how to develop each approach further. Several of these authors push beyond the traditional limits of their techniques, or stretch them to explore nontraditional objects, thereby illustrating their capacity for evolution to match varying types of text. Both Meg L. Thomas and Ted Nannicelli and Mukherjee, for instance, take approaches more commonly associated with other media—historical poetics and film, and postcolonialism and literature, respectively—and apply them to nontraditional objects, namely TikToks and board games. Meanwhile, as already noted, Gray and Rens integrate their analyses with other approaches, but still invite readers to play, experiment, and innovate with these "older" approaches.

The seventh and eighth chapters in Part II, by Soraya Murray and by Paul Frosh and Lillian Boxman-Shabtai, then innovate by inviting us to reconsider the *subject* of textual analysis. Too often, they note, textual analysis has been assumed to be practiced by a neutral, unremarked-upon agent whose commentary is framed as objective, even pseudo-omniscient, but both call for reconsideration of the *who* of textual analysis. First Murray calls for an autotheoretical approach that reflects on the analyst in question, and that acknowledges and explores the unique chemistry that is produced between text and analyst. Then Frosh and Boxman-Shabtai propose a form of "collaborative disputation" that multiplies the subject of analysis, and that highlights disagreements and differences of opinion rather than sweeping them under the methodological carpet to help hold up a myth of the singularity and simplicity of meaning. Each approach can be overlaid with any other—an autotheoretical postcolonial analysis, a collaborative narratological analysis, and so forth—and we offer them precisely to disturb the "business as usual" of solitary analysis, encouraging analysts to consider their own connections to the text as they try to elucidate its meanings.

Together, the section aims to (re)introduce and revisit several key approaches to textual analysis and offer them new life and renewed relevance for the contemporary media environment. Collectively, they offer an overview of several of the most widely used approaches to textual analysis, while also encouraging readers to see each as far from moribund.

4

The Upside-Down Comic Book

A Narratological Analysis of M. Night Shyamalan's Unbreakable

PATRICK KEATING

Keating introduces and mobilizes the tools of narratology to focus on an especially dynamic plot device, the narrative twist, and turns to director M. Night Shyamalan's "upside-down" superhero story Unbreakable *as an example. In doing so, he offers techniques for charting how plots unfold, how point of view is established, and how meaning is created by a film's organization of time and narrative.*

Narratological analysis is the study of storytelling: what stories are and how they are told. The approach has a long history, stretching back to Aristotle's analysis of tragedy as the "representation of an action."[1] In the twentieth century, Russian formalist and French structuralist scholars made literary narrative a central topic of research, addressing such issues as time, causality, and point of view.[2] More recent scholarship, sometimes known as "postclassical narratology," has extended these insights to a much wider range of media, including movies, television shows, comic books, advertisements, podcasts, and more.[3]

Movies with bold plot twists are ideal candidates for narratological analysis because they demonstrate the power of narrative organization, which controls when and how information is disclosed to viewers. A twist is not an event so much as it is a revelation, dependent on timing. Reveal the twist too soon, and the surprise will disappear. Since his breakout hit *The Sixth Sense* (1999), the writer-director M. Night Shyamalan has developed a formidable reputation, for better or worse, as a contemporary master of the twist. His 2001 superhero movie *Unbreakable* contains a particularly memorable example: a revelation that the hero's mentor is actually a criminal mastermind who has orchestrated most of the movie's events. By explaining how the film guides (and misleads) our understanding moment by moment, narratological analysis can help us understand how the twist works. More importantly, it can bring to the fore the film's underlying reflexivity. *Unbreakable* is a story about storytelling—about the impact that stories can have on those who tell them and those who hear them.

Introduction to Narratological Analysis

The starting point for much narratological analysis in film studies is the distinction between story and plot.[4] A narrative movie is typically about a sequence of events, known as a *story*. For instance, a crime movie might be about the following sequence:

1. a murder
2. a detective's investigation
3. the killer's efforts to evade the investigation
4. the capture of the murderer.

Narratology's crucial insight is that any given movie might represent this sequence in many different ways depending on how it organizes these events into a *plot*. The plot, in this context, refers to the organization of events as they unfold on-screen. For instance, a Philip Marlowe movie might skip the murder and keep the attention on the detective throughout:

2. a detective's investigation
4. the capture of the murderer.

We would still learn about the murder (1) and the killer's efforts to escape (3), but only indirectly, as mediated by the detective's investigation. The larger sequence of events (1, 2, 3, 4) constitutes the movie's story; this narrower set of events (2, 4) constitutes the movie's plot.

Alternatively, a psychological thriller might plot the story differently, revealing the identity of the murderer right away:

1. a murder
3. the killer's efforts to evade the investigation
4. the capture of the murderer

In this scenario, our knowledge of the detective's investigation (2) would be indirect, filtered through the experiences of the killer. This new plot might shift the emotional register toward suspense, rather than mystery.

Because story and plot are conceptually distinct, narratological analysis must consider three things at once: the story, the plot, and the interplay between them.

Analyzing the Story

Some narrative theorists define the concept of story very broadly, as any kind of change over time.[5] Watching a narrative film, we might ask, What is the world like at the beginning of the story? What is it like at the end? How has the story-world changed? Other theorists define the concept of story more narrowly, insisting on a causally linked series of events.[6] With this narrower definition in mind, we might ask, How many events are in the story? What causes link the events together? Do any events happen by chance? Still other theorists add further requirements, such as the call for a protagonist with a goal.[7] This definition brings its own questions to the fore: Does the story have only one protagonist? What does the protagonist want? What sorts of obstacles does the protagonist face?

All of these questions can help us better understand Hollywood movies, which typically tell stories about goal-oriented protagonists encountering obstacles as they head toward a definitive conclusion.[8] But these questions can also help us understand movies that break from the Hollywood norm. In *Jeanne Dielman, 23 Commerce Quay, 1080 Brussels* (dir. Chantal Akerman, 1975), many scenes depict repetitive actions such as household chores. Challenging our expectation that stories are about impactful events, the bulk of the movie emphasizes mundane sameness. *Run Lola Run* (dir. Tom Tykwer, 1998) initially appears to be more conventional, featuring a committed protagonist pursuing a high-stakes goal. However, the story ends up being about a series of chance events that the protagonist is nearly powerless to control. Making things even stranger, these chance events appear to happen in three alternate timelines. The end result is a movie that defies our expectations about agency and causality.

Analyzing the Plot

Plotting brings up a different set of questions involving the organization of story material. An otherwise ordinary story might unfold in an unexpected way: out of order, say, or from the point of view of a secondary character. Regarding the organization of time, we might ask, Does the plot present story events in chronological order or not? Does the plot skip a crucial story event? Does the plot select story events from a relatively narrow period, such as a day or two, or does it range more widely over decades or centuries?[9] Even a plot that respects the chronology of story events must guide our experience of story construction, precisely by helping us recognize that the chronology has been respected.

The term *point of view* may refer quite literally to the use of a point-of-view shot, but it also refers more broadly to the idea that a plot may regulate our understanding of story-world events by filtering our access through a particular character's knowledge or experience. Does the plot restrict our access to what a single character sees or knows? Or does the plot expand our access, going beyond a single character's purview? Does the plot give us access to a character's subjective states, as in a dream sequence? Or is the plot restricted to showing the character's behavior from the outside? These sorts of questions draw a distinction between range and depth.[10] Questions about range ask whether our knowledge is restricted to what a character knows, while questions about depth ask whether the plot represents a character's subjective experience or not.

These two principles—time and point of view—may be closely intertwined. The plot of *Bonjour Tristesse* (dir. Otto Preminger, 1958) jumps to the past because the protagonist is remembering previous events. In this way, the movie's point of view motivates its shifting timeline. By contrast, *The Godfather Part II* (dir. Francis Ford Coppola, 1974) jumps back and forth between two timelines, not to suggest that any one character is remembering the past, but to make a larger rhetorical argument about the development of American capitalism. The point of view is wide-ranging, and so is the temporal structure.

Narrative Dynamics: The Interplay between Story and Plot

For the eminent narratologist Meir Sternberg, the interplay between story and plot produces a trio of characteristic narrative effects: prospection, retrospection, and re-cognition.[11] With prospection, the viewer looks ahead to future events, as in a suspense movie that plays on our fears that a bomb will go off. With retrospection, the viewer looks back toward some marked gap in the past, as in a mystery with an off-screen murder that prompts two hours of wondering who held the knife. Recognition also involves a look toward the past, but in a different way, because the gap is initially unmarked. It comes as a complete surprise when we learn that James McAvoy's character died at Dunkirk in *Atonement* (dir. Joe Wright, 2007) and that the rest of his life was imagined by another character. After this revelation, we must rethink some previous sequences and ask again what really happened.

With these three effects in mind, we may formulate one more cluster of questions, centered on the concept of the gap: How does the movie conceal crucial information? How and when does it reveal that information? Is the gap located in the future or the past? Does the movie answer the questions it raises, or does it leave them open at the end? *Charulata* (dir. Satyajit Ray, 1964) ends on a series of freeze-frames, stopping moments before the protagonist touches her husband's hand. The gesture raises the possibility that they will reconcile, and yet the final images leave that possibility unconfirmed.

All of this talk of gaps and information may make it seem that narratives are little more than puzzles, like exercises for our brains. However, narratological analysis can also help us understand a movie's emotional appeals. Stories may generate hopes and fears by representing likable characters who pursue worthy goals, or they may muddy those hopes and fears by representing flawed characters pursuing dubious goals. Plots may organize point of view to encourage sympathy for the protagonist or to make identification maddeningly difficult. The technical-sounding terms prospection, retrospection, and re-cognition each come with an emotional corollary: suspense, curiosity, and surprise.

Unbreakable: Story

The basic story of *Unbreakable* follows a familiar template: the superhero's origin story. The protagonist is David Dunn, played by Bruce Willis. Chronologically, David's journey proceeds through three stages, each one typical of the superhero movie: discovery, training, and confrontation. First, David realizes that he has extraordinary powers: he survives a devastating train crash. Second, with the help of a mentor, David learns how to harness those powers. Elijah, played by Samuel L. Jackson, is an expert in comic books, and he convinces David that comics are merely exaggerations of real-world phenomena. Third, David uses his powers to defeat the Orange Suit Man (Chance Kelly), who has assaulted and imprisoned a family in their home.

David's origin story gains richness from several personal subplots. He overcomes his initial mistrust and builds a friendship with Elijah. He reconciles with his wife, Audrey (Robin Wright). And he deepens his bond with his son, Joseph (Spencer Treat Clark), who believes in the superhero mythology more readily than David does. There is also an important backstory involving a car crash that happened when David and Audrey were in college.

Before turning to Elijah's role in the story, it is worth pausing to reflect on the summary so far. I have broken David's story into various parts. Together, these parts seem well suited for a particular kind of emotional appeal, grounded in hope and fear. David is not just a protagonist: he is a hero. It never occurs to him to use his powers for selfish reasons; instead, he uses his powers to help people in danger. David's personal subplots function to make him more relatable and sympathetic. The story generates a series of well-defined hopes: viewers are asked to hope that David has veritable powers, to hope that he learns to use them more effectively, and to hope that he defeats the thoroughly despicable abductor in the climactic fight scene. Each hope is paired with a corresponding fear: the fear that David might not be a superhero after all, the fear that he might abandon his training, and the fear that he might lose the fight with the Orange Suit Man.

To some extent, I am pointing out the elements of David's story that are conventional, or even clichéd. Dozens of superhero movies depict a flawed but well-intentioned man learning to use his powers for good.

Unbreakable's version of the story feels different because David's superpowers remain within plausible human limits. He is unusually strong, durable, and intuitive, but he cannot fly or shoot laser beams. Ambiguity is built right into the story-world, and David's status as a bona fide superhero remains unclear, even to himself.

Even more striking is the reflexivity of *Unbreakable*'s story. The story is conventional for a very important reason: this movie is *about* narrative conventions. Elijah knows all of the rules of the superhero genre, and he believes that they are meaningful but fictionalized representations of real-world phenomena. Elijah spends most of the movie reading David's life and looking for signs of conventionality. The more closely David's story conforms to the superhero template, the more willing Elijah is to conclude that David is a superhero. The final scene reveals that Elijah has been doing the same thing with his own life for years, looking for signs that he fits into another template: that of the supervillain. Characters look to stories to guide them in their actions.

The movie's reflexivity turns Elijah into a marvelously complex figure, simultaneously a reader, a narrator, and an author. As a reader, he learns the conventions of the genre and looks for someone who fits them closely. As a narrator, he spends much of the movie telling different versions of David's story. In one version, David is just an ordinary man; in another, he is a superhero. Like a good narrator, he illustrates his claims with well-chosen examples, emphasizing David's limitations when he tells the ordinary-man version of David's life and emphasizing David's exceptional abilities when he tells the superhero version of that same life. The movie's final scene reveals that Elijah has been something of an author-figure all along. He does not just tell the story to David; he orchestrates events to fit the narrative pattern that he has had in mind all along.

Unbreakable: Plot

Because David is the protagonist, we might expect the plot to focus on him squarely, giving him more screen time and granting viewers more access to his thoughts. The plot does indeed center on David, but not exclusively. Its construction always leaves an opening, hinting that it might have been Elijah's movie all along. For instance, the duration of the plot is mostly quite limited. Almost every event that we see takes place within a few weeks of story time, spanning from the train crash to the final scene.[12] The tight duration centers the action on David—not on his life as a whole, but on his experience of discovery. And yet this organizing principle allows several exceptions. Prior to the opening title, the movie begins with a scene set in 1961, decades before the main action. Elijah's mother (known as Mrs. Price, played by Charlayne Woodard) gives birth to Elijah in a department store dressing room, and the doctor informs her that the infant has several broken bones. Later, a sequence set in 1974 shows Mrs. Price using comic books to encourage her son to go outside, in defiance of his osteogenesis imperfecta. These scenes show us that the movie we are watching could have been plotted differently, focusing not on David's weeks-long discovery, but on Elijah's years-long journey of living with a physical ailment.

Rather than filtering our access to the story-world exclusively through David, the movie's range is quite expansive. David is absent from several scenes: Elijah's scenes from 1961 and 1974, of course, but also the scene of Joseph learning about the train crash, the scene of Elijah following a mysterious man outside the stadium, a conversation scene between Elijah and Audrey, and a scene of Elijah sitting in despair in a comic book store. If the movie appears to prioritize David's point of view, it is more because of a conspicuous difference in depth. Several times, the movie grants us access to David's thoughts, in the form of flashbacks or visions. Whenever he touches a passerby who has committed a crime, the movie cuts abruptly to the crime. The style of the movie then shifts: the camera is usually at a high angle, and the colors appear desaturated. These markers put the event in David's mind. He is imagining the crime, in a flash, right at the moment he makes contact with the passerby. The subjectivity of the presentation emphasizes the possibility of doubt. For much of the film, David will question the veracity of these flashes. Only the confrontation with the Orange Suit Man will confirm his suspicions. By contrast, the extended flashback to the car crash appears in the long-take style that is more characteristic of the film as a whole. Again, David remembers a past event, but here his memory is marked as unambiguously accurate. This is the true story of the car crash.

Both of these flashbacks differ from the scenes of Elijah's childhood, which are not motivated as memories. When the movie opens with Elijah's birth in 1961, there is no suggestion that Elijah or anyone else is remembering the incident, accurately or inaccurately. It is simply the first story event that we see. Later, when the movie flashes back to the sequence from 1974, there is again no suggestion that Elijah or anyone else is remembering the incident. The previous scene showed David receiving a raise from his boss. David is certainly not thinking about 1974; he has not even met Elijah. The subsequent scene shows Elijah in his gallery. Elijah is not thinking about 1974, either; he is busy explaining comic-book aesthetics. The relationship between the 1974 scene and the gallery scene is not subjective, but causal. Mrs. Price's hard work as a mother has resulted in Elijah's successful career.

We might summarize this contrast in subjectivity by saying that we have access to David's internal experiences, and we do not have access to Elijah's. There is some truth to this statement, but it fails to capture what it feels like to watch the movie unfold. For most of the movie, it feels like the reverse is true. Samuel L. Jackson gives a charismatic performance, making Elijah's emotions easy to read. In the gallery scene, Jackson vividly conveys Elijah's pride in his collection, an emotion that shifts rapidly to disgust when Elijah realizes that a prospective client fails to appreciate the artistry of comics. We may not dip into Elijah's memories, but his external behavior makes his emotions transparent. By contrast, David seems unreadable. In many scenes, it is difficult to see David's face at all, which remains half hidden underneath a hooded raincoat. Even when we do see David's face, Willis relies on understatement to convey the character's hesitation and doubt. On the surface, it is David, not Elijah, who seems mysterious. The contrast makes it all the more surprising when we realize that we have been misreading Elijah's character all along.

Unbreakable: Narrative Dynamics

As a filmmaker with a reputation for surprise twists, Shyamalan has faced a specific storytelling problem for much of his career: How do you engage the audience for the full one hundred minutes or so *before* the twist is revealed? For most of its running time, *Unbreakable* does not try to shock us with twists; its primary appeals are rooted in curiosity and suspense. Like a good mystery, *Unbreakable* organizes its curiosity plot around a marked gap in the past. Elijah wants to know if David is a superhero. To find out, Elijah does not ask David to leap off a tall building or stop a speeding train. He asks David questions, seeking to uncover the mysteries of the car crash and of a near drowning that David suffered as a child. Approximately two-thirds of the way through the movie, these two questions are answered in quick succession. Elijah explains the near drowning by noting that every superhero has a fatal weakness, and David explains the car crash by admitting that his love for Audrey made him lie about his injury.

With these twin mysteries resolved, the movie shifts from curiosity to suspense. Now the driving question centers on the future: What is David going to do with his newly confirmed superpowers? Very quickly, the movie turns this open-ended question into something much more specific: Can David defeat the Orange Suit Man and rescue the survivors? There are two possible outcomes: David wins, or he loses. The first outcome is marked as very good, and the second is marked as very bad. Having created this tightly focused uncertainty, the movie stretches out (literally, suspends) the uncertainty for several minutes, during which time it seems very likely that our worst fears will come true.[13]

Unbreakable delivers several small surprises as it unfolds. It is a surprise when we learn that Joseph has put extra weights on the bar in the exercise scene, and it is a surprise when we learn that two children have come downstairs to rescue David from the pool. The movie's biggest surprise, by far, comes in the final scene. In narrative theory, a surprise is not just a shocking turn of events. It is a shocking turn of events that prompts an act of retrospection. As the movie comes to a close, Elijah loudly declares, "They called me Mr. Glass." He has mentioned this experience with childhood bullying before, to his mother in the 1974 sequence and then to Audrey in the physical therapy scene. Previously, the line seemed like backstory, generating sympathy for Elijah. Now, after the surprise revelation, it seems like a crucial key to Elijah's character. He has taken the insult and turned it into a source of strength, both impressive and disturbing. The bullying has become a core element of his origin story.

The movie's ending strives for a difficult balance: predictable in principle but unpredicted in practice, delivering a surprise that will feel like it has been planted all along. To be sure, some viewers will find that the movie has missed the mark. Some may guess the twist an hour in advance; others may argue that the movie has cheated by leaving out certain information. For my part, I am always impressed by the way Shyamalan has used two visual motifs to prepare us for the final twist: the reflection motif and the upside-down motif. Reflections appear in almost all of Elijah's scenes. In the opening scene, the handheld camera pans to show a mirror in the room where Mrs. Price has given birth. In the 1974 sequence, a static camera focuses on Elijah, not directly, but via the reflection on the front of a television set. When David visits Elijah's gallery for the first time, the camera remains outside the shop for several moments, looking through reflective glass. These scenes provide visual reinforcement for the movie's verbal references to glass, and they evoke the idea that Elijah and David are, in some sense, reflections of one another.

Symbolically, a reflection can suggest similarity, but it can also suggest opposition, since a reflection inverts the subject. The theme of inversion also informs the upside-down motif, which appears several times over the course of the movie. On the train, David smiles at a child who is looking at him upside down. Later, another child—David's son Joseph—is upside down when he learns of the car crash. Then, a third child—Elijah in 1974—sees an upside-down comic book, which he turns aright. Already the upside-down motif has tied together children, crashes, and comics. When Elijah suffers a serious fall in the subway station, he is upside down again. David then appears upside down when he lifts weights in his basement. A major repetition occurs when Elijah sees a comic book that reignites his faith in David; the upside-down view of the comic book recalls Elijah's first comic book from 1974. Still later, David walks by an upside-down sign when he visits the train yard, and then he remembers Audrey in an upside-down car after the car crash.

Several of these upside-down motifs appear in inverted point-of-view shots. Because they are so clearly subjective, these inverted shots raise a question that gets at the heart of the story: Are David and Elijah really opposites? Or are they only opposites because various characters *perceive* them that way? Joseph and Elijah both desperately want to believe that David is a superhero. Audrey does not, and David is unsure. The upside-down shot links Joseph's admiring view of his father to Elijah's proud view of the antagonist he has created. The ending of the story suggests that Joseph and Elijah were right all along: David is a superhero. But the recurring upside-down motif may undercut our confidence in

Joseph and Elijah by hinting that they may have been seeing the world the wrong way.

Is David Dunn a superhero or not? The movie has posed this question, and not in a neutral way. It has nudged us to hope for a positive answer, partly because being a superhero will make David Dunn happier and partly because seeing a superhero will fulfill our generic expectations. If we find ourselves wanting David to be a superhero, then we find ourselves in the same position as Joseph (a child) and Elijah (a villain). The doubts we have about them must extend to us. Our perceptions, too, may be upside down.

Notes

1. Aristotle, *The Poetics of Aristotle*, translated by Stephen Halliwell (Chapel Hill: University of North Carolina Press, 1987), 37.
2. See, for instance, *Russian Formalist Criticism: Four Essays*, edited by Lee T. Lemon and Marion J. Reis (Lincoln: University of Nebraska Press, 1965); and Gérard Genette, *Narrative Discourse: An Essay in Method*, translated by Jane E. Lewin (Ithaca, NY: Cornell University Press, 1980).
3. On "postclassical narratology," see Jan Alber and Monika Fludernik, "Introduction," in *Postclassical Narratology: Approaches and Analyses*, edited by Jan Alber and Monika Fludernik (Columbus: The Ohio State University Press, 2010), 3.
4. I borrow the terms *story* and *plot* from David Bordwell, Kristin Thompson, and Jeff Smith, *Film Art: An Introduction*, 12th ed. (New York: McGraw-Hill, 2020), 75.
5. Peter Verstraten, *Film Narratology*, translated by Stefan van der Lecq (Toronto: University of Toronto Press, 2009), 9.
6. Brian Richardson, *Unlikely Stories: Causality and the Nature of Modern Narrative* (Newark: University of Delaware Press, 1997), 106.
7. Marie-Laure Ryan proposes a scalar theory of narrativity, whereby certain traits can make a work seem "more" or "less" narrative than another. One trait that increases narrativity is the presence of "agents, motivated by identifiable goals and plans." See Ryan, *Avatars of Story* (Minneapolis: University of Minnesota Press, 2006), 8.
8. On narrative construction in contemporary Hollywood, see Kristin Thompson, *Storytelling in New Hollywood: Understanding Classical Narrative Technique* (Cambridge, MA: Harvard University Press, 1999), 10–21. On narrative construction in 1940s Hollywood, see David Bordwell, *Reinventing Hollywood: How 1940s Filmmakers Changed Movie Storytelling* (Chicago: University of Chicago Press, 2017), 126–30.

9   See the discussion of order, frequency, and duration in Bordwell, Thompson, and Smith, *Film Art*, 80–82.
10 Bordwell, Thompson, and Smith, *Film Art*, 88–94.
11 Meir Sternberg, "Narrativity: From Objectivist to Functional Paradigm," *Poetics Today* 31, no. 3 (Fall 2010): 640–41.
12 The movie does not specify the exact duration of these events, but it gives us enough clues to make an educated guess. David is on the train because he was in New York for a job interview. Later, around two-thirds of the way into the movie, David learns that he got the job. Presumably, this happens just a few weeks later.
13 My account of suspense is indebted to Noël Carroll, "Toward a Theory of Film Suspense," in *Theorizing the Moving Image* (New York: Cambridge University Press, 1996), 94–117.

5

At the First Sign

Analyzing Television Posters with Semiotics

JONATHAN GRAY

Gray revisits semiotics, a technique often employed to make sense of ads, music videos, or underlying binaries, structures, and ideologies in longer texts, and makes the case for semiotics' utility in exploring paratexts, all those elements that surround a text, that are often not considered "the text itself," yet that frame and position it. Gray then illustrates this by analyzing a second-season poster for The Walking Dead.

"Don't judge a book by its cover," we're told, precisely because we all regularly do judge books by their covers—and movies, television shows, podcasts, radio shows, video games, and all media by their trailers, posters, and other promotional entourage. For analysts, though, these materials that advertise, introduce us to, and direct us toward media— these paratexts—can thus tell us a great deal about what pitches various media products are employing, what they want us to expect, what frames they propose we evaluate them by, what meanings they want to share and circulate in advance of "the thing itself."[1] As Gerard Genette wrote of the paratext in proposing the term, it is "an airlock that helps the reader pass without too much difficulty from one world to the other," creating our early experiences with this other world's atmosphere, or preparing those who have been there before for reentry.[2]

This chapter considers how to analyze paratexts, or more specifically it focuses on how to analyze posters as one particular instance of paratextuality. Posters are designed to seek us out in banal, everyday moments and places: they sit next to us at bus shelters, perch overhead on public transit, or cling to the sides of buses; in the form of billboards, they add themselves to our commutes or holiday travels; in smaller form, they inhabit magazines and newspapers, sandwiched between articles, or they pop up at us online; in even smaller form, as thumbnails, they constitute much of the graphic interface of streaming media platforms. If they work as successfully as their creators hope, they will usher us toward their texts, but more than just pointing us in a direction, they'll send us to them with expectations, hopes, concerns, and meanings, around and with which the text will then need to work. But they also speak to those who don't follow their directions, forming public meanings about their texts and thereby situating their texts culturally. Regardless, then, of whether we care only about the products they point to or more broadly about the meanings circulated in and through media, they contribute significantly, at times vitally, to media meaning-making, and as such they can and should be subjected to textual analysis themselves.

One can approach this analysis in many ways. But this chapter proposes the particular effectiveness of semiotic analysis. Semiotics works by deconstructing any image, phrase, or text into its many parts, asking what each part brings to the collective. This fine-grained approach makes it ideal for analyzing "smaller," short-form texts such as ads, music videos, or, here, posters. Semiotics was posed as a science of signs/meaning, but whereas many social scientific approaches to analyzing texts, such as content analysis, struggle to account for vital elements such as context, form, culture, and interpretation, a semiotic approach handily offers both the scientific rigor of a method that considers each part of a text and a humanistic sensitivity to and interest in a text's place in cultural and textual systems. It moves from a micro focus on each constitutive part of a text to ask larger, macro questions about the ideologies and norms that a text is variously championing, relying upon, or challenging, and thus it helps analysts see the stakes that a (para)text is establishing, the atmosphere it is creating.

Semiotic Analysis

Semiotics stems from early-twentieth-century linguist Ferdinand de Saussure's interest in the science of signs.[3] Language, he noted, is largely arbitrary, by which he didn't mean that in practice we can use any word to mean anything, just that in theory we could. This chapter is about posters, for instance, and I write with a fair degree of comfort that you understand what a poster is. But first, it's not hard to imagine another language in which the combined letters "poster" refer instead to, for instance, the feeling of not wanting to get out of bed, or perhaps a mischievous pet. It's only through usage and culture that "poster" has come to mean a sheet of paper (or a digital equivalent), likely advertising something. Google Translate tells me that in Sanskrit, a poster is written as पोस्टर, while in Swahili, it is *bango*. But other languages don't just necessarily have a different *word* for the exact same content; they might instead divide the world up differently. Maybe the concept of "posterness" is specific in some ways to English, to a particular group of languages of which English is one, or even just to this specific moment in time in English, and translating that word to other languages or times may not allow for the subtleties of how the nearest equivalent of "posterness" might entail other concepts in other languages. Perhaps elsewhere, for example, what I call a brochure might be referred to with the same word that signals what I call a poster, or perhaps other languages or times distinguish(ed) between posters with different purposes, giving each their own word.

Thus, while Saussure's semiotics involves the *signifier* as that which we use to represent a concept or thing ("poster") and the *signified* as the concept itself ("posterness"), his assertion that language is arbitrary insists that not only the word but the concept itself is in no way set, except through linguistic and cultural convention. Language, in short, gives meaning to the world; it is not a neutral system of applying words to things, but it creates meaning. Those things become distinct concepts *through* language and through the assignation of words or of other signs such as pictures, images, or any other communication system: a red light need not mean "Stop," a rose need not signify love, and an outstretched middle finger need not be a rude gesture. Granted, some signs are "motivated," not entirely arbitrary, as with onomatopoeias, metonyms, and synecdoches, for instance. But even then, different languages use different onomatopoeias (English cats purr, *les chats français ronronnent*), and we have all probably seen many metonymic signs used to distinguish men's and women's restrooms, not just stick figures with or without dresses. No sign can boast deep, unchanging ontology.

However, if all signs operate by cultural convention, on the one hand, they must all continually replicate themselves—if "poster" means the same thing fifty years from now, it will be because usage across culture has kept it stable. On the other hand, all sign systems are thus open to being changed over time. Each use contributes variously to holding a sign in place or to recoding it. And while the stakes of the word "poster" may seem small, abstract concepts such as justice, strength, or equality, and contested descriptive terms related to concepts such as gender, race, sexuality, or nationality, matter far more. Semiotics tells us that none of these terms "is what it is": if they are to keep their current meanings, that must be through concerted effort, just as concerted effort will be required to change those meanings. That effort will occur in many venues—anywhere a sign system is used—but media become especially important sites to study precisely because of their capacity to reach so many. Semiotic analysis examines how signs work, both individually and together, variously to hold in place or to challenge the cultural world around us.

A key focus of semiotic analysis can be the syntagmatic and paradigmatic associations between signs, recognizing that much cultural meaning stems from those associations. To examine syntagmatic associations is to focus on which signs "team up" together; to examine paradigmatic associations is to focus on signs that contrast with or replace one another. To return to the icons on restroom doors, for example, the most common pairing of stick figures, with or without a dress, relies upon *and hence perpetuates* a syntagmatic association between men and trousers, which is opposed paradigmatically to a second syntagmatic association between women and dresses. First, then, these icons work to normalize certain forms of dress for certain people, implying women *should* wear dresses, not trousers (and vice versa for men). Second, it insists that there are only two options and that the world divides between them. Third, the ubiquity of these icons worldwide succeeds in suggesting a universal truth: this isn't just how gender works in this one place, but "everywhere." Or consider a sophomoric alternative I saw in a bar, where the men's restroom had a picture of a pencil and the women's, a pencil sharpener. These signs refer to genitals, and so on the one hand they work to normalize a distinction between genders according to genitals, and indeed they suggest genitals matter, decisively dividing the world into two. But since signs work through associations, it's also worth noting that pencils are the "doers" of the writing world, pencil sharpeners the mere aids, and thus *whether intended or not*, men are syntagmatically associated with writing/creating, women with assistance. Yet another pair of bathroom door icons I saw presented stylized pictures of Little Red Riding Hood and the Big Bad Wolf. These relied on users' awareness of the fairy tale and again carried a host of syntagmatic associations—Little Red Riding Hood is innocent, under threat, and often sexualized in Halloween costumes and such, whereas the Big Bad Wolf is associated with a raw, aggressive, predatorial power and with craftiness—in ways that superimpose those associations onto gendered distinctions.

Examining syntagmatic and paradigmatic associations also invites us to consider what is missing and hence to consider the specificity of this choice of sign. Because syntagmatic groupings suture various signs together, the absence of one or more members of a usual grouping may at times be conspicuous. We can, for instance, anthropomorphize a salt shaker to signify loneliness by depicting it with no pepper shaker in attendance. Meanwhile, paradigmatic contrasts may be rendered clear in some depictions—as when a sign for men exists next door to a sign for women—but they also exist in what was chosen and what was not. Consider our choice of what to wear in the morning, for example. The pair of jeans you decide to put on is related paradigmatically to the skirt, tuxedo trousers, or cargo shorts you do not. Similarly, then, in media analysis, we should always think about what was chosen and what wasn't and consider effects: How might this scene have been different if shot another way? What would be signified differently about this character if they wore that top instead of this one? What is signaled by starting the story (or advertising it) with this scene instead of another one? One must be careful not to allow hypotheticals to overwhelm one's analysis, but a good analyst will always be thinking about choices, impacts, and consequences and about how these various associations work in concert to communicate grander messages.

Certainly, another famed name in semiotic analysis is that of Roland Barthes, who in his book *Mythologies* suggests that we are surrounded by the "myths" created by such semiotic associations.[4] Barthes's book served as an important early invitation to scholars to textually analyze a wide range of objects that few others considered meaningful. He wrote multiple short analyses of, for example, toys, wine and milk, the semiotics attached to Einstein's brain, and a prominent magazine cover. Barthes saw media as perpetuating numerous dominant ideologies and used textual analysis not for aesthetic appreciation but to unpack what roles media and popular culture were playing in perpetuating ideologies of, for example, class, gender, race, childhood, and nationalism. *Mythologies* invites us, too, to employ semiotic analysis to explore the mythologies that surround us and media's roles either in further embedding sign associations that do the work of various ideologies or, perhaps, in disarticulating associations, pulling them apart, and resignifying them to disrupt prevailing ideologies.

For some excellent examples of semiotic analysis at work, see Gillian Dyer's analysis of ads, John Fiske and John Hartley's analyses of television shows, Jane Gravells's analysis of news reporting, Michael Betancourt's analysis of title sequences, Arthur Asa Berger's and Jonathan Bignell's varying semiotic analyses, and Pete Bennett and Julian McDougall's collection updating Barthes's *Mythologies*.[5] However, semiotics never quite caught on as much as it could have, and a key reason may be precisely because it breaks texts down into their constitutive parts and thereby risks being exhaustive and overwhelming to practice with longer-form texts with so many parts. It can, of course, be employed in far more targeted ways: when an object in a text really seems to matter, one can analyze it semiotically; one can examine costuming, sets, lighting, shot choice, or any other production element alone; one can home in on particularly important scenes, or so forth. But we can also embrace its utility for smaller, more compact texts that have fewer parts and hence that allow a more "complete" analysis, such as ads, music videos, memes (see Baishya's analysis in chapter 16 of this volume), logos, and all manner of paratexts, including trailers, merchandise, previously-on segments, opening credit or title sequences, and posters. Here, I consider the last of these.

Case Study: *The Walking Dead*'s Season 2 Poster

Posters can be remarkably evocative, communicating a great deal about a show in little time. We should see their role as dual, though: both to encourage new viewers, and to set expectations, mobilize myths, and propose key meanings or even questions for new and returning viewers. Consider this 2012 poster for season 2 of AMC's hit zombie apocalypse television show, *The Walking Dead* (2011–22; see figure 5.1).

Figure 5.1: A U.S. poster advertising the second season of *The Walking Dead* prior to its release.

First, what do we see? Much of the top two-thirds of the poster is occupied by clouds—dark and stormy in the bottom left, clear and breaking in the top right. In the bottom third, a lone figure runs along a dirt road, away from the viewer, toward the sun and a darkened country house and weather vane. The figure is in silhouette but wears a cowboy hat, holds a revolver, and is clearly wearing a (gun?) belt, off which two other, unidentifiable items hang. The rest of the landscape is desolate, grassy and hilly, but hard to make out because it is backlit. Superimposed over the clouds are the show's title; four stars, attributed to *People*; and the following quotation: "... Full-Throttle Suspense and Terror...," attributed to *TV Guide*. Broadcast information and AMC's logo adorn the bottom of the ad.

This deceptively simple ad has a lot going on semiotically, especially in representing genre. The figure appears to be a cowboy, which metonymically suggests a Western (as does the grey-and-sepia color tone)... and yet the likely tire-not–wagon wheel tracks in the dirt road suggest this is not in the usual time period of a Western. The lone country house is a semiotic cypher: on one hand, country houses like this regularly represent honest-to-goodness middle America, while on the other hand, it's enshrouded in darkness and surrounded by a flock of birds having just taken flight, both signifying a horror movie. Is this *Little House on the Prairie* (NBC, 1974–83) or *Texas Chainsaw Massacre* (dir. Tobe Hooper, 1974)? We're left to wonder. Similarly, we are left to ask whether the cowboy is running away from something or toward something. The dual presence of the sun and the country house in the distance further confuses us: is the figure running toward the light (signifying hope) or toward the house (which, as we've said, could represent safety but could also represent danger)? The clouds, too, offer a semiotic duel of the fates, with one-half of the formation representing danger, one-half hope.

In terms of the words in the ad, the quoted reviews first signify high quality, and since Westerns and horror movies are often derided as mere generic fare, the reviews thereby work to ameliorate that frame. And yet as they're adding terms such as "quality" or "prestige television" to this generic hybrid mix, they also add terms relating to action ("full-throttle") and thriller ("suspense") movies while confirming the horror ("terror"). The title, meanwhile, further confirms the horror, "the walking dead" being a phrase used to signify zombies while also playing into the above-noted duel of fates by asking us whether our cowboy's days are numbered—the "walking dead" can also suggest inevitable demise.

Syntagmatically, all of these signs unite to signify a show that generically mixes horror, the (probably nonhistorical) Western, action, and the thriller, while further suggesting that the binaries of hope versus despair and safety versus danger will figure heavily. And since cowboys signify not just men but the apex of rugged masculinity, in Barthesian terms, the cowboy invokes a powerful myth of a specific kind of masculinity, mobilizing it and suggesting that it will undergird the show's action. With no other characters around, we are promised a male lead and promised that this show will be, at least in part, about masculinity.

For returning viewers, meanwhile, a whole host of meanings are suggested by what is *not* a part of this syntagm. Most notably, this character is alone. Returning viewers, or even those who have just seen previews or other paratexts, will likely identify the running figure as Rick (Andrew Lincoln), a sheriff adorned with cowboy hat, gun belt, and revolver. But where is the rest of the cast? In its opening season, *The Walking Dead* was often lauded for its ensemble cast. Within this context, therefore, what does Rick's isolation signify? That the rest of the characters are all dead or turned into zombies seems unlikely: even edgy dramas fond of killing characters rarely wipe out all but one of their key cast. Instead, then, it seems more likely that Rick is either running to save them or leading them away from peril. Either way, this strengthens an association between Rick and heroism, insisting that he is not just a hero but the central hero, the one who matters. Indeed, if he is leading them, then "we" as viewers are elided with "them." The point of view gives us their eyes, thereby craftily inviting viewers to see him as "our" leader. For potential viewers debating whether to start watching the show, this gives a determined framing to Rick; for returning viewers, it underlines his heroism. Or perhaps not, for as we have said, he just might be fleeing, which just might signal lack of heroism: Is Rick a coward, abandoning his friends? Such a reading seems less likely—Rick's left hand is poised on his belt, his right hand out with gun at the ready, together signifying battle-readiness, not a fearful dash away from the scene. The cowboy myth further works to discount such a reading. But its slight possibility as an interpretation, I'd suggest, is intriguing, acting once again to signify tension: new viewers are largely encouraged to see Rick as a hero, and the poster largely works to insist to returning viewers that Rick is the leader, yet both groups are invited to have a few lingering doubts about him, or more generally they are invited not to trust anyone, but to expect "anything."

Much meaning can also be gleaned paradigmatically by asking what the ad is *not* doing or showing. The syntagm presented is a rural one, which contrasts paradigmatically with the first season's setting in Atlanta and its suburbs. Even nonviewers may have seen and recalled one of the first season's more striking posters, in which a lone cowboy figure rides toward Atlanta. His side of the highway is empty, while the other side is packed with cars, all of which seem to have been fleeing the city and then gotten caught in a traffic jam, their drivers all now missing. Thus, to shift from this urban paradigm to a rural one is striking. Within the context of the series, this signifies new challenges, a new location, and, perhaps with it, a whole new dynamic and set of governing expectations and norms. And since cowboys are more commonly syntagmatically associated with country farms than with cities, maybe our cowboy is even arriving at his "proper" environment, signaling he is coming into his own.

Another set of meanings are generated by comparing the ad paradigmatically to other television posters. Here I am aided by the act of collecting almost six hundred television posters from *Entertainment Weekly* between 2011 and 2021. While semiotics allows us to analyze single ads, the method is also helpful for examining common and widely reused signs, in this case across these posters. One thing that becomes quickly evident looking at the six hundred ads is that television posters overwhelmingly center cast members; indeed, a striking majority of television posters consist solely of photos of the cast, with no or minimal background. Another commonality is that television posters tend to be colorful, whether in an attempt to arrest magazine readers who were otherwise leafing onwards to the next article or to signify a "colorful"— interesting, vibrant—medium. Thus, this poster's solitary, faceless figure and its drab grey-and-sepia tone make it stand out or, in semiotic terms, place it in a different paradigm. The paradigm is that of quality/prestige television, as it is the more stylized productions that more commonly adopt such a strategy, and the poster's grey and sepia signify edginess and realism, not vibrancy or happiness. The implication is that the story, feel, and aura of the show are stars, not only a given cast member. Even in posing questions—Is he running toward or away from danger? Is he a hero or a coward? What happened to the rest of the cast? What has disturbed the birds?—the poster eschews a norm of being more definitive. And by doing so, it therefore posits that its plot will similarly contain more complexity, not simplicity, and that it exists in a world of more moral questions and uncertainties than does much other television. In short, the ad works not just in and of itself, but in relation to other ads, performing distinctiveness and difference to insist that the show itself stands apart from other television.

In terms of myths, as already noted, this poster relies upon associations of Westerns and cowboys with a certain notion of masculinity and/as leadership, since our lone figure is either facing the elements alone or leading a group behind him. With little in the poster to suggest a contestation of that myth, by nature it therefore recirculates and hence gently reinscribes that myth. In doing so, it proposes that myth as a heuristic device for making sense of the show at large, encouraging new and returning viewers alike to consider the show and its characters in relationship to the cowboy myth. Since this occurs alongside numerous signs of quality television, the poster therefore also contributes, slightly, toward solidifying a syntagmatic connection between quality, "complex" television and a focus on men and masculinity (see *The Sopranos* (HBO, 1999–2007), *Breaking Bad* (AMC, 2008–13), *Mad Men* (AMC, 2007–15), or *Dexter* (Showtime, 2006–13) for other famed examples).[6]

In addition, the poster plays with the idea of middle America, again mobilizing that myth to propose that viewers decode the action of the series in relation to it. Here, though, the poster's messages are too murky to constitute a clear reification of such a myth. Perhaps that country house represents safety, in which case the myth of middle America as pleasant safe harbor would be recirculated, but its depiction leaves it worryingly close to the isolated house of a horror movie in ways that might suggest a challenge to such a myth. We could imagine adding details to move the sign one way or the other: a proudly flying American flag outside, for instance, might strengthen nationalist ties of the image to safety, just as a tattered flag might signify a house (and myth) in disrepair. At the level of the poster, no resolution is offered, but questions are posed to those who might voyage onwards into season 2 of *The Walking Dead*: *can* one find safety in this new world? *Is* this rural landscape any safer than the urban one of season 1? What *has* become of the American dream?

Conclusion

As audience studies insists, textual analysis shows us what *offers* are made by a text, never necessarily which offers are accepted by readers. Paratextual analysis must contend with yet another challenge: namely, it is hard to predict—or even retroactively ascertain—which paratexts an audience member encounters. In the case of *The Walking Dead*, surely some new or returning audience members never saw this poster or quickly glossed over it. As such, we should be careful not to overestimate its power. Yet it still has powers: to frame or reframe the show, to suggest genre, or to propose central myths, ideologies, and meanings. Paratexts are thus rich sites for textual analysis, helping us to explore the atmospheres and environments for which they prepare audiences on their journeys to the program (or movie or game or podcast or other media). We might analyze them to get a better understanding of the meanings that producers would prefer we glean from their texts—or, alternatively, we might study audience-created paratexts to see those preferred meanings being contested or challenged. We might look *across* paratexts to find dominant themes or patterns that relate to specific genres, images, or concepts. We can also explore differences between paratexts for the same text, seeing in them either tensions with regard to the preferred meaning(s) or specific pitches to specific audiences: what did season 2 posters for *The Walking Dead* look like in other countries, for instance, or what collection of thumbnails does Netflix use for it? In all such endeavors, semiotics can help us.

Notes

1   See Jonathan Gray, *Show Sold Separately: Promos, Spoilers, and Other Media Paratexts* (New York: New York University Press, 2010).
2   Gerard Genette, *Paratexts: The Thresholds of Interpretation*, translated by Jane E. Lewin (Cambridge: Cambridge University Press, 1997), 408.
3   Ferdinand de Saussure, *Course in General Linguistics*, translated by Wade Baskin (London: McGraw-Hill, 1983).

4   Roland Barthes, *Mythologies*, translated by Annette Lavers (St. Albans: Paladin, 1973).
5   Gillian Dyer, *Advertising as Communication* (London: Routledge, 1982); John Fiske and John Hartley, *Reading Television* (London: Methuen, 1978); Jane Gravells, *Semiotics and Verbal Texts: How the News Media Construct a Crisis* (Basingstoke, UK: Palgrave MacMillan, 2017); Michael Betancourt, *Semiotics and Title Sequences: Text-Image Composites in Motion Graphics* (New York: Routledge, 2017); Arthur Asa Berger, *Signs in Contemporary Culture: An Introduction to Semiotics*, 2nd ed. (Salem, WI: Sheffield, 1999); Jonathan Bignell, *Media Semiotics: An Introduction*, 2nd ed. (Manchester: Manchester University Press, 2002); Pete Bennett and Julian McDougall, eds., *Barthes' Mythologies Today: Readings of Contemporary Culture* (London: Routledge, 2015).
6   See Amanda D. Lotz, *Cable Guys: Television and Masculinities in the 21st Century* (New York: New York University Press, 2014).

6

Fragmented, Playful, Uncomfortable

The Textual Analysis of Digital Games

DIANE CARR

Carr takes a fragmentary/lexial approach to analyzing video games, adopting a method that homes in on particular moments that invite and welcome deep scrutiny and reflexive interpretation. Carr illustrates this method by focusing on numerous cases in which fantastical games offer messages about normative and nonnormative bodies and their uses.

Playing a digital game can involve experimenting and making mistakes, getting lost, and testing out strategies. Clearly, digital games differ from other kinds of screen media. This chapter describes a version of textual analysis that reflects these differences. It's an approach that lends itself to arguments about representation, and probably works best for single-player games set in fictional worlds with characters and narrative elements, as well as rules and scores. This chapter takes something of a behind-the-scenes approach, exploring questions about the relationship between textuality and play, games and interpretation, rather than providing an exemplar analysis.

While game researchers have used different approaches to close analysis, the need to begin by playing the game is generally acknowledged, because "being up close and personal with a given game forces you to think through its specificity, helping thereby to ensure against the temptations of over generalization and testing the validity of top-down analyses of "games" as a general category. Even empirical studies of gamers might benefit from such analysis, necessary if they are to understand the role of different player styles and the ways players might subvert "preferred" modes of play and interpretation."[1] As these references to play, interpretation, and subversion suggest, games are not neutral, and neither is the player, or the textual analyst. The textual analyst is *somebody*, situated in time, space, language, institutions, and culture. The game researcher using textual analysis selects and plays a game and opts to treat it as a text in order to generate an interpretation. Each of these steps involves choices, and these choices will shape the eventual analysis.

Within game studies, as in other fields, textual analysis has meant various things. Game researchers with links to the social sciences might associate the term with forms of content analysis.[2] This can involve looking across a sizable collection of games to map the frequency or omission of a particular element. Arts and humanities–oriented game researchers might use the same term to describe the in-depth, up-close analysis of representations within a single game. They might apply a set of concepts drawn from, for example, feminist horror studies, critical race theory, or queer studies to a selected game.[3] The version of textual analysis explored in this chapter is compatible with this approach, although it might involve a different starting position.

Here, textual analysis starts with "fragmenting" a game and then unraveling these fragments using a set of codes. This approach is adapted from the work of literary theorist Roland Barthes.[4] Unraveling fragments involves reiteration and reflection, mess, and plurality. In this way, the process resembles play. Because it is messy, it can be difficult to reconcile with deadlines. It can be an uncomfortable process that drags the analyst in unexpected directions. Yet, by doing so, it offers the analyst a chance to address "the complexity and elusiveness, the real political difficulty, of representations."[5] This chapter begins with an outline of Barthes's approach and a discussion of the ways that games and play complicate analysis, before addressing some issues of adaptation, and then sharing some examples of fragmentation and analysis.

Borrowing from Barthes

Barthes connects a particular idea about what a text is, with suggestions for how it might be analyzed. Barthes describes the "text" as a virtual fabric (a textile, an illusionary whole) that can be pulled apart and unraveled. Imagine approaching a mural and discovering that it is a mosaic, composed of tiny fragments. For Barthes, "To interpret a text is not to give it a (more or less justified, more or less free) meaning, but on the contrary to appreciate what *plural* constitutes it."[6]

In *S/Z*, Barthes demonstrates a version of textual analysis that involves breaking up a novel into tiny fragments ("lexia") and then scrutinizing these using a series of five codes.[7] These codes work like lenses, helping the analyst to explore, unpack, and unravel the different facets or senses of each fragment. Briefly, the five codes are the code of actions (acts, events, consequences, progression, etc.), the code of enigma (the questions posed, suspense, and disclosure), the semic code (adjectives, labels, descriptions, attributes), the symbolic code (antithesis, the play of opposites), and the cultural or referential code (references to forms of knowledge, perhaps cultural, "commonsense," medical, or scientific).

By applying these codes to fragments of a text, the analyst can begin to make conventions discernible. As Julie Lesage has explained when writing about the adaptation of Barthes's approach for film analysis, "In daily life and in art, conventions establish what is probable, plausible or obvious. They provide whole clusters of seemingly natural details. The fact that these details and the conventions behind them are unremarkable means that ordinarily we do not notice or discuss them, that they are lost until named."[8] Lesage's points about noticing and naming naturalized conventions indicate why this version of textual analysis is well suited to studies of power and representation. As part of "reading off" fragments, the analyst might eventually connect with relevant conceptual resources (for example, feminist literature on race and representation in science fiction) to further explore, for instance, the bodies, societies, technologies, and fantasies encountered in a science fiction game. The advantage of starting with fragmentation is that it supports depth and granularity, and foregrounds interpretation-as-process. Interpretation mixes connotation with association, where connotation is a property of the text, and association is a property of the subject/analyst.[9] Interpretation is something that happens between the text and the subject, so (assuming an embodied, culturally situated analyst) it will be local and partial rather than fully determined or universal. Plus, because Barthes's approach takes a pluralistic approach to interpretation, it is relatively compatible with gameplay.

To explore this further, imagine playing a science fiction game that features a mission set in a secret research laboratory. The playable game protagonist (the avatar) must break in and retrieve a briefcase. One of the first obstacles the player faces is a guard dog named Dora. Perhaps Dora's main job is to look intimidating. Or perhaps Dora is programmed to bark to alert the human guards if she detects noise or movement. As an obstacle, Dora has the role of encouraging the player to devise and test strategies. She might be coaching the player to try stealth, potholing, or parkour. If Dora is programmed to bite the avatar, the amount of damage that she inflicts might be more important to the player than what she looks like. Even so, Dora's appearance could be important if her role is to intimidate while representing a particular kind of militant corporate power within the game world. Perhaps (after replaying this section of the game and being exposed, chased, thwarted, and bitten), the player discovers that it is possible to alter Dora's behavior by whistling or giving her sausages. Yet, the player's decision to avoid or engage with Dora in the first place might be shaped by their real-world feelings about actual dogs. What matters here is that Dora is not "one thing." Dora is an amalgamation of programming, graphics, and associations. By running away, using stealth, or throwing sausages, the player can produce different Doras, as well as different versions of the game's protagonist (as accident prone, dog friendly, reckless, or cautious, for instance).

The player can manifest different versions of Dora. So, the player-analyst has decisions to make. They could select one aspect of Dora to focus on and argue (or imply, or simply assume) that *this* version of Dora is definitive. Games invite this kind of claim because games measure performance, quantify outcomes, rate bodies, penalize errors, and reward achievement with points and scores. By doing so, a game depicts some actions, actors, and outcomes as quantifiably better than others. Progress in a game might require adherence to a role and a set of rules. Does it always follow that the "winning" version of a game (or the rewarded version of an action) is inevitably the most significant or indicative? For the analyst, do replayed encounters, failed attempts, and accidents count? Is playing a game more about agency, obedience, or some kind of combination? These questions about agency are relevant to claims about interpretation and meaning-making. Playing might involve obeying the rules, striving for goals, and studiously playing "in role," but it could also involve trying on different outfits while testing out a flamethrower in an inappropriate location just to see what happens.

Suppressing this kind of playfulness from an account of the game might make it easier to produce an authoritative interpretation, but the performance of authority within knowledge production is something that a reflexive textual analyst might prefer to query. Experience is messy, and research and analysis involve omission.[10] Analysts make decisions as they go, positioning themselves and their work in the process. Decisions about how to analyze a game and what to omit are bound up with decisions about the status of play and the agency of players. Game analysis happens in context, as do game development and game play. This has implications for who plays, how games are played, and the conventions that might emerge within player communities— and some of these conventions relate to meaning and interpretation:

> There are player communities where only goal-directed play is considered acceptable, just as there are forms of analysis that presuppose particular modes of play. . . . This is one of the reasons why it might be important to continue to reflect on and distinguish between claims about meaning-making that pertain to games-as-designed, claims about meaning-making during play, and claims about the interpretation of games as a situated practice. These distinctions will have implications for game scholars wishing to engage in game interpretation while acknowledging the complexity of the relationship between meaning and the game-as-structure, the game-as-played, and play as a variable, multiple, embodied and contextual mode of engagement.[11]

As a process, fragmentation helps to foreground the plurality of the game-as-text. If I want to conduct a critical analysis without steamrolling play and playfulness out of my account, I need an approach that allows for plurality. Fragmenting a game, and unpacking and unraveling those fragments, might feel complicated, counterintuitive, or disorientating, but what this "slow-motion" process offers is a space that allows the analyst to be attentive to that which might otherwise have been overlooked. It supports the finding, naming, and denaturalizing of conventions. If the cultural politics of a game reside in what is naturalized and embedded, rather than (or alongside) what is evident, obvious, or overt, then this approach is appropriate, because it helps equip the analyst to engage with what might otherwise have remained unnoticed.

This approach to textual analysis requires reflecting on how interpretation works, while trying to produce an interpretation. It is not straightforward. If the purpose of analysis is to help build a compelling, assertive argument about what something means, then making space for plurality can feel counterproductive. It can feel difficult to forcefully interrogate the cultural politics of a game while using concepts that acknowledge plurality. Playing a game is an experience that potentially incorporates repetition, mistakes, and accidents, as well as honing skills, scoring strategies, and goals. Games have rules and yet play generates ephemera and ambiguity. Perhaps an aversion to this ambiguity is partly why some players in online multiplayer games are so committed to policing the actions of others. Such players might argue at length about the "best" or most efficient way to play a game, and yet the means permitted to attain a game's goals might have little to do with efficiency.[12]

Attempting the textual analysis of a game can involve trying to hold open the potential interpretations of a game fragment to accommodate the chimeric aspects of play and replay. It can entail an uncomfortable feeling of relinquishing what you already know, in the hope that you arrive at an insight that you did not expect. It is worth trying, however, because popular media reflect the contexts they emerge from. The textual analysis of popular media, including games, offers a way to articulate aspects of our experience that might otherwise remain difficult to articulate, and perhaps doubly so if we belong to communities that have exploitative, difficult histories with authoritative forms of knowledge production.[13]

Adaptation, Fragments, and Codes

Applying Barthes's work to games is not straightforward. As discussed above, Barthes's approach to textual analysis involves fragmentation (breaking the text into lexia) and then scrutinizing these fragments through a series of codes. The first problem is that it is not obvious what a "fragment" of a game would be. Is Dora the guard dog a fragment? Or would Dora herself need to be fragmented? The second problem is that Barthes's codes are not a precise fit. For these reasons, it might be helpful to envisage this approach as a kind of stepped, reflexive scaffolding, rather than as a fixed set of instructions to be followed.

As already discussed, Dora combines coding, rules, and the capacity to damage, with references to working dog breeds, sinister corporate power, and a weakness for sausages. During play, the player might experiment with different strategies, producing a different version of Dora (and the protagonist) each time. For these reasons, deciding what counts as a fragment is not straightforward. Embracing fragmentation can mean relinquishing claims conventionally associated with rigor—this approach is not systematic or exhaustive. What might help with working through these problems of adaptation, is reflecting on the *purpose* of fragmentation. The aim is not to capture and catalog every potential instantiation of the game. The point is to slow down, disrupt, or resist progress through the game. Fragmentation might mean replaying a particular section of a game, making time to wander around, and giving up on the idea of arriving anywhere in particular. It could mean forgetting goals or progress, getting lost, distracted, or stuck. Imagine, for instance, "completing" a particular area within a game (e.g., sneaking through a suite of offices to recover a stolen briefcase) and then refusing to leave until all the desk drawers have been opened, the security guards knocked unconscious, puzzles solved, computers hacked, toilets flushed, the kitchenette set on fire, and the cupboards raided. Fragmentation "unglues" the player-analyst from in-game progression, navigation, or goal attainment. A screenshot might work as a fragment, and it may help as a memory aid or a form of note-taking, but a screenshot will not necessarily show rules and accumulated scores, the character's acquired abilities, their available currency, inventory items, journal entries, or their capacity to interact with objects in the game-world. Yet these could all be part of the fragment under consideration.

Consider, for instance, this example of one game fragment drawn from *Deus Ex: Human Revolution*.[14] This moment-as-fragment was selected (at the time) partly because (as a player-analyst) I was distracted by some graffiti that seemed out of place yet strangely apt. This fragment offered me-as-analyst a chance to unravel different aspects of the body of the protagonist (Adam Jensen) and his fictional, graphically rendered location, the narrative and characterization, and the game's rules and goals:

> [Adam] is interrupted as he makes his way through an industrial research and development facility. . . . His colleague, Pritchard, exploits an implant

in Adam's head to explain that there has been a security breach. Pritchard reports that his attempts to unlock a laboratory door have been thwarted. Adam turns a corner and is faced by the phrase "control decontamination" stencilled on the wall ahead. Pritchard explains that Jenson is required to hack his way into the laboratory. The hack minigame involves moving components through an array while attempting to avoid detection. So, this example of a sequence-as-fragment incorporates references to locks, overrides, breached security, hacking, boundaries, constraints, invasion, contamination, thwarted restrictions, and trespass. All of which tie to issues of control and consent and contribute toward the representation of Adam's own impaired, augmented body as a contested location.[15]

Treating this moment of the game as a fragment made it possible to see, reconsider, and cross-reference aspects of Adam's body, abilities, location, mission, and role. It helped to make certain conventions "visible" and contributed toward the building of a particular argument about the representation of disability within this game.

Fragmentation is not simply the division of the game into manageable portions. Games generate new versions of events when played, and games (from the screen to the interface and platform) are multilayered. For these reasons, fragmentation is selective, and the analyst's decisions as to what constitutes a fragment, and how fragments would be selected, would require reflexive adaptation, game to game. Sometimes a fragment might be a kind of knot or convergence (as with the example from *Deus Ex: Human Revolution*). At other times, a fragment might be a moment or sequence that resonates for no clear reason or that stands out because it is particularly pleasing or annoying.

The creation and selection of fragments is not straightforward, and neither is the use of Barthes's codes. For instance, the code of actions would differ in novels and games, because actions in a game might be initiated by a player, and sequences can be replayed (generating multiple sets of potentially contradictory actions). The codes are not precisely delineated in Barthes's work, and the application of the codes to a game fragment is more likely to involve playful contingency than a tidy process of classification.

Consider this moment early in *Rise of the Tomb Raider*.[16] The avatar Lara Croft has climbed halfway up a mountain in a blizzard and is now casually hanging from an ice axe. This is an example of a moment treated as a fragment selected simply because of how it felt. Watching Lara sway felt uncanny (uncanny in the Freudian sense—it gave me a feeling of eerie yet ambiguous recognition or doubling). Lara's silhouette is human, but calmly dangling by one hand over an abyss is not. Once I have opted to treat this moment as a fragment, the next step for me would be to apply Barthes's codes. As noted, it would not be an exhaustive account, and the codes are not a perfect fit. I start with the code of actions: as the player, I'm responsible for suspending and pausing Lara. I push the buttons. I'm implicated in the acts and actions on-screen, but those acts are shaped by the game rules, design, and programming. Some of the actions present in this fragment are pausing, hanging, swaying, dangling, and gripping. Next, I might apply the enigma code to ask, where is she going? The short answer is "up." Then, I apply the cultural or referential code: there are references to extreme sports and expensive travel, privilege associated with nationality and class, displays of "health," gendered youth, race, wealth, and leisure. Next, I apply the semic code: Lara's gentle swaying implies improbable, disproportionate strength. Her relaxed stance suggests an ability to effortlessly carry many times her own body weight. In this, Lara resembles an insect (hence that initial moment of uncanny "doubling"—human and beetle). Lara is inhumanely strong, hollow, or both. Finally, I apply the symbolic code (opposites, antithesis): full/empty, rise/fall, insect/human, naturalistic/fantastical. Hollowed out and carrying a backpack, Lara is built for appropriation. Being empty, she can rise and raid.

The haphazard process of applying the codes allowed me to "unpack" this fragment, and to arrive at an interpretation. The problem is that I am confronted by a certain amount of redundancy, because Lara's aptitude for rising and raiding is made clear in the title of the game. In my experience, vacillating between excitement (Lara is an empty bug!) and deflation (yes, Lara is a thief who can climb things, hence the title of the game) is part of doing textual analysis. Yet, my eventual analysis would not rely on the unpacking of a single fragment. A reiterative process of fragmentation and unraveling would make it possible to explore the ways that Lara's emptiness plays out and connects with different threads (e.g., emptiness and grief, loss and the inability to age, voids and vertigo, hunger, Lara's compulsive drive to please her ghostly parents, emptiness and theft, history and empire). Such connections would become the basis of the analysis, and the analysis would be used to support the development of an argument about representations in the game. These leads—grounded in play, generated through fragmentation and code use—could then be deepened with reference to relevant critical literature, concepts, and frameworks.

Applications: From Fragmentation to Analysis

In this final section, some examples drawn from prior analysis are shared, linking example fragments with eventual arguments. In this chapter, I've proposed that this version of textual analysis can support a critical engagement with aspects of the text that would otherwise remain overlooked. It can help the analyst to access the naturalized conventions that underpin the representations on offer. I'm interested in the representation of bodies, culture, and technology, so I tend to work with science fiction, zombie, and horror games. Textual analysis has helped me to critique that which is presented as plausible, natural, normal, or unremarkable in these games, including the tendency to associate authority and status with able bodies and ability, and the extent to which this privileging relies on the role of disability as Other—as threat, deviance, deficiency, or spectacle. Here are some examples of those fragments, and the eventual arguments made.

There's a moment quite early in the zombie game *Resident Evil 4* when the protagonist Leon enters an unfamiliar village.[17] When the grim, zombified locals notice Leon, they attack. As I was playing, this was compelling and disconcerting to me because the villagers resembled my family and a person who looked like my mother assaulted my blond, male, North American avatar with a hoe. When I treated this moment as a fragment, alternative interpretations became possible. Using the codes helped me to notice, for example, that the zombified villagers attacked Leon using farmyard tools and gardening implements. Following references to "tools" and "work" across the game made it possible to trace the ways that the game links deviant technologies and malevolent authority with disability, while at the same time naturalizing the authority of able bodies and the validity of associated authority and enabling technologies. Before this, I had never thought about zombie otherness in relation to disability and ableism, which seems strange in retrospect, but that is the power of convention and conventional metaphors.[18]

When I was analyzing *Dead Space*, a zombie horror game set on a mining spacecraft, some of the fragments I worked with related to the avatar's spectacular deaths.[19] These moments were selected because the amount of creative elaboration taking place suggested a kind of frantic overkill. The avatar's name was Isaac. Unraveling Isaac's deaths and his tendency to burst led to reflections on the avatar's spacesuit, and especially its role in enforcing Isaac's boundaries: his skin, the edges of his body, and his capacity to "hold it together" under pressure. Unraveling the spacesuit-as-fragment became the starting point for an exploration of the fragile status of normate bodies in games, and the various kinds of knowledge (about bodies and their relative value) that were being represented as valid or corruptible.[20] The idea of the "normate"—a subject position that is unmarked by difference—is drawn from Rosemarie Garland Thomson's work on spectacular bodies, and relates to histories of looking, disability, and intersectional difference (of race, gender, and class, for example), so this is an example of an analysis that began with in-game fragmentation, and then connected with relevant concepts and literature to further develop an argument.[21]

Later, unraveling fragments in the zombie games *The Last of Us* and *The Walking Dead* made it possible to explore the significance of assessment to representations of able bodies and disability.[22] I was working with fragments that involve characters getting drawn toward wrecked schools, universities, pharmacies, and hospitals. Using codes to unravel these fragments made it possible to argue that, in these games, the zombie apocalypse is equated with the dissolving of institutions that are conventionally associated with assessment of various kinds. Furthermore, it became possible to argue that the destruction of these institutions and the demise of these conventional forms of assessment (or "the death of the clinic") means that the male characters can then access alternative forms of assessment and validation, this time linked to fatherhood.[23]

The notion that "ability is good" is so normalized and so conventional that it is difficult to critique (or even "register"), while the use of disability as a shorthand for deviance or inadequacy is so common that it can be difficult to call out, extricate, or name.[24] Taken together, the examples shared here demonstrate that working with fragmentation and codes can help the player-analyst to engage critically with conventions that might otherwise remain unnoticed and overlooked. Textual analysis made it possible to argue that, in these games, the status associated with normate subjectivity is depicted as natural, and yet highly conditional. Play, reflexivity, fragmentation, and unraveling made it possible to build arguments about the instability of able bodies, the significance of assessment, and the association of disability with monstrosity, loss, deviance, and threat.

Conclusion

In this chapter, a version of textual analysis has been introduced, based on the processes demonstrated by Barthes in his book *S/Z*. Different approaches to close analysis have emerged within game studies since the field's emergence more than twenty years ago. Some of these are compatible with the version of textual analysis outlined here. For instance, this approach can be combined with forms of structural, paratextual, transtextual, and intertextual analysis. It can be combined with different conceptual frameworks.

Adapting Barthes's work for games is not straightforward, and what has been proposed is a provisional rather than a perfect fit. Fragmenting the game, and unraveling fragments through the application of codes, can feel haphazard and counterproductive; this process is imprecise, and it makes a mess. As an imperfect process, it requires reflexivity and cycles of choice and omission, just as playing a game involves repetition, agency, and experimentation. This version of textual analysis invites entanglement and embraces plurality. Selecting a game, playing it, and replaying it, and hoping to wander into an insight that feels useful within a specific time frame by bringing a set of adapted codes to bear on a nominally random fragment, does entail risk. Uncomfortable as taking these risks might be, it's worthwhile if it becomes the means of arriving somewhere unexpected, because the unexpected might be exactly what is required if the effective critiquing of representations relies on attempts to excavate conventions, name the unnoticed, and upset the obvious.

This approach to textual analysis offers ways to name and critique what the analyst might otherwise have missed, including that which is conventional and naturalized in representations of bodies, cultures, locations, and fantasies, and it is a chance for the analyst to build toward an argument about representations in games that is reflexive, contextual, and grounded in gameplay.

Notes

1. Tanya Krzywinska, "The Pleasures and Dangers of the Game," *Games and Culture* 1, no. 1 (2006): 121.
2. Martyn Denscombe, *Good Research Guide: For Small-Scale Social Research Projects*, 5th ed. (London: McGraw-Hill Education, 2014).
3. For examples, see Hans-Joachim Backe, "A Redneck Head on a Nazi Body: Subversive Ludo-Narrative Strategies in *Wolfenstein II: The New Colossus*," *Arts* 7, no. 4 (2018), https://www.mdpi.com/2076-0752/7/4/76; Alexander Champlin, "Playing with Feelings: Porn, Emotion, and Disability in *Katawa Shoujo*," *Well Played* 3, no. 2 (2014): 63–81; Hanli Geyser and Pippa Tshabalala, "Return to Darkness: Representations of Africa in *Resident Evil 5*," *DiGRA Conference* (September 2011), https://dl.digra.org/index.php/dl/article/view/565; Theresa Krampe, "No Straight Answers: Queering Hegemonic Masculinity in BioWare's *Mass Effect*," *Game Studies* 18, no. 2 (2018), http://gamestudies.org/1802/articles/krampe; Paul Martin, "Race, Colonial History and National Identity: *Resident Evil 5* as a Japanese Game," *Games and Culture* 13, no. 6 (2018): 568–86, https://doi.org/10.1177/1555412016631648; Ewan Kirkland, "Restless Dreams in *Silent Hill*: Approaches to Video Game Analysis," *Journal of Media Practice* 6, no. 3 (2005): 167–78; Ewan Kirkland, "Masculinity in Video Games: The Gendered Gameplay of *Silent Hill*," *Camera Obscura: Feminism, Culture, and Media Studies* 24, no. 2 (2009): 161–83; and Souvik Mukherjee, "The Playing Fields of Empire: Empire and Spatiality in Video Games," *Journal of Games and Virtual Worlds* 7, no. 3 (2015): 299–315, https://doi.org/10.1386/jgvw.7.3.299_1. For more examples of digital game analysis, try searching the library at the Digital Games Research Association (https://dl.digra.org/index.php/dl), where information can also be found about game studies conferences and different national chapters. For relevant journals, see *Game Studies, Games and Culture, . . . Loading*, or *Well Played*. The approach to textual analysis outlined in this chapter is an abridged adaptation of Diane Carr, "Methodology, Representation, and Games," *Games and Culture* 14, no. 7–8 (2019): 707–23, https://doi.org/10.1177/1555412017728641.
4. Roland Barthes, *S/Z*, translated by Richard Miller (London: Blackwell, 1990).
5. Richard Dyer, *The Matter of Images: Essays on Representations*, 2nd ed. (London: Routledge, 2002 [1993]), 2.

6   Barthes, *S/Z*, 5, emphasis in original.
7   Barthes, *S/Z*, 18.
8   Julia Lesage, "*S/Z* and *Rules of the Game*," *Jump Cut: A Review of Contemporary Media* 12–13 (Winter 1976–77): 45–51, www.ejumpcut.org/archive/jc55.2013/LesageRulesOfGame/.
9   Barthes, *S/Z*, 8. For a discussion of association, reading, and misreading in Barthes's earlier work, see Lydie Moudileno, "Barthes's Black Soldier: The Making of a Mythological Celebrity," *The Yearbook of Comparative Literature* 62, no. 1 (2016): 57–72, https://doi.org/10.3138/ycl.62.017.
10 See John Law, "Making a Mess with Method," in *The SAGE Handbook of Social Science Methodology*, edited by William Outhwaite and Stephen Turner (London: SAGE, 2007), 595–606.
11 Diane Carr and Cheesycat Puff, "Games, Play, Meaning and *Minecraft*," *Well Played* 8, no. 2 (2019): 20–21, https://press.etc.cmu.edu/search?keys=carr+puff.
12 See Bernard Suits's definition of games in *The Grasshopper: Games, Life and Utopia* (Peterborough, ON: Broadview Press, 2014).
13 See Sharon L. Snyder and David T. Mitchell, *Cultural Locations of Disability* (Chicago: University of Chicago Press, 2019); Carr, "Methodology, Representation, and Games," 2019; Ruha Benjamin, "Informed Refusal: Toward a Justice-Based Bioethics," *Science, Technology, & Human Values* 41, no. 6 (2016): 967–90, https://doi.org/10.1177/0162243916656059; and Nick Taylor, "I'd Rather be a Cyborg Than a Gamerbro: How Masculinity Mediates Research on Digital Play," *MedieKultur: Journal of Media and Communication Research* 34, no. 64 (2018), https://doi.org/10.7146/mediekultur.v34i64.96990.
14 *Deux Ex: Human Revolution*, developer: Eidos-Montreal, publisher: Square Enix, PlayStation 3 version, 2011.
15 Carr, "Methodology, Representation, and Games," 171.
16 *Rise of the Tomb Raider*, developer: Crystal Dynamics, publisher: Microsoft Studios and Square Enix, PlayStation 4 version, 2015.
17 *Resident Evil* 4, developer: Capcom Production Studio, publisher: Capcom, Wii version, 2007.
18 Diane Carr, "Textual Analysis, Digital Games, Zombies," presented at DiGRA 2009, UK.
19 *Dead Space*, developer: EA Redwood Shores, publisher: Electronic Arts, PlayStation 3 version, 2008.
20 Diane Carr, "Ability, Disability and *Dead Space*," *Game Studies* 14, no. 2 (December 2014), https://gamestudies.org/1402/articles/carr.
21 Rosemarie Garland Thomson, *Extraordinary Bodies: Figuring Physical Disability in American Culture and Literature* (New York: Columbia University Press, 2017).
22 *The Last of Us*, developer: Naughty Dog, publisher: Sony Computer Entertainment, PlayStation 3 version, 2013; *The Walking Dead*, episode 1–5, developer: Telltale Games, publisher: Telltale Games, PlayStation 4 version, 2012.

23 Diane Carr, "Representations of Ability in Digital Games," originally presented at the Critical Evaluation of Game Studies Seminar, April 28–29, 2014, University of Tampere, Finland. Published as a chapter in *Gaming Disability: Disability Perspectives on Contemporary Video Games*, edited by Katie Ellis, Tama Leaver, and Mike Kent (London: Routledge, 2023), 92–102. "The death of the clinic" is a reference to Michel Foucault's work on power and bodies in *The Birth of the Clinic* (London: Routledge, 2002).

24 See Fiona Kumari Campbell, "Stalking Ableism: Using Disability to Expose 'Abled' Narcissism," in *Disability and Social Theory*, edited by Dan Goodley, Bill Hughes, and Lennard Davis (London: Palgrave Macmillan, 2012), 212–30.

7

Historical Poetics and TikTok

MEG L. THOMAS AND TED NANNICELLI

Thomas and Nannicelli illustrate how to analyze TikTok videos using historical poetics, a film studies approach innovated by David Bordwell to make sense of the principles by which films are constructed and through which they are able to create meaning. Using a case study of several ads for the musical film Mean Girls, *they interrogate how the platform's policies and parameters establish the prospects for what is possible.*

An Overview of Historical Poetics

"Historical poetics" is an approach to the analysis of artwork that tries to understand their structural, formal, stylistic, and semantic features as the result of the decisions and actions of individuals who are embedded in particular historical contexts and, as such, subject to various conditions and constraints of an artistic, cultural, industrial, or social nature. One of the primary values of the approach is that, rather than imposing a preestablished theoretical or methodological framework, it takes artworks on their own terms, seeking evidence-based causal and functional explanations of how and why artworks have the features they do and how those features are designed to achieve particular aims or effects.

In media studies (including film studies), film historian and theorist David Bordwell first used the term "historical poetics" to describe a research program he developed over a series of articles and books between the 1980s and the 2000s.[1] Given the title of the present volume, and its aim to rejuvenate textual analysis in media studies, it is somewhat ironic that one of Bordwell's early statements of historical poetics was included in a chapter titled "Why Not to Read a Film."[2] Writing in 1989, Bordwell was proposing a new methodological direction for a discipline in which the primary focus had become "readings" of films.

By "readings," however, Bordwell really meant "interpretations," which, he flatly stated, historical poetics "does not seek to produce."[3] However, there is another, more capacious understanding of textual "readings" that roughly equates to "textual analyses," and in this sense, at least, historical poetics might sit within this book more easily than it would first appear. Part of our aim in this chapter is to show just how.

Historical poetics is a research program within the larger tradition of poetics. The term *poetics* comes from the Greek *poiêsis*, which means "making" and has likely stayed with us thanks to the influence of Aristotle's *Poetics* (ca. 335 CE), the Greek title (*Poêtikê*) of which translates to "the art of composing poetry." Extrapolating a bit from Aristotle, a poetics of any art form (in a descriptive, value-neutral sense of that term), then, "studies the finished work as a result of a process of construction."[4] Less formally, poetics might be thought of as a reverse-engineering approach; it analyzes the finished product in ways that try to account for its structural, formal, stylistic, and semantic features.

According to Bordwell, the broad tradition of poetics just sketched, which he calls "analytic poetics," is characterized by the fundamental research question, "What are the principles according to which films are constructed and through which they achieve particular effects?"[5] Analytic poetics thus traffics in functional explanations; the poetician attempts to account for the purpose and intended function of various formal and stylistic qualities. In this "analytic" sense, poetics is "a practice-based theory of art."[6]

As Bordwell acknowledges, though, artistic traditions and practices, and the principles that attend them, are neither static nor universal; rather, they are historically embedded: "That's why we need a historically inflected poetics, one that recognizes that art is made differently under different circumstances."[7] The central question guiding *historical* poetics, then, is, "How and why have these principles [according to which films are constructed and achieve particular effects] arisen and changed in particular empirical circumstances?"[8] Thus, historical poetics trades in causal explanations; the poetician aims at identifying the relevant principles and their proximate causes.

On the one hand, Bordwell's formulation of historical poetics sits within a long, intellectually diverse tradition of scholarship that includes (just to mention the influences he cites) German-language art history from the late nineteenth to the mid-twentieth century (E. H. Gombrich, Erwin Panofsky, Alois Riegl, and Henrich Wölfflin) and twentieth-century Slavic literary theory (Russian formalists such as Boris Eikhenbaum, Viktor Shklovsky, and Yuri Tynyanov, as well as Prague structuralists such as Roman Jakobson and Jan Mukarovsky).[9] Indeed, several of the Russian formalists went on to contribute to the 1927 volume *The Poetics of Cinema*, edited by Eikhenbaum, from which Bordwell's project takes its name.[10] Yet, on the other hand, given the variety of thinkers whose ideas he has synthesized, Bordwell's approach is also profoundly original, so some of the specifics of his account bear further elaboration.

To elucidate the nature of historical poetics, then, and to begin to show more concretely how one might use it to analyze media, let us focus on two key aspects of the approach—constructional principles and empirical circumstances.[11] (We'll return to the question of "art" versus "media" at the end of this section.) Constructional principles are, roughly speaking, the rules, conventions, and norms that govern the creation of a certain sort of artwork or artifact. For some theorists, such principles derive from the supposed nature of the medium. For others, they are largely socially determined and consist in the rules of thumb of craft practices that get formalized in, say, trade publications, books, courses, and so forth. In any case, the historical poetician's interest in these rules, conventions, and norms is that they figure into causal explanations of why and how an object of inquiry comes to have the features that it does. As Bordwell puts it, "The poetician makes these norms explicit as a way of explaining why films have certain features."[12]

What about "empirical circumstances"? Simply put, they are the facts about the contexts in which artists or artisans work. Relevant contexts here include (but are not limited to) historical, social, cultural, national, political, and industrial. Depending upon the object of our inquiry, some such contexts may be more pertinent than others. These contexts delimit the constructional principles that are available to artists or artisans, and they make some constructional principles more salient than others. In other words, historical poetics situates artists or artisans within the contexts in which they work and against a background of norms and conventions operative in those contexts; it offers causal explanations of the features of particular works or artifacts that appeal to those contexts and norms.

So far, this may sound very abstract, but formulated in these broad terms, historical poetics is a more capacious approach than is sometimes recognized, and the approach can be shaped to address the specific research questions one wants to ask. In the case of film, historical poetics may pitch questions at varying levels of generality—from questions about the corpus of a single director (Bordwell's *Ozu and the Poetics of Cinema*) to questions about films of a defined time period within a particular industry (Todd Berliner's *Hollywood Incoherent*) or questions about national cinemas (Gary Bettinson and James Udden's *The Poetics of Chinese Cinema*). Moreover, it can be adapted to other media (Jason Mittell's *Complex TV*).[13] The level of generality at which the poetician formulates their research questions in turn establishes the level of generality of the principles or conventions to be investigated. An historical poetics approach to the work of a single film director, such as Wes Anderson, may need to key in on *internal* norms established within the director's corpus; an historical poetics approach to, say, Chinese-language cinema may need to look at consistency and variation of industrial norms across several national contexts.

Although Bordwell's own poetics often emphasizes formal and stylistic analysis, he explicitly acknowledges that his program represents merely one option for pursuing historical poetics.[14] Bordwell describes poetics, in general, as comprising three distinct domains or areas of inquiry—thematics, large-scale form, and stylistics.[15] Poetics-based scholarship in television studies, for example, suggests ways that the approach can emphasize thematics or the semantic features of a work—more simply put, subject matter or theme. Influenced by Robert C. Allen's "reader-oriented poetics" as well as Bordwell's historical poetics, television scholar Jason Mittell conceives of poetics as involving "a focus on the specific ways that texts make meaning, concerned with formal aspects of media more than issues of content or broader cultural forces."[16]

Allen's work on soap opera and Mittell's work on television in general provide a good segue to the question of "art" within historical poetics, as well as to our own analysis of TikTok videos. The "fine arts" (often regarded as drama, literature, music, painting, and sculpture) have tended to be the objects of studies in poetics. Following the Russian formalists, Bordwell's historical poetics also regards film as an art form. But what does this mean for the poetics of cultural practices and forms that are regarded as popular art or, perhaps, not art at all? Is the poetics of those forms a possibility? The short answer is "yes." The term *art* and adjacent terms such as *artistic medium* and *art form* should be understood capaciously to include all sorts of sociohistorically embedded artisanal and craft practices that result in intentionally designed artifacts. As composer Igor Stravinsky put it in his *Poetics of Music*, "The poetics of the classical philosophers did not consist of lyrical dissertations about natural talent and about the essence of beauty. For them, the single word *techné* embraced both the fine arts and the useful arts and was applied to the knowledge and study of the certain and inevitable rules of the craft."[17] In the next section of this chapter, we argue that even in forms of popular media production and content creation outside of what we have historically recognized as art, the form and style of a work (or text) are still heavily shaped by regulative and industrial norms and its social, technical, and infrastructural contexts. As a result, we hope to demonstrate the usefulness of a historical poetics approach to textual analysis in more lateral applications—in this case, to analyzing short-form videos such as TikToks.

Historical Poetics in Practice

If historical poetics prompts us to ask how a work's production context influences its form and style, then it makes sense to first decipher what exactly constitutes a work's production conditions. In the case of a TikTok video, we might ask questions such as, What aspects of TikTok's policies, licensing agreements, user practices, and platform infrastructure might influence or constrain the kinds of content a user (including influencers and business accounts) might produce?[18] What design parameters does the platform enforce for users producing content? For what kinds of stylistic and formal features does the platform reward users through increased visibility and reach? What sociocultural norms exist on the platform that might influence a user's creative decisions when producing content?

We then turn to the work's stylistic and formal features. In the context of a TikTok video, we might ask questions such as, What music, audio, or licensed or unlicensed "sound" does the video incorporate?[19] What is the video's duration? What filters or templates does the video incorporate? What graphics, text, transitions, or visual effects does the video use? What is the rhythm or tempo of the video's editing? How has the composition of the video been designed? When we start to ask why these specific design decisions have been made, we can start to draw explicit connections between the production conditions and constraints that exist within the TikTok platform and the stylistic and formal features in the resulting TikTok video.

Platformization has ushered in significant changes in how films and television shows are being produced, distributed, and consumed. This means that producers need to cater to a new media landscape, one in which platforms such as TikTok powerfully shape the popular reception of film and television content. For production companies, this means building a fan base and a following for films or TV shows on social media platforms such as TikTok ahead of their official release. This context has significantly influenced the way promotional content for films or TV shows is designed. Consider the 2024 remake of the film *Mean Girls* (dir. Samantha Jayne and Arturo Perez, Jr.). How has the TikTok platform—as a production context—influenced the look and sound of this film's promotional content created specifically for this platform? We'll analyze three different promotional videos uploaded by the official Mean Girls TikTok account, @MeanGirls—with each example exploring the relationship between a different set of stylistic features and the TikTok platform as the relevant production context.

The remake of *Mean Girls* (dir. Mark Waters, 2004) follows the same storyline as the original film. However, unlike the original, the 2024 *Mean Girls* is a musical, incorporating much of the music and script from the 2017 Broadway musical adaptation of the original film, directed by Casey Nicholaw. The story follows the life of high-schooler Cady Heron, who, having been homeschooled in Africa up until this point, begins her first year at a public school in the United States. The comedy explores Cady's experience transitioning into high-school life and navigating social cliques—including the popular-girls clique, "the Plastics."

In the lead-up to the film's release, the official Mean Girls TikTok account was uploading promotional videos to the platform. These videos had been strategically designed to appear in TikTok users' feeds seamlessly and organically. While the account was certainly using paid advertising features on the platform, such as the "promote" feature, which allows users to pay to increase the visibility of their content, this feature is restricted to videos that contain only original sounds or sounds from the TikTok Commercial Music Library. This means that, for at least two of the videos we will analyze, the account relied exclusively on organic reach.[20] Therefore, the videos had to be designed in such a way that they gained traction and visibility organically on the platform. This production context yielded a unique set of aesthetic characteristics, or what one might argue constitutes a "group style."[21]

The first of these videos (see figure 7.1) is a four-second clip from the film in which character Kevin Gnapoor approaches the Plastics' table. The video opens with a close-up on the character Regina George. She looks Kevin (off-screen) up and down and asks in disgust, "What is he still doing by our table?" We cut to a close-up of Kevin looking sheepish. He replies, "I can hear you by the way." The video cuts back to a close-up

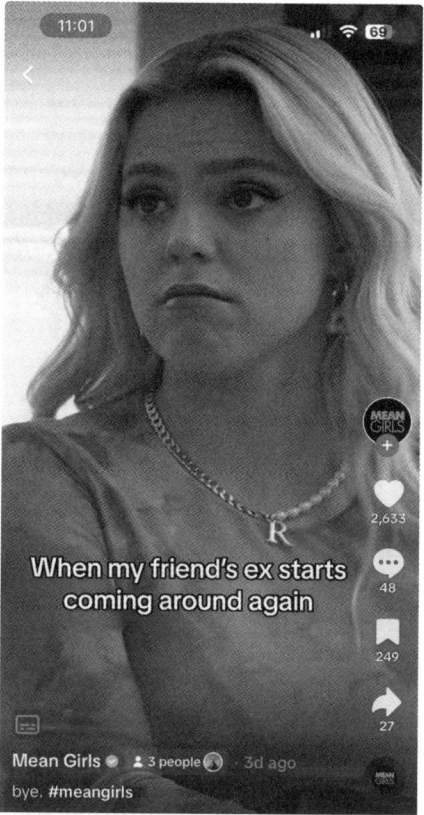

Figure 7.1: A video uploaded by the Mean Girls TikTok account on January 15, 2024, https://www.tiktok.com/@meangirls/video/7324047708174486827.

of Regina, who smirks and asks, "Can you hear me now?" She waves her fingers and whispers, "Bye," before turning to her friends and laughing. The words "When my friend's ex starts coming around again" are overlaid on the video.

The video's sound (audio pulled from the film) is classed as an "original sound"—meaning that this is the first instance of the sound's use on the platform and that the account holder owns the copyright. The video had approximately 214,100 views as of January 23, 2024, making it relatively successful as an organic form of promotion. The video was designed to maximize shareability and relatability while providing a template for users to take up the sound and create their own videos with it. This means the sound should be clear and free of background noise, short, punchy, and relatable or amusing. Writing for *Business Insider*, Abigail Abesamis Demarest explains that "sounds are central to TikTok. A video paired with just the right sound can increase shareability of your post, and viral sounds can inspire creators from all over the TikTok community to use your sound in their own videos."[22]

The video is a demonstration of how the sound can be used by others; in this case, the sound is used as a way to make a joke about shunning a friend's ex-partner. The format or template this video encourages users to adopt is to upload the user's own footage, accompanied with the sound from the original video uploaded by the Mean Girls account, and paired with the user's own unique text overlaid on the video. The platform facilitates this kind of engagement by providing a "use this sound" button, while prohibiting the use of the footage for "stitched" or "dueted" videos.[23]

The Mean Girls account has made strategic decisions about the design of this video that are driven by replicability and shareability. The video offers a replicable template that exploits an already-popular meme format on the platform; it bolsters shareability by creating meaning that can exist independently of the film's context—in this case, a joke about ex-partners. This form of video slots seamlessly into the stream of videos already on the platform.

The second post we will analyze reflects a style and format unique to TikTok's platform infrastructure and, consequently, the sociocultural norms of the platform. This post uses the "slideshow" function where users can upload a series of images that play in a loop while a looped sound also plays in the background. The video exploits a popular TikTok trend that involves users uploading a series of images, beginning with a screenshot of a message from "Mom" that reads, "Start making your Christmas list." The following photo in the trend is a Christmas-themed stock photo with text such as "Say less," "Bet," or "OK." The remaining images in the slideshow generally feature a satirical or otherwise comedic Christmas wish list.

The Christmas-list TikTok uploaded by the Mean Girls account piggybacks on the preexisting momentum behind the trend. The first image features a screenshot of a lock screen with a still from the *Mean Girls* (2024) film as the background and the standard message preview from "Mom" (figure 7.2). The following image uses a stock photo of pink and red presents with the word "Bet" overlaid on it (figure 7.3). This is followed by nine other images, all memes that relate in some capacity to either an actor from the film (figure 7.4) or a recognizable image or symbol from the film such as the Burn Book or cheese fries. The post was received relatively well by other TikTok users, with most users engaging positively with the post in the comments section.

This style of slideshow post is unique to TikTok's platform infrastructure. Posts that adopt these unique stylistic traits are generally successful on the platform because they are perceived by users as more authentic or entertaining and are less likely to be perceived as "advertising." This motivates TikTok accounts to avoid using excerpts pulled straight from official film trailers. Instead, they should produce promotional material independently of the film trailer or, at a minimum, recut, recompose, or otherwise edit it to more authentically emulate the unique style of content that appears on the target platform (TikTok). This means abandoning a wide-screen aspect ratio and prioritizing clips from the film that already embody the look and feel of other popular videos on the platform (such as fan edits with TikTok transitions or effects, composition that suits a 9:16 aspect ratio, dance scenes with clear and replicable choreography, clear and punchy original sounds that can be taken up by other users, or newly created content based on preexisting TikTok trends or meme formats).

The last video we will analyze offers another example of a common video style on TikTok—the fan edit. Writing for *Pitchfork*, Cat Zhang explains that "fan edits often take the form of montages or simple videos

Figures 7.2, 7.3, 7.4: Stills from the Mean Girls TikTok post uploaded December 24, 2024, http://www.tiktok.com/@meangirls/photo/7315856209783950635.

layered with effects, their movements synced to a popular song.... They are often visually engaging and easy to grasp, especially ones made to flaunt the sexual appeal of a celebrity or character."²⁴ The difference, in this case, is that while the video emulates the style of a fan edit, it has been made and uploaded by the official Mean Girls account—the owners of the copyright rather than a fan.

This video emulates the style of a fan edit in a number of explicit ways. It uses a viral sound from an account that exclusively creates fan edits of films and television shows, contains a series of slowed-down close-ups of Chris Briney from the *Mean Girls* remake, and uses highly stylized TikTok effects and transitions (figure 7.5). The sound comes from a viral fan edit that features Briney as Conrad in the show *The Summer I Turned Pretty* (Amazon Prime Video, 2022–), taking advantage of his preexisting fan base. In the sound, a teenage girl says, "This is 100 percent your look, Connie baby" before fading into the song "Family Affair" by Mary J. Blige.

Figure 7.5: Screenshot from the Mean Girls TikTok post uploaded November 21, 2024, https://www.tiktok.com/@meangirls/video/7303667580705803563.

Looking at these three videos together highlights a significant stylistic departure from more traditional promotional material such as film trailers, commentary, or interviews with cast and crew. The design of these videos is explicitly informed by TikTok's licensing and copyright rules (around audio and images), its platform infrastructure (how a user navigates and produces content on the platform), and the cultural norms of the platform (the kind of content that is successful and how users are encouraged to engage with the content). Understanding these aspects of the conditions in which these videos were produced and distributed helps us understand why they might look and sound as they do. These videos conform to a restricted range of stylistic options that TikTok users have to choose from.

While this case study has been predominantly descriptive, we hope these brief examples demonstrate how historical poetics as a method of textual analysis allows researchers to observe and make claims about emerging stylistic patterns over a corpus of works. While this approach has traditionally been used in the context of fine arts, historical poetics proves useful in a much broader range of contexts—including new forms of digital media and popular culture. Understanding the political, social, cultural, economic, or infrastructural contexts that underpin stylistic patterns across a corpus of works can change how we understand, interpret, or appreciate a work of art or popular text. For example, an understanding of the strict censorship rules in Francoist Spain offers insight into the patterns of allegorical storytelling that emerged in Spanish cinema between 1939 and 1975. Similarly, a deeper understanding of how TikTok's algorithms, copyright rules, licensing agreements, and platform infrastructure operate can provide insight into why certain kinds of content might be successful on the platform and others might be censored or removed entirely. Thus, a historical poetics approach may also (perhaps surprisingly) afford researchers the opportunity to reveal or critique production conditions that may contribute to politically or culturally harmful patterns of representation in artwork or popular texts.[25]

Notes

1 Key texts include David Bordwell, *Ozu and the Poetics of Cinema* (Princeton, NJ: Princeton University Press, 1988); David Bordwell, "Historical Poetics of Cinema,"

in *The Cinematic Text: Methods and Approaches*, edited by R. Barton Palmer (New York: AMS Press, 1989), 369–98; and David Bordwell, *Poetics of Cinema* (New York: Routledge, 2008). The term "historical poetics" was first used in a related, but distinct, sense by the Russian literary theorist Alexander Veselovsky, who preceded the Russian formalists who had a more significant influence on Bordwell, as we explain below. See, for discussion, Igor Shaitanov, "Aleksandr Veselovskii's Historical Poetics," *New Literary History* 32, no. 2 (Spring 2001): 429–43.

2 David Bordwell, *Making Meaning: Inference and Rhetoric in the Interpretation of Cinema* (Cambridge, MA: Harvard University Press, 1989), 263–74.
3 Bordwell, "Historical Poetics," 370.
4 Bordwell, *Poetics*, 12.
5 Bordwell, *Poetics*, 23.
6 Bordwell, *Poetics*, 22.
7 Bordwell, *Poetics*, 22.
8 Bordwell, *Poetics*, 23.
9 See Ladislav Matejka and Krysyna Pomorska, eds., *Readings in Russian Poetics: Formalist and Structuralist Views* (Cambridge, MA: MIT Press, 1971).
10 Richard Taylor, ed., *The Poetics of Cinema* (Oxford: Russian Poetics in Translation Publications, 1982).
11 Explaining the place of "effects" in Bordwell's poetics would require a discussion that is beyond the scope of this chapter. If our aim were to give a full account of Bordwell's views, including an elaboration of his conception of *analytic poetics*, we'd be obliged to address the matter of effects. However, because *historical poetics* is characterized (in part) by causal rather than functional explanations, we can safely circumvent the question of effects here. Interested readers could consult Bordwell's *Narration in the Fiction Film* (Madison: University of Wisconsin Press, 1985), especially chapter 3.
12 Bordwell, *Ozu*, 21.
13 Bordwell, *Ozu*, 21; Todd Berliner, *Hollywood Incoherent: Narration in Seventies Cinema* (Austin: University of Texas Press, 2010); Gary Bettinson and James Udden, eds., *The Poetics of Chinese Cinema* (New York: Palgrave Macmillan, 2016); Jason Mittell, *Complex TV: The Poetics of Contemporary Television Storytelling* (New York: New York University Press, 2015).
14 David Bordwell, "Five Lessons from Stealth Poetics," in Bettinson and Udden, *Poetics of Chinese Cinema*, 15. Likewise, the "neoformalism" Bordwell and Kristin Thompson at times embrace is one way of doing historical poetics; see Bordwell, "Historical Poetics," 378–85.
15 Bordwell, *Poetics*, 17.
16 Mittell, *Complex TV*, 5. Also see Robert C. Allen, *Speaking of Soap Operas* (Chapel Hill: University of North Carolina Press, 1985), 61–95.
17 Igor Stravinsky, *Poetics of Music*, translated by Arthur Knodel and Ingolf Dahl (Cambridge, MA: Harvard University Press, 1947), 4.

18 For a detailed breakdown of the technological elements that constitute a media platform, readers should refer to José van Dijck, *The Culture of Connectivity: A Critical History of Social Media* (New York: Oxford University Press, 2013), 29–32.
19 A "sound" on TikTok is a preexisting sound bite from TikTok's general user or commercial user library—with strict licensing rules around sounds being used for commercial purposes.
20 TikTok, "Use Promote to Grow Your TikTok Audience," accessed January 22, 2024, https://support.tiktok.com/en/using-tiktok/growing-your-audience/use-promote-to-grow-your-tiktok-audience.
21 Bordwell explains that a group style can be described as a paradigm, "a set of elements which can, according to rules, substitute for one another," a unified system that offers creatives "bounded alternatives": "The Classical Hollywood Style, 1917–1960," in *The Classical Hollywood Cinema: Film Style and Mode of Production to 1960*, edited by David Bordwell, Janet Staiger, and Kristin Thompson (London: Routledge, 1988), 4. While making a case for a group style would require a comprehensive analysis of a broad range of works, it is still a useful and relevant concept for this case study.
22 Abigail Abesamis Demarest, "How to Make Your Own Sound on TikTok, or Add Music and Voiceover to Your Videos," *Business Insider*, October 15, 2022, www.businessinsider.com/guides/tech/how-to-make-a-sound-on-tiktok.
23 The "stitch" and "duet" functions on TikTok allow other TikTok users to incorporate the original poster's video into new TikTok videos. Users can choose to prohibit their content from being "stitched" or "dueted" to protect their copyright.
24 Cat Zhang, "Thirst Traps, Anime, and the Viral Power of TikTok Fan Edit Communities," *Pitchfork*, April 14, 2022, https://pitchfork.com/thepitch/anime-fan-edits-tiktok/.
25 We dedicate this chapter to the memory of David Bordwell, who passed away during its production.

8

Reading Gender Relations in an Afrobeats Music Video

A Multimodal Textual Analysis

SIMPHIWE RENS

Rens argues for the value of a multimodal approach to the study of music videos, which examines the textual layer of lyrics and the video's images and storyline. Combining this approach with a form of quantitative content analysis, Rens analyzes the messages of sexual objectification in Rema's hit Afrobeats music video "Calm Down."

For music fans and followers, there is no reason to doubt that the artists producing music videos invest in the production of said videos mainly to entertain us and to market their music catalogs in hopes of gaining profit and fame. However, for media and communication studies scholars and students, it is important to understand that music videos are effective in dynamically staging topical dialogues via images, sound, lyrics, and storyline cues, collaboratively functioning as emotional registers that resonate with their target audiences. Music videos can effectively—sometimes inadvertently—reiterate thoughts and beliefs that are either loyal or subversive to existing dominant ideologies concerning social and cultural—including gendered—experiences and interactions. Depending on how we read them, the multilayered messages emanating from music videos can offer us insights into what and who are regarded as important in the cultures from whence these videos emerge.

With this in mind, this chapter uses a two-pronged method, including quantitative content analysis and qualitative multimodal analysis, and outlines its value for delving further into the textual structures and meanings of music videos. I then operationalize this approach by examining the music video for the song "Calm Down" performed by the Nigerian musician Rema.[1] This approach to music video analysis allows us to study the selected music video as a multilayered (that is, multimodal) media text that presents ideologically charged narratives and discourses through visuals, sound, lyrical content, textual elements, and storyline progressions. This is important because music videos can be saturated with biases, ideologies, and prejudices that either reiterate or refute existing societal inequalities, stereotypes, and gender roles. Knowing this, I use this chapter to demonstrate that there is value in paying continuous attention to gendered representations in music videos, as these videos provide material that helps us to observe, and be critical of, our cultural values regarding the social categories of "woman" (or femininity) and "man" (or masculinity), for example. Thus, through continuous critical analyses of present-day popular messages of gender, sex difference, and sexuality in music videos, researchers can contribute fresh perspectives to our understandings of present-day media messages that may variously contribute to the ways in which young, avid consumers of these videos are socialized to see themselves.[2]

Interdisciplinary studies have variously explored the role and impact of the music video text—and its sociocultural and ideological contents—on young people's social and gender identity constructions. For many of these studies, the content analysis method is a key approach.[3] Music video analyses have carried out varying objectives: for instance, to explore the "effects of gender and music video imagery on sexual attitudes," the "contributions of music video exposure to Black adolescents' gender and sexual schemas," and the "influence of sexual music videos on adolescents' misogynistic beliefs."[4] In this chapter, the multimodally expressed messages concerning gender performance and expressions of sexuality as captured in the most viewed Afrobeats music video will be placed under the spotlight. This decision stems from observation of the ways that critical feminist interpretations of popular media texts—like music videos from youth-dominated musical genres such as hip-hop and rap, for instance—have debated the degree to which producers of these texts sexually objectify women's bodies using camera shots and a sexualized male gaze, and promote the "thingification of femaleness" and women's sexualities.[5] In addition, they highlight the public(ized) degradation of women through music video scenes and song lyrics that violently and vulgarly address women with whom the screen is shared.[6] Recent studies of Afrobeats music videos, specifically, have also demonstrated the presence of misogynistic themes and patterns of sexual objectification of women's bodies.[7]

This chapter places specific focus on messages in relation to gender and sexuality and how these sociocultural categories are represented in Rema's music video for his popular Afrobeats song "Calm Down." Afrobeats is an increasingly globalizing musical genre owing its origins to the West African countries of Nigeria and Ghana. Focus is specifically placed on *this* music video because, with over 653 million views at the time of writing, this video is the most viewed Afrobeats music video on YouTube. This platform attracts billions of users who are clocking more than a billion hours of daily video viewing, and Afrobeats music videos enjoy a notable portion of these views.[8]

As such, the African youth on the continent and across the diaspora who produce these videos widely circulate multilayered messages about their lived experiences through the visual discourses captured in their videos' multiple frames and also in the song lyrics, the beat and tempo undergirding the songs, and the plot progressions driving the music video storylines. Using a feminist analytical approach, I consider Rema's music video as a valuable, albeit ungeneralizable, conduit through which to examine present-day performances of gender in the African context. With this goal in mind, the multimodal textual analysis carried out in this chapter is underpinned by the following research question: In a time of increasing feminist sensibilities across the African continent, what messages concerning gender and sexuality are prioritized in Rema's "Calm Down" music video?

The analysis carried out in this chapter helps the reader come to grips with the overt and covert gender-relational depictions in the sampled music video as they relate to women and men's on-screen interactions, their (sexualized) bodily positionings and movements, and their ways of looking and being looked at in the hyperreal context of the music video. That way, we may gain a better understanding of what characterizes some of the current social norms and ideals concerning gender relations as they circulate in popular cultural texts.

Analyzing Music Videos: A Two-Pronged Methodological Approach

To achieve its critical reading of the chosen video, this chapter relies on a two-pronged analysis strategy. The first part of the analysis involves a brief *quantitative content analysis* of the video to account for the presence and frequency of overtly observable gender-relational behaviors that relate to expressions of sexuality. Few would question the value of using content analysis to map trends and patterns in media texts, but quantitative approaches are notably underused in the humanities, as this method supposedly is unable to interrogate multilayered communication texts in depth. However, I believe that the quantitative content analysis method is suitable for deeper analyses of media effects by researchers who are interested in assessing the sociocultural image and positioning of certain societal groups over others. That said, this method of analysis neglects to account for context, intent, and intensity in relation to what is being counted; therefore, I propose that it be followed by a deeper multimodal analysis, as shall be demonstrated later. The quantitative content analysis approach is inspired by long-standing music video content analysis approaches used by scholars who were—similar to myself in this chapter—interested in partly quantifying the occurrence of actions described in the designated content categories.[9]

It should be noted that researchers using this approach usually analyze a large corpus of texts, rather than (just) a single text, to code for themes aligning with their analyses. In this chapter, I simplify and shorten this process of coding by examining just this single video, but a key reason to engage in such quantitative analysis is so that it can be aggregated with coding of other videos, thereby allowing the analyst to see patterns, contrasts, and larger narratives being created across videos that might then direct the analyst to specific topics for further and deeper multimodal analysis. My hope is that the reader will see the utility of combining the data in this chapter with those from other videos.

Considering the length and format of a music video—with many fast-moving visual frames per second—a frame-by-frame content analysis is not feasible due to the time that the content analyst would need to spend on the video. Analyses of music videos may involve large samples of texts, accounting for hundreds of minutes of screen time to be scrutinized and coded. Therefore, to approach the data in a more manageable manner, music videos can be analyzed across intervals of ten, twenty, or thirty seconds during the coding process. This chapter opts for a ten-second segmentation approach. This means that each ten-second segment of the analyzed text will be considered as an independent visual frame wherein each content category will be coded for only once.

For instance, when coding for screen time dedicated to women's or men's sexual objectification through camera positioning, the presence of this theme is counted once for every ten-second segment throughout the music video, irrespective of the number of individual times the theme occurs during that segment. Objectification is conveyed when the camera renders body parts often associated with acts of sexual engagement (e.g., breast/chest area, lips, buttocks, thighs, pelvis, crotch area) on display through tight shots that are strategically zoomed in to focus specifically on these isolated body parts (or a cluster of body parts) instead of the body as a whole. These types of camera shots drive the viewer's attention to revolve mainly around the depicted body part(s) and may trigger thoughts about the (sexualized) use of the depicted body part(s) in the viewer's mind.

The second, and more elaborate, part of the analysis is a *multimodal discourse analysis* of the various communicative layers of the video: visual, lyrical, sonic, and contextual. This more qualitatively swayed reading is deployed to systematically carry out what this chapter considers a multimodal textual analysis to explore how the messages creatively embedded in the visuals, the lyrics, the beats, and the plot progressions of the chosen text depict gender relations in a time of increasing feminist sensibilities that have for decades called for, and still continue to call for, the just treatment and representations of women and their bodies, bodily autonomy, and expressions of their sexualities in popular media texts and platforms.

To ensure a context-sensitive analysis of a text through multimodal discourse analysis, it is helpful to base the analysis on theoretical insights stemming from previous studies that advanced a similar goal and research question(s) as your study. As such, the multimodal discourse analysis performed in this chapter is anchored by cultural studies scholarship guided by feminist theory, representation theory, and gender performativity theory. This framework adds to the richness of the findings regarding the dominant representations of African gendered lived experiences in the multimodal messages emanating from "Calm Down."

Multimodal discourse analysis, as a form of textual analysis, is a technique used to closely observe the combination of visual, sonic, and textual forms in texts and to evaluate the manners in which discourse is circulated, legitimized, and naturalized to create specific meanings about the world.[10] This cross-disciplinary technique is more focused on depth than breadth, calling for a deep, critical engagement with the empirical object of focus in a study. A combination of this method with another one is useful, more so if a study aims to evaluate factors such as patterns or trends with respect to a specific communication text stemming from a particular genre. For this chapter, identifying representational patterns in the selected Afrobeats music video (in relation to gender and sexuality) is pivotal in tackling my research question. Therefore, a content analysis provides an evidence-based point of departure into the deeper discourse analysis that I carry out on the multilayered data.

I dissect and analyze the identified video across its multiple layers. The visual layer contains all the image-based frames forming part of the video's progression from the first to the last second; these frames can communicate to viewers without the involvement of sound or written text and may thus still be "understood" when the video is consumed while muted. The sonic layer contains all the sound-based elements that form part of the video's progression from beginning to end; these elements include the beats, rhythm, and tempo making up the chord progression of the song for which the video is developed. This element also incorporates the spoken word, which is expressed in the verbalized lyrics of the song. Then there is the more ideological layer of the plot progression behind the "story" being told by the music video. This layer is reliant on the combination of the visual (via the actions committed by the featured humans with one another and the objects in the physical spaces where these actions are carried out) and the sonic (the beat, tempo, rhythm, and lyrics of the song, which collaboratively communicate the mood of the song) to communicate a comprehensive narrative that has a beginning, a middle, and an end.

A Multimodal Textual Analysis of Rema's "Calm Down" Music Video

For the quantitative content analysis of observable, quantifiable gender-relational behaviors, I developed a list of thematic categories (or codes) through the guidance of existing studies and literature that similarly adopted a feminist lens to critically explore the contents of popular media texts. For this analysis, I focused on six categorical behaviors: 1) sexual objectification via camera angles; 2) implicit sexuality/acts of sexual expression; 3) explicit sexuality/acts of sexual expression; 4) homoerotic expressions/acts indicative of same-sex desire; 5) men/women as bearers of the active desiring gaze; and 6) women/men as decorative/background subjects in their roles in the video's storyline. The developed codes deliberately focus on observable gender-relational portrayals in relation to sexuality expression by women and men; these are outlined in Table 8.1 in detail.

In terms of screen time, the analyzed music video is three minutes and thirty-nine seconds in duration, accounting for 219 seconds of analyzable content. For coding, the 219 seconds of content was divided into twenty-two ten-second segments. The coding of "categorical behaviors" was done to arrive at descriptive statistics about the presence and potential prevalence of said categorical behaviors within the analyzed visual data to trace dominant representational patterns and aid this chapter's eventual deeper assessments of the additional layers of the video, beyond the visual.

The results from the content analysis of the music video's visual layers are presented in Table 8.2. The rate of occurrence is determined in relation to the total amount of screen time of the video.

Based on the content analysis of the observable behaviors in the video, it is apparent that this video exemplifies one of the key criticisms leveled against music videos from musical genres appealing to youth: their insistence on sexually objectifying women's bodies. In terms of women's sexual objectification through strategic camera shots, for instance, there is a 14 percent rate of occurrence of this theme. The music video, on the whole, also promotes the "thingification of femaleness" in depicting the male protagonist, Rema, as relying on a sexualized, strategically positioned woman's body as a background "object" to boost his own masculine expression in a scene of the video.

Table 8.1: Content categories used for data coding

Content Categories/Themes Coded Across Twenty-Two Video Segments

Women	Men
Sexual objectification via camera angles: When the camera renders body parts (chest area, stomach, lips, buttocks, thighs, pelvis, crotch area) on display by focusing in on an isolated body part (or a cluster of body parts) of a featured woman instead of her body as a whole.	**Sexual objectification via camera angles**: Same description applied to men featured in the video.
Implicit sexuality/acts of sexual expression: When sexual impulses and innuendo are portrayed. Scenes wherein female characters suggest or seem to elicit sexual appeal, arousal, and desire through eroticized behaviors such as hip/pelvic thrusts, or long/slow-motioned licking/biting of lip or finger. These may be implicit but strongly suggestive of sex and sexuality.	**Implicit sexuality/acts of sexual expression**: Same description applied to men featured in the video.
Explicit sexuality/acts of sexual expression: When sexual actions are portrayed. Scenes wherein female characters explicitly engage in the stroking/grabbing of breasts, genitalia, buttocks, thighs, and moving in ways suggestive of sexual intercourse: grinding of bodies against others; kissing a man on screen; being sexually alluring in explicit ways.	**Explicit sexuality/acts of sexual expression**: Same description applied to men featured in the video.
Homoerotic expressions/acts indicative of same-sex desire: When sexual actions are portrayed as occurring between two or more women. These include scenes depicting implicit and explicit actions of a sexualized nature: moving in ways suggestive of sexual intercourse: grinding of bodies; kissing on screen; visual cues of same-sex, nonheterosexual romantic intimacy.	**Homoerotic expressions/acts indicative of same-sex desire**: Same description applied to men featured in the video.
Women as bearers of the active desiring gaze: When women featured in the video enact an active gaze upon men. Scenes wherein women are portrayed as actively staring/fawning over men's bodies in ways suggestive of desire, curiosity, or interest, thereby relegating men's bodies to the status of passive objects to be looked at.	**Men as bearers of the active desiring gaze**: Same description applied to men featured in the video.
Women as decorative/background subjects in their roles in the video's storyline: When women are portrayed as mere decorative, unimportant "objects" only there to "flank" the main artist(s) in the video (i.e., background dancers, provocatively dressed video extras to merely show off their looks and enhance the sexual and aesthetic bravado of the main artist).	**Men as decorative/background subjects in their role in the video's storyline**: Same description applied to men featured in the video.

Table 8.2: Frequency of occurrence (in screen time) of content categories

Categories Coded Across the Twenty-Two Ten-Second Segments	Frequency Count	Rate of Occurrence (%)*	Combined Screen Time (3 minutes, 39 seconds in total)
Women's sexual objectification by camera	3	14%	48 seconds
Men's sexual objectification by camera	0	0%	0 seconds
Women's implicit sexuality/acts of sexual expression	2	9%	31 seconds
Men's implicit sexuality/acts of sexual expression	1	5%	17 seconds
Women's explicit sexuality/acts of sexual expression	10	45%	1 minute, 53 seconds
Men's explicit sexuality/acts of sexual expression	9	41%	1 minute, 39 seconds
Women on women homoerotic expressions/ acts indicative of same-sex desire	0	0%	0 seconds
Men on men homoerotic expressions/acts indicative of same-sex desire	0	0%	0 seconds
Women as bearers of the active desiring gaze	1	5%	17 seconds
Men as bearers of the active desiring gaze	5	23%	78 seconds
Women as decorative/background subjects in the video's plots/narrative progression	1	5%	17 seconds
Men as decorative/background subjects in their role in the video's plots/narrative progression	0	0%	0 seconds

*Rate of occurrence: frequency count ÷ total number of segments × 100

The text also relies on explicit sexual behaviors by women (at a 45 percent rate of occurrence) and men (41 percent rate of occurrence) to advance the video's plot. For instance, visual depictions in the music video include the featured partygoers grinding their bodies against each other while dancing, the two main characters sensually kissing on screen, and the sexually suggestive caressing and explicit sexual allurement by the woman playing the main character.

This thematic pattern in Rema's "Calm Down" music video is, arguably, relied on to visually capture the atmosphere of romance that undergirds the video's central storyline of a young heterosexual couple in love. These overt, quantifiable behavioral patterns presented in the video's visual layer give a helpful preliminary look into the kinds of messages concerning gender and sexuality that are prioritized in the video. This, however, offers what many a scholar in the humanities would regard as a surface-based analysis. Therefore, I now embark on a deeper reading of the music video through close analysis of the lyrics, the plot progression, and the sonic layers that collaboratively accompany the visual layer, which viewers may regard as the dominant communicative layer of the music video. That way, a more comprehensive reading of the text is achieved, allowing for deeper ideological readings that transcend the text's obvious visual depictions.

In terms of plot progression, the central storyline for "Calm Down" revolves around a young man's romantic pursuit of a young woman whom he meets for the first time at a party. This initial meeting is depicted early in the music video, at the 0:27 mark, and sets the tone for the rest of the activities taking place in the storyline. The protagonist, played by Rema, is romantically attracted to the woman. Rema proclaims, in the lyrics of his first verse, that her attractive yellow dress, as well as her "mellow" disposition and calmness, make her stand out from the rest of the girls in the room at the depicted party, who Rema claims are acting wild and all over the place. These lyrics, and the visual frames up to this point, are layered with the song's medium-tempo rhythm, anchored by a catchy melody with a chord progression made of heavy bass guitar and percussion that can inspire a viewer/listener to break into "smooth" hip-based dance moves.

The combination of visual frames over which the song's opening chorus and first verse are layered help communicate the idea that, immediately upon first seeing this woman, Rema decides to build up the courage to romantically pursue her. A visual display of his "courage" is especially evident at the 0:37 point of the video when Rema climbs off the couch he was sitting on, stands in front of his two friends, and proceeds to imitate what can be described as a pose done by bodybuilders: the tense curving of both arms in the front of the stomach to lift the chest up and out so as to display the muscles in the torso. It is following this visual gesturing of "strength" that Rema proceeds to romantically pursue this woman. The sequence of events that follow this moment in the narrative, visually and sonically (through the song's upbeat rhythm and melody), depicts the new romantic pairing engaging in different social activities as a couple.

For instance, the two are depicted in scenes where they are exploring the city on a motorcycle, and the woman is shown to lovingly embrace Rema from behind by locking both arms around his midsection and gently laying her head over his shoulder to plant a kiss on his cheek. Other scenes depict the two being jovial as they attempt to paint portraits of one another using hand-held canvases and paintbrushes. There are also scenes depicting the two while playing a game of pool, during which Rema romantically embraces his love interest to teach her how to successfully shoot the balls, which she initially struggles to do. Characterizing much of these scenes are moments of random kisses between the two, extended moments of hugs and embraces, and visible laughter and joy on their faces.

Visually, and in terms of storyline, Rema's music video portrays various scenes of gender-relational interactions characterized by a romance-oriented sensibility that constructs an antioppressive environment for women and their bodies. Rema is visually depicted as an affectionate man preoccupied with the emotional fulfillment of the woman portraying his love interest. If we read the aforementioned visual and sonic layers of the analyzed video through a lens of (heteronormative) gender relations, we may conclude that these depictions are tantamount to typical popular media representations and tropes of heterosexual romance characterized by the themes of "boy-meets-girl," "boy-falls-in-love-with-girl," "boy-romantically-pursues-girl," "girl-falls-for-boy," and "they-live-happily-ever-after." However, a closer look at the lyrical contents of the song indicates a contradictory ideological undertone that contrasts the romantic overtones of the storyline and visual depictions with an implicit embodiment of misogyny by Rema, the main protagonist.

As part of his first verse wherein he explains how he met and fell in love with this "mellow" and calm woman in a yellow dress, Rema goes on to describe how, even after he finally managed to get this woman to talk to him, he still struggled to get her to give in to his romantic advances. Adamant to get her to fall for him, Rema's lyrics in this same verse admit:

> *Then I start to feel her bum-bum (warm)*
> [I then start to feel her buttocks (they're warm)]
> *But she dey gimme small-small*
> [But she is only minimally giving into my advances]

As part of his efforts to get her to reciprocate his romantic advances, Rema proceeds to touch this woman's "warm" buttocks. Rema's unwarranted, implicitly violent touching of this woman's intimate body parts is indicative of a misogynistic disregard of women's boundaries and may be read as sexual harassment. This observation from the video's lyrical content disrupts the more egalitarian gender relations that the visual mode successfully constructs in tandem with the sonic mode. As such, Rema's "Calm Down" music video portrays gender-relational interactions as implicitly misogynistic and benevolently sexist, but these regressive elements are masked by visual imagery tantamount to welcomed romanticism and care.

We can see, then, how at times, different layers of a music video can contradict one another in terms of their ideological meanings. In this case, the video's visual, sonic, and storyline elements tell the story of a mutual and consensual romance while the lyrical contents advance a misogynistic and regressive view of women's sexual objectification. It is important, then, that researchers continue to critically dissect music videos beyond just their visual layers (often the dominant layer for analysts) because, as is the case with the video analyzed in this chapter, implicit forms of misogyny and sexism may be present and may contribute to such behavior being socially normalized and overlooked because they are strategically veiled with overt romanticism. Granted, the overwhelming presence of themes of love and romance in popular culture can be celebrated because they arguably inspire the much-needed absence of elements of violence-oriented and publicly degrading gender relations depicted in popular texts such as music videos. While viewers of music videos may appreciate these texts for their "innocent" entertainment value, this should be done with caution, as such depictions may derail the feminist fight toward women's *actual* just treatment across their diverse contexts in and beyond popular media texts.

Notes

1 Rema, "Rema—Calm Down (Official Music Video)," February 11, 2022, YouTube, 3 min., 39 sec., www.youtube.com/watch?v=CQLsdm1ZYAw.
2 Cynthia M. Frisby and Jennifer Stevens Aubrey, "Race and Genre in the Use of Sexual Objectification in Female Artists' Music Videos." *Howard Journal of Communications* 23, no. 1 (2012): 66–87, https://doi.org/10.1080/10646175.2012.641880.
3 Cara Wallis, "Performing Gender: A Content Analysis of Gender Display in Music Videos," *Sex Roles* 64 (2011): 160–72, https://doi.org/10.1007/s11199-010-9814-2.
4 Linda Kalof, "The Effects of Gender and Music Video Imagery on Sexual Attitudes," *Journal of Social Psychology* 139, no. 3 (1999): 378, https://doi.org/10.1080/00224549909598393; Monique L. Ward, Edwina Hansbrough, and Eboni Walker, "Contributions of Music Video Exposure to Black Adolescents' Gender and Sexual Schemas," *Journal of Adolescent Research* 20, no. 2 (2005): 143, https://doi.org/10.1177/0743558404271135; and Johanna M. F. Van Oosten, Jochen Peter, and Patti M. Valkenburg, "The Influence of Sexual Music Videos on Adolescents' Misogynistic Beliefs: The Role of Video Content, Gender, and Affective Engagement," *Communication Research* 42, no. 7 (2015): 986, https://doi.org/10.1177/0093650214565893.
5 Emmanuel Adeniyi, "Nigerian Afrobeats and Religious Stereotypes: Pushing the Boundaries of a Music Genre Beyond the Locus of Libertinism," *Contemporary Music Review* 39, no. 1 (2020): 59–90, https://doi.org/10.1080/07494467.2020.1753475.
6 Kate Conrad, Travis L. Dixon, and Yuanyuan Zhang, "Controversial Rap Themes, Gender Portrayals and Skin Tone Distortion: A Content Analysis of Rap Music Videos," *Journal of Broadcasting & Electronic Media* 53, no. 1 (2009): 134, https://doi.org/10.1080/08838150802643795.
7 Simphiwe Emmanuel Rens, "Women's Empowerment, Agency and Self-Determination in Afrobeats Music Videos: A Multimodal Critical Discourse Analysis," *Frontiers in Sociology* 6 (May 2, 2021), https://doi.org/10.3389/fsoc.2021.646899.
8 Rodney Duffett, "The YouTube Marketing Communication Effect on Cognitive, Affective and Behavioural Attitudes among Generation Z Consumers," *Sustainability* 12, no. 12 (2020): 5075, https://doi.org/10.3390/su12125075.
9 Wallis, "Performing Gender," 160–72; Rita Sommers-Flanagan, John Sommers-Flanagan, and Britta Davis, "What's Happening on Music Television? A Gender Role Content Analysis," *Sex Roles* 28 (1993): 748, https://doi.org/10.1007/BF00289991.
10 David Machin, "What Is Multimodal Critical Discourse Studies?" *Critical Discourse Studies* 10, no. 4 (2013): 347–55, https://doi.org/10.1080/17405904.2013.813770.

9

How to Read a Colony on a Game Board

Settlers of Catan *and Postcolonial Thinking*

SOUVIK MUKHERJEE

Mukherjee demonstrates how we can apply postcolonial theory—which is more commonly used to consider film and literature's geopolitical, racial imaginaries, and power structures—to board games and their own icons of power, especially given the medium's fondness for exploration and conquest. Mukherjee turns to the Eurogame hit Settlers of Catan *as an example.*

Introducing *Settlers of Catan* in a Postcolonial Milieu

Klaus Teuber's epic board game *Settlers of Catan*, now renamed *Catan* (see figure 9.1), became a blockbuster success in Europe and the US when it was released in 1995, and generations have grown up having hours of fun in the fictitious world of Catan; however, it did not make a stir at all in most countries of the Global South. The 1980s and 1990s were also the heyday of postcolonialism, a theoretical framework that makes clear the inherited power relations of nineteenth-century European imperialism and their continuing effects on modern global culture and politics, and they saw the publication of seminal work by scholars such as Homi Bhabha and Gayatri Spivak.[1] The message of postcolonialism, despite being so contemporary, does not seem to have influenced the original thinking behind *Catan*, and the game is quite simply and straightforwardly about colonizing a settlement and reenacting the European myth of settling in a fertile land and encountering no meaningful resistance, as if it were part of their destiny. When viewed through a postcolonial lens, the *Catan* board begins to unravel a set of ethical and geopolitical problems. Also coming into play (literally and metaphorically) are new sets

Figure 9.1: A *Catan* board showing the salient elements of gameplay and its imperialist construction. Photo by Jonathan Gray.

of questions regarding the logic of the game—its algorithm, as it were. Board games, of course, have existed since antiquity, and *Catan* takes its place in a long series of games beginning with the Royal Game of Ur (ca. 2600 BC) and Senet (ca. 2620 BC) that have been political and are characterized by what Ian Bogost calls a "procedural rhetoric."[2] These games have been described as "narrative" by Pawel Bornstedt because "a board game's theme always belongs to the narrative level, because otherwise, as far as the ludic aspects are concerned, it would be irrelevant whether single-colored cards were simply drawn instead of cards with colored moves."[3] In recent board games scholarship, Paul Booth has made a strong case for board games as media.[4] Writing decades earlier, however, Roland Barthes described the "text" as a plural entity that "is experienced only in an activity of production" and described even a wrestling match as text.[5] As such, given the long tradition of board games to function as narrative media and convey a rhetorical message, it is evident that board games such as *Catan*, too, are an important textual medium worthy of academic analysis, and multiple critical lenses, such as the postcolonial, need to be deployed.

That *Catan* has a distinct colonial connection has already been established by Bruno Faidutti in his article "Postcolonial Catan" and by academics such as William Robinson and Greg Loring-Albright in their discussions of Orientalism in the so-called Eurogames and explorations of postcolonial responses through counterplaying the game.[6] That scholarship shall be explored at length later, but it is indeed intriguing to see that all the colonial critiques took such a long while to surface and that postcolonialism, which was in its heyday at the time of *Catan*'s release, seemed largely oblivious to the game's overt promotion of the colonial agenda. Peter Barry outlines some of the key arguments of postcolonialist critics in his introductory book on literary theory, as follows:

1. They reject the claims to universalism made on behalf of canonical Western literature and seek to show its limitations of outlook, especially its general inability to empathise across boundaries of cultural and ethnic difference.
2. They examine the representation of other cultures in literature as a way of achieving this end.
3. They show how such literature is often evasively and crucially silent on matters concerned with colonization and imperialism.
4. They foreground questions of cultural difference and diversity and examine their treatment in relevant literary works.
5. They celebrate hybridity and "cultural polyvalency", that is, the situation whereby individuals and groups belong simultaneously to more than one culture (for instance, that of the colonizer, through a colonial school system, and that of the colonized, through local and oral traditions).
6. They develop a perspective, not just applicable to postcolonial literatures, whereby states of marginality, plurality and perceived 'Otherness' are seen as sources of energy and potential change.[7]

Barry constrains his criteria to literature, but these can generally apply to other categories as well where the colony and the metropole come into contact and conflict. Mary Louise Pratt's concept of "contact zones" captures the scenario well in identifying that the colonizer and colonized are not in a simple *versus* relationship but one where there is addition, subtraction, and the creation of new cultural elements in an unequal and often violent platform of interaction.[8] Barry also does not mention a core thought behind postcolonialism: that of subaltern studies. Subaltern studies brings to the forefront those discourses of the colonized that are routinely written out and silenced by the archival and historiographical apparatus of the European colonizing powers.[9] Similarly, another influential concept in postcolonial thought is that of Orientalism; Edward Said articulates this as the fictitious (re)construction of the East by European cultures, many of which were involved in colonialism.[10] Commentators such as Faidutti are struck by the similarity between our initial reactions to *Catan* and what Said says of nineteenth-century European novels, and specifically of Jane Austen's *Mansfield Park*, where he thought slaves, though nowhere to be seen, are always in the background, but it is indeed surprising, as Faidutti notes, that "world literature has largely become postcolonial, and the same could probably be said of music (rap is something like postcolonial rock) and movies. There's nothing like this in games, and the image they show of the Orient is plain orientalist exoticism, of a kind that has disappeared from literature, movies, and even comics."[11] As Walter Mignolo points out, it is important to read against the grain of Western conceptions of knowledge, in an approach that he describes as decoloniality.[12] The colonial overtones of *Catan* have already been commented on; this chapter will develop earlier commentary to illustrate in detail how the board game can be read as a (post/de)colonial text.

Postcolonialism and Its Ambivalent Attitude to Board Games

Why postcolonial thinkers did not pay attention to this perpetuation of colonial discourse among millions of board game players is probably connected to the neglect of board games across disciplines and theoretical positions. However, this contrasts with the attention given to sports such as football and cricket by leading postcolonial thinkers, from the very earliest discussions by C. L. R. James to Ramchandra Guha, Simon Gikandi, and Arjun Appadurai more recently.[13] There could be multiple explanations for the neglect of board games, ranging from plain ignorance to the conscious or unconscious perpetuation of colonial notions.

After all, "sedentary games" were looked down upon by colonial historians such as James Mill because they were considered pursuits of laziness and physical and moral debility.[14] This situation leaves game designers such as Faidutti awaiting the Salman Rushdie of board games! Of course, as far as Eurogames such as *Catan* are concerned, many of them did not reach the Global South until very recently, and they continue to be expensive and still out of reach for a large section of people.

Colonialism in board games, however, predates these Eurogames by centuries. One only has to look at games such as William Spooner's *Voyage of Discovery* (1836), which shows the profit-laden nature of the European interactions with Indigenous people and the inherent violence in their exploration.[15] Speaking of older as well as more recent Eurogames, Mary Flanagan and Mikael Jakobsson note that "while our research reaches hundreds of years back to explore historical examples, a surprising—indeed, shocking—number of the most insidious colonialist games were released in the last two decades. In fact, the number of colonial-themed board games released each year is increasing."[16] Also, the perpetuation of Orientalist iconography, even in recent board games such as *Jaipur* (Sébastien Pauchon, 2009) and *Afrikan Tähti* (Kari Mannerla, 1951), is surprising.[17] Although neglected by mainstream cultural studies, including studies of popular culture, board games have focused on major cultural issues since time immemorial. The Dutch historian Johan Huizinga remarked that culture is "sub specie ludii," loosely translated as a "game in disguise"; a game also can be a phenomenon in the deeper study of culture.[18] For instance, *Monopoly* (Charles Darrow, 1935), which originated as the *Landlord's Game* (Elizabeth Magie, 1904), now carries a clear capitalistic message, and the notorious Nazi game *Juden Raus* (Günther and Co., 1936) is about xenophobia and extermination.

Applying the lens of postcolonial theory to board games, particularly Eurogames such as *Catan* or *Puerto Rico*, helps unpack some key characteristics of these games. The first is the game mechanic of the four Xs: eXplore, eXpand, eXploit, and eXterminate, as video game scholar Dom Ford points out.[19] One of the major issues is that of how space is constructed in board games and then navigated. Elsewhere, I comment on the power of maps in video games: "The power is not only connected to the illumination of the dark spaces or the 'fog of war' of the game's map but also to the agency to change the interface through interaction."[20] The clearing of the "fog of war" and the expansion of territory are directly associated with colonialism, especially when they are associated with resource collection and the conquest of territory. Often the end goal of the games is to remove the other player from the board: when this is represented through the interface of a board game, the implications of colonial extermination are clear.

The first element of these board games that needs to be questioned is the quadruple-X game mechanic; although it is not obvious at first sight, it is soon evident. As Nancy Foasberg comments, "Many Eurogames—including those critiqued here—are mathematically beautiful, strategically rich, and socially engaging. However, they are frequently set in a colonial past which is approached uncritically."[21] Will Robinson points out another important characteristic, perhaps a stratagem, of Eurogames wherein they eschew displays of violence in the game. Unlike their digital counterparts, where players of *Half Life*, *Doom*, or *Mass Effect* shoot monsters to bits, in Eurogames there is little or no overt violence. Robinson contends that these games "often contain the problematic presentation of European expansionism without including the indigenous other."[22] This also brings up the concept of *terra nullius*, where the map is viewed as an empty space that can be (and should be) occupied without resistance in games such as *Risk* (Parker Brothers, 1959). Postcolonial commentators on cartography have brought up many pertinent questions regarding the way maps allow viewers to construct space.

Many Eurogames are based on cartography and have historical maps or abstract maps as their play spaces. Graham Huggan criticizes the eighteenth- and nineteenth-century European cartographers whose attempts to fill in the blank spaces on the map of the world show "conspicuous gaps, absences and inconsistencies in the presented text as a means of exposing flaws in the wider discursive system it exemplifies."[23] He also points out that the projection system still used in many of these maps is Eurocentric and follows the system outlined by Dutch cartographer Gerardus Mercator in 1589. Both in board game studies and video game studies, such maps are crucial play spaces, but from a postcolonialist lens, these are also the playing fields of Empire. The narratives of the subaltern and the Other do not figure on the game boards, or, at least, not until perhaps one invokes the perspective of subaltern studies and unravels the stories that remain untold on the game boards and cards. Indeed, often these games and their deep-seated colonial bias remain unnoticed or are accepted as the norm. In the seventeenth and eighteenth century, as Megan A. Norcia observes, these colonial tropes were considered usual and acceptable, as the games made by Spooner and Betts indicate. Centuries later, however, the same assumptions continue in board games published in Europe.[24] For example, *Afrikan Tähti* is about the finding of a diamond on a map of the African continent, which is quite clearly colonial and connects exploitation of resources to success in the game. As Sabine Harrer and Outi Lahti note, Africa is still the continent from which resources are extracted by meeples (playing pieces, often stylized), and Orientalism and colonial privilege are evident "in the design of *Afrikan Tähti*'s game board, which adopts the visual language of colonial-style cartography, including racist caricatures of Black tribes' people on the original map."[25] *Afrikan Tähti* still continues to be popular in Finland and the rest of Scandinavia despite recent controversies. Karen E. French and William R. Stanley's *Game on the European Colonization of Africa*, published as late as 1974 (by when most of the African countries had gained independence), depicts the colonies on a *Monopoly* board setting wherein the regions or countries are effectively turned into real estate.

In sum, the tool kit that postcolonialism offers is one that enables a reappraisal of existing games, their algorithms, and their play cultures in the light of more inclusive, diverse, and global parameters. It also helps unpack the sometimes-intrinsic colonial bias in some of these games. In games studies, which is increasingly beginning to include discussions of board games alongside its vaster body of work on video games, there are many examples of research into this question. For example, Rebecca Mir and Trevor Owens contend that in Sid Meier's game *Colonization*, "what is interesting about this particular way of setting up and building *Colonization* is that Natives are largely explicitly created by the negation of rules that grant particular characteristics to the colonial powers. From the perspective of the game's source code there are normal peoples (colonial powers) who come with a range of abilities and characteristics and then a set of exceptions that strip many of those abilities away from peoples who are flagged as 'isNative.'"[26] Deeply problematic as this is, there are many such examples in video games, and game developer Meghna Jayanth rightly points out that the video game is characterized by white protagonism and an imperialist agenda.[27] Using these examples from digital games, it is possible to reexamine how game mechanics and rule sets (algorithms) in board games often have a colonial bias that pervades the very logic of a game.

Colonial *Catan*, Postcolonial *Catan*: Playing Through Different Lens

In a board game such as *Catan*, the principal logic of the game is that of settler colonialism. The land is considered unoccupied and abstract pieces represent terrain and resources. The concept of using tiles to create custom maps dates back centuries and the German *Kriegspiel*, literally "war game," as conceptualized by Georg Leopold von Reisswitz and his son, simulated actual battlefield maps using a set of tiles. The introduction of hexagonal tiles was crucial because of the increased affordances that the combination of hexagons provided. *Catan* may not incorporate the logic of these games, but it is not possible to ignore the antecedents of war-gaming and the maximizing of resource gathering and management in the way it has been conceived. The main point-gathering mechanic of the game is centered around resources—brick, wool, ore, grain, and wood (lumber)—and the player is expected to build cities and roads at the intersections of the hexagonal tiles. In fact, some of the key achievements that count toward victory points are the building of the longest road and possession of the largest army, both of which are characteristic of imperialism.

The "robber" pawn in the game blocks resource gathering for the players adjacent to a certain hexagon tile and also allows the player who moves the robber to steal the resources of those other players. The robber pawn (which was earlier black or grey, colors that could have a racial significance) could be thought of as an already-inbuilt mechanism of counterplay in the game, although it, too, furthers the ends of the player who uses it. The *Catan Wiki* describes the robber thus:

> Some say that the Robber established a base in the desert soon after the very first settlement, Candamir, was built on Catan. Others state that the Robber came only later when the rival powers came to divide the island. Either way, the original threat of the Robber disappeared once the cities

of Catan were established and settled. However, when the first barbarians invaded the land, robbery returned and, it is said, the Robber of old returned once more to ravage the lands of Catan. None truly know who the Robber is, but it is certain that the base of the Robber lies somewhere deep in the Catanian desert, a place that settlers have long avoided because of its harsh soil and dangerous climate.... The truth is that the robber is a harmless fellow who is merely taken advantage of by the players, for the sake of their own benefit. He is pushed around from terrain hex to terrain hex, unable to escape his sometimes quite harsh destiny.[28]

From the additional fictional context that players (presumably) have given the piece, there is the sense that the robber is perhaps the Othered subaltern who exists in Catan and whose presence and needs are not heeded until a special situation arises (in this case, a throw of seven).

Inserting a counterplay mechanism, Loring-Albright has adapted *Catan* in a mod to include the Indigenous First Nations, which occupy the spaces in the middle of the hexagon. Being in the middle, however, reduces the resource-gathering capabilities of the First Nations, whereas the hexagonal tiles enable more connections for the settler factions because they are placed at the intersecting points. Loring-Albright gives the First Nations a new card called the "tribes card" that enables them to collect resources; additionally, the tribes card can initiate military action while the settlers can only defend themselves. I would argue that this process of counterplay is, nevertheless, a perpetuation of colonial logic and that in itself it poses quite a few problems.

Loring-Albright explains placing the First Nations in the center of the tile as reflecting the historical disadvantages that these peoples suffered. There is, however, a flaw in the reasoning—historically, colonized peoples did not necessarily have less access to resources—in many cases, they were denied access to resources. Loring-Albright, of course, argues that the decreased access to resources was due to the First Nations being forced out of their original homelands. Adding a tribes card that can help collect resources or fight battles also does not reflect what happened historically, and neither is the fact that only the First Nations can initiate battles. Finally, the question of settlers is more complicated: often peoples from other colonized nations were forced to settle in foreign lands by the colonizing powers—often in conflict with the original inhabitants. These issues are left ignored in Loring-Albright's mod for *Catan*, and the fact that the entire thinking around the game mechanics is linked to resource collection reflects the same logic as the original game: that of colonization and expansionism.

Whether it is the absent Other in the *terra nullius* of *Catan*, the dark-colored robber who is the Other-figure, or a counterplay that nevertheless perpetuates colonial questions, the logic of *Catan* carries within it the inherent question that has always vexed imperialism: how to accommodate (or expel) the Other and the hybrid. From the game, as from other games about settler colonies, the mechanic of expansion and resource exploitation that emerges is one that is described as the "coloniality of power" by Latin American thinker Anibal Quijano, who highlights "the intimate relation that the coloniality of power constructs among race, global capitalism, and Eurocentered modernity and knowledge."[29]

Walter Mignolo's concept of decoloniality draws on Quijano's thinking of epistemic subversion of the Global North knowledge systems. So far, academic discussions of decoloniality do not address games as much, especially outside the still-nascent but growing discussions within game studies. There have been some studies of cricket; for example, Priya Dixit identifies the writings of C. L. R. James as the site where "in the writing and playing of cricket, various strategies of decolonizing world politics such as reworking established hierarchies, emphasizing autobiography as method of critique and resistance, and thinking about standpoint and positionality in generating knowledge can be illustrated."[30] The algorithmic bias of game mechanics originating in Europe is, however, not easy to counter. Commenting on video games and decoloniality (in the work of Rhett Loban and Tom Apperley), Samuel Poirier-Poulin observes that although "modding can be a pedagogical tool to expose players to histories and cultures that are too often erased, it is limited by the Eurocentric mechanics of many games."[31] Decolonial gaming strategies and mechanics are difficult to imagine, although some clear examples exist, as the recent work on Gyan Chaupar has shown.[32] So where can one place decolonial play? Does the game-text prescribe play through its rules and contexts? Is the decolonial play a space of promise where the colonial and imperial bias no longer exist? Or can play and mods only go so far, for the game-text that is still at root deeply colonial/imperial?

The answer may be sought in subaltern studies although, regrettably, subaltern studies scholars rarely engage in discussion of play, as discussed earlier. One of the key points to consider is to understand the lack of or denial of agency as a game mechanic. In game studies, after an initial optimism about the player being invested with free choice and agency, the question of agency has been treated in much more complex ways: the algorithm and the nonhuman agents are given due consideration and agency itself is viewed as being illusory. In postcolonialism, the subaltern is denied agency, and it is only through the margins and fissures that the subaltern identity can be perceived. Such readings can also be compared to the way in which the robber pawn has been understood earlier in this chapter. Where existing notions of play tend to describe it as a free activity (with its implications of agency), there are nevertheless many non-Western notions of play where such freedom is not a precondition of play. One such example is Aaron Trammell's notion of "repairing play" where, through instances from play in American slave narratives, he exposes how play can consist of denying the subjectivity of others and how even torture can be described as play. Trammell writes eloquently about "the more insidious ways that play has functioned as a tool of subjugation. A tool that hurts as much as it heals and has been complicit in the systemic erasure of BIPOC people from the domain of leisure."[33] In playing *Catan* in the sense of a "repairing," the latent insidiousness of the play mechanic is laid bare. Trammell describes the process of repairing as a coalition of many different postcolonial responses to the games of empire: whether one plays cricket by totally subverting the colonial rules of the game (the Samoan version called Kilikiti is a case in point) or plays *Europa Universalis* (Philippe Thibaut, 1993) using a mod that evens out the play scenario for the oppressed nationalities and peoples. Playing *Catan* could be such an act of repairing once the players understand and appreciate the covert colonialist agenda in the game and seek to subvert them through the gameplay. In a game such as *Spirit Island* (R. Eric Reuss, 2017), however, the island itself is populated by spirits through whom players actively resist the very arrival of colonial powers, thus making the basic premise of settling quite difficult. As one looks beyond *Catan* to its mod, *First Nations of Catan* (Greg Loring-Albright, 2015), or new games such as *Spirit Island*, the postcolonial response to the game is evident. But I argue that, provided that its algorithmic concerns are kept in mind, *Settlers of Catan* or *Catan* itself ironically functions as a postcolonial text in the sense that being a game, it is open to mechanisms of counterplay and also invites a critical response to its basic colonial underpinnings, albeit one that has been ignored as such and mostly viewed through other lenses.

Notes

1. Homi K. Bhabha, *The Location of Culture*, 2nd ed. (London: Routledge, 2004); Gayatri Chakravorty Spivak, "Can the Subaltern Speak?," in *Colonial Discourse and Post-Colonial Theory: A Reader*, edited by Patrick Williams and Laura Chrisman (London: Routledge, 2015), 66–111.
2. Ian Bogost, *Persuasive Games: The Expressive Power of Videogames* (Cambridge, MA: MIT Press, 2007), 3.
3. Pawel Bornstedt, "The Board Game as a Narrative Medium," *Analog Game Studies* 11 (January 2024), https://analoggamestudies.org/2024/01/the-board-game-as-a-narrative-medium/.
4. Paul Booth, *Board Games as Media* (New York: Bloomsbury, 2021).
5. Roland Barthes, "From Work to Text," in *Textual Strategies: Perspectives in Post-Structuralist Criticism*, edited by Josue V. Harari (Ithaca, NY: Cornell University Press, 2019), 73–81.
6. Eurogames are a genre of late twentieth-century strategy and organization board games mainly originating in Europe, especially Germany, where "instead of chance, players would be given a small range of options for what to do on their turn and their success in the game rested on how good their decision-making and planning were, relative to that of other players": Tristan Donovan, *It's All a Game: A Short History of Board Games* (London: Atlantic Books, 2018), 247. Also see Bruno Faidutti, "Postcolonial Catan," in *Analog Game Studies: Volume 2*, edited by Aaron Trammell, Emma Leigh Waldron, and Evan Torner (Pittsburgh: ETC Press, 2017), 3–34, www.lulu.com/shop/evan-torner-and-emma-leigh-waldron-and-aaron-trammell/analog-game-studies-volume-2/ebook/product-23267378.html; Will Robinson, "Orientalism and Abstraction in Eurogames," *Analog Game Studies* 1, no. 5 (2014): 55–63; and Greg Loring-Albright, "The First Nations of Catan: Practices in Critical Modification," *Analog Game Studies* 2 (November 9, 2015), 35–42, https://analoggamestudies.org/2015/11/the-first-nations-of-catan-practices-in-critical-modification/.
7. Peter Barry, *Beginning Theory*, 3rd rev. ed. (Delhi: Viva Books, 2010), 198.
8. Mary Louise Pratt, *Imperial Eyes: Travel Writing and Transculturation*, 2nd ed. (London: Routledge, 2007).
9. Dipesh Chakrabarty, "Subaltern Studies and Postcolonial Historiography," *Nepantla: Views from South* 1, no. 1 (2000): 9–32.
10. Edward W. Said, *Orientalism* (New York: Vintage Books: 1979).

11 Faidutti, "Postcolonial Catan."
12 Walter D. Mignolo, "Introduction: Coloniality of Power and de-Colonial Thinking," *Cultural Studies* 21, no. 2–3 (2007): 155–67, https://doi.org/10.1080/09502380601162498.
13 C. L. R. James, *Beyond a Boundary* (London: Hutchinson, 1963); Simon Gikandi, *Maps of Englishness: Writing Identity in the Culture of Colonialism* (New York: Columbia University Press, 1996); Ramchandra Guha, *A Corner of a Foreign Field: The Indian History of a British Sport* (London: Macmillan, 2002); Arjun Appadurai, "Playing with Modernity: The Decolonization of Indian Cricket," in *Consuming Modernity: Public Culture in a South Asian World*, edited by Carol A. Breckenridge (Minneapolis: University of Minnesota Press, 1995), 23–48.
14 James Mill, *The History of British India* (London: J. Madden, 1848), http://archive.org/details/historybritishi23wilsgoog; see also Nirbed Ray and Projit Bihari Mukharji, "Sedentary Games and the Nationalist Project: A Silent History," *International Journal of the History of Sport* 22, no. 4 (2005): 699–707, https://doi.org/10.1080/09523360500123119.
15 William Spooner, *A Voyage of Discovery or The Five Navigators*, hand-colored engraving mounted on linen, 1836, Victoria and Albert Museum Young V&A Collection, https://collections.vam.ac.uk/item/O26352/a-voyage-of-discovery-or-board-game-spooner-william/.
16 Mary Flanagan and Mikael Jakobsson, *Playing Oppression: The Legacy of Conquest and Empire in Colonialist Board Games* (Cambridge, MA: MIT Press, 2023).
17 Sébastien Pauchon, *Jaipur* (Switzerland: GameWorks SàRL, 2009), https://boardgamegeek.com/boardgamepublisher/6347/gameworks-sarl; Kari Mannerla, *Afrikan Tähti* (Raisio, Finland: Peliko, 1951).
18 Johan Huizinga, *Homo Ludens: A Study of the Play-Element in Culture* (London: Routledge and Kegan Paul, 1949).
19 Dom Ford, "'EXplore, EXpand, EXploit, EXterminate': Affective Writing of Postcolonial History and Education in *Civilization V*," *Game Studies* 16, no. 2 (2016), https://gamestudies.org/1602/articles/ford.
20 Souvik Mukherjee, "The Cartography of Virtual Empires. Video Game Maps, Paratexts, and Colonialism," in *Paratextualizing Games: Investigations on the Paraphernalia and Peripheries of Play*, edited by Benjamin Beil, Gundolf S. Freyermuth, and Hanns Christian Schmidt (Bielefeld: Transcript Publishing, 2022), 81.
21 Nancy Foasberg, "The Problematic Pleasures of Productivity and Efficiency in Goa and Navegador," *Analog Game Studies* 9, no. 1 (2016), https://analoggamestudies.org/2016/01/the-problematic-pleasures-of-productivity-and-efficiency-in-goa-and-navegador/.
22 Robinson, "Orientalism and Abstraction."
23 Graham Huggan, *Interdisciplinary Measures: Literature and the Future of Postcolonial Studies* (Liverpool: Liverpool University Press, 2008), 25.

24 Megan A. Norcia, *Gaming Empire in Children's British Board Games, 1836–1860* (New York: Routledge, 2019).

25 Sabine Harrer and Outi Laiti, "Outside the Racist Nostalgia Box: Rethinking Afrikan Tähti's Cultural Depictions," *Journal of Games Criticism* (August 2023), https://gamescriticism.org/2023/08/22/harrer-laiti-5a/.

26 Rebecca Mir and Trevor Owens, "Modelling Indigenous Peoples: Unpacking Ideology in Sid Meier's Colonization," in *Playing with the Past: Digital Games and the Simulation of History*, edited by Matthew Wilhelm Kapell and Andrew B. R. Elliott (New York: Bloomsbury, 2013), 91–106.

27 Meghna Jayanth, "White Protagonism and Imperial Pleasures in Game Design," *Medium,* December 7, 2021, https://medium.com/@betterthemask/white-protagonism-and-imperial-pleasures-in-game-design-digra21-a4bdb3f5583c.

28 "The Robber," *World of Catan Wiki*, accessed March 1, 2024, https://catan.fandom.com/wiki/The_Robber.

29 Aníbal Quijano, *Aníbal Quijano: Foundational Essays on the Coloniality of Power*, edited by Walter D. Mignolo, Rita Segato, and Catherine E. Walsh (Durham, NC: Duke University Press, 2024), 2.

30 Priya Dixit, "Decolonial Strategies in World Politics: C. L. R. James and the Writing and Playing of Cricket," *Globalizations* 15, no. 3 (2018): 377–89, https://doi.org/10.1080/14747731.2018.1424284.

31 Samuel Poirier-Poulin, "Review: Game Studies and Decoloniality," *Antares* 12, no. 28 (2020): 366–70, http://dx.doi.org/10.18226/19844921.v12.n28.18.

32 See Flanagan and Jakobsson, *Playing Oppression*; and Souvik Mukherjee, "EReading Karma in Snakes and Ladders: Two South Asian Game Boards in the British Library Collections," British Library Asian and African Studies Blog, September 11, 2020, https://blogs.bl.uk/asian-and-african/2020/09/ereading-karma-in-snakes-and-ladders-two-game-boards-in-the-british-library-collections.html.

33 Aaron Trammell, *Repairing Play: A Black Phenomenology* (Cambridge, MA: MIT Press, 2023).

10

An Autotheory for Game Studies

Shadow of the Colossus

SORAYA MURRAY

Murray takes issue with textual analysis's troubling presumption of objectivity, whereby a reader/listener/user/player is imagined but only mysteriously, and never nominated. Murray instead posits autotheory as a way of explicitly naming the user, thereby centering the experiences of a particular body in a particular time and place, and then uses her own response to and relationship with the video game Shadow of the Colossus *as an example.*

Theorizing Room for the Personal in Game Analysis

Playing a video game is highly personal and becomes an experience—maybe not the same as in the lived world, but an experience nonetheless. Games build worlds and generate emotional charges that gather intensity across long periods of time. Cultural, social, political, and other contextual cues inform these experiences. Yet more often than not, games writing tends to privilege a smooth, standardized "expert" engagement with a game as most authoritative. How does one make room for the self-referential in video game analysis, inflected through theory, creativity, and self-awareness? What possible exploits can a sustained, sometimes conflicted relation to a video game offer? What about unexpected or even unacceptable engagements? What about players who have fraught relationships with the games they play or see those games as ideologically antagonistic worlds? How can these intense personal relations be meaningfully accounted for in textual analyses of video games?

As a visual culture scholar, I see video games as embedded in larger cultural, social, and political intensities of the lived world. Understanding why games matter—their stakes as mass culture objects—is complex. Plus, while meaning in games can be conveyed through representation, it is also communicated through rules, mechanics, texture, touch, temporality, narrative, atmosphere, spatial relations, mapping, aesthetics, and borrowed visual literacies of preexisting media.[1] Their potential meanings also change unexpectedly across time, gathering relevance, falling in or out of favor, and becoming emblematic products of their own time.

Further complicating any textual analysis, gameplay experience is highly individualized. Some researchers are innovating useful methods to capture the performances of people playing games. Playthroughs, with their distinctive personal dimensions, offer an invaluable resource for players and those who want to study games. Stuart Moulthrop and Dene Grigar have created what they call "traversals" of digital literature, or as they define them, "audio and video recording of demonstrations performed on historically appropriate platforms" by the makers that can offer documentation, elucidate maker intentions, and capture the material uniqueness of the original medium itself.[2] This documentation becomes critical for the historical record, since times change and platforms become obsolete. However, people engage with games in various contexts and experience them in vastly different ways. Video games can become theoretical objects to think with or simulated spaces for contending with difficult topics and societal struggles.[3] This contemplative mode can open up another valuable way of understanding how and why games of the past moved players—perhaps even despite their technical limitations—and why certain games remain resonant. This also provides a way of valuing, cultivating, and documenting a form of knowing deeply rooted in aesthetic engagement with the textual object.

In this chapter, I demonstrate how the personal and theoretical come together in an analysis through autotheory, or what writer Teresa Carmody describes as "art/writing that combines theory or philosophy with autobiography."[4] I'll first share how some key thinkers have defined what autotheory is and then consider why it matters for the analysis of video games. Finally, with the iconic action-adventure game *Shadow of the Colossus* (Ico, 2005) as a critical object of analysis, I show how critical game studies, with theory and the centrality of the self as vital elements, can better account for how one works through their engagement with video games.⁵ I offer an example of textual analysis that folds in vital components of visual studies: a close reading that centers visual elements and their contextual interpretation and illumination, as well as the role of the personal, autobiographical, and subjective relations to the game embedded in a context. Put another way, this chapter proposes and then demonstrates an autotheory for critical game studies.

An Autotheory for Critical Game Studies

First, why would an autotheory of game studies matter? What good work can it do? What new knowledge can it reveal? And how can it be helpful if it does not lead to a generalizable model that can be implemented to understand other games?

Beyond games, many have theorized and modeled ways of bringing the subjective more firmly into the analysis of visual objects in their own critical methodologies. In art and its discourses, there is some precedent for creating pathways for understanding the role of the personal and contemplative in textual analysis. Art history and visual studies scholar Joanne Morra has identified what she calls a "working-through" required for sitting with particular aesthetic objects of study. This points to the value of an intensely personal and idiosyncratic framing to spark novel interpretations. Morra describes repeated looking, thinking, failing, free association, sitting with, procrastination, and other working practices as necessary processes for grasping what art objects mean.⁶ Documentarian and scholar Mieke Bal, who writes about what the autotheoretical is for her work, describes a "spiral-like activity" of self-reflexive process: "a form of thinking that integrates my own practice of art making as a form of thinking, and reflection on what I have made as a continuation of the making."⁷

Scholar Jennifer Doyle has brought her personal experiences of "difficult" art into productive tension with conventional art-historical understandings of what constitutes their legitimate analysis. She thinks about the role of criticism and centers an understanding that artists craft affective intensities, not just objects—and that one's experience of these intensities is highly personal and idiosyncratic. Doyle's definition of affect is helpful in thinking about those intensities: "the diffuse nature of emotion and feeling, in which a mood can saturate a space, for example, or in which an institutional setting such as a museum might impose its own set of rules regarding proper comportment, expressivity, and emotionality."[8] How we connect with those intensities happens through our bodies. Arianne Zwartjes writes of this as a way to "metabolize theory through lived experience."[9] There are many forms autotheory can take. But uniting all these approaches is the prioritization of slow theorization: self-reflexive, sustained, internal, embodied, contemplative, relational, and contingent. And, this personal/theoretical mode requires a component of vulnerability, which may feel riskier for the writer and intellectually messy for the reader.[10]

I believe that the more nebulous elements of games—like affect—are a massive part of how they capture the public imagination and become meaningful to people. Yet, there are currently few tools in game scholarship for articulating what games actually mean to us. Maybe that is because of the personal component, which can be thought of as either self-reflexive (contemplative and bearing more positive associations) or self-absorbed (bearing more negative connotations). We need to observe and document these diffuse affective intensities as they gather up in video games within their own cultural moment. This is because the contextual circumstances of a video game change across time, and while playthroughs and traversals are helpful, the individual testimonial of gameplay in an autotheoretical mode can offer another significant meditation on why games matter, in context.

While no robust discourse links critical game studies and autotheory, theorists have addressed other creative practices in ways that could be generative for games. Notably, Lauren Fournier has recently expanded our understanding of the autotheoretical impulse as a feminist intervention in art. Her ideas may also open up new possibilities for understanding video games as a visual culture form. Fournier's critical interventions gather up and extend the many vital ideas of those committed to the role of the personal and theoretical. She defines autotheory as an "integration of theory and philosophy with autobiography, the body, and other so-called personal and explicitly subjective modes . . . a self-conscious way of engaging with theory—as a discourse, frame, or mode of thinking and practice."[11] As described by Fournier, a key component of the "personal-theoretical, incidental [and] gut-centered" is the focus on what she calls "reparative forms of critique."[12] She explains that these critical approaches are rooted in contemporary art and its traditions, in things that have been variously termed "conceptual criticism" and "performative philosophy"—transdisciplinary methods that meld theory and autobiography while rejecting the false duality between art and life. Fournier thinks about what possibilities the autotheoretical offers, considering, for example, how lived experience informs a personal and self-reflective interpretation.

Admittedly, in a time of ubiquitous social media and public oversharing, such a subjective and highly personal approach might inspire criticism. In her book, Fournier thinks about the troubling connection made between autotheory and narcissism, which, incidentally, has also become a highly gendered critique.[13] But I see the personal as a necessary component of an inclusive and varied understanding of creative practice, in this case, video games. A second question that may arise is about how such a method might be historically or interpretively "useful" or how it maintains "rigor," especially in the face of normative standards of acceptable scholarship, which are more associated with objectivity. Is this "personal" approach somehow implicitly ideologically encoded as belonging to the "feminine" realm and therefore doomed to be regarded as a less valid form of knowing, insofar as scholarship is concerned? What if we think of video games as theoretical objects? How does this approach intersect with feminist ethics?

For Fournier, autotheory challenges the acceptable understanding of what constitutes legitimate erudition, which she sees as bound up in identity. "Historically, for one's work to be considered intellectual and critical, as a philosopher, historian, critic, or professor, one had to have an air of objective authority," Fournier writes.[14] She suggests that, in fact, the autotheoretical impulse is employed by the so-called fathers of high theory, incorporating personal experience—it's just that their perspectives are held as universal and rational. But this creation of a dualism between the objective and disembodied, as opposed to the personal and embodied, reinforces a dysfunctional set of relations. I would take her point even further and assert that there is little possibility of entirely excising the personal investment from the theoretical and philosophical despite the clinging tendency to believe the exact opposite.

Fournier's words point to a certain bias against the worth of the personal and the embodied as legitimate ways of knowing and understanding when that knowing is cast against normative, universal, or "objective" subject positions. So, this means an autotheoretical approach is connected to equity in modes of knowing: its impulse is a focus on specificity, the personal and the subjective, rather than using theory to distill generalizable "objective" principles. This pursuit of the generalizable tenets is also tied to troublesome presumptions that everything should be translatable into some form of capital or capitalist notions of marketability or interchangeable commodity value. The autotheoretical, on the other hand, refuses hierarchal authoritativeness and opens up a valuable conversation around other ways of knowing.

What the autotheoretical can do is provide unique tools to capture the ethos of a particular (not generalizable) space and time, which will pass away and whose documentation will eventually take on its own idiosyncratic value. Autotheory is also valuable because games are playable—and played by *people*, who necessarily bring their subjectivities to the game scenarios they encounter. In all their variety, autotheoretical interpretations can break from rote understandings of video games by embracing contingency and encouraging us to playfully hold master narratives at arm's length. The approach is necessarily slow and intentional, with its spiral-like returns, working-throughs, and repetitions. Such an approach rejects smooth, frictionless modes of play as markers of expertise and mastery and opens up an expanded sense of who may have the authority to speak on games and which experiences count. At its best, autotheory is radically inclusive.

As I have mentioned, game studies has suffered from an implicit expectation that its forms of knowledge production have more value if they can be distilled into general theories and applicable principles. But this leaves out other forms of knowing and understanding that can open up new ways of understanding our deeply personal relations to games. As scholar Vilashini Cooppan puts it, "Autotheory catalyzes voice, demands hearing, reconstitutes the self through self-expression, and in that very act calls for the world to change through recognition."[15] There is a vital role for the circuit connecting the game as a textual object, theory, and memoir or autobiographical elements. In the next section, I look at one of the most iconic video games of all time: *Shadow of the Colossus*. Modeling an autotheoretical approach, I reflect on playing *Shadow* as a graduate student in the context of its original release, considering core themes of striving and consequences in both the game and my life during that time.

Shadow of the Colossus: An Autotheoretical Look

Enter a Forbidden Land. Strike a grave bargain in exchange for the revival of a dead maiden. Slay the Colossi. Return, irrevocably transformed. Wander, the playable character, ventures into a monumental landscape on his trusted horse, Agro. The young hero carries with him the maiden Mono, hoping to entreat the god Dormin to summon her mortal soul back to the living. The god agrees, but only if Wander destroys icons of the sixteen colossi that trap Dormin's divided spirit. With the help of Agro and an ancient stolen sword that gathers beams of light to guide his journey, Wander sets out into a compelling world to kill the ancient and mysterious creatures (see figure 10.1).

Shadow of the Colossus, first published in 2005 by Sony Computer Entertainment for the PlayStation 2, remains one of the most revered works in video game history. Highly reviewed and awarded in its own time, *Shadow* presents a pared-down hero's journey, allowing the player to engage with monomyth. So beloved is this work by game director Fumito

Figure 10.1: Wander encounters the Third Colossus, Gaius. Screenshot by Jocque Jefferson.

Ueda, and so enduring its themes for players, that *Shadow* was remastered in 2011 for the PlayStation 3 and then again in 2018 for the PlayStation 4.[16]

The game's intensely allegorical quality makes it an ideal object for autotheoretical analysis. Everything about the game feels distilled and concentrated, as though one is moving around in the symbolic rather than the literal. Nick Suttner, who wrote a dedicated book on *Shadow*, discusses the "plainness" of Wander compared to the colossi, which favors a player's ability to project themselves onto the hero more effectively.[17] As I'll show, in its overall reductiveness, *Shadow* as a whole creates an effective "screen" for projecting meaning onto it, becoming a game-world symbolically rich with notions of working-through, free association, repeating and failing, and trying again.

You strike colossi down and they each collapse, with a deafening stone crash, sending brownish-grey clouds of debris in all directions. *Shadow* takes place in an open world with ruins of some unknown, long-gone empire; the characters bear the vague qualities of anime fantasy in their shape and proportion. Spaces are bathed in a golden light; riding solitary across vast lands to the location of each colossus takes longer than a typical video game of the time would allow. Colossi are made of magic and stone, moss and fur. They are sublime, mammoth creatures, illuminated from within, the light beaming from their flat disc-like eyes and from elaborate markings that indicate vulnerable places to strike. I free-climb up, gripping handfuls of fur and grasping at stone ridges, clinging for dear life while each titan tries to shake me off. Being careful, lest my grip weaken, I crouch and plunge my sword into their illuminated magic sigils (see figure 10.2).[18] They roar, buck, and moan in pain as their injuries spew inky blackness like oil geysers. The colossus topples in a rumbling avalanche. Then, unexpectedly, I am pierced by tendrils of shadow; I collapse and am hurled through a tunnel of light to be returned to Dormin's fortress. The victory feels bittersweet at best but also like a punishment.

At the time of its release, there was a buzz about *Shadow of the Colossus* as an auteurish game, one developed after the 2001 release of the game studio's previous successful title, *Ico*. *Shadow* is an action-adventure, and it is single-player—which indulges my fondness for solitary quests. The game is instantly satisfying for its grandeur, brooding fantasy, and emphasis on cinematic world-building and drama. Galloping across large spaces for long durations was an innovative gameplay component

Figure 10.2: Wander plunges his sword into the magic sigil of a colossus. Screenshot by Jocque Jefferson.

for the time, and it lends a sense of grand scale to the landscape. Its vastness and long stretches of open space suspend one in the contemplative, between isolated sections of heroic action. And game mechanics, such as weakening grip stamina as one tiredly clings to a colossus body and climbs up, serve to heighten tension.

Using thoughtful elements like these, the game gathers an intense affective charge, experienced as a sustained engagement with epic historical forces at play in one's life and far beyond one's control. With sustained play, the familiarity of a game filled with apparently recognizable tropes and formulaic dimensions (find a monster, destroy it, find an even bigger monster, destroy it) soon gives way to observing, working through, and contending with resistances in the game. The game becomes an object that mobilizes its expressive dimensions toward confronting something more profound and more troubling. Through its repetitive dimensions of exploration, encounter, challenge, and destruction of something wondrous and otherworldly, the player begins to question Wander's choices. As the game wears on, the cyclical slaying of ancient creatures becomes morally questionable at best, in what appears a Pyrrhic pursuit for achieving a dubious goal.

This scenario feels like a pattern of playing and replaying of a traumatic display: a small entity strikes, a monolith collapses, a small entity strikes, a monolith collapses. . . . I do this sixteen times across the game, toppling one colossus after another. A small entity strikes, a thick black substance spews forth from the creature, giants tumble, a painfully invasive transformation occurs . . . and it all happens again and again. Wander completes the task but is punished by pursuing warriors who have come to stop him. He is killed by his own clan for entering a forbidden territory and for interfering with creatures that should have been left unbothered. The victory of completing the cycle of sacrifices comes at a great cost.

Sustaining myself in the gamespace, I begin to project onto its generic quest much more personal notions of striving. It is 2005, and I am in graduate school at Cornell University. I am writing my doctoral dissertation on contemporary art and visual culture while I am playing *Shadow*. I am in an art history department but thinking about what it will mean, now that I know for certain that video games are important visual culture forms and that not enough people are writing about them. My first scholarly essay has just been published—which possibly portends future success.[19] But it is about video games, and I am thinking of what it means to deviate from the discipline that I am right now trying to master and of the stakes involved in achieving one's goals. I am in a strange intellectual territory. I am climbing giants; I am in their shadows. The visual shock of a diminutive underdog warrior, gigantic goals, my interest in games, my striving to master an academic discipline, and my concern for the outcome of that striving are all entangled.

Shadow is an early game that I encountered and played during a time when I was endeavoring to better myself and my life in an environment that was geographically, culturally, and intellectually strange to me. The game became a mental model, a poignant allegory for perseverance in my daily life and, most of all, for dashing in headlong, taking my shot, and facing an unknown future. The game captures this, distills it, and reduces it to its core struggle. Shadow pricks my sense of striving and overcoming. Problem-solving each new challenge in the game and in the institution, I negotiate resistances. I slay, and I slay, and I slay. And I win. The immersive nature of the game made it possible to reframe a problem within an autotheoretical scenario, a (game)space where I creatively negotiated the complexity of an ineffable intellectual impulse coming from within.

Through the game, I practiced being at ease while, again and again, finding myself in over my head. I learned to always see there is a goal, even if you don't yet know where it is; follow where the light points you. Then, locate the objective, get there, and self-consciously steel yourself to charge in and defeat it. Metaphorically, the grip stamina mechanic became meaningful; philosophical, even. At first, I would grip for dear life to the colossus, barely making it to safe spots to release and briefly recharge. But with each victory over a colossus, my grip would grow stronger—the better to meet the next challenge. This is a small element of the overall game, but extremely well thought through, understated yet something that creeps into significance across the course of the heroic journey. This "spiral-like activity" of engaging with *Shadow*, returning to the emotional intensity of trying and failing, resetting then trying again, helped shape a philosophy about the terms by which a person fixes one's determination to succeed.

Of course, the striving was not without its consequences. Over the course of the game, the quest exacts a visible toll on Wander, whose physical appearance changes with each monumental goal achieved. Nick Fortugno describes the potency of *Shadow of the Colossus* as rooted in what he calls its futility and dramatic necessity.[20] He talks about a game dynamic achieved in which, as a player, one must push forward, even while realizing there is an unintended consequence of the game's goal orientation—a deeply tragic one. In this case, it is the killing of ancient mythic creatures and the corrupted thing that our hero Wander becomes as a result. Fortugno writes, "All of the suffering—the obvious pain and struggle attached to the hunt and assault, the destruction of relatively harmless or isolated creatures of great beauty and scale, the bodily deterioration of Wander, the loss of [his horse] Agro—all of this could be avoided if the quest was given up."[21] Yet Wander wants his love back at any cost and thinks neither of what it means to destroy mythic beings nor to avoid his fate. At least, regardless of how a player may feel about killing colossi, there is no way to continue the game without also continuing to destroy them. But there is productive friction because, as a player, reflection on consequential costs stirs in me. In the end, Mono lives again. Wander becomes a colossus, then is reborn strange: as a child with horns. He is, as one scholar observes, "marked" by his deeds in a way that is ever legible to others.[22]

I, too, complete my quest. I'm older now, looking and feeling much different than when I set foot in that almost mythical, elite educational space. I have learned to follow my intellectual instincts, pursue unexpected directions, and face those challenges, even for long durations when others might not comprehend my choices . . . or even why the quest itself is so important to me. But now I, too, am marked by my deeds in a way ever legible to others. I've slain my colossi, and it shows.

* * *

This chapter includes one autotheoretical contemplation of using a video game to read contextual elements alongside affective components of the game and the self-reflexive. The text connects the traumatic, conflicted dimensions of collapsing colossi with the strains of engaging in academic disciplinary mastery and being changed by the experience. The writing models self-reflexivity by engaging the symbolic to convey an embodied sense of engaging in a quest for knowledge. It also engages autobiography and allegorically connects it to the striving and consequences that are core to the game.[23] The autotheoretical provides insight for game designers, players, and scholars because the affective dimensions of video games play a meaningful role in overall game experience. Making theoretical space for the subjective or personal as an authentic and consequential aspect of game experience enriches game analysis and builds language for understanding a critical dimension of how games expressively move players. Through the autotheoretical, we access not only simple gameplay experience, but also the function of prior cultural, social, and political triggers that shape a holistic understanding of what happens during play—ultimately affording another way of knowing why particular games mean so much to us.

Notes

1 There are now many approaches to these aspects of video games. For an introduction, see Matthew Thomas Payne and Nina Huntemann, eds., *How to Play Video Games* (New York: New York University Press, 2019).
2 Stuart Moulthrop and Dene Grigar, "Pathfinders: Documenting the Experience of Early Digital Literature," *Nouspace Publications*, 2015, https://doi.org/10.7273

/WFoB-TQ14. See also Stuart Moulthrop, Dene Grigar, and Joseph Tabbi, eds. *Traversals: The Use of Preservation for Early Electronic Writing* (Cambridge MA: MIT Press, 2017).

3   Soraya Murray, "No Country for Old Tropes: Representation and Political Affect in Red Dead Redemption 2," in *Red Dead Redemption: History, Myth and Violence in the Videogame West*, edited by John Wills and Esther Wright (Norman: University of Oklahoma Press, 2023) 203–20.

4   Teresa Carmody, "On Autotheory and Autofiction: Staking Genre," *Los Angeles Review of Books*, September 17, 2021, https://lareviewofbooks.org/article/on-autotheory-and-autofiction-staking-genre/.

5   For the sake of this analysis, I will be using the 2018 remaster of *Shadow of the Colossus*, originally released in 2005, developed by Japan Studio and Team Ico, and published by Sony Computer Entertainment for the PlayStation 2. The remastered version was developed by Bluepoint Games and published by Sony Interactive Entertainment for PlayStation 4, which updates the visual and aural quality but is effectively the identical gameplay.

6   Joanne Morra, "The Work of Research: Remembering, Repeating, and Working-Through," in *What Is Research in the Visual Arts? Obsession, Archive, Encounter*, edited by Michael Ann Holly, Marquard Smith, Clark Studies in the Visual Arts (Williamstown, MA: Sterling and Francine Clark Art Institute, 2008), 47–63.

7   Mieke Bal, "Documenting What? Auto-Theory and Migratory Aesthetics," in *A Companion to Contemporary Documentary Film*, edited by Alexandra Juhasz and Alisa Lebow (Oxford: Wiley-Blackwell, 2015), 124, 133–34.

8   Jennifer Doyle, *Hold It Against Me: Difficulty and Emotion in Contemporary Art* (Durham, NC: Duke University Press, 2013), 146n3.

9   Arianne Zwartjes, *These Dark Skies: Reckoning with Identity, Violence, and Power from Abroad* (Iowa City: University of Iowa Press, 2022), xiv.

10 Zwartjes talks about the critical component of vulnerability in an author's self-positioning, as needed for autotheory to work: Arianne Zwartjes and Megan Sweeney, "The Contact Zone," *Feminist Studies* 49, no. 2 (2023): 356.

11 Lauren Fournier, *Autotheory as Feminist Practice in Art, Writing, and Criticism* (Cambridge, MA: MIT Press, 2021), 7.

12 Fournier, *Autotheory as Feminist Practice*, 1, 5.

13 Derek Conrad Murray, "Selfie Consumerism in a Narcissistic Age," *Consumption Markets & Culture* 23, no. 1 (January 2, 2020): 21–43, https://doi.org/10.1080/10253866.2018.1467318.

14 Fournier, *Autotheory as Feminist Practice*, 47.

15 Vilashini Cooppan, "Skin, Kin, Kind, I/You/We: Autotheory's Compositional Grammar," *ASAP/Journal* 6, no. 3 (2021): 585.

16 *Shadow of the Colossus* (2018) remaster developed by Bluepoint Games, published by Sony Interactive Entertainment for PlayStation 4. Originally released in 2005, developed by Japan Studio and Team Ico, and published by Sony Computer Entertainment for the PlayStation 2.

17 Nick Suttner, *Shadow of the Colossus* (Los Angeles: Boss Fight Books, 2016), 48.
18 A sigil is an elaborate pattern that glows with light, marking the vulnerable parts of a colossus's body.
19 Soraya Murray, "High Art/Low Life: The Art of Playing Grand Theft Auto," *PAJ: A Journal of Performance and Art* 27, no. 2 (May 1, 2005): 91–98.
20 Nick Fortugno, "Losing Your Grip: Futility and Dramatic Necessity in Shadow of the Colossus," in *Well Played 1.0: Video Games, Value and Meaning* (Pittsburgh: ETC Press, 2009), 171.
21 Fortugno, "Losing Your Grip," 181.
22 Alexander Lehner discusses this idea of being "marked" in "A Short Theory of Ecocritical Metagames: Shadow of the Colossus and Everything," *Paidia— Zeitschrift für Computerspielforschung* (blog), February 28, 2018, www.paidia.de/a-short-theory-of-ecocritical-metagames-shadow-of-the-colossus-and-everything/.
23 The author wishes to thank Jonathan Gray, Daphne Gershon, and Derek Conrad Murray, as well as Jocque Jefferson for assisting with image capture.

11

Is There an Argument about This Text?

Textual Analysis as Collaborative Disputation

PAUL FROSH AND LILLIAN BOXMAN-SHABTAI

Frosh and Boxman-Shabtai ask why the reader and analyst must be singular. Inspired by paired textual study practices in Talmudic seminaries, they propose a similar dialogical approach for textual analysis—"collaborative disputation"—where two or more analysts articulate diverse and contrasting interpretations. They operationalize this with a discussion of Palestinians' and Jewish Israelis' group interpretation and analysis of TikTok videos about the 2021 Israel-Hamas war.

Textual analysis, as it is mainly practiced among "qualitative" researchers and humanities-oriented scholars, is individualistic, silent, and solitary.[1] It is founded on a restricted understanding of interpretation that falls short of fully recognizing its embodied and social character. Even if it is learned in groups, and includes conversations with colleagues and friends, textual analysis is usually performed alone. There are important exceptions, such as ethnographies of reading and co-authored studies. Unfortunately, for reasons outlined below, the embodied and social character of interpretation underpinning these alternatives is also circumscribed, primarily by the pursuit of consensus. Overall, the assumptions, constraints, and subject-positions implied by routine practices of textual analysis are scarcely recognized by textual scholars and are rarely interrogated.

Consider a potted biographical sketch that illustrates these claims. Trained in literary analysis, Paul learned to conduct "close readings" and "practical criticism" in high school and university, and he has continued to rely on these approaches in his research to this day. These techniques largely require him to sit on his own, usually in silence, in front of a book or computer screen (or both), physically framing interpretation as a solitary hermeneutic encounter with the text that results—ideally—in a piece of individual writing that is offered up on the altar of publishable scholarship. Many of his academic peers would recognize this framework as applying to themselves as well, professionally legitimizing and regulating their scholarly encounters with texts.

Lilly (Lillian), trained in the communication (inter)discipline, had been taught that quantitative content analysis was the field's flagship method and gold standard for textual analysis. This method involves coding (i.e., assigning a value to the text, or segments of it, according to predetermined categories in a code book) and achieving "intercoder reliability," namely an agreement about coding decisions between at least two coders that is statistically measured. However, an early experience working with this method for the analysis of digital humor was marked by a failure to reach sufficient levels of agreement between coders. This fortunate flop inspired a study on the polysemic qualities of humorous texts that placed disagreement at the forefront.[2] More recently, Lilly returned to content analysis for a project exploring a large corpus of wartime communication on TikTok. Again, intercoder reliability proved to be elusive, and again, Lilly found herself drawn to the disagreements.

In this chapter we propose *collaborative disputation* as an epistemology for textual analysis that reinjects sociality and the voice of the other into scholarly close reading. We contemplate the *hevruta* method of paired textual study found in Talmudic seminaries, seeing it as a historically rich interpretive tradition whose stark differences from academic textual scholarship can usefully shed light on the latter's deepest assumptions and consequences. In contrast to the potential solipsism of the hermeneutic scholar, and to the consensus-oriented teams in most coproduced quantitative and qualitative content analysis, *hevruta* pairs are guided by disputation. Their aim is to clarify differences in understanding, to articulate distinctive responses, to expose and critique ambiguities and lacunae, and to sharpen interpretive competencies through engagement with a text in dialogue and disagreement with another's intuitions and ideas. In what follows, after a brief exposition of the "solitary paradigm" of academic textual scholarship, we explore the practicalities, benefits, and limitations of collaborative disputation by discussing some of the attributes of *hevruta* study. We then offer a comparison to a current project in which Palestinian (Arabic-speaking) and Jewish (Hebrew-speaking) Israelis co-analyzed TikTok videos posted by members and supporters of both national groups during the 2021 Israel-Hamas war. This case, we argue, demonstrates the relevance of *hevruta* to studies of new media and the value of collaborative disputation for analyzing contemporary texts.

The Hermeneut as Hermit: The Solitary Paradigm of Textual Analysis

The "solitary paradigm" of academic textual analysis and close reading, honed and internalized through the intellectual biographies and habituated practices of textual scholars, is rarely acknowledged by these scholars as a constraining framework for engaging with cultural objects. It privileges an intensely focused, attentive encounter between the consciousness and sensibility of an individual reader and the signs on the page or screen, and downplays—in fact, usually neglects entirely—the possibility that interpretation is an overtly intersubjective and social practice. This model of textual engagement produces a distinctive subject-position for the scholar at the *pertinent moment of performing a reading*. It is a deeply individualistic subjectivity, closed off at that point from interaction with empirical others; but it is open in two other dimensions, which it privileges: first, a dialogic encounter with the "virtual" otherness of the text and any implied personae it conjures (e.g., God, the author, hegemonic ideology, destabilizing subtexts); and second, thanks to the surrounding silence (and the scholar's own learned practice of silent reading), it is open to the voice of the scholar's own refined interiority as it resonates and intertwines with the voices of the text. Violation of this silence can threaten to drown out the interior auditory drama; hence the complaint hurled at noisemakers: "I can't hear myself think!" Indeed, the university library—the most sacred common institutional locus for textual scholars to practice their craft in the physical presence of others—is a space of solitariness: individuals, sharing the same room and often the same tables, nevertheless act as though they are physically and socially apart, pervaded by a silence that they have inculcated over time and that is policed by the library staff.

There are important exceptions to this paradigm of scholarly textual analysis, perhaps the most obvious being the move away from the literary-style interpretation of primary texts to the analysis of "empirical" readers.[3] This work has great value for our understanding of the structured *variety* of reading practices among diverse populations—especially populations denigrated in the past by literary establishments, such as women and working-class readers. However, the character of the reading practices that this work frequently observes—convivial, lively, often agonistic interaction between people in their encounters with texts—seems barely to have influenced the solitary procedures of academic textual scholarship.

A second obvious exception to the solitary paradigm is scholarship published by two or more researchers, which has become prevalent in the social sciences. This co-authorship is clearly not individualistic or antisocial. However, in both its procedures and its published outcomes, qualitative textual co-analysis is oriented around the production of *consensus* between scholars about their interpretations (notwithstanding the influential work of literary theorists on the multiplication of different potential meanings that reading activates).[4] This drive to consensus has become increasingly enshrined in procedures for systematic "consensual qualitative research," perhaps echoing the (statistically measurable) aspiration of quantitative content analysis to achieve consensual intercoder reliability as the key marker of acceptable (i.e., publishable) interpretation.[5] Even where no such procedures are followed, however, consensus is still produced in the final outcome; it is extremely rare to find co-authored publications that highlight disagreements between co-authors, whether theoretical, methodological, or analytical.[6] The aim seems to be, and the result usually is, the construction of a "collective individual," a singular interpretive authorial voice fused together from the readings of different people during the research or in the published work. This construction of a collective individual disavows the importance of difference and disagreement for interpretation as an intersubjective and social activity.

Hevruta as Collaborative Disputation: Key Parameters

What ways of conceptualizing and practicing interpretive textual analysis can, by virtue of glaring contrast, shed light on the solitary paradigm and indicate possible alternatives? Another biographical note leads us to the example of Talmudic study: Paul grew up in an Orthodox Jewish household and spent some time in yeshiva—Talmudic seminary—and similar study frameworks. In these settings, while individual textual analysis certainly occurs, studying the text of the Talmud with a study partner, frequently (and ideally) the same partner over many years, is the central mode of textual engagement and learning. This learning in pairs is called the *hevruta* or *chevrusa* method (*hevruta* means "friend" or "companion" in Aramaic), and it is famously contentious in character, often vociferously so, with disagreement as a primary value. The emphasis on collaborative disputation in *hevruta* pairs is very different from the solitary paradigm of academic textual scholarship outlined earlier, as well as to the consensual aspirations of co-authored research. There are in fact several interconnected characteristics of the *hevruta* method that throw the constraining parameters of conventional textual scholarship into sharp relief.

1. *The primacy of disputation.* Agonistic argument is the default and most privileged mode of discussion, in which the partners civilly (usually) but nevertheless passionately express variety and divergence in interpretation. This does not mean that members of the pair never agree with one another's interpretations, but that disagreement is valued for its own sake, as its own end; it is not a starting point on the road to persuading another in order to achieve consensus. As Shoshana Blum-Kulka, Menahem Blondheim, and Gonen Hacohen observe: "The ideal of *Torah li-shmah* (Torah study as an end unto itself) underscores the perception that time spent on disagreement is of the same religious value as that expended on reaching an agreement. At the same time, the rigor, exertion, and intensity of the study process are considered to carry positive religious value (*amalah shel torah*). Combined, these constraints (or rather, the lack thereof), tend to enhance rigorous disagreement rather than consensus."[7]

2. *Sociality and textuality.* Disagreement is a collaborative framework for discourse, but it is also a sociable activity that binds interlocutors together over time, frequently into very strong friendships. The Talmud gives examples of the strength of this adversarial affection: as Hershey H. Friedman notes, it contains hundreds of arguments between Abaye (ca. 278–339 CE) and Rava (ca. 270–350 CE), yet they were described as friends and were buried in the same cave.[8] Disputation is not merely

deeply collaborative but is also an intensifier of affection between those who perform it together.

Moreover, while *hevruta* means study in pairs, there are always at least *three* "participants" in this social interaction—two humans, and one text (sometimes more). In fact, the Talmudic text itself is a written version of conversations and disagreements among rabbinical sages across hundreds of years. The very format of the Talmudic text on the page (see figure 11.1), in which commentary and exegesis surround the records of the discussions at the page's center, link intertextual readings to ongoing disputation over centuries in a "virtual study hall."[9]

3. *Vocalization and soundscape.* The text is given voice when it is read out loud. Readings are therefore pro-*vocative* in a literal sense. They are not silent or performed alone; the text is externalized through one's own voice and the voice of the other articulating it. This vocalization is connected to a distinctive location and soundscape. *Hevruta* pairs usually study in a specially designated physical space—the main seminary study hall (*Bet Hamidrash*, "house of study")—in the company of other pairs, all involved in simultaneous, lively argument and engagement with texts.[10] This boisterous hubbub of articulation and discussion is the natural state. Pairs stake out their space within this soundscape of interpretation through attention and proximity, but they are not indifferent to the conversations (often about the same text) going on among pairs around them. Each pair thus inhabits a porous acoustic envelope that enables them to hear each other without filtering out others. In addition to the soundscape, the crowded space of the study hall enhances the sense of intimacy not only with one's immediate companion, but with a larger community of others simultaneously engaged in the same activity. The soundscape and embodied proximity typical of *hevruta* contrast starkly with the silence and distant spacing between readers in Western university libraries.

4. *Multiplicity of roles.* The human participants are never just readers but also listeners and speakers. While the interchanges and modulations between these positions are guided by the process of reading through the text, they are heavily improvised in relation to one another and are not pre-scripted.

5. *Clarification, association, rhetoric, ritual.* It is probably simplistic to describe what *hevruta* pairs do as textual "analysis." The activity is simultaneously *clarificatory* (what is the message? The Talmud can be very

Figure 11.1: Oz Vehadar edition of the first page of the Babylonian Talmud with textual elements (e.g., Mishnah, Gemara) and interpretive commentary (e.g., by Rashi, Nissim Ben Jacob) numbered in a spiralling rainbow. GordonGlottal, Labeled Talmud, 2022, digital image, Wikipedia, accessed May 20, 2024, https://commons.wikimedia.org/wiki/File:Labeled_talmud.png.

opaque), *hermeneutic* (what is the meaning?), *associative* (what other texts and phenomena does this connect to?), *rhetorical* (disputation is a method for sharpening one's persuasive powers), and *ritualistic* (the activity continually assembles and reaffirms an interpretive community).

6. *Time*. In addition to the simultaneity of engagement in the study hall, the social relationships between pairs are constructed and refined

over time—hours, days, and often years. Interpretive work is continually enhanced through the ongoing performance of a social relationship. It is therefore not a simple matter to find the right *hevruta* companion, and it can take time to find someone with whom there is an interpretive and discursive "click," with whom disagreement is consistently productive. Learning and interpretation are inherently social, multivocal, and processual.

7. *Mobility and enframing.* *Hevruta* is moveable (one can learn in pairs in many physical contexts; it is not restricted to the main study hall), and it is marked by movement and embodiment (*yeshiva* literally means "sitting," but much of the conversation involves bodies moving, swaying, and vocalizing texts as part of their disputation). Also, however, *hevruta* is open to *additional individuals* (especially more learned people, including rabbis and teachers) joining in briefly for consultation and argumentation; it is "networked," though it is still based around the core nucleus of two students. It is also enframed by individual "private" reading and larger class discussions following the *hevruta* sessions, during which the discussions and disagreements of the pairs are amplified for (and often contradicted by) others.

8. *Media.* Traditional *hevruta* study uses books and printed texts. These media are easily shareable in traditional spaces of copresence: everyone is on the same page. But there is no reason that this should not be extended to digital contexts or to different kinds of readers. *Hevruta* learning is ideally live, but using digital tools—live audiovisual streaming, for instance—it can be radically extended. It can also be expanded beyond its focus on the Talmud to other texts and topics. One current example is an international (and gender-equal) project called *Zug* ("couple" in Hebrew), which enables both in-person and online *hevruta* pairings on topics such as money and power, criminal justice, Torah and social media, and the works of Bob Dylan and Leonard Cohen.[11]

Collaborative Disputation and the 2021 Israel-Hamas War as Seen on TikTok

How might we think about collaborative disputation, and the parameters of the *hevruta* model outlined above, in relation to media and cultural research? How does it intersect with and differ from the practicalities of collaborative interpretive analysis of contemporary media texts? And how can it offer potential alternatives to the solitary paradigm and consensual bias? In this section we address these questions through a particularly rich and challenging example: a research project that brought together an Israeli Jewish principal investigator (Lilly) and four research assistants (all female students in the department's honors track): Amit Turgeman and Lee Matan, who are Hebrew-speaking Jewish Israelis, and Noor Gommed and Yara Daas, who are Arabic-speaking Muslim Palestinians with Israeli citizenship. The texts they set out to interpret were TikTok videos posted by members and supporters of both national groups during the 2021 Israel-Hamas war.

The context and conditions of this project are clearly very different to those of Talmudic study. First, Talmudic texts are sources of religious sanctity and legal authority. One may be invited to question particular opinions in the Talmud; however, one is not permitted to critique or dismiss the Talmud as a whole, or the rabbinical sages who comment on it—at least not in Orthodox Judaism. In contrast, sanctity and authority are not words usually associated with TikTok. Whereas Talmudic study is motivated by the "hermeneutics of love" typical of theology, Lilly's research team was mainly motivated by "hermeneutics of suspicion" prevalent in academia.[12] Second, unlike the Talmud, which is written, TikTok "texts" are overtly multimodal audiovisual objects. Third, although the Talmud combines Aramaic, Hebrew, and other languages, it is linguistically fairly homogenous: if you can read one section of the Talmud, you can read most other sections. The TikTok project encompasses a multilingual sphere including mainly Arabic, English, and Hebrew but also other languages (e.g., French and Malay). Finally, and perhaps most obviously, the TikTok videos refer to and *participate in* an actual violent national conflict. While the Talmud and its students are argumentative, the TikTok videos are deliberate extensions of warfare into the symbolic realm. "Disputation" risks being a facile understatement of the hostility and rancor they express. Joint discussion by Israelis and Palestinians of war-related texts is certainly not common; as we elaborate below, the achievement of collaborative and respectful disputation stemmed from a collective passion for scholarship, a continuous effort to maintain positive social relations, and the commitment to a polyvocal space where contrasting interpretations could be heard.

To be clear, the TikTok project was not based on the idea of *hevruta*; a serendipitous chain of events linked the two. However, it does illustrate some important parallels with the *hevruta* model and, in particular, the benefits of the Talmudic spirit of collaborative disputation for the analysis of complex, multimodal, and multivocal texts. *Similar to* hevruta*, the TikTok project saw disagreement as a primary value, and it was designed to encourage disputation.* The project research team was interested in the polysemic qualities of wartime communication on TikTok—namely, how TikTok texts sustained different meanings and how different readers interpreted them. Content analysis, specifically the idea of intercoder reliability, was used as a point of reference. Whereas classic content analysis views analytical categories that fail to reach intercoder reliability as garbage, this project saw disagreement as treasure. Following the notion of "valid disagreement," it viewed polysemy and lack of consensus as objects of study in their own right.[13]

In practice, the team developed a code book that explored different aspects of the texts. The four research assistants independently coded an identical corpus of fifty TikTok videos, and their interpretations were compared. The team members met for four two-hour meetings on Zoom in November 2023 to discuss disagreements. As in *hevruta*, the purpose of the meetings was not exactly analysis but rather a combination of *clarification* (what are these TikTok videos saying? Is it accurately captured by the code book's analytical categories?), *association* (have we seen a similar message or aesthetic in other TikTok videos?), and *rhetoric* (coders "make a case" about their coding decisions and might passionately argue about them).

The meetings were also largely *ritualistic*, following a routine procedure: Lilly displayed the spreadsheet with the coding decisions and asked the research assistants to elaborate on their interpretations. Typically, a conversation between coders ensued; banter about coding "troublemakers" may have arisen. Lilly weighed in after the conversation reached saturation. She sometimes assumed the "underdog" position (e.g., siding with the one coder who diverged from the other three), sometimes went back and forth between competing interpretations, sometimes added another interpretation into the mix. She shared her ambivalence often and admitted to being easily persuaded by almost any reading.

Convened a month after the October 7, 2023, massacre waged by Hamas and during Israel's subsequent deadly offensive in Gaza, the meetings also provided odd ritualistic relief. During these intense weeks, team members (who were grappling with the events in various ways) found comfort and ease in the normalcy of analytic group discussion. We bitterly joked that the project about the 2021 war was a "nice distraction" from the 2023 war.

The collaborative disputation underpinning the TikTok project illustrates *the intersection between sociality and textuality* characteristic of *hevruta*. With diverse backgrounds and characteristics, the research assistants came with important social and cultural capital. While providing textual interpretations, they themselves were also "texts." They represented diverse demographic attributes such as ethnicity, religiosity, and geographical origins, both within and across the Muslim and Jewish populations. For example, Noor and Yara, hailing respectively from Nazareth and East Jerusalem, represented different identities among Palestinians with Israeli citizenship. Moreover, the group's personality traits, hobbies, and academic interests highlighted different perspectives not only on the conflict but also on ways of approaching it. Take their academic interests: Yara in English and Islamic literature, Noor in technology and gaming, Lee in social media marketing, and Amit in language and discourse. These and other characteristics bear on textual interpretation, which often diverged in line with the Israeli-Palestinian divide but also often in terms of reading style (Lee and Yara tended to be more rule oriented, Amit and Noor more intuitive).

This hermeneutic and social drama is captured by an Excel spreadsheet, a format much more prosaic than the Talmudic page yet similarly preoccupied with the identification and layering of interpretations (see figure 11.2). The spreadsheet's multivocality is manifested in several dimensions. A column for each coder represents their coding decisions on a given text. Another column summarizes points that emerged in the deliberation and its results: consensus versus disagreement. Comments in cells elaborate, when necessary, thoughts and questions that emerged during the coding (or, in other words, the voices within the coder's head).

Though an institutional hierarchy existed between Lilly and the team, attempts to loosen it were made to enable openness and *a multiplicity of*

	A	AG	AH	AI	AJ	AK
1	Serial number hashtagname_hashtagnumber	Criticism	Criticism Amit	Criticism Lee	Criticism Noor	Criticism Yara
2	ISRAEL_25	Noor: tagret - messi, object - criticism of Messi implied by praise to Ronaldo for supporting PL. Contextual knowledg about rivalry; paradigmatic pair	(0) no criticism	(0) no criticism	(3) yes both/othe	(0) no criticism
3	ISRAEL_27		(1) yes at PA	(1) yes at PA	(1) yes at PA	(1) yes at PA
4	26_القدس		(0) no criticism	(0) no criticism	(0) no criticism	(0) no criticism
5	27_القدس_لنا	Noor- chronology/evolution of Tamimi points at the reality of grwoing up under occupation - criticms through the construction of a life narrative. BUT no clear target (soldiers? IDF? Israel?), Amit - the point is to praise Tamimi, this doesn't directly imply criticism of ISR (similar to Messi vs Ronaldo)	(0) no criticism	(0) no criticism	(2) yes at ISR	(0) no criticism
6	פוריישראל_19		(0) no criticism	(0) no criticism	(0) no criticism	(0) no criticism
7	פוריישראל_20		(0) no criticism	(0) no criticism	(0) no criticism	(0) no criticism
8	sheikhjarrah_25	target: IDF and/or specific lipsyncing soldier (Yael Edri), settlers(?) object (Amit) - being a loser/failure isn't criticism, also lipsyncing soldier - criticism of army is too broad to have a speific attribute / is mockery=criticism? Noor - satire rather than parody	(0) no criticism	(1) yes at PA	(2) yes at ISR	(2) yes at ISR
9	sheikhjarrah_26	also media criticism (Lee comment)	(2) yes at ISR	(2) yes at ISR	(2) yes at ISR	(2) yes at ISR
10	26_שומרונים	Noor, Lee - criticism of platform for blocking video Yara - agrees with platform interpretation Amit - this is complaint not criticism; act of resistance (doing something inspite)	(0) no criticism	(3) yes both/othe	(3) yes both/othe	(0) no criticism
11	27_שומרונים		(0) no criticism	(0) no criticism	(0) no criticism	(0) no criticism

Figure 11.2: Coding spreadsheet: each text (column A) is coded by multiple coders (columns AH–AK). After comparing coding decisions (in this case about the existence of criticism in the text), the team discusses disagreements (column AG).

roles. Bonding activities (e.g., a day trip to Noor's hometown of Nazareth), the power of the group (which could collectively approach Lilly), and Lilly's constant encouragement of (and enthusiasm around) disagreement and alternative interpretations fostered an environment in which coders gradually shook off the fear of making coding "mistakes" (a feeling they reported in early stages of coding) and took turns playing devil's advocate "against" one another (including Lilly).

Time is an important aspect in the refinement of social relationships needed for productive collaborative reading. By the time the team met on Zoom to discuss disagreements, it had been working together for a year and half. The team had its own humor and ways of doing things, and the coders had developed unique interpretive voices. Moreover, the voices of their friends reverberated in their minds. In group reflections about the project, coders expressed the feeling of pondering one another's interpretations when making coding decisions and working hard to sustain their own readings alongside an intuition about others' readings. Multivocality was thus not only the result but also a feature of the interpretive process.

The project's working model was *mobile* and *enframed*. Thanks to their remote setting on Zoom, disagreements in meetings were accessible to guests. The discussions often invoked other individuals, such as faculty members who are experts on topics pertaining to the codebook, and Lilly often consulted them and returned to the group with their interpretations (which might be still challenged by group members). The project was thus intertwined within the general social connectivity of academia and a collective commitment to research and knowledge-building. In conversations dedicated to airing feelings (which might be quite negative given the nature of the texts), team members often reiterated the ethos of scientific inquiry, reminding themselves—and the group—of their purpose.

While *textual articulation* is straightforward in Zoom sessions (rather than text being read out, the TikTok video is played and the coding sheet displayed on a shared screen), the overall *soundscape of interpretation* is complex. Zoom is a noisy space in which conversational turn-taking can be quite awkward, and connectivity issues may freeze interlocutors in bad Wi-Fi limbo. Furthermore, noise from the outside world spills into the conversation as the backstage of participants impinges into the meeting. Team members were already seasoned Zoom conversers by the time the disagreement sessions were convened, so synchronicity was usually achieved. But the noise of the "home front" during conflict echoed throughout the Zoom sessions. Air-raid sirens blared out; participants apologized and disappeared to their safe rooms or bomb shelters. Disconnectivity also sometimes disrupted conversations. With schools closed due to the ongoing war, Lilly's kids occasionally demanded attention and amused the team. All these sources of disruption inserted randomness into group discussion, forcing breaks that could at times distract from and at times invite further reflection on a particular text about which a conversation had been cut off.

The TikTok war project illustrates the applicability of the *hevruta* method beyond books and printed texts and the study of the Talmud. The project in itself is a bustling *multimedia* environment, encompassing emails, Zoom meetings, a shared Google Drive with shared documents and spreadsheets, a WhatsApp group, and face-to-face encounters. Each of these spaces provides another channel for collaborative disputation between group members.

Conclusion

The TikTok project and the *hevruta* tradition offer clear alternatives to the conventional solitary paradigm of textual scholarship and to the requirement for consensus characterizing qualitative and quantitative co-authorship in social scientific content analysis. By privileging disputation as a collaborative mode of textual engagement, they provide frameworks for interpretation as fundamentally interpersonal, multivocal, and sociable. The TikTok project and the *hevruta* tradition therefore approximate more closely the collaboratively disputatious modes of textual interpretation routinely performed across diverse publics, and they highlight the generative and dynamic connections among texts, meanings, and social relations for audiences in many nonacademic contexts. Crucially, they turn these insights about interpretation into methods for performing scholarly interpretation itself.

Of course, achieving collaborative disputation in a research setting is not an easy feat. The procedure is resource heavy, as it requires a team of highly competent (both intellectually and emotionally) coders/readers and it takes more time than solitary or consensus-oriented research. Moreover, striking a balance between "collaboration" and "disputation" (in other words, encouraging participants to be both friendly and opinionated) requires ongoing investment and supervision from the team leader, who must be alert to tensions that are bound to arise when treating sensitive topics, and quick to respond to them. A dialogical approach to textual analysis can be difficult to accomplish, but revelatory when done well. Hopefully, this chapter has shown the potential and necessity of such an approach for texts underscored by broad histories of conflict and deep cultural meanings.

Another challenge to this approach arises from a key difference between *hevruta* and the TikTok project. *Hevruta* has historically co-evolved with an authoritative text—the Talmud—whose printed layout preserves and animates recorded disagreements: disputation is literally inscribed into its very pages. In contrast, the TikTok project encounters a serious dilemma. Unlike the Talmud, the Excel file illustrated in figure 11.2 is a format internal to the research team itself, not intended for communicating the debates and viewpoints of the team members to outside readers. While it could be made legible for a broader audience, maybe as a digital appendix to a published paper (following open access conventions), there is no way to publish the interpretive disagreements of its team members in an academically "sanctified" format that does not lead to a unified, consensual conclusion. The project's multivocality certainly could be conveyed in audiovisual formats, such as conference presentations, podcasts, and videos. But, given the hierarchical structures by which scholarly authority is conferred and academic careers furthered, it would most likely require much broader cultural, epistemic, and institutional shifts before major humanities and social science publishers become open, as a matter of routine, to publishing textual analyses fractured with interpretive disagreements between scholars. Hopefully, this article will help generate new thinking, and more collaborative disputation, toward that end.

Notes

1. This chapter was written while Paul was a Core Fellow at the Helsinki Collegium for Advanced Studies at the University of Helsinki.
2. Lillian Boxman-Shabtai and Limor Shifman, "Evasive Targets: Deciphering Polysemy in Mediated Humor," *Journal of Communication* 64, no. 5 (October 2014): 977–98, https://doi.org/10.1111/jcom.12116.
3. Leah Ceccarelli, *Shaping Science with Rhetoric: The Cases of Dobzhansky, Schrodinger, and Wilson* (Chicago: University of Chicago Press, 2001), https://press.uchicago.edu/ucp/books/book/chicago/S/bo3612788.html; Wendy Griswold, "The Fabrication of Meaning: Literary Interpretation in the United States, Great Britain, and the West Indies," *American Journal of Sociology* 92, no. 5 (March 1987): 1077–117, https://doi.org/10.1086/228628; María Angélica Thumala Olave, "Reading Matters: Towards a Cultural Sociology of Reading," *American Journal of Cultural Sociology* 6, no. 3 (October 1, 2018): 417–54, https://doi.org/10.1057/s41290-017-0034-x; Janice A. Radway, *Reading the Romance: Women, Patriarchy, and Popular Literature* (Chapel Hill: University of North Carolina Press, 1984).
4. Roland Barthes, *S/Z: An Essay*, translated by Richard Miller (London: Macmillan, 1974).
5. Clara E. Hill, Barbara J. Thompson, and Elizabeth Nutt Williams, "A Guide to Conducting Consensual Qualitative Research," *The Counseling Psychologist* 25, no. 4 (October 1, 1997): 517–72, https://doi.org/10.1177/0011000097254001.

6   For one of those exceptions, though in the context of experimental research, see Barbara Mellers, Ralph Hertwig, and Daniel Kahneman, "Do Frequency Representations Eliminate Conjunction Effects? An Exercise in Adversarial Collaboration," *Psychological Science* 12, no. 4 (2001): 269–75, https://doi.org/10.1111/1467-9280.00350.
7   Shoshana Blum-Kulka, Menahem Blondheim, and Gonen Hacohen, "Traditions of Dispute: From Negotiations of Talmudic Texts to the Arena of Political Discourse in the Media," *Journal of Pragmatics, Negation and Disagreement* 34, nos. 10–11 (October 1, 2002): 1576, https://doi.org/10.1016/S0378-2166(02)00076-0.
8   Hershey H. Friedman, "The Art of Constructive Arguing: Lessons from the Talmud," SSRN Scholarly Paper (July 27, 2014), https://doi.org/10.2139/ssrn.2472735.
9   Blum-Kulka, Blondheim, and Hacohen, "Traditions of Dispute."
10 For a sense of what this looks and especially sounds like, see "Havruta," posted May 24, 2017, by Keren Levy, 40 sec., YouTube, https://www.youtube.com/watch?v=BYBLXuGaXhY. For different and longer examples, see "Learning in Yeshiva," posted June 19, 2019, by Yeshiva Amidei Dgirsa, 4 min., YouTube, https://www.youtube.com/watch?v=3zufVdaARvA ("White noise—studying in a Yeshiva study hall"), posted September 3, 2019, by Arye Minkov, 1 hr., 35 min., 36 sec., YouTube, https://www.youtube.com/watch?v=hwLJYk5OevU. These examples are from ultra-Orthodox Talmudic academies and are hence exclusively male. *Hevruta*, however, is today commonly utilized as a key interpretive method across Jewish denominations (including secular academies for Jewish learning) where women are equal participants.
11 Project ZUG, November 24, 2015, www.projectzug.org.
12 Rita Felski, *The Limits of Critique* (Chicago: University of Chicago Press, 2015), https://press.uchicago.edu/ucp/books/book/chicago/L/bo21386290.html.
13 Christian Baden, Lillian Boxman-Shabtai, Keren Tenenboim-Weinblatt, Maximilian Overbeck, and Tali Aharoni, "Meaning Multiplicity and Valid Disagreement in Textual Measurement: A Plea for a Revised Notion of Reliability," *Studies in Communication and Media* 12, no. 4 (2023): 305–26.

PART III

New and Underexplored Objects for Textual Analysis

Introduction

As the language of "texts" and "reading" clearly indicates, textual analysis was first developed with written literary texts in mind. Later in the twentieth century, it was claimed and widely practiced by scholars of film and television. But the method is open to use on a much wider range of texts, media, and technologies, as suggested by Roland Barthes's famed *Mythologies*, which includes essays analyzing texts as diverse as milk, Einstein's brain, toys, and wrestling matches.[1] The chapters in this section similarly encourage a broader application, acknowledging that media and popular culture exist in much more than "just" films and television programs.

In some cases, this calls for us to consider materials in space. The section begins, for instance, with Mehita Iqani's reminder that our consumption economy is one that produces ever more waste and refuse. But Iqani sagely argues that such items do not simply lose their meaning as waste, and she invites us to explore the textual meanings and appropriations of trash. From garbage by the roadside to huge looming structures and theme parks, Colin Burnett considers amusement park rides and their own meanings. What plots and storylines do they offer, he asks, and how best to consider them?

Eszter Zimanyi and Julie Turnock offer us yet more "new" objects for analysis. They address some of the limitations other methods pose in studying these objects and how textual analysis manages to circumvent such limitations. Zimanyi turns to a very common type of text: the selfie. Expanding our understanding of this ubiquitous kind of text, Zimanyi centers on migrant and refugee selfies, and explores the ethical affordances of textual analysis as a way to avoid ethnographic methods that at times risk surveilling and locating precarious populations. Turnock, meanwhile, considers what she calls an "effects program," a discourse that often fetishizes and mythologizes filmic stunts and effects, and how these features can be deconstructed and reconsidered through analyzing press and other paratextual discussions of the effects, taking them as objects of analysis as much as the spectacle of the effects in the films themselves.

We encourage readers to follow in these authors' tracks, both by considering other texts that are too rarely analyzed or whose meanings are foolishly assumed to be simple, and by seeing the capacity for some such analyses to bypass methodological challenges such as ethical dilemmas or problematic mythologies.

Note

1 Roland Barthes, *Mythologies*, translated by Annette Lavers (St. Albans, UK: Paladin, 1973).

12

What Could Rubbish Say?

On the Textual Politics of Plastic Waste

MEHITA IQANI

Iqani makes the case for the importance of studying garbage, trash, or rubbish: as humans dispose of ever more objects, filling the world with ever more garbage, Iqani argues, those objects' textual meanings only increase after being discarded. Iqani turns to Elize Vossgätter's fine art collection Gutter Pop *to offer an example of the textual resonance of trash.*

Among many horrors, the age of the Anthropocene has ushered in apocalyptic quantities of consumer waste.[1] Garbage, rubbish, or trash, as it is variously referred to in different cultures, is produced by intensive consumption and unsustainable practices of disposal. It is a key aesthetic feature of popular culture.[2] Rubbish, largely but not only constituted by plastic, which cannot biodegrade, chokes up rivers, litters beaches, swirls into huge gyres in the ocean, and piles into ever-growing toxic landfills around urban areas. Trash is a matter of concern to environmental policy, urban planning, and government regulation. As this chapter will show, it should also be of concern to textual analysis. Precisely because many waste items are the products of consumption—that is, matter left over by processes and practices of market exchange—there are always traces of texts left over therein. Branding, advertising claims, bar codes, nutritional information, graphic design, and images all constitute the textuality of commodities, that is, of pre-rubbish.[3] But beyond this inherent textuality, trash must also be understood as a discursive resource, that is, as something that can produce and carry meaning. Rubbish "speaks" through its very materiality, through its monumental excess as polluting agent, through its ability to be reworked into new forms and values, and through the ways in which it connects, for better or worse, humans with other organisms and planetary materials.

The Textual Afterlives of Plastic Commodities

It is well established in textual analysis that a text is defined as a piece of communication that travels through space and time and is somehow sent and somehow received. Various consumer products certainly fit into this understanding of textuality. Plastic in particular carries a specific postmodern and late capitalist resonance of textuality. More things are made of polymers than many realize: our clothing, our cars, our foods are packaged in it, medical equipment and sex toys inserted into our bodies, and so on.[4] Plastic carries brand messaging emblazoned on its malleable surfaces, but also in its very being, its ability to be turned into any shape, texture, color. A toothbrush is a text: the smooth plastic lines of its handle speak to the heart of the project of modernity; in other words, plastic is a mode of communication.[5] A five-dollar H&M T-shirt is a text: it may carry words and images on its surface, and, even if not, its color, shape, texture, and even size carry messages about fashionability, bodies, and self-identity. Plastic can say anything that can be imagined by and in late modernity.

Arjun Appadurai famously argues that all things have social lives.[6] This is patently true for the many commodities that populate lived experience during late capitalism. What is also true is that every commodity, from the plainest unbranded minimal item to the most garishly decorated, is textual. Even though we do not ordinarily read them for deeper meaning in our everyday lives, the material and symbolic properties of commodities say a lot and can of course be analyzed as important carriers of meanings, ideologies, and identity markers. The preponderance of commodities that populate life in many cultures around the world is evidence of the hypertextuality of modern life: every item we exchange has a name, a brand, a message, an idea, and all of those are coded through a variety of communicative forms. Even unbranded items speak volumes about their placement in the world and ideas about how to be in it. Even the simplest forms of packaging, say, a wrapping for a chocolate bar, carry great intentionality in their messaging (as the designer who created that wrapping will testify). When the chocolate wrapper is thrown away, is it no longer a text? And if it is, what does, or could, it say? What kinds of new meanings can emerge from the afterlives of the many commodities that we desire, acquire, use up, and throw away?

Studying trash as a textual form requires both the application of existing methods of text analysis to discarded items and the forging of new ways of looking at garbage. Garbologists, and archaeologists of the future, will learn a great deal about Western consumer capitalism by picking through the mountainous landfills we have created.[7] The traces of textuality attendant to the trash heap are there, whether analysts look at them or not. The work of reading trash can be archaeological: as detectives might pick through domestic trash to find clues or evidence, so too can social scientists pick through landfills to find clues and evidence about the lives and practices of people from previous generations or the present. Trash is layered in the landfill much like geological strata, and digging down through the layers can offer windows into other times. Indeed, all archaeology excavates, to some extent or another, the waste and textual castoffs of history.

The tools of textual analysis should actively extend beyond the framing of texts as texts by those who produce them, into the afterlives of those texts. This requires a new theoretical framework about what constitutes a text and also a willingness to use the tools of textual analysis in new social domains. If commodities, fashion items, and advertisements are texts, then so they remain once chucked out.[8] If texts can be found in stinking rubbish dumps as much as in gleaming department stores, in oceanic gyres of microplastics as well as on the nonchalant hips and shoulders of runway models, then it seems that we must reach for new modalities of reading as well as new theories about what it means to write.

The Generative Possibilities of Plastic Waste

In Western capitalist societies, and those of the Global South that aspire to be like them, rubbish is typically thrown away.[9] Even recycled items often end up on the rubbish dumps of Global South cities, after having been shipped there to extract them from societies used to having their trash collected and taken away.[10] Landfills are usually situated out of sight of the majority of well-off consumers, although they are increasingly a site of subsistence (and suffering) for many socioeconomically marginalized people.[11]

But: *there is no away.*

Planet Earth is a closed system, and everything that is created on this planet stays here. For organic materials, that means being reintegrated through decomposition, but for the billions of items that have been, and are being, manufactured from plastic, this is impossible. Plastics do not biodegrade but photodegrade. This means that light from the sun breaks plastic up into even tinier pieces—microplastics, nanoplastics—which, although not visible to the human eye, are still present in various natural substances (water, the flesh of fish and animals and humans, the air).[12] Plastics are washed into rivers, then into oceans, where they photodegrade and irreparably change ecologies and organisms. But plastic is not a substance that exists outside of textuality: as one of the central materials in consumer culture, it is constantly written upon and with; it is both a carrier of meaning and a thing with which meaning is made. There is an ethics to plastic trash.[13] That textuality does not simply disappear when the item is thrown away, but neither is that textuality untransformed. Water, air, and other natural resources have been theorized as elemental media: they are the original organic materials that connect all living creatures.[14] When consumer waste merges with the ecological, what new forms of textuality and meaning creation and transmission become possible? Human-made substances (made from oil, no less) are increasingly becoming part of elemental media. When plastic soaks into water, earth, and flesh, the elements are arguably being mediated in a new way.

Plastic has been integrated into so many communicative objects and practices of everyday life that it has become a media form; furthermore, its microscopic presence in our own bodies means that we also might need to start thinking about how plastic is defining human selfhood, materially as well as morally.[15] Plastic has been found in human placentas.[16] Plastic is a conglomerate of material form and meaning: a plastiglomerate.[17] Plastic skids between toxicity and frivolity; it coats, shapes, and inserts itself in multiple forms across organic life. Plastic waste is thus more than simply a resource that can be recycled; it transforms into a new kind of deeply textual substance that interacts and integrates with natural substances and is processed at the molecular level. Plastic was textual when it was manufactured, it was textual when it was transformed into a commodity, it was textual when it photodegraded, it was textual when it was absorbed into microorganisms, and it was textual when it worked its way up the food chain into the human body. Does that then mean that plastic is starting to write us and, indeed, the world?

Reading Waste for Feeling and Future

Although many tools of textual analysis are relevant to the project of reading waste, one useful entry point is to work with its affect. Waste is an item that provokes intense feeling in humans. When confronted with a broken bag of trash near our front doors, we might get angry. If we get a whiff of a passing garbage truck on a hot day, we might feel disgust. When we see images of plastic-choked rivers, or plastic choking wildlife, we may feel indescribable sadness. We may feel pride if we recycle or manage to reduce plastic in our personal consumption, or judgment if our neighbor does not. In these ways, waste is a substance full of affect: it produces bodily and embodied emotional responses and forms of relation.[18] And yet another thing that produces affect are the new landscapes of waste that have been, and are being, produced by consumer capitalism: the ocean plastic gyres, the growing landfills, the e-waste hellscapes.[19] These landscapes are astounding in ways at once similar and different to the affect produced by the wild, beautiful, and sometimes terrifying natural landscapes on our planet Earth. As such, reading waste for its emotional and bodily impact is a useful analytic strategy.

Art is also affective. Visual art is a form of textuality that bears detailed engagement. Artists are consummate producers of "texts" in that they create new aesthetic forms that are often challenging and abstract and that invite strategies and regimes of reception. The traditions of art criticism are useful to the analyst of texts and to the analysis of waste.[20] One must pay attention to the form and content of the item in question, considering composition, light, materiality, texture, color, and many other features. A close and detailed description of these qualities forms a useful first step toward a deeper consideration of the politics and feelings produced by the work and to which it responds. Many artists are turning to waste not only as a resource for creating things of beauty or intensity that may move us but also as a site for exploring new assemblages of meaning and value among humans, the natural world, and the regimes of waste that humans have created, which are changing that natural world, ourselves included (for let us not forget that we are animals, textual animals perhaps, but animals still). Waste art is a genre that has received significant attention from media analysts, especially those writing in the realm of ecomedia studies.[21]

What can trash say? How is rubbish repurposed and given new textual meanings? What are the life cycles of certain materials, from production through disposal and reuse? How can waste be used as a tool for artistic, political, even cultural expression? To explore some of these questions and offer an example of the meaning-making power of waste, I turn to a case study of a body of art made with and speaking about trash that is especially receptive to textual analysis. But the points made are applicable to analyses of all waste.

Gutter Pop by Elize Vossgätter

Gutter Pop was a solo fine art collection produced by the artist Elize Vossgätter and first exhibited at the University of Cape Town's Michaelis Gallery in November 2023. The show explored questions of the interconnectedness of natural and synthetic materials and human and other forms of life through sculptural paintings and painterly sculptures made with beeswax, paraffin wax, found branches and twigs, and animation. Of the project, Vossgätter stated:

> Gutter Pop refers to my intrigue in the things left behind in the wake of excess and the systems we put in place to control and preserve them in order to remake, recombine and redirect. Assemblages of our disposable detritus, methane mountains of stewing Styrofoam and poly-polymers, the liquid lubricants of sewage, dyes and detergents that are digested through the interlocking matrix of constipated gutters, drainpipes, ducts, and discharges where these toxic puddings translocate and assimilate—these are the vulgar reminders of our industrial effluvia. Within them lie the generative bacteria of emerging biomes, which ceaselessly continue the cycles and generate potential hybrid ecosystems such as the plastiglomerate islands in our oceans or the calcified fatbergs that clog our culverts. The stuff of gutters colonize each other and make something new: in this is both death and emergence.[22]

The exhibition comprised several large-scale paintings, including a series of diptychs and triptychs, sculptural formations of "stones" scattered on the floor and "sticks" suspended from the ceiling, waxily enribboned plant remains encased in Perspex cubes, and animations featuring these characters. Densely, the paintings integrated layers and layers of wax paint, carefully carved to show various hues layered one beneath the other. The color palette was vibrant, vibrating, with tones of shocking pink, yellow, and green overlaid above and behind darker solemnities of black and green. Onto and into these thick layers of waxy paint, Vossgätter carved intricate swirling and patterns, reminiscent of river rapids, lichen whorls, the patterns of tree bark, leaves filtering sunlight, swallow and weaver nests, long shots of the layers of rock comprising mountains. But instead of the palette of the natural world, wildly manufactured colors shined through. Similarly synthetic colors wrapped around the organic shapes of twigs and branches or narrow columns were made from recycled papier-mâché to forge new alien-pop creatures, snakelike or with multiple limbs, screened into boxes and touched up through the Perspex filter of neon pink, acid green, or bright yellow.

One key materiality in the works was the use of found objects, specifically dead plants from a neglected nearby garden and the leftover, discarded lost wax (a synthetic substance made from paraffin) used in bronze casting from other artists in the same studio. The lost wax was shaped into roughly textured balls, which were strewn onto the gallery floor, only to be buffered and knocked about by little roving vacuum cleaners as well as the feet of exhibition visitors, who may have kicked them about (intentionally or mistakenly) while viewing the rest of the show. These balls littering the floor—reminiscent of scrunched-up and thrown-out paper waste—were perhaps the most literal nod to the materiality of waste: "Robbed of their capability to disintegrate, they remain frozen in this state of passive-action: doing-something-yet-doing-nothing."[23] Hanging in space above them were totem-like long sticks wrapped in multicolored wax strings, which hugged the form of the knobs and bumps characteristic of tree branches and twigs, wholly transformed into magical wands, implying the wizardry of holy staves or croziers, and floating unperturbed above the bumbling detritus below (see figure 12.1).

Figure 12.1: *Gutter Pop* installation view, November 2023, Michaelis Gallery, University of Cape Town. Photograph by Nicole Fraser, reproduced with the kind permission of Elize Vossgätter.

Whose Waste Is It Anyway? Interspecies Art Collaboration

Many of the textures created in the *Gutter Pop* collection reference the aesthetic of plastic: they looked at once smooth and stretchable, moldable and molded. Yet although reminiscent of chewed gum or the holds in a climbing gym, the artworks were mostly not made of plastic; they were made of wax mixed with a small ratio of natural rubber latex. But by looking plastic, and by referencing plastic, these works said something about plasticity. In addition to the deployment of certain found objects (dead flora, lost wax), the content of the works spoke powerfully to questions of plastic waste and the detritus of consumer capitalism. Although wildly attractive in their texture and color appeals, and very pleasing to the eye, the paintings in their rough abstraction arguably called to mind the colorful mayhem of the landfill more than the peaceful hues of natural patterns. Indeed, the whirling gyres of the plastic ocean were cited by Vossgätter as a key, yet devastating, aesthetic reference: "I contrast this synthetic-color-sensibility with a sensuality of organic form."²⁴ It is perhaps the most potent commentary of all that *Gutter Pop* looked like a beautiful garbage dump. While other waste artists created beauty out of trash, Vossgätter succeeded in beautifully referencing trash with largely natural materials, which forced a reconsideration of the textuality of rubbish.

Although attendant conceptually to notions of waste in the ways described above and incorporating found and discarded materials, *Gutter Pop* was largely created from art-making materials sourced from suppliers, most notably beeswax and synthetic pigments. Although these materials were not "found," in that they were not discarded by someone else, they form part of long and complex entanglements between nature and culture, much like almost every other material from cobalt to charcoal and beyond. Vossgätter's artistic process for her paintings used to entail "splicing natural beeswax with synthetic pigments" through a process that required "soaking bleached beeswax pellets in mineral turpentine overnight," then impregnating the mix with "raw, synthetic pigment powders."²⁵ This new mixture would be applied to the canvas in thin layers, over and over again, to create a carveable, malleable surface. This artistic process used around 100 kilograms (220 pounds) of wax a year.

Vossgätter became increasingly interested in the source of the wax, and she started tracing the supply chain from hive to studio, finding that it involved a great deal of human and technical intervention for the wax to arrive in its pellet form.²⁶ This process also led to an understanding of the links between bee farming and the use of pesticides, which were wiping out bees and pushing up the price of their wax. When the turpentine and other toxins used in the process started to poison the artist, manifesting in a range of toxemia symptoms, she explored new, less toxic processes of integrating the wax and synthetic colors. When the price of wax pellets tripled, she also explored new local sources of wax. Wanting to better understand her key material, Vossgätter was drawn to spend time with beekeepers, and to learn more about honeybees and the wax that is a by-product of their reproduction and honey-making. By getting to know, in this way, one of the substances central to her creative process, she also started to "make kin" with the bees and forge an affection and affinity for them.²⁷

It was a huge surprise—although in hindsight perhaps attuned to the artistic process—when bees started to turn up in Vossgätter's studio and began to interact with the works in progress. The fresh pigmented wax being applied to canvas, and the artist's less toxic approaches to processing it into colors, attracted bees, and they in turn would collect and carry off tiny packages of colored wax. As long as Vossgätter was using wax, the bees kept coming, interacting with and acting on the paintings and sculptures and digging into the surface of the works with their little legs, until they began to feel like "active participants in the art making process."[28] Observing and interacting with the bees began to guide Vossgätter's process in overt and subtle ways. This led her to question the idea of authorship and also notions of materiality: the artist imagined the bees taking her psychedelic wax back to their hive, and she wondered, "What strange nature was I making?"[29]

Bees were more than simply the source of wax for an artist: they were also coming to mine some of that wax back, but the wax they were mining was not the same wax that had been taken from them; this wax was bright with color, laden with dye. Scientists have observed bees' wax collection processes, and through communication with these scientists and close observation of the visiting bees, Vossgätter was able to deduce the likely distance and direction of the wax-collecting bees' hive.[30] She followed the bees and found the hive just 80 meters (87 yards) away from her studio, in an old oak tree in the Company's Garden, just behind the University of Cape Town's Hiddingh Campus. At the entrance to the hive were many of the colors Vossgätter was working with in her studio: "The neon pink, of course, was unmissable."[31] There it was: a new text, written by the bees with excess matter from Vossgätter's art materials.

The question of whether it was the artist creating with the beeswax or the bees creating with the artist's pigmented wax forces us to reconsider what is waste and to whom or what it belongs, especially when materialities merge. Organic forms (seawater, animal flesh) have become blended with plastic molecules, and synthetic pigment has become blended with natural wax. Are humans using polymers to create meaning, or is plastic rewriting humanity and in turn integrating itself with animal and insect communicative codes to create new forms of textuality?

Reading Waste as/with Art

The case study discussed, *Gutter Pop* by Elize Vossgätter, illuminates new routes for textual analysis as mode and method, as signaled by the many questions included in this chapter. These are offered as an open-ended set of pathways for thinking about how waste, and the new integrated materialities that it forms when discarded, readopted, and reintegrated, can speak and what it might say.

Rubbish, trash, waste, whatever we wish to call it, must be theorized and analyzed as a textual resource. Waste art reveals how garbage is a special genre of text that deserves analytical attention as well as a special form of writing that can produce texts through a new modality of communication: waste. This means that waste can both write and be written with. The creative and communicative possibilities of waste are vast, and artistic experimentation in this realm can be instructive for analysts of trash as text.

The very materiality of waste reveals how it is a communicative material that can be deployed to create meaning. It can be repurposed to create beauty, it can be gestured to in creativity, it can serve as a blazing sign of apocalypse and demise. The affective potential of trash makes it an excessively fertile resource that can provoke intense and deep emotional responses.

Like other elemental media, trash is also a medium in its own right, which offers specific resonance as a channel for distributing information and making connections. Through its monumental and microscopic excess, rubbish not only pollutes natural environments but also transforms them, and as such it offers (and indeed threatens) to remake communicative modalities in ways that might yet be unknown and unknowable to human intelligence.

By all means, there will be ongoing value to the project of treating the creations of waste-artists as texts: critically discussing them in relation to culture in the age of the Anthropocene. But beyond this, I urge textual analysts to think with garbage to extend our very understandings of textuality itself.[32]

Notes

1 Christophe Bonneuil and Jean-Baptiste Fressoz, *The Shock of the Anthropocene: The Earth, History and Us* (London: Verso Books, 2016); Timothy Clark, *Ecocriticism on the Edge: The Anthropocene as a Threshold Concept* (London: Bloomsbury Publishing, 2015).

2. Mehita Iqani, *Garbage in Popular Culture: Consumption and the Aesthetics of Waste* (Albany: State University of New York Press, 2020).
3. Mehita Iqani, *Consumer Culture and the Media: Magazines in the Public Eye* (London: Palgrave Macmillan, 2012).
4. Susan Freinkel, *Plastic: A Toxic Love Story* (Boston: Houghton Mifflin Harcourt, 2011); Jennifer Gabrys, Gay Hawkins, and Mike Michael, *Accumulation: The Material Politics of Plastic* (London: Routledge, 2013).
5. Gunther Kress, *Multimodality: A Social Semiotic Approach to Contemporary Communication* (London: Routledge, 2013).
6. Arjun Appadurai, "Introduction: Commodities and the Politics of Value," in *The Social Life of Things: Commodities in Cultural Perspective*, edited by Arjun Appadurai (Cambridge: Cambridge University Press, 1986), 3–63.
7. Edward Humes, *Garbology: Our Dirty Love Affair with Trash*, repr. ed. (New York: Avery Publishing Group, 2013).
8. Roland Barthes, *Mythologies* (Boulder, CO: Paladin, 1973).
9. Mehita Iqani, *Consumption, Media and the Global South: Aspiration Contested* (London: Palgrave Macmillan, 2016).
10. Karen McVeigh, "Huge Rise in US Plastic Waste Shipments to Poor Countries Following China Ban," *The Guardian*, October 5, 2018, www.theguardian.com/global-development/2018/oct/05/huge-rise-us-plastic-waste-shipments-to-poor-countries-china-ban-thailand-malaysia-vietnam.
11. Velvette De Laney, "Landfill Waste Is a Design Choice: Or, There Is No 'Away,'" *Design Management Review* 29, no. 1 (March 2018): 12–17, https://doi.org/10.1111/drev.12103.
12. Katie Schaag, "Plastiglomerates, Microplastics, Nanoplastics: Toward a Dark Ecology of Plastic Performativity," *Performance Research* 25, no. 2 (February 17, 2020): 14–21, https://doi.org/10.1080/13528165.2020.1752572; Charles Moore, "Trashed: Across the Pacific Ocean, Plastics, Plastics, Everywhere," *Natural History* 112, no. 9 (2003): 46–51; Damian Carrington, "Alarm as Study Shows How Microplastics Are Blown Across The World," *The Guardian*, April 15, 2019, www.theguardian.com/environment/2019/apr/15/winds-can-carry-microplastics-anywhere-and-everywhere; Philip Hoare, "Microplastics in Our Mussels: The Sea Is Feeding Human Garbage Back to Us," *The Guardian*, June 8, 2018, www.theguardian.com/environment/shortcuts/2018/jun/08/microplastics-in-our-mussels-the-sea-is-feeding-human-garbage-back-to-us.
13. Gay Hawkins, *The Ethics of Waste: How We Relate to Rubbish* (Lanham: Rowman & Littlefield, 2006).
14. Melody Jue, *Wild Blue Media: Thinking through Seawater* (Durham, NC: Duke University Press, 2020); Melody Jue and Rafico Ruiz, eds., *Saturation: An Elemental Politics* (Durham, NC: Duke University Press, 2021).
15. Allison Cobb, *Plastic: An Autobiography* (New York: Nightboat Books, 2021).

16 Antonio Ragusa et al., "Plasticenta: First Evidence of Microplastics in Human Placenta," *Environment International* 146 (January 2021): 106274, https://doi.org/10.1016/j.envint.2020.106274.
17 Kirsty Robertson, "PLASTIGLOMERATE," *CSPA Quarterly*, no. 19 (2017): 38–44; Schaag, "Plastiglomerates, Microplastics, Nanoplastics."
18 Melissa Gregg and Gregory J. Seigworth, *The Affect Theory Reader* (Durham, NC: Duke University Press, 2010); Brian Massumi, *Politics of Affect* (Cambridge: Polity, 2015).
19 Iqani, *Garbage in Popular Culture*; Maggie Kainulainen, "Saying Climate Change: Ethics of the Sublime and the Problem of Representation," *Symploke* 21, no. 1 (December 22, 2013): 109–23.
20 Jonathan E. Schroeder, "Critical Visual Analysis," in *Handbook of Qualitative Research Methods in Marketing*, edited by Russell W. Belk (London: Edward Elgar Publishing, 2007), 303–21.
21 Maite Zubiaurre, "Trashtopia: Global Garbage/Art in Francisco de Pájaro and Daniel Canogar," in *Global Garbage: Urban Imaginaries of Waste, Excess, and Abandonment*, edited by Christoph Lindner and Miriam Meissner (Abingdon: Routledge, 2016) 17–34; Mehita Iqani, "Core Dump: The Global Aesthetics and Politics of e-Waste," in *Handbook of EcoMedia*, edited by Antonio López, Adrian Ivakhiv, Stephen Rust, Miriam Tola, Alenda Y. Chang, and Kiu-wai Chu (New York: Routledge, 2023), 160–7; Cajetan Iheka, *African Ecomedia: Network Forms, Planetary Politics* (Durham, NC: Duke University Press, 2021).
22 Elize Vossgätter, "Gutter Pop" (MFA Thesis, Cape Town, University of Cape Town, 2023), 13.
23 Vossgätter, "Gutter Pop," 38.
24 Vossgätter, "Gutter Pop," 33.
25 Vossgätter, "Gutter Pop," 15, 19.
26 Vossgätter, "Gutter Pop," 19.
27 Donna Haraway, *When Species Meet* (Minneapolis: University of Minnesota Press, 2008).
28 Vossgätter, "Gutter Pop," 21.
29 Vossgätter, "Gutter Pop," 23.
30 Krzysztof Olszewski, Piotr Dziechciarz, Mariusz Trytek, and Grezegorz Borsuk, "A Scientific Note on the Strategy of Wax Collection as Rare Behavior of Apis Mellifera," *Apidologie* 53, no. 4 (August 2022), article 40, https://doi.org/10.1007/s13592-022-00948-z.
31 Vossgätter, "Gutter Pop," 25.
32 I am indebted to Elize Vossgätter for creating *Gutter Pop* and her elegant writings on her process and vision, endorsing my desire to write on her work, and welcoming me into her studio for private viewings of the work in progress as well as postinstallation.

13

"That's What We Storytellers Do. We Restore Order with Imagination"

Analyzing Decoration and Plot in Walt Disney World Resort's Pandora: The Valley of Mo'ara

COLIN BURNETT

Burnett asks what is the narrative experience or plot of a theme park ride, and conducts an analysis of Walt Disney World Resort's Pandora: The Valley of Mo'ara, including the ride, queue, and entire area in his study. In doing so, he gives us a blueprint for how to textually analyze a theme park ride, as well as any number of other designed experiences or physical spaces.

"That's what we storytellers do. We restore order with imagination."
—Tom Hanks as Walt Disney, in *Saving Mr. Banks* (dir. John
  Lee Hancock, 2013)

It is often said that Disney parks tell stories. How? What strategies does Disney use to transform physical spaces such as parks into a storytelling medium? In this chapter, I adopt two analytical concepts that narratologists commonly employ to make sense of narrative strategies in various media but that are not normally found in studies of theme parks. I refer to the Russian formalist terms plot (*syuzhet*) and story (*fabula*). Disney parks create narrative experiences differently from film or television. Yet they share with these media the ability to organize audiovisual cues into patterns that formalists call plots; that is, they structure narrative information *within the work itself.* By strategically controlling the flow of information, Disney encourages guests to the park to grasp the "crux or fundamental features" of the narrative.¹ Seeking to comprehend this crux, guests build a mental model that takes the form of a related pattern, what formalists call stories.

In a nutshell, the story of a film, TV show, or theme park isn't *in* the work. It's in our minds. It's an "extraction"—the "gist" of the work inferred in our effort to comprehend it.² Narrative media use plots to click in an active process in which we create, through perception and inferential elaboration, a rough sketch of characters and the chain of fictional events that binds them.³ This activity is what permits us to feel a work's fictional power—its ability to grab hold of us emotionally, through anticipation, suspense, and surprise.

I will argue that Disney parks tell stories in the specific sense that their physical environments—spaces, buildings, monuments, and rides—are organized as plots that invite a variety of cognitive and affective responses in guests. Yet, as physical spaces in real life, theme parks face a distinct storytelling challenge; they are highly *ergodic*, bursting with random perceptual possibilities.⁴ Guests find their gazes continually distracted—pulled toward incidental or functional elements of the experience, such as other guests, their clothing, the day's weather, and opportunities to stop for a meal. Theme parks must work to contain the ergodic plenitude of their entertainment experiences.

My case study is Pandora: The Valley of Mo'ara, a themed land based on James Cameron's *Avatar* (2009) that was added in 2017 to the Animal Kingdom division of the Walt Disney World Resort near Orlando, Florida. Valley of Mo'ara solves the problem of ergodicity through an unusually well-structured plot that, as I will reveal, depends on two distinct but interconnected layers of formal patterning. First, Valley of Mo'ara, though initially presented as a wild, *un*structured fictional environment, quickly organizes into a *decorative* experience in which local details of the land (its shapes, colors, angles of view, etc.) reward active pattern-seeking *for its own sake*. In the language of narratologists, Valley of Mo'ara's storytelling is relatively self-conscious. By structuring its visual cues decoratively, as patterns stimulating in themselves, the land's design channels attention to the *order* lent to the theme park experience.⁵

This first layer of formal patterning is integrated into a second. The land embeds these fictionalized decorative patterns, as well as its main attractions (Disney's term for rides), within a more immersive pattern—a chain of fictional events first expressed through three design techniques employed by Disney Imagineers (members of the company's research and development team): a *peripheral berm*, a *narrow opening walkway*, and an *entrance sign*. Valley of Mo'ara's peripheral berm, or surrounding mound, and its opening walkway limit the ergodicity of the land's entrance by steering guests flowing into the land toward a detailed sign comprising narrative text, a map, a series of icons, and, crucially, diegetic temporal markers that clarify when events transpire in the *Avatar* story. These elements function as the land's opening "scene," to borrow the cinematic term preferred in Disney Imagineering; they prime guests to imagine themselves playing a clearly defined diegetic role while navigating the land.[6] Guests are on an expedition and guided tour of a new area of Pandora, the world introduced in the 2009 film.

This second layer of formal patterning, as we will see, is highly structured in an additional way. The three design elements that open the land cue guests' recollection of the 2009 film, suggesting a *transmedia* chain of events, but one whose gist guests can't fully grasp as they navigate past the land's entryway. A question lingers in their minds: *How did the* Avatar *story develop after the events of the 2009 movie?*

Thus, the land positions guests both *within a diegesis* as tourists traveling to Pandora and as *builders of* the *Avatar* diegesis, as active story-makers pursuing answers to questions essential to the construction of a complete chain of events. The missing links are furnished as guests navigate the land's many decorative stimuli, queues, and waiting areas, especially those of the main attraction, a four-dimensional experience titled *Avatar: Flight of Passage*. By this point, Valley of Mo'ara repays two forms of active engagement: a deeper regard for pattern and the effort to comprehend a larger transmedia story.

How Theme Parks Construct Plots: A Primer on Design Elements and Macrolevel Forms

Disney parks depend on cinematic strategies to build their plots. Consider the screen-based 4-D attraction *Avatar: Flight of Passage*. A 3-D headset, along with real motion simulation, concrete sound and music cues, and atmospheric effects such as mist and wind, positions the guest in the virtual point of view of a diegetic avatar, mounted, in the plot, on a dragon-like flying banshee, or *ikran*. As the ride commences, the guest, now in character, is guided by a tribal Na'vi character on a high-energy journey through the thrilling vistas of Pandora.

In Disney parks, screen-based attractions are strategically integrated into physical realms also structured to communicate plot cues. These realms require their own analytical language, some of which is cinematic (Disney Imagineers were originally set designers from the movie industry) and some of which derive from the arts of amusement parks, live theater, miniatures, gaming, home design, architecture, and Imagineering itself.[7] We enter Disney parks and lands through *gateways*. There, we read *signs* and peer up at faraway *wienies* (the tall vertical or long horizontal icons that serve as visual centerpieces of parks and lands). We navigate past, walk through, and cross the thresholds of buildings constructed as scaled-up models—large *toy edifices* that both trick and dazzle the eye with forced perspective and decorative detail. Outside and inside these toy edifices, we weave through *queues* toward *waiting rooms*, which further prepare us for *attractions* that act as focal points of the entertainment experience. Attractions consist of, and at times combine, many genres: *dark rides, flat rides, VR (virtual reality) rides, roller coasters, motion simulator rides, drop tower rides, water rides, flying theater rides, transportation rides*, and *carousels*. In these spaces, we observe live-action performers (costumed *cast members*) and *audio-animatronic figures* (mechanical bodies, at times with multifunctional screen projections for faces, performing repetitious actions or lines of dialogue). We also play *games* (interactive objects such as spindles, switches, and lights), and find our attention steered to detailed *murals, wall art* (posters, paintings, and miniscreens), *thematized decorations* (settings with architectural designs or faux-natural flora and fauna), and the *hidden show lights* adding mood and channeling our gaze within these spaces. Once we exit the toy edifices, we continue on to the park's numerous *show sites* (theaters and outdoor stages), *shops*, and *dining halls*.

Parks are also composed of urban design elements that contain additional plot cues, such as *walkways* (the basic path structures organizing the orderly movements of visitors), *edges* or *berms* (the borders around lands and parks), *hubs* or *étoiles* (central plazas that lead off into main walkways), *nodes* (defined spaces that connect, and create intervals between, walkways), and *landmarks*, which in Disney parks consist of primary and secondary wienies and toy edifices derived from Disney movies or shows. Additional elements of park design are of a more functional nature: *restrooms, service animal stations*, and so on.

These formal languages—at once cinematic, theatrical, amusement park, and urban design-based—form the basis of a theme park narratology, in which plot patterns are communicated via the macrolevel and microlevel of park design. At the macrolevel, Disney employs urban design elements to produce various spatial structures, such as the *hub-and-spoke*, *loop*, and *divergent hubs* park designs.[8] California's Disneyland, for example, depends on a highly controlled hub-and-spoke form, making manifest the "planned narrative sequence of spaces" that remains a defining aspect of Disney Imagineering.[9] Each phase of the journey along Disneyland's central "spoke," Main Street, as it leads up to Sleeping Beauty's Castle, carries guests through distinct fictional scenes or beats, together comprising a discontinuous diegetic space. As Disney historian Karal Ann Marling writes, "Scene One" of Disneyland comes as guests "stand outside the Main Street Emporium, looking north toward the Hub," whereas "Scene Two" begins "where Main Street flows gently into the Hub at a corner soda fountain."[10] Between these two points, the idea—at least originally—was to employ a narrative of American progress in reverse order from machine-made goods (in the Emporium) to hand-made goods (a cabinetmaker's shop).[11] "Scene Three" is, in part, anticipated. Disneyland's primary wienie, Sleeping Beauty's Castle, is visible from all points along Main Street, promising to carry guests from a reassuring past based on phases of U.S. history to a realm of fantasy. But the fictional options for the next scene are about to burst. The guest leaves Main Street and passes into the hub (a roundabout with a commemorative statue of Mickey Mouse and Walt Disney), and, from there, the plot is structured as one of "choice and change."[12] In the hub, new spokes, in the form of walkways, shoot out in four directions, each with its own fictional offerings. The experience is televisual, with the guest positioned "like an impatient viewer in front of the [TV] set."[13] We are able to choose one channel over the others or take each in turn—Frontierland, Adventureland, Tomorrowland, or Fantasyland, with their secondary wienies visible from the hub.

Analyses of this kind, which read distinct points of interest in Disney parks as plot beats or scenes, are highly metaphorical and rather common in Disney commentary. Macrolevel designs, such as Disneyland's hub-and-spoke, structure *some kind of* plot experience. We're invited to perceive toy edifices as containing *plot elements* and to perceive these elements as *ordered* (Main Street traverses a sequence of historical periods, and the hub gives us fictions to choose from). Yet it remains unclear whether at this level of analysis Disney parks construct plots in the form of clearly linked chains of events. In Disneyland's opening scenes, plot cues remain *undermotivated*, perceived by guests as only faintly narrativized.

Over time, Imagineers have developed several distinct styles for parks, ranging from more to less plot-motivated designs. Theme park historian David Younger distinguishes between "experiential" and "explicit" plots, the first characteristic of Disney's "traditional style" and the second of the "new traditional style."[14] Both styles rely on plot cues. Thus they differ from a third style, the "presentational style," which eschews plot construction in favor of expo-inspired attractions that are largely expository or educational in nature, such as EPCOT's *Horizons* ride (1983–99).[15] With the traditional style, a loose plot is integrated into the park design through isolated plot elements that do not cohere as a firm chain of events and provide no clear character role for visitors. This is the style adopted in early Disney designs such as Disneyland's *Mr. Toad's Wild Ride* (1955–). Like the traditional style, the "themed amusement park style," a fourth style, also uses experiential plots, but minimally so, to enhance amusement park attractions such as roller coasters "while never suggesting the attraction is anything other than its ride system."[16] In recent decades, Disney parks have shifted to the new traditional style, characterized by a high degree of plot motivation for design elements, thus giving rise to an explicit plot with a clear character or fictional role for visitors and a clearly motivated chain of events. An example of the new traditional style is Pandora: The Valley of Mo'ara.

The causal chain of Valley of Mo'ara, on first glance, can appear slightly ambiguous because this land, a subdivision of Animal Kingdom, is designed at the macrolevel to be jungle-like, taking the form of a visually occluded loop. A loop park design usually consists of a simple binary choice for guests—*this way around, or that way?*—as the basis for its plot construction. In the case of Valley of Mo'ara, the loop design remains hidden during the "setup" portion of the experience.[17] Initially, the land gives off a sense of immensity, whether one enters the northside entryway from Animal Kingdom's Africa or from Discovery Island. With thick flora towering above, the guest's angles of view are limited. The park's wienie—the gravity-defying Floating Mountains—isn't visible for several dozen paces, especially along the Africa entrance, inviting the impression of unending and unstructured possibility. Through sound effects—unidentifiable chirps, whistles, croaks, and vibrations—one's attention is steered toward a dense horticulture where otherworldly fauna lurk. In contrast to the hub-and-spoke layout of Disneyland, macrolevel design urges us to stay on our toes. The natural world is unruly.

The Valley of Mo'ara's apparent inefficiency at communicating a plot is something of a diversion, however. The park, in its first moments, is already organizing our experience. Imagineers risk ergodicity at the highest level of design because the experience is being balanced out, with order arising from local decorative patterns.

Analyzing Pandora's Decorations: A First Layer of Microlevel Patterning

The "setup" of The Valley of Mo'ara cues guests to perceive a strange balance at the heart of this themed land. On the one hand, there's the unruly wild of Pandora. On the other, there's a beauty and sense of refined culture expressed through decoration—through unity and variety of design elements. The walkway into the land is lined at uneven intervals with oversized pendant light fixtures, all individualized and hanging high above the path from rudimentary wooden poles. The sheer variety of the fixtures connotes a culture, that of the fictional Na'vi people, at once traditional and experimental: a common design, but within that commonality a flourishing of unrestricted variety. Na'vi culture is also prone to analogy, inspired by organic forms. The light fixtures overtly mimic flowers, drooping like an array of bell flowers—twin flowers, Canterbury bells, and lilies of the valley.

These fixtures permit decorative patterns—the variety of colors and shapes and the perceptual experiences they stimulate—to gently rise in

Figure 13.1: Valley of Mo'ara's *flaska reclinata*.

the guest's attention. The light fixtures, in earthy tones such as beige and brown, meld with their natural surroundings despite their obviously handmade features. For guests entering from Discovery Island, color suddenly bursts from the land's flora, such that variations in hue and tone draw our attention there. The sight, along the right side of the walkway, of an oversized seed plant with rosy pedals protruding from tightly wrapped green sepals, lures the eye (in *Avatar* lore, the massive plant is referred to as a *flaska reclinata*, a species that detoxifies Pandora's volcanic air; see figure 13.1). Imagineers are giving guests reason to "make order" of the fictional land's flora. Red and other vibrant accents will lunge into view against a backdrop of dominant hues—greens and fairly sedate, desaturated earth tones.

Just above the *flaska reclinata*, guests are given an angle view of something they've come to expect from Disney parks. For the first time, we see the land's wienie, Pandora's spectacular Floating Mountains. The design relies on forced perspective, what is called "peaking" (themed tops are made to seem inaccessible to visitors), and "faded chroma" (desaturated hues on the rocks mimic aerial perspective), all to generate the striking impression of great spatial depth in the land and thus anticipation that almost unlimited decorative pattern-seeking lies ahead.[18]

Now that guests have come to expect that decorations will stimulate their senses from above their heads, their senses are also stimulated from decorations positioned down below. As we continue along the main walkway toward the center of the land—a center we likely still can't quite grasp spatially—more wooden designs such as Na'vi huts come into view, as does, again to our right, more exotic, colorfully adorned vegetation. Our eyes are pulled into a pulsating creek carving a trench through the land, itself lined with green-leafed plants sprouting a plethora of rosy shoots. As we round a bend, a brighter tint of green catches the eye, again from a lower position. It's a Pandora plant known as a vein pod. The blurring of the line between real and fictive flora is crucial to the land's decorative effect.

Decorative patterning is spatially arranged to continually invite us to look up, then down, then up, then down again. Right above the vein pod, emphasized by a conspicuously tall palm tree running up our field of view, are the Floating Mountains, several massive boulders reaching dozens of meters into the sky, with roots from trees living there stretching down to the ground. Glancing again below, we note, to the left of the path, a new color—a great purple blueberry-like plant known as a puffball tree, which in story is a keystone species on Pandora, again detoxifying the air.

Decorations—systematically varied patterns—are multiplied and refined in this way as one continues to navigate the park's loop, visible at last, carrying us around and under the Floating Mountains. The themes of handmade objects integrated within the natural realm and saturated accents against green/neutral backdrops organize the guest's perceptions not just in the walkways but also in live performances (during the *Swotu Wayä* drum circle, for example, an outdoor theater performance in which guests are invited to play drums that connect with Na'vi ancestors) and queues as well (in the queue for the land's main ride, *Avatar: Flight of Passage*, saturated color is expressed in a series of intricate Na'vi murals). As we are about to see, these decorations—as attention grabbing as they are—function as *amuse-bouches*. They lend order to prepare the way for the plot-focused main course.

Analyzing Pandora's Plot: A Second Layer of Microlevel Patterning

Microlevel decorative patterns sustain the guest's search for detail ahead of, and in between, another emerging pattern—namely, that of plot—that further offsets the potential unruliness and ergodicity of the land's hidden-loop structure. To understand this layered effect, we must look again at the land's entryway. As guests cross the bridge from Animal Kingdom's Discovery Island and the peripheral berm that surrounds the Valley of Mo'ara, their eyes are soon drawn from the surrounding decorations to a large, well-positioned entrance sign just left of the walkway (see figure 13.2)—purple in color, to contrast with the surrounding foliage. The sign embeds the land's decorations within a clearly articulated plot, giving guests a character to play and a chain of events to cognitively model.

The map is rich in plot cues, containing temporal and causal information that links the areas guests will navigate with a backstory related to but not shown in the original film (see figure 13.3). The gist of 2009's *Avatar*—particularly its ending—is worth recalling here. In his blue-bodied avatar, Jake Sully (Sam Worthington); the Na'vi character Neytiri (Zoe Saldaña), who throughout the film laments humanity's pillaging of Pandora and desecration of sacred Na'vi ritual sites; and various Na'vi clans defeat the exploitative RDA (Resource Development Administration), ousting its leadership and military forces from Pandora and sending them back to Earth. The map guides guests in locating the film's plot within a larger narrative gist. It reveals that the area of Valley of Mo'ara that is open to guests is sandwiched between two blue-coded zones. In the upper left, we observe a zone described as an "old" RDA mine access. In the lower right, we perceive a zone under restoration, which at one time was an RDA refinery. These plot cues invite guests to infer that events from the film's conclusion—namely, the RDA's expulsion from Pandora—are part of the story-world's *history*. They also simultaneously update guests on events that have transpired since the film's ending. Areas of Pandora once exploited by the RDA are now being returned to their natural resplendence. For guests who turn their attention to the land's formal patterns, the pleasure of crafting a story—a mental model of events—begins to drive much of the experience.

Figures 13.2 and 13.3: Valley of Mo'ara's entranceway sign and detail of its map.

The chain of events—the RDA's expulsion and the subsequent welcoming of humans back to a Pandora now under restoration—remains incomplete. *What occurred between the expulsion and restoration? What made this reversal of Na'vi sentiment toward humanity possible?* The upper and lower panels of the sign contain additional plot cues. The icons of two organizations not presented in the film—and hence unfamiliar to guests—adorn the sign. The first is that of the ACE (Alpha Centauri Expeditions), which, as the text reveals, has partnered with the Na'vi to make our expedition possible. The second icon, that of the PCI (Pandora Conservation Initiative), is strategically left unexplained to guests. They are being cued to form questions and anticipate outcomes: *What role does the PCI play in the Valley?*

Valley of Mo'ara's entrance sign is designed to trigger inferential elaboration in the form of an incomplete transmedia story that integrates the

Figures 13.2 and 13.3: (*continued*)

2009 film. We are invited to situate the Valley and our expedition there in the film's future. But the chain of events remains an open one. The sign presents guests with an enigma surrounding the Na'vi's newfound hospitality.

This first scene isn't followed immediately by a second. The park's plot relies on the technique of *delay*. The enigma leaves guests in suspension. The guest's dual roles, as a diegetic character on expedition and an extradiegetic builder of the larger *Avatar* story, are kept in careful balance as we take in the decorative patterns of the Valley while also looking for plot information that will take us into scene two.

Scene two comes in the queue to the land's main attraction, *Avatar: Flight of Passage*, located centrally in the land, just beyond the Floating

Figure 13.4: A sign in the queue for Valley of Mo'ara's *Avatar: Flight of Passage*.

Mountains. Guests enter a space not depicted in the film: a sacred cavern ornately decorated with Na'vi cultural artifacts such as flying wood sculptures and vividly colored wall paintings. At this stage, decorations draw attention in and of themselves *and* subtly refine the plot enigma: *Why are humans such as us being admitted to this site of Na'vi ritual?*

The queue descends into what appears to be a bunker—scene three. We pass through airlock doors equipped with elaborate keypads. Bearing the mark of the RDA, these doors reveal that humanity had once defiled *this* sacred Na'vi site, too. We learn moments later, however, as we continue along the queue, that quite a bit of time has passed since the RDA was ejected from Pandora. Remnants of RDA signage and equipment stand in ruin, strangled by vegetation.

Guests come upon a different sign—the start of scene four. We are given a closer look at the Pandora Conservation Initiative's logo (see figure 13.4). It contains a woodsprite, in *Avatar* a symbol of Eywa (the deity worshipped by the Na'vi), being cradled by two sets of leaves curved to resemble human hands. The bunker is currently occupied by a scientific society that promotes harmony between humans and the Na'vi.

Still in the queue, guests circle past workspaces of PCI scientists, rich in plot detail, and a full-sized avatar in incubation. Moments later, we discover a waiting room, which presents the fifth and penultimate scene of Valley of Mo'ara's plot. We find ourselves in a genetic matching room; we will be fitted with an avatar and fly a banshee. Our attention is directed at a video wall. One of the lead PCI scientists, Dr. Stevens (David Danipour), appears on the screen and narrates the causal history of the Valley of Mo'ara, describing how the actions of characters in the aftermath of the film changed the course of human-Na'vi relations:

> *Using avatars to fly this way was all figured out by my boss, Dr. Jackie Ogden. She leads our science team, part of the Pandora Conservation Initiative. And we're here in the Valley of Mo'ara, studying banshees and their environment. Over a generation ago, this enormous company called the RDA created a lot of damage to the area through their bad mining practices and conflicts with the Na'vi. Just like on Earth, it can take decades for ecosystems to recover. One way to understand what's going on with an ecosystem is to study what are called keystone species. [. . .] It was Dr. Odgen who restarted the avatar program. It's because of her that you're able to go through this rite of passage today.*

In one of its final scenes, Valley of Mo'ara cues guests to infer the gist of the larger *Avatar* story (at least prior to the release of the sequel film, 2022's *Avatar: The Way of Water*, also directed by Cameron). Moments before we link with a banshee, the sixth and final scene—*Flight of Passage*'s waiting room—reveals that, since 2009's *Avatar*, humanity has returned to Pandora on the promise that the PCI will help restore Pandora's ravaged ecosystems, using the study of the banshee as a crucial area of scientific inquiry. Building on the themes of the film, human science has at last trumped militarized colonialism.

In short, what guests experience is a transmedia story that spans a full generation, beginning with the RDA's mining of Pandora, followed by its expulsion. This expulsion sets up the PCI's return decades later to assist in the restoration and Dr. Ogden's resumption of the avatar program under the auspices of the PCI, ending with the ACE's hosting of human expeditions to Pandora thanks to the PCI's discoveries.

Using perhaps the most efficient means available—written and spoken language in key signs and video presentations placed at strategic points throughout the land—Valley of Mo'ara is a fully developed plot in the Russian formalist sense. Through that plot, the land *tells a story*. Its entrances, walkways, queues, waiting rooms, and attractions prompt guests, often alongside an array of decorative patterns, to focus their attention and piece together *the gist*—the events and causality of the *Avatar* story.

Notes

1 David Bordwell, "Cognition and Comprehension: Viewing and Forgetting in *Mildred Pierce*," in *Poetics of Cinema* (New York: Routledge, 2008), 137.
2 Bordwell, "Cognition and Comprehension," 137.
3 Kristin Thompson, *Breaking the Glass Armor: Neoformalist Film Analysis* (Princeton, NJ: Princeton University Press, 1988), 38–39.
4 Espen J. Aarseth, *Cybertext: Perspectives on Ergodic Literature* (Baltimore: Johns Hopkins University Press, 1997), 1–2.
5 David Bordwell, *Narration in the Fiction Film* (Madison: University of Wisconsin Press, 1985), 283.
6 Karal Ann Marling, "Imagineering the Disney Theme Parks," in *Designing Disney Theme Parks: The Architecture of Reassurance*, edited by Karal Ann Marling (Paris: Flammarion, 1997), 60.
7 Sabrina Mittermeier, *A Cultural History of the Disneyland Theme Parks: Middle Class Kingdoms* (Chicago: Intellect, 2021), 24–25.
8 Timothy Fuerst, "It All Started with the Hub and Spoke: An Analysis of Park Forms," *Imagineerland: Themed Design Blog*, July 30, 2018, http://imagineerland.blogspot.com/2018/07/it-all-started-with-hub-and-spoke.html#google_vignette.
9 Marling, "Imagineering the Disney Theme Parks," 68.
10 Marling, "Imagineering the Disney Theme Parks," 83.
11 Marling, "Imagineering the Disney Theme Parks," 92.
12 Marling, "Imagineering the Disney Theme Parks," 74.
13 Marling, "Imagineering the Disney Theme Parks," 74.
14 David Younger, *Theme Park Design and the Art of Themed Entertainment* (Inklingwood Press, 2016), 99–100, 150, 156.
15 Younger, *Theme Park Design*, 152.
16 Younger, *Theme Park Design*, 155.
17 Younger, *Theme Park Design*, 109.
18 Younger, *Theme Park Design*, 170, 172.

14

Images on the Move

Close Reading Migrant- and Refugee-Authored Media Online

ESZTER ZIMANYI

Zimanyi considers migrant- and refugee-authored media, especially selfies distributed via social media, encouraging us to see the depths of meaning in even the most seemingly banal photos. Indeed, Zimanyi notes the importance of textual analysis as a method for studying a precarious population whose safety might be further imperiled by other, perhaps more obvious methods.

When you hear the words "migrant" or "refugee," what images come to your mind, and what ideas do you associate with these terms? How do you expect migrants and refugees to look, speak, and behave? Perhaps, like many people, the first things you think of are the dramatic images that have dominated global news media coverage of various mass displacement events throughout the 2010s and 2020s. For years, we have seen countless scenes of asylum seekers desperately seeking to be rescued from overcrowded inflatable boats that frequently capsize in choppy waters at sea. We have also seen unsettling images of border police violently pushing back and detaining asylum seekers in various international border zones. In sympathetic portrayals of migrants and refugees, journalists often choose to emphasize photographs and videos that show women and children in states of exhaustion or distress or those that feature families stuck in unsanitary, makeshift tent encampments near border crossing sites. In more skeptical reporting on migration, we might only see images of overwhelmingly large crowds of people on the move, walking through forests, fields, or deserts toward their desired destinations. Across these portrayals, however, is a tendency to focus on emergency situations, wherein migrants and refugees are figured either as people in need of being rescued or as people who need to be managed and contained. As such, their individual desires, experiences, and lives prior to, and following, being displaced are often minimized or erased from our view.[1]

These spectacular images of emergency help drive clicks and sell stories in a digital economy where human attention is increasingly the most valuable currency. But journalists are not the only ones documenting human displacement. Migrants and refugees, equipped with personal smartphones, are using a range of new media tactics to produce and share their own firsthand accounts of seeking safety. These include photographs, video diaries, and mapmaking practices that primarily circulate across social media platforms (such as Instagram and TikTok), as well as films that find audiences in theaters, on television, and across the festival circuit.[2] Yet, echoing the experiences they document, these media objects exist in varying states of ephemerality and precarity, making them difficult objects to study at length.

With these considerations in mind, this chapter makes a case for *why* we should use textual analysis as a method for studying migrant- and refugee-authored media. In the first section, I consider some of the practical challenges and ethical concerns that arise in researching media produced by vulnerable populations and circulated on social networking platforms. In the second section, I draw on specific examples to consider how close reading practices that account for both the image and its unstable location on a given social media platform allow for a thoughtful exploration of the formal and narrative tropes that migrants and refugees employ in their posts. These include decisions about framing, color, sound, and text (in the form of spoken testimony as well as image captions), which are often made with multiple audiences in mind. Much like the memes discussed by Anirban K. Baishya in chapter 16 of this book, closely reading migrant and refugee media online requires paying attention to the "text" of the object (its formal and aesthetic qualities); the context in which it is circulating (the historical and geopolitical circumstances within which a particular mass displacement event unfolds and the ways in which that event is reported on by news media); and "intertextuality," or the ways migrant- and refugee-authored media strategically take up, and unsettle, familiar forms of address in order to reach audiences and, increasingly, to outsmart algorithmic "shadowbanning."³ I take a phenomenological approach by centering my own experiences with encountering migrant media in my personal social network feeds and compare migrant- and refugee-authored social media posts from two different major (and ongoing) sites of displacement to consider how migrant social media practices have changed over time and in relation to the type of displacement being experienced.

The first example I close read is an Instagram post made by a Syrian refugee while transiting across Europe in 2015, during what became known as the "long summer of migration."⁴ Then, I analyze one video that was cross-posted on TikTok and Instagram by Nisreen Shehada, a young Palestinian woman who was displaced from her home within Gaza after October 7, 2023.⁵ By comparing migrant- and refugee-authored media from these two time periods, I demonstrate how comparative textual analysis methods can help reveal, situate, and unpack the media practices of migrants and refugees that wide-scale data mining might miss. While all the images and videos I reference have been shared publicly online, to protect the privacy of the authors of these media, I am choosing to rely on description only for posts made by people who have not spoken to journalists about their experiences and social media use. In my analysis of Nisreen Shehada's content, I have chosen to reproduce one still image from her video because she has been "blue check verified" as a public figure online and has encouraged viewers to share her content widely.

Mapping a Methodological Route (or, Why Textual Analysis?)

There are many conditions that impact the audience reach of migrant- and refugee-authored media online, as well as the duration that content is accessible to the public. Sometimes, the unstable nature of migrant-authored media is due to a platform's design. Posts shared on Snapchat or through Instagram's "stories" feature, for example, automatically "expire" after twenty-four hours. Other times, the disappearance of these media objects is due to corporate choices. Content moderators regularly remove posts they deem to be in violation of a platform's terms of service, and some platforms—like Instagram and X (formerly Twitter)—now censor posts that show or discuss distressing topics behind "sensitive content" warning labels.⁶ Media can vanish when platforms choose to eliminate certain features of their service entirely or when they suspend certain functions within specific geographic areas.

This was the case in March 2022, when Snapchat disabled its public "heatmap" feature in Ukraine in direct response to Russia's invasion of the country that February. Snapchat's heatmap typically allows individual users to contribute posts that have been geotagged onto a public global map. These posts are then amalgamated with other posts tagged to that location, so that users can view many different people's posts in succession as they virtually explore different places. Snapchat's developer, Snap Inc., stated that it disabled posting to the global heatmap page within the borders of Ukraine in order to protect the safety of civilians living there.[7] However, the decision has also prevented people in Ukraine from circulating their firsthand accounts of life under war to a wider audience on Snapchat, which raises important questions about whether social media platforms should have the power to decide who gets to be visible, and when, on such a large scale. Of course, migrant and refugee content creators may also decide to remove their own posts, change their usernames, or change the privacy settings of their accounts, making it difficult for researchers to locate and view migrant- and refugee-authored media in their original context over time. These are just some of the factors that make migrant- and refugee-authored digital media such challenging objects to research; yet, these media provide invaluable insights about contemporary experiences of displacement and migration around the world.

For researchers, the instability of migrant- and refugee-authored media online perhaps makes mass data scraping seem like a necessity: on the surface, collecting as much media as possible, as quickly as possible, provides an opportunity to "save" posts that are at risk of disappearing and to identify broader trends in the ways migrants and refugees make use of social media platforms, as well as in the general types of content they post. However, large-scale data extraction presents practical and, more importantly, ethical concerns related to the informed consent and safety of vulnerable populations. Just as migrants and refugees increasingly depend on digital communication technologies to plan and navigate their journeys, governments use these same technologies to fortify their control over their borders and to surveil and manage migrant and refugee populations.[8] With this in mind, scholars in new subfields of inquiry, such as digital migration studies, have raised salient questions about the ethics of conducting digital humanities research with and about migrant and refugee populations.

As digital migration studies scholars Sandra Ponzanesi and Koen Leurs remind us, data-driven research "infringes not only on the privacy of 'users' (actual people) but also generates results and analyses that can be manipulated for other purposes" by governments and organizations seeking to curtail migration.[9] Leurs and Madhuri Prabhakar further point out that Big Data methods leave consent in a gray zone.[10] Although the terms of service agreements that social media users agree to typically grant corporations and researchers permission to obtain and study users' personal data, most users are unaware of what such permission actually entails. Migrants and refugees who have not yet received legal recognition from a host country may not wish to have their social media posts included in a particular study, even if the data is anonymized. And contacting every user whose data has been scraped to ask for informed consent may not always be feasible for researchers working with large sets of data. Remaining cognizant of these risks to the privacy and safety of migrant and refugee social media users is key to ensuring, as much as possible, that our research and writing do not exploit vulnerable populations further.

What do these practical and ethical questions mean for media studies scholars, in particular, who are interested in studying the *media objects* (videos, photographs, social media posts, and audio recordings) that migrants and refugees circulate online? And what insights would a more modest approach to these objects, using methods of textual analysis, provide that mass data scraping might overlook? While data scraping may give us a sense of broad patterns—for example, the frequency with which certain words or hashtags are used by migrants and refugees in their social media posts—it also separates media objects from the visual and textual digital media environments in which they are embedded as they circulate. Textual analysis methods emphasize the importance of studying texts *within* the contexts of their creation and circulation in order to draw informed conclusions about how "members of various cultures and subcultures . . . make sense of the world around them."[11] While we can certainly close read images and videos as independent objects, digital media content cannot be easily separated from the platforms on which they are created and shared. Migrant- and refugee-authored media distributed on social media networks exist in relation to the many other media circulating on those same platforms, from GIFs and memes to infographics and news articles. That said, algorithms increasingly individuate users' feeds, making it difficult to predict the exact context in which any one user might encounter migrant- and refugee-authored media. Considering these evolving challenges, what affordances does textual analysis provide for scholars studying migrant- and refugee-authored media online, and how can we apply methods of textual analysis in our research? In the next section, I reflect on my own approach to searching for, examining, and writing about refugee media from two different mass displacement events of the early twenty-first century.

Moving Images of People on the Move

In the summer of 2015, more than one million people seeking refuge, primarily from Syria, Afghanistan, and Iraq, arrived to the European continent, and nearly four thousand people drowned in the Mediterranean while attempting to reach Europe's shores.[12] The seemingly sudden influx of so many asylum seekers became a global media fixation and was alternately called Europe's "refugee crisis" or "migrant crisis" by politicians and journalists alike. Around the world, news organizations published shocking photographs and videos of migrants in distress; in September that year, the image of three-year-old Aylan Kurdi, whose lifeless body washed ashore in Turkey, went viral on social networking sites and became an icon of the crisis.[13] At the same time, migrants and refugees were actively documenting their own journeys using smartphones, often in the form of taking selfies when arriving to new locations. These selfies typically displayed none of the overt crisis imagery that mainstream news media focused on in coverage of the "migrant crisis." Instead, at first glance, the "refugee selfies" posted throughout the summer and fall of 2015 often appeared entirely mundane, depicting individual migrants (or sometimes small groups of people) posing by European buildings or resting by rivers and in seemingly idyllic open fields. These selfies simultaneously emphasized a generic everydayness, one that easily blended in with the selfies taken by locals and tourists, and the precarity of the refugee subject—a precarity that often only became fully legible if viewers of a selfie noticed the image's accompanying captions and hashtags referencing migration and clicked through to the subject's profile page. There, the selfie would become contextualized by the refugee subject's other posts documenting their forced displacement from their home.[14]

At the time, many refugee selfie captions and hashtags were written in the subject-author's native language, which may have limited the circulation of the images to a wider international audience. However, refugee selfies posted publicly on Instagram were frequently geotagged, such that they would appear in Instagram's "Explore" tab when countries, cities, or towns were typed into the search bar. This is how I came to discover refugee selfies during 2015 and 2016: while searching under the "Recent" tab for locations as broad as "Macedonia" and as specific as "Röszke, Hungary," I found refugee selfies mixed in with other images of the crisis, such as tent encampments, border fences, aid workers, and journalistic images of refugees walking along roadways. When I noticed these selfies appearing in close proximity to other images from the crisis, I began clicking on each user's name to view their selfie within the context of their full Instagram profile and to see what other images they had shared. Until September 2016, Instagram displayed a "photo map" on individual users' profile pages that showed all their geotagged photos on a world map.[15] Through this feature, I was able to see the migration routes of multiple refugees from Syria, Iraq, and Afghanistan mapped across their Instagram uploads. While the process was slow and painstaking, I discovered photographs that stood in stark contrast to other social media images and journalistic photographs of the crisis (which mainly emphasized large groups of people and moments of distress). Although most of these refugee selfies did not circulate widely, I write about them because they offer intimate portraits of individual migrants and refugees during moments of respite, boredom, and even joy that complicate the spectacular images of suffering we often see in the news.

One selfie, posted on Instagram by a young Syrian man I call Amer, shows him sitting along a riverbank on a sunny autumn day. He holds the camera out to his right-hand side to frame the river and the stone sidewalk on which he sits, and looks into the camera, smiling with one eyebrow arched upward. He is by himself, but farther down the sidewalk, we can make out the shapes of other people sitting along the river. On first look, the photo signifies little more than a snapshot of someone enjoying nice weather in early September 2015. However, on Instagram, Amer captioned the image "Surviving regensburg."[16]

Regensburg, a city in eastern Bavaria, contains a reception center for asylum seekers who are awaiting decisions on their applications for asylum in Germany.[17] Embedded in this context, Amer's expression, framing, and caption perhaps signify something more ambiguous than I initially thought. He is smiling, but he suddenly seems incredibly isolated in the frame. His arched brow conveys a look of exhaustion as much as it does a playful personality. He is one of the lucky ones who made it safely to Germany, but, nevertheless, he is still only "surviving" there.

While there is no spectacular violence or danger represented in the image, Amer's caption reminds us that the challenges faced by migrants and refugees do not entirely end once they reach a place of safe haven. Deriving this reading from his post, however, is only possible if we read his image and caption within the context of his *other* posts, which archive both his migration and the life and family he left behind in Syria, *as well as* the wider context of images and news reports on the "migrant crisis" that circulated in 2015 and 2016, to which Amer's selfies respond. It requires that we take the time to engage with both the specific image and the migrant user's full profile page. Still, when taken together with other media that document Europe's "migrant crisis," I argue that refugee selfies are one media form through which migrants and refugees make a public claim to existence and take agency over the authorship of their individual refugee stories, resisting the essentializing discourses of both victimhood and "security threat" that frame most discussions about mass migration.[18]

By paying attention to what languages and stylistic elements migrants and refugees choose to use when crafting their social media posts, as well as whether or how these posts employ a direct address to the viewer, we can make educated guesses about the audiences that particular users are imagining for their content. In 2015, most refugee users of social media platforms seemed to be posting with their friends and family in mind; however, by 2023, a growing number of migrants and refugees had begun actively targeting international publics with content made to raise awareness about specific displacement events. These social media users, some of whom have become known as "war influencers," strategically use the English language and often appropriate social media trends and formats to reach the widest audiences possible. They use audiovisual memes made popular primarily on TikTok "as templates for war storytelling" as well as to "draw algorithmic attention to critical sociopolitical issues and traumatic events [by] leveraging [TikTok's] viral dissemination and exposure of sounds."[19]

One contemporary mass displacement event where social media platforms such as TikTok and Instagram have become vital spaces for sharing first-person accounts of the refugee experience is Israel's war in Gaza, also referred to as the Israel-Hamas War. The war began on October 7, 2023, after Hamas fighters carried out a surprise attack on southern Israel, killing an estimated 1,200 people. As I write this chapter, in May 2024, the Israeli military's devastating campaign in the besieged enclave of Gaza is still ongoing and has killed more than an estimated 35,000 Palestinians.[20] The war has internally displaced approximately 1.5 million Palestinian civilians, who have been pushed south into the Rafah district, an area that previously housed only 275,000 people.[21] It has also led to the total collapse of Gaza's healthcare system and widespread starvation.[22]

In the weeks following October 7, a number of young Palestinians turned citizen-journalists gained international recognition for their documentation of everyday life during the war; they include twenty-five-year-old Bisan Owda, twenty-five-year-old Motaz Azaiza, twenty-two-year-old Plestia Alaqad, and twenty-seven-year-old Nisreen Shehada.[23] While Azaiza, Owda, and Alaqad have operated as freelance journalists for international news agencies, Nisreen Shehada—who describes herself as a "dentist and food blogger" in her TikTok and Instagram bios—has tactically appropriated recognizable TikTok/Instagram video trends to encourage viewers to keep talking about Gaza. In one video, Shehada appropriates the "POV/Day-in-the-life" video trend to provide a glimpse into her daily life as a displaced Gazan in Rafah.[24] The video uses the same music (an excerpt from Michael Giacchino's score to Disney Pixar's 2009 animated feature *Up* [dir. Pete Docter, 2009]) and introductory phrase ("Join me as I . . .") as other day-in-the-life videos circulating across both platforms. But where most viral videos following the day-in-the-life trend demonstrate the skin care, fitness routines, and fine dining experiences of wealthy young people, Shehada's opening line invites us to join her "for a baking day in the tent," signaling that her circumstances are highly unusual.[25]

In a small mirror hanging by a wire from the tent pole, we catch a glimpse of Shehada's face as she records the video on her phone and waves to her viewers (see figure 14.1). The video cuts to a flour mixture in a plastic bucket as Shehada's upbeat voiceover narrates as follows: "With bakeries closed for the past three months, due to the scarcity of electricity and flour, we have to make our bread. Each morning, mothers bake fresh bread, and the smell is simply captivating. Young children find joy in the process. Here's young Jaffa playing with a small piece of dough." As the video continues, we move from a point-of-view shot of hands mixing the dough in the plastic bucket to a toddler playing with a small piece of dough while sitting on the ground. Then, Shehada shows us a small metal oven, as she states, "This baker used to work on electricity, but we found a way to modify it to bake using coal. Everyone loves fresh bread.... And, of course, a cup of tea will make things even better. Here is Aboud and his cat saying goodbye!" In Shehada's video, we see how the lack of electricity has required Palestinians to create makeshift ovens to cook food; we learn that the scarcity of food and ingredients is an issue even in the areas of Gaza that were designated as "safe zones" by the Israeli military; and we glimpse the sparsity inside the tent within which a whole family must reside. Her simple day-in-the-life format excludes any graphic content that might risk being censored, shadowbanned, or outright removed by social media platforms. Yet it still successfully communicates the exceedingly difficult circumstances under which internally displaced Gazans have been forced to live since the beginning of the war, making it both an important archival document and a salient example of how and why refugees use social media to record their experiences.

Conclusion

While migrant and refugee media, like all social media content, remain at risk of erasure as platforms change and evolve, textual analysis methods allow us to situate how social media users experiencing forced displacement are thoughtfully mobilizing the affordances of digital media to document and bear witness to the immensely challenging

Figure 14.1: Nisreen Shehada shows viewers how her family navigates food shortages and limited supplies after being displaced to the Rafah district of Gaza.

circumstances they must navigate, from war, famine, and disease to rebuilding their lives in temporary or long-term homes away from home. Nisreen Shehada's "baking day in the tent" video has gained over one million views combined on TikTok and Instagram, demonstrating how the appropriation of a preexisting format can ensure the widespread circulation of migrant- and refugee-authored media, even if mainstream news outlets do not republish migrants' and refugees' social media content. Indeed, Shehada's video entered my personal Instagram feed not because I was actively looking for such content but because Instagram's algorithm had already identified me as someone who would be interested in it. This was a marked shift from the refugee selfies of 2015, which required a much more active search process to be found. Textual analysis methods provide us with the tools to recognize and examine detailed elements of a media object's composition, while placing that object in conversation with broader formal and generic conventions, shifts in platform functionality and governance, and world events. By engaging the text, context, and intertextuality of Amer's selfie and Shehada's video, as just two examples, we can begin to build a more nuanced analysis of the habits, motivations, tactics, and feelings that underlie migrant- and refugee-authored media online.

Notes

1. Throughout this chapter, I oscillate between, or combine, the terms "migrant" and "refugee." While they have distinct legal definitions, it is not always possible to determine from social media posts whether the subject of the post is legally considered one or the other.
2. *Midnight Traveler* (dir. Hassan Fazili, 2019) and *Purple Sea* (dir. Amel Alzakout, 2020) are two examples of critically acclaimed films that document the experiences of their refugee directors. *Midnight Traveler* was shot using three different cell phones, while *Purple Sea* is composed entirely of GoPro footage.
3. Geoffrey A. Fowler, "Shadowbanning Is Real: Here's How You End Up Muted by Social Media," *Washington Post*, December 27, 2022, www.washingtonpost.com/technology/2022/12/27/shadowban/.
4. Bernd Kasparek and Mark Speer, "Of Hope, Hungary, and the Long Summer of Migration," *Border Monitoring EU*, September 9, 2015, https://bordermonitoring.eu/ungarn/2015/09/of-hope-en/.
5. As I am writing this chapter in May 2024, Israel's war in the besieged enclave is still ongoing. In January of 2024, the International Court of Justice ruled that

there is a "plausible risk" that the state of Israel is committing genocide in Gaza. See Fatima Al-Kassab, "A Top U.N. Court Says Gaza Genocide Is 'Plausible' But Does Not Order Cease-Fire," NPR, January 26, 2024, www.npr.org/2024/01/26/1227078791/icj-israel-genocide-gaza-palestinians-south-africa.

6 Imad Khan, "Instagram Expands Sensitive Content Controls: Here's How to Apply Them," *CNET*, June 6, 2022, www.cnet.com/news/social-media/instagram-expands-sensitive-content-controls-heres-how-to-apply/. See also Chris Morris, "Twitter/X Previews What 'Shadowbans' Will Look Like," *Fortune*, September 27, 2023, https://fortune.com/2023/09/27/twitter-x-shadowban-preview-visibility-limiting-elon-musk/.

7 Mitchell Clark, "Snapchat Turns Off Public 'Heatmap' for Ukraine," *The Verge*, March 5, 2022, www.theverge.com/2022/3/4/22962384/snapchat-heatmap-ukraine-disabled-privacy-advertising.

8 Mark Latonero and Paula Kift, "On Digital Passages and Borders: Refugees and the New Infrastructure of Movement and Control," *Social Media + Society* (2018): 1–11.

9 Sandra Ponzanesi and Koen Leurs, "On Digital Crossings in Europe," *Crossings: Journal of Migration & Culture* 5, no. 1 (2014): 15.

10 Koen Leurs and Madhuri Prabhakar, "Doing Digital Migration Studies: Methodological Considerations for an Emerging Research Focus," in *Qualitative Research in European Migration Studies*, edited by Ricard Zapata-Barrero and Evren Yalaz (Cham, Switzerland: Springer, IMISCOE Research Series, 2018), 260.

11 Alan McKee, *Textual Analysis: A Beginner's Guide* (London: Sage Publications, 2003), 1.

12 Jonathan Clayton, Hereward Holland, and Tim Gaynor, "Over One Million Sea Arrivals Reach Europe in 2015," UNHCR, December 30, 2015, www.unhcr.org/news/stories/over-one-million-sea-arrivals-reach-europe-2015.

13 Bishnupriya Ghosh, "A Sensible Politics: Image Operations of Europe's Refugee Crisis," in *Moving Images: Mediating Migration as Crisis*, edited by Krista Lynes, Tyler Morgenstern, and Ian Alan Paul (New York: Columbia University Press, 2020), 57–70.

14 Eszter Zimanyi, "Digital Transience: Emplacement and Authorship in Refugee Selfies," *Media Fields Journal* no. 12 (2017): 1–16, http://mediafieldsjournal.org/digital-transience/.

15 Emma Hinchife, "Instagram Is Killing Photo Maps," *Mashable*, September 6, 2016, http://mashable.com/2016/09/06/instagram-kills-photo-maps/.

16 I discuss more of Amer's selfies in "Digital Transience." In that essay, I reproduced a screenshot of Amer's Facebook post containing the same image, with his permission. On Facebook, Amer did not include a caption alongside the photo.

17 Paula Hoffmeyer-Zlotnik and Marlene Stiller, "Conditions in Reception Facilities," AIDA (Asylum Information Database), April 6, 2023, https://asylumineurope.org/reports/country/germany/reception-conditions/housing/conditions-reception-facilities/.

18 I expand this argument in Zimanyi, "Digital Transience."
19 Tom Divon and Moa Eriksson Krutrök, "TikTok(ing) Ukraine: Meme-Based Expressions of Cultural Trauma on Social Media," in *Media and the War in Ukraine*, edited by Mette Mortensen and Mervi Pantti (Bristol: Peter Lang, 2023), 119, 126.
20 See AJLabs, "Israel-Gaza War in Maps and Charts: Live Tracker," Al Jazeera, accessed March 22, 2024, www.aljazeera.com/news/longform/2023/10/9/israel-hamas-war-in-maps-and-charts-live-tracker; and Aya Batrway, "Gaza's Death Toll Now Exceeds 30,000. Here's Why It's an Incomplete Count," NPR, February 29, 2024, www.npr.org/2024/02/29/1234159514/gaza-death-toll-30000-palestinians-israel-hamas-war.
21 Mohammed Hussein, Mohammed Haddad, and Jadd Chahal, "Nowhere Safe in Gaza: How Israeli Attacks Have Pushed More Than 1.5 Million People into Rafah," Al Jazeera, March 4, 2024, https://interactive.aljazeera.com/aje/2024/displacement-israel-war-on-gaza-no-safe-place/.
22 Nidal Al-Mughrabi, "Fighting, Fuel Shortages Knock Out Gaza's Second-Largest Hospital," Reuters, February 19, 2024, www.reuters.com/world/middle-east/gazas-second-largest-hospital-completely-out-service-health-ministry-says-2024-02-18/. See also Edith M. Lederer, "A Quarter of Gaza's Population Is One Step Away from Famine and Aid Trucks Are Looted, UN Says," Associated Press, February 28, 2024, https://apnews.com/article/israel-palestinians-un-humanitarian-famine-gaza-malnutrition-cf622f843fe531fb6dbd5657a39d6b49.
23 Ruth Michaelson, "'I'm Not Just Covering The News—I'm Living It': Gaza's Citizen Journalists Chronicling Life In War," *The Guardian*, December 12, 2023, www.theguardian.com/world/2023/dec/12/gaza-citizen-journalists-war-footage-israel.
24 Nisreen Shehada (@nisreendiary), "Join me for a baking day in the tent," Instagram, January 23, 2024, www.instagram.com/reel/C2bp-bR0xgt/?igsh=MWowbDIydWw4cXMzdA==.
25 David Mack, "TikTokers Are Showing Their Typical Daily Life, But There's Nothing Typical about It," *Buzzfeed News*, August 30, 2022, www.buzzfeednews.com/article/davidmack/tiktok-day-in-life-videos-parody.

15

Reading the Effects Program

The Mission: Impossible *Series and Special/Visual Effects Discourse*

JULIE TURNOCK

Turnock turns ostensibly to special effects in blockbuster movies, focusing in particular on those in the Mission: Impossible *franchise; however, Turnock counsels us to look beyond the effects in the films alone, instead putting forward a mode of analysis that considers the entire "effects program," including producers' and advertisers' rhetorical positioning of those effects as vital contributions to their meaning.*

"People actually fall for this s***."
—August Walker (Henry Cavill) in *Mission: Impossible—Fallout* (dir. Christopher McQuarrie, 2018)

In a well-known sequence in *Mission: Impossible—Rogue Nation* (dir. Christopher McQuarrie, 2015), Tom Cruise appears to be hanging off the side of an airplane as it takes off, carrying him thousands of feet into the air.[1] A well-circulated behind-the-scenes video for the film available on YouTube is introduced with a title card stating, "Why do the stunts look real? Because they ARE real." The video shows this sequence with carefully edited production footage alongside talking-head interviews with the stunt coordinator and effects supervisor as well as Tom Cruise's voiceover to "prove" that Cruise really did the stunt that he appears to do in the movie. The shot is complete with camera code information and a counter bar at the bottom of the frame, suggesting we are looking at raw production footage.[2] Simple logic that the film's megastar cannot be endangered, plus knowledge of how films' insurance policies dictate what stunts actors can and cannot perform, should be enough to make one doubt the *Mission: Impossible* production's claims.³ However, it is not the purpose of this chapter to establish that Tom Cruise did not "really" hang on to the side of an airplane as it actually left the ground as it appears to do in the movie. Rather, it is to acknowledge that even when we are not sure of the effects used, we can recognize the contexts where effects are most likely to be used, for purposes of spectacle, danger, budget, or convenience. Moreover, even if the effects are imperceptible, when we analyze such "impossible" sequences in the film as part of the diegetic (on-screen) narrative, we inevitably bring to it paratextual information about the film's making.⁴ French literary theorist Gérard Genette identifies paratexts as elements that accompany the text but are outside of the text proper. For example, the reader brings certain associations and interpretations to the book through the title, author's name, publisher, introduction, marketing material, blurbs, and so forth.⁵ Likewise, most film viewers bring an interpretive schema through what they already know of the star, director, franchise, trailer, poster, publicity on social media, and so forth. The *Mission: Impossible* series is an appropriate object to demonstrate that when we analyze films in terms of their special/visual effects work, narrative, effects technology, publicity, and other paratexts cannot be easily separated.⁶ Rhetorically, the *Mission: Impossible* franchise does not just use effects but also has a lot to say about them. This is especially apt in a film series that is about a secret paramilitary force that, alongside action derring-do, uses visual trickery including high-tech gadgets and illusionistic technology (most famously, identity-changing masks) to commit subterfuge against its shadowy enemy.

How does one study and analyze a film's effects, especially the invisible or disavowed ones, in the face of all this rhetorical confusion? Rather than see the often-misleading effects publicity rhetoric as distracting, instead I see it as a necessary part of understanding and analyzing what we are seeing on the screen. While I will be pulling examples from the series of action films starring Tom Cruise, we can use the method deployed here for other action films and other kinds of films as well (for which I will provide examples at the end of the chapter). In order to generate meaning from these sequences, I propose that the media scholar combines narrative thematics with publicity discourse and the film's on-screen effects to produce a film's (or series of films') special/visual effects "program." The effects program is generated through textual analysis, which may or may not be at odds with the filmmakers' intentions.

The visible effects work in films, what we might call the movies' "wow" moments, such as exploding fireballs, thrilling action sequences, and imaginary creatures and locations, is often received by critics as "empty" spectacle.[7] Nevertheless, filmmaking teams and effects artists in their public statements frequently contradict this assertion, insisting their job is to "tell a story" and "support the director's vision." Certainly, as we shall see, on various levels, movies tell a story with their effects. However, the relationship between effects work and narrative is not always so direct or even deliberate—nor so visible. The effects program we as media scholars produce through analysis is sometimes in harmony with the explicit narrative but sometimes in conflict with it. Perhaps perversely, the more profuse and cutting edge a film's technology is, the more antitechnology the film's narrative is likely to be. From the killer humanoid robots in *Metropolis* (dir. Fritz Lang, 1927) and *Terminator 2: Judgment Day* (dir. James Cameron, 1991); the valorization of plucky technological underdogs in *Star Wars* (dir. George Lucas, 1977) and *Avatar* (dir. James Cameron, 2009); and the organic-seeming but technologically engineered humanoids and creatures of *Blade Runner* (dir. Ridley Scott, 1982) and *Jurassic Park* (dir. Steven Spielberg, 1993); to the terrifying AI in *2001: A Space Odyssey* (dir. Stanley Kubrick, 1968), *The Matrix* (dir. Lana and Lilly Wachowski, 1999), and *Mission: Impossible–Dead Reckoning Part I* (dir. Christopher McQuarrie, 2023), visualizing new effects technologies usually means assuaging audiences' anxieties about those visualized technologies by making "humanity" triumph over "artificial" technology by the time the credits roll.

Nevertheless, "artificially" generated (whether digital or analog) effects elements are overwhelmingly designed to match or complement ("profilmic") live-action footage, with the ethos "If *x* (an alien, a spaceship, etc.) existed in the world and then was photographed, how would that look?" In other words, the effects should look seamless—as if filmed without effects, even in imaginary or impossible contexts like fantasy realms or nonexistent creatures. As many effects artists say, if they have done their job correctly most of their work goes unnoticed as effects. Effects-heavy film productions likewise reinforce this seamlessness ethos in their publicity rhetoric by deciding how much and what information to release and promote. In the late 1990s and early 2000s, digital technology's novelty era, the productions of the *Star Wars* prequels and the *Lord of the Rings* films, for example, released hours of behind-the-scenes videos (as DVD extras) to promote their cutting-edge digital technology and CGI (computer-generated imagery) creatures and environments. In a later era of greater CGI fatigue, *Star Wars: Episode VII—The Force Awakens* (dir. J. J. Abrams, 2015) and its sequels limited much of their effects publicity to practical effects and location shots, downplaying their (considerable) CGI. Likewise, many productions, including those in the *Fast and Furious* franchise, Christopher Nolan films, and *Top Gun: Maverick* (dir. Joseph Kosinski, 2022), all films with thousands of effects shots as well as large effects teams, put out carefully worded statements and selective video that claim minimal (and even no) CGI was used in the films.[8] The successful execution of the seamlessness ethos makes these statements plausible.

Although all productions pick and choose what effects to publicly highlight or not, as we saw at the beginning of this chapter, the *Mission: Impossible* films go to lengths of misinformation that are unusually elaborate. Moreover, analysis of key moments across the film franchise strongly suggests the production delights in hoodwinking its audience as much as its audience apparently delights in being fooled. Nevertheless, the production's rhetorical trickery reaches toward the nearly impossible—convincing viewers that we are not seeing any or minimal effects work, despite what they think they know about effects work and simple logic. This is hand in hand with the overall *Mission: Impossible* public-relations agenda, of which the effects are a part.

In other words, when it comes to analyzing effects discourse, the films' public rhetoric plays a crucial role in what we think we are seeing on the screen. The particular challenge of analyzing visual effects sequences in movies is both their obvious visibility (material like life-threatening stunts that would indeed be "impossible") and their aesthetic of seamless invisibility. In late 2023, Danish effects artist and VFX supervisor Jonas Ussing posted a video essay, or YouTube explainer, titled "'No CGI' is Really Just INVISIBLE CGI" in response to recent behind-the-scenes promotional videos and production claims that denied use of CGI for films such as *Gran Turismo* (dir. Neill Blomkamp, 2023) and *Oppenheimer* (dir. Christopher Nolan, 2023). Using the Tom Cruise vehicle *Top Gun: Maverick* as his primary example, the video essay carefully breaks down the actual copious use of CGI in this film and many others as well as the misleading, if not fallacious, discursive strategies productions use to suggest digital effects were done profilmically "for real."[9] This and similar videos and testimony from effects artists are important in our analysis to help us recognize the role of promotional information and misinformation in what we are seeing on the screen.

Effects Analysis Methodology

The *Mission: Impossible* series demonstrates how the promotional, technological, and narrative thematic forms of discourse find reflections of one another in the films' many effects-heavy sequences. However, it may be helpful to start with a more familiar schema. The most typical effects program pattern deployed by effects productions (particularly in the digital age) can be generalized as follows:

1) Prime the audience for the "wow" (e.g., a new technology, a beloved character, a fantasy locale) before the film.
2) Diegetically reveal the wow.
3) Domesticate the wow through repetition in the narrative integration.
4) Interrogate the wow through the film's thematics.

The 1993 film *Jurassic Park* provides an emblematic example:

Prerelease publicity touts CGI innovation: The film's prerelease publicity primed moviegoers in featurettes, magazine articles, trailers, and interviews to expect digitally generated dinosaurs from Steven Spielberg, the director known for reliably providing entertainment, popular artistry, and technological wonder.

Spectacular diegetic sequence early in the film reveals the new CGI technology to both the characters (as diegetic wonder) and the viewers (as technological wonder): The first dinosaur is presented to the guest paleontologists (Laura Dern and Sam Neill) as a spectacle that turns their heads and leaves their mouths agape, anticipating the response of the publicity-primed movie audience who will be seeing a fully CGI, organic creature in action for the first time.

Repetition of display of the new technology in equally spectacular but more narratively integrated sequences: After the initial wonderment reveal, the dinosaurs exist matter-of-factly (though menacingly) in the film's diegesis as quasi characters. Most notably, in the T-Rex attack, the dinosaur appearing does not provoke the response "Wow, look at the dinosaur!" but "Eek! The dinosaur is coming to kill us!" where the dinosaur plays the "role" not only of spectacle to be gaped at but of active antagonist.

Finally, throughout the film, the script and the narrative repeat thematically the stakes of the new CGI technology, both diegetically and extranarratively. This can be summed up by the famous quote uttered by Ian Malcolm (Jeff Goldblum): "[The] scientists were so preoccupied with whether or not they could that they didn't stop to think if they should."

Mission: Impossible in Action

The consistently successful *Mission: Impossible* franchise takes advantage of viewers' familiarity with the pattern exemplified in *Jurassic Park* for product differentiation: 1) The prerelease strategy denies copious use of typical CGI "tricks," insisting the film's stunts are done "for real"; 2) diegetic sequences reveal how the team is tricking the villains; and 3) undivulged tricks are re-concealed as "real," thereby 4) thematically demonstrating to the viewer over and over that they are being tricked and should not trust what they see.

The *Mission: Impossible* series serves as a metonym for the broader way effects material within films acts as a push/pull, displaying the films' effects before the viewers' very eyes in order to conceal them. In fact, despite the "We're doing all these effects for real" publicity rhetoric, films in the franchise consistently show the characters within the diegesis not only that they are being fooled, but the methods used to fool them.

The *Mission: Impossible* blockbuster film series has been promoted nearly since the series's inception as staging high-octane action sequences that appear to put its star in actual physical danger. This began in earnest with its second installment, the John Woo–directed *Mission: Impossible II* (2000), when producer Paula Wagner insisted in *Entertainment Weekly* that "it was all Tom up there," doing the rock-climbing stunt, as well as "dangling from a helicopter six stories above the ground."[10] By 2018's *Mission: Impossible—Fallout*, the "Tom Cruise is willing to die for your entertainment" and "These effects were done for real" promotional language had solidified into generally held fact, one that journalists reporting on the film do not appear to question.[11] However, this practice performs another kind of magic trick: erasing the actual (and largely nonunionized) effects artists and stunt performers who complete thousands of hours to make Cruise and the films look good. This is despite the obvious presence of thousands of effects artists' names in the credits of all of these films. Moreover, investment in the films' own narratives relies upon discourse about the *Mission: Impossible* franchise taking the viewer beyond willful suspension of disbelief. The moviegoing public clearly wants to believe that Cruise and the production were really performing dangerous stunts, and the production publicity finds advantage in catering to that belief.

The *Mission: Impossible* film series (based on the 1960s television series of the same name) follows the exploits of the secret paragovernmental group the Impossible Mission Force (IMF)—as the exposition explains in one of the films, the IMF "operates outside of the [intelligence] community and answers directly to the president." The "impossible missions," such as avoiding anarchists' nuclear attack, preventing a global pandemic caused by germ warfare, battling shadowy arms dealers, and taking control of omniscient AI programs, comprise the bulk of the action of the films. The team is led by Tom Cruise's Ethan Hunt, who is aided by a rotating list of operatives, allies, and frenemies. To battle their foes, Hunt and the IMF deploy a combination of advanced technology, physical daring, and theatrical subterfuge.

The films' action requires a great deal of effects work, some of which is displayed to the viewer as effects, some of which remains invisible. In every installment, the film shows the IMF team on a mission that involves deceiving a villain, while showing us, the viewers, how it was done and what technology was used to achieve it. Frequently, there is an action set piece in which the ruse is in danger of discovery and the team frantically scrambles to pull it off. Once the objective of the trick has been achieved, it is often then revealed to the villain, so they realize exactly how they have been deceived. These sequences typically appear in the first part of the film, establishing a trust with the audience and suggesting that we, on the side of the IMF, are privy to their tactics. It is worth noting that another word for "trick" is "stunt." For much of the remainder of the film, the production then takes advantage of that trust to display many action sequences that purport to show Cruise doing his own stunts—complete with the metatexual publicity information that states he has done so. When the film's diegesis does not display for us the trick, logically that suggests the actors really did do it for real. Moreover, since we are on the side of the IMF and not the villain, we believe we are not the ones being tricked. We might characterize the stratagem of the overall effects program in the series as a kind of close-up magic trick (something Cruise is known to enjoy).[12] First, the production shows us a technology it is using, misdirecting us, and then it uses a different, hidden technology or technique to pull off a bigger trick.

Some quick examples of this sleight of hand appear in *Mission: Impossible—Ghost Protocol* (dir. Brad Bird, 2011) when Ethan and teammate Benji (Simon Pegg) infiltrate the Kremlin to get information on the villain. To conceal their presence, they erect a pop-up semitranslucent screen with a digitally rendered projection of the hallway that, from the guard's perspective, conceals the agents' presence.[13] Using a sound device to distract the guard, they move closer and closer until, having fooled his eye and ear, they access the vault from behind the screen unbeknownst to him. Another example is the precredit sequence in *Fallout*, in which Ethan and Luther (Ving Rhames) must trap a villain into believing that his plan to detonate three nuclear bombs has succeeded, so they can learn his plan and foil it. The sequence starts with real-world (extradiegetic) CNN news anchor Wolf Blitzer reporting on air about the coordinated attacks (complete with "live footage") in Rome, Jerusalem, and Mecca. We the viewers also think this is "for real" within the movie's diegesis, until Ethan and Luther have extracted the needed information from the mark. Then, the room's walls fall away, revealing it as a set, complete with Benji taking off his Wolf Blitzer mask and voicebox.

With the Wolf Blitzer mask in mind, perhaps the most emblematic of the *Mission: Impossible* tricks is the consistent trope of face replacement. In fact, the "mask gag," where a character is revealed in the diegesis to be wearing a fully convincing mask and voicebox, is the recurring signature trope of the *Mission: Impossible* franchise. As digital technology presented diegetically as physical, the mask gag appears, often more than once, in every installment of the series. It is the visible ruse that allows us as viewers to feel party to the IMF's tricks of the trade. Many characters are eventually revealed to be concealing their identities behind the ingenious mask, but, most often, the mask-wearer is revealed to be

Hunt. And again, the mask gag most consistently appears in the films' first act. *Mission: Impossible II* already inverts the expectations in the precredit scene by revealing that it is the villain (Dougray Scott) wearing an Ethan Hunt mask to gain the trust of a scientist and then steal a vial of a dangerous virus, setting the action into motion. The very next scene cuts to the "real" Hunt, and purportedly the "real" Tom Cruise, performing a "without a net" rock-climbing stunt, as the publicity had it.[14]

The trope of the face replacement in the mask gag is a perfect example of how the films' strategy is to reveal the trick in one place so as to deny it in the many others. In conventional effects work, digital face replacement is a commonly used (but minimally publicized) technique, most typically to put the star actor's face over the face of a stunt performer, making it appear as though the star actor is performing the stunt.[15] For example, during the motorcycle chase through the streets of Paris in *Fallout*, if one looks carefully one can see the subtle wobbling of Tom Cruise's face as "he" races down the narrow streets as evidence of the digital face replacement (as one of many digital techniques needed for this and every other action sequence in the very dangerous scene).[16] The concealment of identities behind convincing masks is a nice metaphor for what the spy game is all about, seeming to give the viewer a behind-the-scenes look at espionage. However, in special/visual effects analysis, we can take the trope of the mask further when we combine the textual material we see on the screen and the film's extratextual publicity material about its production.

For example, one sequence in *Mission: Impossible—Dead Reckoning, Part I* takes digital face replacement as a concealed effect and turns it into diegetic text that we can analyze as part of the film series' effects program, while remaining a concealed effect elsewhere in the film. In the immediate postcredit sequence about thirty minutes into the film, Ethan and the IMF team are at the Abu Dhabi airport (actually filmed largely in Birmingham, UK) attempting to secure the second half of a key from a mystery buyer that will allow the bearer exclusive control of a powerful AI called "The Entity." It is worth noting that one of the reasons the AI is depicted as dangerous is that it can appear to alter reality: it can manipulate any computer interface to display whatever the AI wants. At the same time, Hunt must elude the CIA operatives also on the scene trying to take him in. As Hunt attempts to meet up with the mystery buyer (among several action threads happening simultaneously, including the defusing of a nuclear bomb, a meet-cute with Grace [the female love interest, played by Hayley Atwell], and a glimpse of a believed-dead nemesis), computer expert Luther hacks into the CIA facial recognition software they are using to find Hunt and swaps his face with that of random travelers, causing the agents to stop decoys instead of Hunt. Hunt wears "smart" aviator sunglasses with a heads-up display, through which Luther feeds him information about his surroundings using facial recognition software and information that appears to be "raw" data they are collecting from travelers around Hunt. The CIA agents are chasing decoys, but the guy they think is Cruise is not; instead, it is Cruise's face on a decoy's body. Humorously, the CIA agent played by Shea Whigham even tries to pull at one of the decoy's faces to be sure he is not Hunt in the kind of realistic mask we have seen throughout the series. At the same time, the AI "Entity" is also digitally face-swapping and manipulating the IMF team's visual feed to confuse them as well. Once again, in an early sequence, the film acknowledges digital face replacement is going on, but delimits it diegetically to the airport sequence. Later, when Cruise's face is (likely) digitally replaced during stunt action sequences (as well as touched up cosmetically), we are supposed to simply believe what we see is real, even though everything in the film's narrative and the film's publicity paratexts suggest we should distrust it.[17]

But why go to such lengths, even as far as outright falsehoods? At the premiere for *Dead Reckoning Part I*, when asked about the stunt work, Cruise responded, "That's just who I am. I'm always . . . you can see everything. That's why I don't have a stunt double. I do it all myself. . . . And I'm just interested, how do I invest an audience in a story? How do I invest them and put them on the edge of their seat?"[18] It is unclear whether the production's impulse can be characterized better as "A sucker is born every minute," or as "Give the people what they want." Nevertheless, the production rhetoric and publicity strategy see a clear connection between belief in the stunt's perceived realness and the viewer's investment. Clearly, as Cruise suggests, we want to believe and invest ourselves in the story, to be on the edge of our seats. While it is a savvy and surprisingly successful strategy, it is also treating the fans like the villain against whom the trick is being played, rather than the IMF allies they feel themselves to be.

Conclusion

Special/visual effects work exists at the intersection of what the viewer knows, what the viewer thinks they know, and what they can see with their eyes. While most films engage in similar trickery to some degree, the *Mission: Impossible* series works the confusion at the heart of this intersection to a more complex degree. However, in the method of analysis I call the special/visual effects program, the effects publicity rhetoric, as part of the film's on-screen effects thematics, can be applied beyond the *Mission: Impossible* franchise. For example, *Terminator 2: Judgment Day*'s "liquid metal" T-1000 emblematizes the constantly shifting potential futures the characters are fighting. More contradictorily, at the technical level *King Kong* (dir. Merian C. Cooper and Ernest B. Schoedsack, 1933) revels in the mixing of styles and approaches, with animated stop-motion puppets mixed with live-action actors, animation mixed with live action, and different composite techniques. However, on the level of the narrative, the possible mixing of the giant ape Kong with human female Ann (Fay Wray) is played as titillating, but also clearly unnatural and horrific, revealing a divided message about heterogeneity and hybridity.

Less obviously effects-intensive films can also be analyzed via this methodology. Publicity around Alfonso Cuarón's 2018 *Roma* centered around the digitally recreated Mexico City neighborhood of the director's youth. The vagaries of CGI-reconstructed memory draw attention to the director's filtering his boyhood experiences through the focus on his indigenous nanny. The set-extending technology allows Cuarón to reexperience his own past by "putting on" another (gendered, classed) body. In the Best Picture Oscar–winning *Parasite* (dir. Bong Joon-ho, 2019), publicity images show that the exterior of the Parks' palatial modern urban oasis was only built as a one-story set, with green-screen extensions for the upper levels and its environs. We can understand the Park house as a fantasy extension of the hardscrabble Kim family's imagination, a projection of the easy life modern capitalism displays for them as an unobtainable mirage, and, moreover, cinema's ability to not just conjure but instigate simplistic fantasies of affluence.

Because nearly all movies are made with varying amounts of effects manipulation, this chapter shows how the media scholar can identify and analyze an effects program for nearly any film, both when its effects are well publicized and when they are not.

Mission: Impossible Filmography

Mission: Impossible (dir. Brian DePalma, 1996)
Mission: Impossible II (dir. John Woo, 2000)
Mission: Impossible III (dir. J. J. Abrams, 2006)
Mission: Impossible—Ghost Protocol (dir. Brad Bird, 2011)
Mission: Impossible—Rogue Nation (dir. Christopher McQuarrie, 2015)
Mission: Impossible—Fallout (dir. Christopher McQuarrie, 2018)
Mission: Impossible—Dead Reckoning Part I (dir. Christopher McQuarrie, 2023)

Notes

1. A complete list of all movies in the *Mission: Impossible* franchise, their directors, and their years of release is included at the end of the chapter.
2. Emphasis in original. The video has had over ten million views as of the time of writing. Mission Impossible, "Mission: Impossible Rogue Nation—Stunt Featurette," July 13, 2015, YouTube, 1 min., https://www.youtube.com/watch?v=afS5ks54tms.
3. However, perhaps the strongest evidence that the production is not totally forthcoming comes from the beginning of an article on *Rogue Nation* in effects industry publication *Cinefex* that starts with a disclaimer regarding the images the production sent them:
   > What we were provided, instead, were stock presskit images, including non-effects movie star shots, artfully faked still composites, and a few digitally falsified "behind the scenes" photos. After countless requests for reconsideration by us and by others on our behalf, all to no avail, we are forced to admit defeat for the first time in our 35-year history. We could have saved face by pulling the article entirely. But it's . . . a fine film with great effects, and so we are going ahead with it. Rather than insult our readers by illustrating the article with patently dishonest photography, however, we have opted to present it without imagery.

   See Jody Duncan, "Keeping it Real: *Mission: Impossible—Rogue Nation*," *Cinefex* 143 (October 2015): 97.
4. Analyzing the relation between effects work in blockbuster films and the promotional discourse is fairly rare. See excellent studies by Lisa Bode, *Making Believe: Screen Performance and Special Effects in Popular Cinema* (New Brunswick, NJ: Rutgers University Press, 2017); and Tanine Allison, "Race and the Digital Face: Facial (Mis)Recognition in *Gemini Man*," *Convergence* 27, no. 4 (2021): 999–1017.

5 See Gérard Genette, *Paratexts: Thresholds of Interpretation*, translated by Jane E. Lewin (Cambridge: Cambridge University Press, 1997): 1–2.

6 While industry nomenclature may vary, I use the term "special/visual effects" to honor the history of the term, as well as to retain the specialness and visibility of effects artistry and labor when conglomerate rhetoric attempts to render it invisible. For more, see Charles Keil and Kristen Whissel, eds., *Editing and Special/Visual Effects* (New Brunswick, NJ: Rutgers University Press, 2016). The ideas presented about photorealism, spectacle, narrative thematics, effects programs, and so forth, are derived from my previous books: *Plastic Reality: Special Effects, Technology, and the Emergence of 1970s Blockbuster Aesthetics* (New York: Columbia University Press, 2015) and *The Empire of Effects: Industrial Light and Magic and the Rendering of Realism* (Austin: University of Texas Press, 2022).

7 *The New Yorker*'s Richard Brody is perhaps the most high-profile critic fond of castigating films for their "empty" effects spectacle. See Brody, "Where 'Godzilla' Meets 'The Immigrant,'" *New Yorker*, May 29, 2014, www.newyorker.com/culture/richard-brody/where-godzilla-meets-the-immigrant; and "The Empty Astonishments of 'X-Men: Apocalypse,'" *New Yorker*, May 29, 2016, www.newyorker.com/culture/richard-brody/the-empty-astonishments-of-x-men-apocalypse.

8 For examples, see: Dirk Libbey, "Fast X's Director Reveals How Much of That 'Giant Bomb' Rolling Scene Was Done Practically, And His Answer Is Shocking," *CINEMABLEND*, May 25, 2023, www.cinemablend.com/movies/fast-xs-director-reveals-how-much-of-that-giant-bomb-rolling-scene-was-done-practically-and-his-answer-is-shocking; Jazz Tangcay, "How 'Oppenheimer' Pulled Off an Atomic Bomb Explosion Without CGI: A Giant Aquarium, Balloons and More," *Variety*, July 22, 2023, https://variety.com/2023/artisans/news/how-oppenheimer-pulled-off-trinity-test-sequence-1235676487/; and Kara Warner, "Top Gun: Maverick's Insane Aerial Stunts: How They Pulled Them Off (With Expert Pilots, Not CGI)," *People*, June 5, 2022, https://people.com/movies/top-gun-maverick-insane-aerial-stunts-how-they-pulled-them-off/.

9 The Movie Rabbit Hole, "'NO CGI' Is Really Just INVISIBLE CGI (1/4)," October 27, 2023, YouTube, 16 min., 29 sec., https://www.youtube.com/watch?v=7ttG9oraCNo. For more on this topic, see my own *Empire of Effects*; Leon Gurevitch, "The Straw That Broke the Tiger's Back?: Skilled Labor, Social Networks, and Protest in the Digital Workshops of the World," in *The Routledge Companion to Labor and Media* (London: Routledge, 2015), https://doi.org/10.4324/9780203404119; and Michael Curtin and John Vanderhoef, "A Vanishing Piece of the Pi: The Globalization of Visual Effects Labor," *Television & New Media* 16, no. 3 (March 1, 2015): 219–39, https://doi.org/10.1177/1527476414524285.

10 Liane Bonin, "The Truth behind *M:I-2*'s Most Dangerous Stunt," *Entertainment Weekly*, May 17, 2000, https://ew.com/article/2000/05/17/truth-behind-mi-2s-most-dangerous-stunt/.

For differing effects discourse regarding the first *Mission: Impossible* film, see Mark Cotta Vaz, "Cruising the Digital Backlot: *Mission: Impossible*" *Cinefex* 67 (September 1996): 90–105.

11   For a few of the countless examples, see Ben Kenigsberg, "Tom Cruise's Most Dangerous Stunts in 'Mission: Impossible,'" *New York Times*, July 30, 2018, www.nytimes.com/2018/07/30/movies/mission-impossible-fallout-stunts-tom-cruise.html; and Carly Thomas, "12 of Tom Cruise's Most Jaw-Dropping Stunts," *Hollywood Reporter*, July 20, 2023, www.hollywoodreporter.com/lists/tom-cruise-most-intense-stunts/.

12   Cruise even performs close-up magic to "Grace" in *Dead Reckoning Part I*.

13   While this imaginary technology is obviously akin to rear projection, the diegetic technology also has parallax-compensating abilities, an actual technology ILM was developing at the time, eventually introduced as under the name Stagecraft in 2019.

14   For a contrary account, see Charles Arthur, "Mission Impossible II Climbing Scenes Special," *UK Climbing*, July 9, 2000, www.ukclimbing.com/articles/features/mission_impossible_ii_climbing_scenes_special-18.

15   Digital face replacement's earliest known and acknowledged use appears in *Jurassic Park,* but it began to be commonplace in the mid-2000s.

16   Although it is not acknowledged by the production, this sequence would have also required a fair number of invisible effects with CGI cars, motorcycles, pedestrians, and so forth, to complete the sequence within acceptable safety parameters. Moreover, as a VFX breakdown reel for *The Killer* (dir. David Fincher, 2023) makes evident, the production does not need to put even a stunt performer on a motorcycle to create a convincingly photorealistic action sequence. VFX Wolves, "The Killer | VFX Breakdown by Wylie Co.," November 27, 2023, YouTube, 1 min., 35 sec., https://www.youtube.com/watch?v=ss3c9a-BTn8.

17   It is worth pointing out the irony that Tom Cruise is frequently the target of unauthorized deepfake videos putting his likeness on other's bodies. For more on this topic see Lisa Bode, Dominic Lees, and Dan Golding, "The Digital Face and Deepfakes on Screen," *Convergence* 27, no. 4 (August 1, 2021): 849–54, https://doi.org/10.1177/13548565211034044.

18   Associated Press, "Tom Cruise Says Fans Will Never See Him Using a Stunt Double," June 23, 2023, YouTube, 32 sec., www.youtube.com/watch?v=TlgEJ57H-i4.

PART IV

Textual Analysis Across Texts

Introduction

A particular challenge with textual analysis in the digital era is posed by the large number of networked texts. From the advent of the hyperlink onwards, digital textualities entail connection and imbrication. All texts—not just digital ones—rest on networks of intertextuality, and all respond to one another to one degree or another, but the digital era puts this basic situation into hyperdrive. And thus, if textual analysis has often been envisioned as a contained activity, involving analyst and text together in solitary congress, the digital era is more chaotic, but therefore also perhaps more exciting, since it demands that textual analysis occur *across* texts. The chapters in this section all engage in such an endeavor.

The first two chapters focus on digital entities that illustrate the dilemma and the challenge of the networked text par excellence, as Anirban K. Baishya considers the meme and Raven Maragh-Lloyd considers the hashtag. Memes and hashtags each bring together and unite many texts, ensuring that all meaning is at some level premised on the responses to and by other texts, and by the rhizomatic whole constantly being created and added to by new entrants. Baishya and Maragh-Lloyd, therefore, each offer approaches to the textual analysis of memes and hashtags that center their lived, active, networked textualities.

However, if the digital era demands that we think across digital texts, it might also encourage us to think about how to similarly consider all texts as beholden to networks of meaning. The next four chapters in the section, therefore, each innovate textual analysis to account for such networks. Laurie Ouellette offers the notion of an "emblematic text," one that is richly meaningful precisely because it is not alone, and is instead a uniquely helpful entry point to analysis of a genre or other network. Then, Kyra Hunting and Daphne Gershon each encourage analysts to explore patterns and situations across texts, using the tool kit of textual analysis but applying it to threads that weave in and out of various texts, with Hunting looking at protogenres in children's television, and Gershon considering narrative situations that repeat across multiple texts. Finally, Henry Jenkins combines various intertextual, paratextual, and genre-based approaches to transmedia texts that were from the outset written across texts and that therefore require analysis across texts.

As Gray and Gershon's introduction notes, the waning of truly mass media may destabilize the rationale by which analysts focus on one text alone, at least if our analysis is premised on the power and reach of any given text. By contrast, though, each of these chapters relocates power and reaches across a network, and offers ways to use textual analysis to track that power. Textual analysis has been used far more often on a single text, but these chapters invite us to devise projects that move across and between texts.

16

"Such Amaze, Much Wow"

(Or How to Read a Meme)

ANIRBAN K. BAISHYA

Though memes are considered by many to be too small, too little, or too insignificant to be "read" with depth, Baishya considers the complex textuality of memes with a three-layered approach based on examining text, context, and intertext. He then applies this approach to locate meaning in the massively multi-authored, ever-developing string of texts that constitutes the "Doge" meme.

Wait . . . What?!

"WHO READS A MEME?!!! AND WHY?! Aren't they just silly little pictures?" Something along the lines of this outburst might have just gone through your mind when you opened this page and read the title. You wouldn't be to blame; memes are funny and fleeting, and there are far too many of them floating around. Once you get past that initial outburst, you might begin to ask other questions. How would you even *read* a meme? Sure, some of them have words—but hardly enough to make any narrative sense. "Reading" is something you might associate with novels, essays, newspapers, comic books—things that have an abundance of words. Or you might consider "reading" to belong to the domain of television shows, films, even music videos that, although they are moving images, allow for the careful construction of meaning through formal, time-based narration. But a meme? Isn't that too small, too little, or too insignificant to read? Again, you wouldn't be the first to ask these questions—I asked them myself when I first encountered memes.

There are at least two interrelated assumptions in the questions above—the first assumption is that memes are not substantially textual to require "reading." Elements of sound (such as a tune or a catchphrase) or human performance (such as internet "challenges") that can also constitute memes complicate things even further—memes don't always need to be primarily visual, let alone "textual," although we may recognize and encounter them visually or textually. Second, and relatedly, it is often also assumed that memes aren't serious enough to be read. After all, reading is thought of as something that requires time, deep engagement, intellectual stimulation, perhaps even solitude. While that is certainly true of some forms of reading, not all texts are read the same way. One could argue that reading a Charles Dickens novel, for example, is a different form of textual engagement than watching a Marvel superhero film. Different objects demand different reading strategies. Memes are a special kind of text that have emerged in the participatory structures of the internet, but they, too, are meaningful expressions of human thought, beliefs, and action. In the semiotic web, memes have emerged as a popular, forceful, and expressive mode that works primarily through humor, satire, and parody. We use them in our day-to-day interactions online, be it in "public" comments on social media posts or in our private messages with friends and family. Marketers use them to reach potential consumers, and their circulation has wide-ranging implications even in rather serious spheres of human activity such as politics and protest (think Pepe the Frog).[1] Memes are everywhere, and to fully understand the digital ecologies we inhabit, it is necessary for us to learn to read them.

The concept of memes first emerged in a nondigital context and was coined by the biologist Richard Dawkins in *The Selfish Gene* (1976). Dawkins used the term—a shortened version of the Greek word *mimeme*—to define units of cultural imitation. Notice that *mimeme* and "mimesis" (another word often used in relation to the arts) carry similar meanings—mimesis is copying or imitating, and *mimeme* refers to that which is copied (or replicated). In Dawkins's original conception, memes constitute a broad category of cultural life, including examples such as "tunes, ideas, catch-phrases, clothes, fashions, ways of making pots or of building arches."[2] While this is a useful starting point, Dawkins's concept is fairly broad and, more importantly, it assumes that these units of culture simply "propagate themselves . . . leaping from brain to brain" without accounting for individual agency.[3]

Memes, of course, work through imitation, replication, and repetition; however, user participation and agency are also key. Memes don't spread by themselves—they are spread by people who make active choices to replicate and spread them. As Ryan Milner points out, memes are, first and foremost, "premised on participation by reappropriation." This has implications for how we "read" memes. Milner continues, "When everyday members of the public contribute their small conversational strands to the vast cultural tapestry, they are memetically making their world."[4] Milner suggests that memes are not only constituents of participatory culture but also *textual* insofar as they are about meaning-making. Individual pieces of text, image, music, and performance don't constitute memes in and of themselves, but they become *memetic* (or meme-like) when enough users speak through (and about) them. Thus, to read memes textually, we first have to understand them as utterances in a cultural conversation.

Taking this idea further, Limor Shifman identifies three components of cultural imitation that we can observe in memes—content, form, and stance.[5] Content and form, respectively, refer to the things that constitute a text and the particular shape or arrangement of the text. We can understand this through nonmeme examples as well. A portrait by Rembrandt, a portrait by Vincent van Gogh, and a portrait by Pablo Picasso all have similar contents—a human face. But the way they approach the human face and arrange it visually (style, color, etc.) varies—they differ formally. Memes vary in similar ways—a popular meme might have a widely recognized textual punchline or idea, but each individual meme might deliver it differently. Some might be still images, some might be videos or GIFs, and some might feature different images (or other elements) reappropriating the main idea of a meme. The final element, stance, refers to the subjective position or leaning of a meme as well as those who "speak" through them—it refers to both the style and rhetoric of a meme in addition to the functions that a meme can perform. For instance, a meme can be parodic or subversive, and each individual utterance of the meme may use it for a different purpose. Considering all this, there's a lot to read in memes!

One way of reading memes is to map out the interaction of text and image and examine how meaning is created through the interplay of the various elements (or signs) in the meme. This method is not born-digital—advertisements, for example, have been read this way—but it remains crucial even for digital objects such as memes. In his influential essay "The Rhetoric of the Image," the French philosopher Roland Barthes describes how a single advertising image can encapsulate a whole universe of potential meanings.[6] There is a linguistic meaning that works through labels and printed text. Visually, there may be denoted (direct) meanings in the image as well as a set of connoted meanings (which are symbolic and open to interpretation).[7] For example, an advertisement for soap may show a red rose, with the denoted meaning being the literal rose itself, while connoted meanings might vary culturally (in many cultures, it may signify love or passion). Further, since such images are open to interpretation, text can sometimes play an anchoring role ("anchorage") to direct the viewer to a particular set of meanings, while at other times, text may facilitate the "relay" of meaning by interacting with images (something seen in comics).[8] This method works perfectly for still images and advertising images—but to use them in the context of digital objects such as memes, we have to modify this slightly. Why? Because internet memes create meaning often, if not always, through systems and structures of social collaboration and participation. Note that most popular memes have "templates" that any user can fill in and circulate. As internet users, we are often encouraged not just to see and consume memes, but to deploy them by sharing, to use them in reactions and comments, even to make them for others to use.

With that in mind, we can arrive at a three-pronged method that requires attention to text, context, and intertext. "Text" refers to the interplay between word and image in a meme as well as between words and images across memes—it includes both alphabetical text (i.e., written or printed text) and the broader understanding of text as a meaning-making system through which cultural objects are interpreted.[9] "Context" is constituted by the historical/cultural milieu in which the meme emerges. These factors imbue texts with very specific meanings—understanding them requires membership in specific cultural and subcultural formations. These meanings are fixed at the point of origin, but they may also be modified when they circulate—memes may be *recontextualized* to mean different things when they enter different cultural systems. Finally, "intertextuality" refers to the meme's ability to speak to other cultural objects; again, this may involve cultural relativism and require membership to codes of popular culture. Memes make references to other circulating media texts, including films, television shows, music, politics, news, and sometimes even other memes. This referential practice is not merely citational but is crucial to meaning-making itself. As Jonathan Gray observes, intertextuality refers to the "interdependence of all textual meaning upon the structures of meaning proposed by other texts."[10] While Gray's focus is on the role of parodic humor in television, Gregory Lukow and Steven Ricci have made similar observations about film genres, noting that the audience's pleasures are conditioned by an "inter-textual relay" in which the pleasure of recognition "reemerges from each viewing event into a continual circuit of exchange."[11] Likewise, memes too can fuel a "memetic relay" by invoking a range of references outside of the denoted content of the meme.[12] Sometimes the memes themselves are reappropriations of images and words from such cultural objects, while at other times, intertextual elements may be added in creative acts of juxtaposition and bricolage.

One crucial thing to remember is that while context and intertext refer to the meme's ability to speak to other cultural objects, they are not outside of "text" broadly conceived. Rather, all memes work through these three modalities (text, context, and intertext) to varying degrees, and what meanings a viewer/user uncovers depends on the level of their investment in the latter two elements. While meanings may be preassigned to certain memes, those meanings are constantly in flux and change based on where memes circulate, who circulates them, and to what end. To turn again to Barthes, no text is fully original—rather, "a text consists of multiple writings, proceeding from several cultures and entering into dialogue, into parody, into contestation."[13] For Barthes, it is not the author but the reader in whom the multiplicity of meaning exists—audiences make meanings out of texts. Barthes did not have memes in mind when he wrote this in "The Death of the Author." In the ecology of the semiotic web, we can supplement "readers" with "users"— this does not mean that all readers today are users, but the current shape of networked culture privileges interactive users as the direct addressees of platformed content (whether blogs, videos, streaming television, or memes). Readers *can* become users, and, as is often the case, many of us "read" on and "use" the affordances of platforms that shape our online experiences. Thus, if the semiotic web thrives on user participation, memes' meanings also derive partly from their audiences and users. So, a textual analysis of memes also needs to be able to account for their viral and participatory aspects.

Enough Already ... Just Tell Me How!

Fair enough! All of that may have sounded a little abstract, so let's get down to business. Let's take the famous "Doge" meme as an example. The meme emerged in 2010 when photographs of a Shiba Inu named Kabosu taken by her owner, Atsuko Sato, were appropriated from her personal blog and reposted on Reddit.[14] In subsequent years, many variations of the meme began to circulate on different social media platforms. Most of the photographs feature the original dog with funny expressions. Subsequent repostings of the image began to include near-nonsensical text in multicolored Comic Sans font, but many also feature the "Image Macro" format with text at the top and bottom halves of the image in Impact font (see figure 16.1).[15]

However, some also circulate without the original Shiba Inu image (being replaced with other dogs), and others include sound instead—more specifically sound of the word "Doge" being pronounced (or mispronounced, depending on how you see it) as *"dohj"* or *"dogeh."*[16] In these later examples, we already see the complexity of the meme as text—the original image does not circulate, but a fragment connected to it does (as sound, no less!). What, then, is the meme-text? The Shiba Inu? The image macros? Modifications in which the Shiba Inu is not even present? One answer is that all of these together are the "text" of the meme (or in memetic language, the "meme pool" itself is the text). Once the meme has circulated enough, none of these constitute the "original." All of them are variations of the same meme-text—not a narrative text, but a social (collaborative and participatory) text that includes a particular tone of humor, (most often) a dog (sometimes this Shiba Inu), and most often badly written text (but not always). As long as one or more of these elements are present, a media artifact can be recognized as a variation of the "Doge" text.

But what can we gain from this recognition? First, reading the Doge meme, trivial as it may seem, helps us understand how internet users

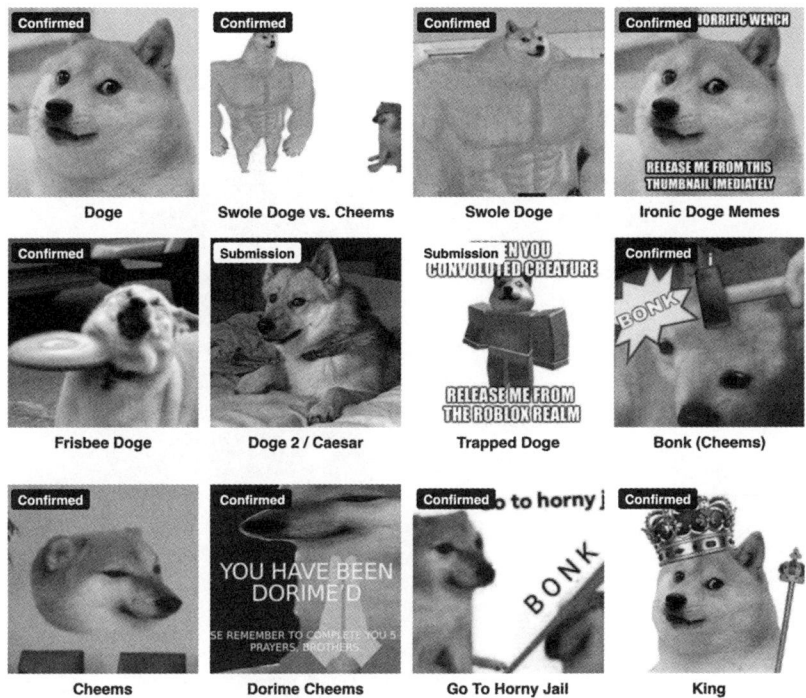

Figure 16.1: Variations of the Doge meme (screenshot of results for "Doge" in KnowYourMeme.com).

(people like you and me) make meaning on the internet through participatory action. At times, this may mean simply partaking in the (parodic) pleasures of meme-making and meme-circulation or perhaps the pleasure of intertextual knowledge (which itself may present as social capital or "clout" online). At other times, this may mean strategically using the preexisting meme text to deploy more serious messages clad in parodic garb. This does not mean that one variant is more valuable than the other—as objects of research (or reading), these variations are value neutral. But the "value" of a meme is also relative to the context of its deployment or use by a user (or users). In other words, its social value may change in the process of memetic relay. For the sake of simplicity, let's first focus on a purely visual example based on the original Shiba Inu image (see figure 16.2).[17]

We'll follow cues from both Shifman and Barthes when we do this. Let's look at this in terms of content first—immediately, two kinds of

Figure 16.2: A variant of the Doge meme, including many of the "original" elements interspersed with others.

signs become apparent: first, the image of the dog and, second, the words. In terms of denoted meanings, there is a dog in the image. However, the image doesn't fully signify if we only say this—it is an image of a dog with a puzzled expression, and one with a history of having circulated as the Doge meme already. The words don't tell us a lot if we do not account for this last point. In terms of grammatical (and rational) sense, "wow . . . such axe . . . wow . . . many murder . . . the shibing . . .

heres doge ... wow" makes little to none. But by the time this meme was posted, this was already part of accepted Doge lingo. In this image, the text plays the role of *both* anchorage and relay. It anchors the image in the tonality of well-known Doge memes by replicating their (deliberately) bad grammar and the multicolored Comic Sans text. "Here's doge" and "the shibing" also signal that we are, in fact, viewing a Doge meme. Along with "such <insert verb/noun>" and "much <insert verb/noun>," "shibe" (a badly spelled variant of Shiba) is also well-recognized Doge terminology. The text anchors the image as a Doge meme, while also relaying elements from other Doge memes.

But there is another layer of relay in this image. The top half of the meme is a still from Stanley Kubrick's *The Shining* (1980). Starring Jack Nicholson as the author Jack Torrance and Shelley Duvall as his wife Wendy, *The Shining* is a cult-classic horror film in which the author is shown spiraling gradually into insanity. In this particular scene, Jack chases Wendy with an axe, and when she locks herself in the bathroom, he hacks down the door. In what is arguably one of the most famous moments in horror film history, Jack sticks his face through the broken wood panel of the door and shouts, with a menacing look on his face, "Here's Johnny!" as Wendy screams in sheer terror. In terms of *stance*, then, the meme is parodic. Even if the bottom half of the meme featuring the dog were not present, the top half would register as a Doge meme simply because of the words "such axe" and "wow." The juxtaposition of these two words in multicolored Comic Sans font over the scene of horror renders it a parody of *The Shining*, but to register as parody, one would have to be familiar with the film in the first place. Thus, the pleasures of the meme are highly intertextual.

Taken in isolation, the words in the top panel trigger a memetic relay between the two "cult" texts—*The Shining* and Doge. This relay is carried forward, like a comic book sequence, in the lower panel, in which Jack Nicholson's iconic face from the scene has been replaced with the Shiba Inu sticking its head through the door. The crazed look of the madman is supplanted with the ironic Doge expression as *The Shining* is transformed into "the shibing." If one were not conversant with the codes of the Doge meme or with *The Shining*, the meme would work only partially. For instance, without knowing about the iconic status of the film, it might still work as some variant of the Doge meme, but the parodic punch would be lost as the circuit of conversation between the two texts would break. Reading this variant of the meme requires intertextual knowledge, and a shared investment in both the lingua franca of Doge-speak and the Hollywood horror film. There are other variants like it—"Snoop Doge" in reference to the rapper Snoop Dogg; Paranormal Activity Doge, which places the Shiba Inu in a scene from the horror film *Paranormal Activity* (dir. Oren Peli, 2007); and a Game of Doge version with the tagline "You Win or You Wow," playing on the HBO series *Game of Thrones* (2011–2019).[18] Such variants show a demonstrable knowledge of, and participation in, codes of popular culture—what Milner describes as the "unique reappropriation of jokes, tropes, archetypes, and references that have come before."[19]

In these examples, we do not know much about the *context* in which the meme was created and circulated, beyond the fact that it has appeared in the official Doge Twitter (now X) account—@DogeTheDog. Here, "Doge" is its own context—we do not need any political or historical knowledge to understand why it was created and circulated, beyond the parodic function. But there are variations in which these contexts become important to be able to fully unpack what is being conveyed. Here, it is important to note that elements of a meme that we are not conversant with are also potential clues. While we may not be privy to the precise meanings of each element in a meme, we can hold onto them as researchers. Color, style, the platform/posting context, and the user handle, as well as intertextual and contextual references, can be examined with a forensic eye as we reverse engineer the many meanings of a meme. Take the following Doge variant from India as an example (see figure 16.3).[20]

This variant retains some features of the original Doge, while others have been significantly modified. For instance, there is no Comic Sans font, and it contains no gibberish text. The fact that it retains the familiar Doge image puts it squarely within a precirculating Doge-text that, as this example shows, had become globally recognized and trafficked. However, compared to the original photograph of Kabosu (see the first image in figure 16.1), the eyes and mouth have been digitally altered to render the expression as one of cunningness and superiority. In terms of image content, the forehead of the dog contains a saffron mark, the face is surrounded by three heart symbols, and all of this is superimposed over the image of a smiling, bespectacled man. To someone unfamiliar

Figure 16.3: Ideologically loaded Doge variant from India.

with the political context of contemporary India, this would be just another user-generated variant of Doge. Reading this meme requires some knowledge of the interwoven signs that create meaning within this one image. This is not unlike intertextual relay, where insider knowledge is mandatory for a full reading of the meme; however, here the nodes in the relay are not other popular cultural texts (though they, too, may be present in some variants) but political signs. The text—"Hey Girl are you Bill to declare India Hindu Rashtra? Because I want to pass you"—has a particularly important anchoring role here. *Hindu Rashtra* translates as "Hindu nation" and is an ideological keystone of the Hindu right wing; saffron, the color of the mark on the dog's forehead, is its political symbol. Further, the image of the man we see here is that of Amit Shah,

India's Minister of Home Affairs, who belongs to the ruling right-wing party, the Bharatiya Janata Party (BJP). The text and superimposed/modified images root this in the ideology of the Hindu right wing.

But there is another historical layer of signification—the words "bill" and "pass" mean very specific things in the context of December 2019, when this meme was posted. On December 11, 2019, the Indian parliament passed the Citizenship Amendment Act (CAA) after protracted controversy. When the bill was introduced in the parliament by Shah, massive protests broke out throughout the country. The Act states that under certain circumstances, persecuted minorities belonging to a "Hindu, Sikh, Buddhist, Jain, Parsi or Christian community from Afghanistan, Bangladesh or Pakistan" would not be considered illegal migrants if they had "entered into India on or before the 31st day of December, 2014."[21] Given the Hindu right's Islamophobic stance, the bill and (subsequently) the Act's exclusion of Muslims were seen as the institutionalization of religious and political bias through the weaponization of legal and constitutional systems.[22] There was also much support for the bill—this Doge variant is an ideological proposition in favor of it. Coming right after the bill's passing into an act, the meme positions itself in a parodic (almost mocking) stance. Further, the account that posted the meme is also part of its ideological signage—the handle is titled "@Kattar Hindu Doggo Memes" (*kattar Hindu* loosely translates as "hardcore Hindu"), and the profile image is a saffronized variant of Doge that we see in this meme. So, this meme radiates meaning both through user participation in global meme culture and through insider knowledge of historically situated political events in India.

That this is a variant of the Doge meme is not insignificant—using Doge imagery and Doge-speak forms an intertextual connection between the realms of global meme cultures and Indian politics. In both examples of Doge memes, intertextual knowledge is a way of speaking across two constituencies—in the previous "shibing" example, those familiar with recent meme eruptions and those invested in the history of the horror film (and, arguably, for those who "get" both levels of the joke, it results in felt membership in both). Likewise, in the second example, the use of the Shiba Inu becomes a way of showcasing familiarity with global digital trends even when the messaging may be conservative or parochial. Further, the preexisting knowledge about the Doge meme's potential for humorous commentary also masks the "heavy" ideological baggage of the political message. In the specifically "Indian" character of this political example, the Doge meme is a variant that exists in a constellation of other forms of toxic humor that are spread across memes, short-form videos, GIFs, and other online utterances. "Doge," here, becomes a connective tissue between local and global meme cultures and points toward the "fundamental and inescapable interdependence of all textual meaning."[23] There are, no doubt, similar political examples elsewhere that must be read within their own contextual ecologies for which the meme is particularly recontextualized.[24]

What happens when such meme-texts expand beyond their original meanings and contexts? Doge, for example, has also transitioned into a form of cryptocurrency—the Dogecoin, which bears the original Doge as its symbol.[25] While it started as a joke in 2013, it later became a legitimate cryptocurrency.[26] Here, the meme-text ceases being *only* a joke and has material, economic effects. Viral circulation and user participation can render any meme culturally and politically significant. Doge, of course, is just one example. Other memes can be read this way too. In the variations discussed above, we have read the Doge meme for linguistic, denoted, and connoted meanings by approaching them through the framework of textual content, context, and intertext. What might such a method of reading memes tell you about digitally mediated communication, society, culture, and politics? What memes would you read using this method? For sure, there is no shortage of memes to analyze. The internet is a vast playing field, and, to quip memetically, "All its memes are belong to us."[27]

Notes

1. Jeffrey Demsky, *Nazi and Holocaust Representations in Anglo-American Popular Culture, 1945–2020: Irreverent Remembrance* (Cham, Switzerland: Palgrave Macmillan, 2021); Katrien Jacobs, Degel Cheung, Vasileios Maltezos, and Cecilia Wong, "The Pepe the Frog Image-Meme in Hong Kong: Visual Recurrences and Gender Fluidity on the LIHKG Forum," *Journal of Digital Social Research* 4, no. 4 (2022): 130–50, https://doi.org/10.33621/jdsr.v4i4.131.
2. Richard Dawkins, *The Selfish Gene* (New York: Oxford University Press, 1976), 192.
3. Dawkins, *The Selfish Gene*, 192.
4. Ryan M. Milner, *The World Made Meme: Public Conversations and Participatory Media* (Cambridge, MA: MIT Press, 2016), 2.

5 Limor Shifman, *Memes in Digital Culture* (Cambridge, MA: MIT Press, 2014), 40.
6 Roland Barthes, "The Rhetoric of the Image," in *Image Music Text*, translated by Stephen Heath (London: Fontana Press, 1977), 32–51.
7 Barthes, "The Rhetoric of the Image," 37.
8 Barthes, "The Rhetoric of the Image," 38.
9 Alan McKee, *Textual Analysis: A Beginner's Guide* (London: Sage Publications, 2003), 4.
10 Jonathan Gray, *Watching with The Simpsons: Television, Parody, and Intertextuality* (New York: Routledge, 2006), 3.
11 Gregory Lukow and Steven Ricci, "The 'Audience' Goes Public: Inter-textuality, Genre and the Responsibilities of Film Literacy," *On Film* 12 (1984): 29.
12 Anirban Baishya, "The Conquest of the World as Meme: Memetic Visuality and Political Humor in Critiques of the Hindu Right Wing in India," *Media, Culture & Society* 43, no. 6 (2021): 1113–35.
13 Roland Barthes, "The Death of the Author," in *The Rustle of Language*, translated by Richard Howard (Berkeley: University of California Press, 1989), 53.
14 Kyle Chayka, "WOW THIS IS DOGE," *The Verge*, December 31, 2013, www.theverge.com/2013/12/31/5248762/doge-meme-rescue-dog-wow.
15 "Search Results: 'doge,'" Know Your Meme, accessed May, 24, 2024, https://knowyourmeme.com/search?q=doge.
16 "You have encountered A DOGE," Tumblr, April 26, 2012, https://dudleyworl-blog.tumblr.com/post/21839641589; E-Lo, "You have encountered A DOGE," YouTube, May 7, https://youtu.be/l-Dmq5ShKuc?si=iMoVpFFny7ehZzD7.
17 @DogeTheDog, "Such movie Many scare The shibing 3spook5u," Twitter, November 23, 2013, https://twitter.com/DogeTheDog/status/404271429715116032/photo/1.
18 @DogeTheDog, "Wow Such snoop Very doge Now is lion So wow Much rap," Twitter, March 31, 2015, https://twitter.com/DogeTheDog/status/583049703702446080; @DogeTheDog, "Wow Such night Very ghost So scare Much spook Pls save doge Sleep tight," Twitter, October 29, 2014, https://twitter.com/DogeTheDog/status/527668839593811968; @DogeTheDog, "Wow Such game Many thrones Much tv So drama," Twitter, June 13, 2015, https://twitter.com/DogeTheDog/status/609814304657805312.
19 Milner, *The World Made Meme*, 79.
20 @khdmemes, "Vro lob reacxx only khi khi . . . ," Twitter, December 22, 2019, https://twitter.com/khdmemes/status/1208767216054726657.
21 "The Citizenship (Amendment) Act, 2019," *The Gazette of India: Extraordinary*, December 12, 2019, https://indiancitizenshiponline.nic.in/Documents/UserGuide/E-gazette_2019_20122019.pdf.
22 "'Shoot the Traitors': Discrimination Against Muslims under India's New Citizenship Policy," *Human Rights Watch*, April 19, 2020, https://hrw.org/report/2020/04/10/shoot-traitors/discrimination-against-muslims-under-indias-new-citizenship-policy.

23 Gray, *Watching with The Simpsons*, 3.
24 See, for instance, Doge deployment by members of the United States Congress in 2013: Brett LoGiurato, "Congress Has Finally Discovered 'Doge,' and It's Going About as Badly as You Would Expect," *Business Insider*, December 23, 2013, www.businessinsider.com/doge-memes-congress-steve-stockman-massie-2013-12.
25 "What is Dogecoin?," Dogecoin, https://dogecoin.com/.
26 Albi Nani, "The Doge Worth 88 Billion Dollars: A Case Study of Dogecoin," *Convergence: The International Journal of Research into New Media Technologies* 28, no. 6 (2022): 1719–36.
27 "All Your Base Are Belong to Us," Know Your Meme, https://knowyourmeme.com/memes/all-your-base-are-belong-to-us.

17

A Textual Analysis of #RIPTwitter

RAVEN MARAGH-LLOYD

Maragh-Lloyd considers a massively collaborative and often community-based text unique to the digital, online era: the hashtag. Focusing on Black Twitter and the use of the hashtag #RIPTwitter as a case study, Maragh-Lloyd argues for the importance of studying hashtags to hear from marginalized communities whose contributions to other, more austere media might otherwise have been limited and curtailed precisely due to their marginalization.

On August 5, 2023, the hashtag "#MontgomeryBrawl" circulated among thousands of internet users after a video went viral of Dameion Pickett, a Black riverfront dock worker, being attacked by white boaters in Alabama.[1] Black folks online were paying attention to the viral video for this and another reason, however. In posted videos of the attack, a legion of unrelated Black onlookers came into focus seemingly from out of nowhere to defend Pickett, which seemed to spark catharsis and joy among Black internet users.

The meanings and functions of the hashtag were varied. On one level, the hashtag and its related tweets seemed to hail online users familiar with the event as close to real time as possible. On another, #MontgomeryBrawl signaled a longer history of Black bodies attacked in public and the spectacularly rare circumstances when those bodies get defended. It also signaled the use of Black humor as a strategy to deal with such a painful history.[2] For researchers, studying a hashtag like this one requires data collection methods beyond the surface-level recognition of its content due to the complexities of cultural phenomena and the related identities, priorities, and histories embedded therein.

Part I: The Stakes of Textual Analysis Online

Media scholars and students who use hashtags as sites of analysis enter an epistemological landscape that is ostensibly less favorable to textual analysis. First, both the study of technology and the object itself are uniquely wrapped up in a discourse of "objective," quantifiable, and reproducible bits of data.³ That is, the lure of mass amounts of information that social network sites offer can tempt researchers to defer to big data analyses, despite the robust critical cultural scholarship that demonstrates the benefits of rich textual analysis.⁴

Even within qualitative digital scholarship, though, textual analysis remains somewhat elusive. In Yarimar Bonilla and Jonathan Rosa's "#Ferguson," the authors argue for hashtags as an indexing system, which functions in the semiotic and clerical sense.⁵ Of the semiotic, the authors write that hashtags allow users to "performatively frame what these comments are 'really about,' thereby enabling users to indicate a meaning that might not be otherwise apparent."⁶ While their article discusses the intertextual potentials of hashtags, the method used is digital ethnography, not textual analysis. This chapter will build on digital scholarship like Bonilla and Rosa's to explicitly tie hashtags to the method of textual analysis. André Brock's formulation of critical technocultural discourse analysis (CTDA) perhaps comes closest to the explicit use of textual analysis in critical cultural internet research.⁷ For Brock, both the information and communication technologies (ICTs) and online discourse itself should be treated as "text." ICTs-as-text, Brock contends, are made up of artifact, practice, and belief. For example, he examines Twitter's "artifact" through historical contextualization and modes of production, while "practice" lends itself to users' engagement with the interface through symbols. Lastly, Brock analyzes "belief" through a Black linguistic framework to ascertain the cultural discourse of Twitter's users and observers. Through CTDA, Brock marries the real limitations of a technology with the possibilities of users shaping that technology "within the artifact [itself]."⁸ Textual analysis, in this sense, is multimodal. CTDA will be useful in this chapter in that I treat both Twitter and the hashtag as texts under examination, as I demonstrate in my analysis of #RIPTwitter, a hashtag that circulated widely in 2022 after Tesla CEO Elon Musk officially (and tumultuously) acquired Twitter.

Textual analysis offers critical cultural studies students and researchers rich ground to understand the ways in which a text is situated in a particular set of power dynamics, opening and foreclosing a host of interventions.[9] Building on the rich work of media textual analysis, this chapter takes into account the unique position of technology and will first outline how to do a textual analysis of hashtags before performing an analysis of #RIPTwitter.

First, when conducting a textual analysis of a hashtag (or perhaps of any kind), it is useful to start with a question. Depending on your inductive or deductive sensibilities, this question might be driven by the text itself or by a theoretical premise. For example, in the case of #RIPTwitter, I was curious about the use of a platform to decry that platform's death. I asked questions related to Black users' relationship to Twitter (which was rebranded to "X" in July 2023) and the meanings and invocations of Black funerary rituals (e.g., the homegoing) to mourn the site's demise. I could have also asked these questions squarely from the theoretical premise of Black ritual. To cite another example, a researcher interested in, say, the relationship between social media and young girls might start by asking questions related to a particular hashtag, such as #cleangirlaesthetic.[10] In this instance, the researcher might already be familiar with these online communities and specific phrases used by them. Or, perhaps the researcher might start with theories of beauty, race, and idealism and integrate specific keywords or hashtags as gleaned from the literature. In either case, a close relationship with the literature *and* the online community is important. Simply searching for a hashtag or keyword online provides an incomplete analysis, given the ways that users negotiate language as culturally specific. That is, because online affordances such as retweets and shares lead to texts' wide and fast circulation, online communities—and especially those who are historically marginalized—have become adept at culturally safeguarding themselves.[11] Without reading, researching, and experiencing the contours of Black Twitter and the use of humor online, for example, any attempt to capture the relationship between something like #RIPTwitter and Black users would be sorely incomplete. Thus, in crafting one's research question, a deep knowledge about the communities, when appropriate, behind the hashtag under examination is paramount.

Second, a textual analysis of online hashtags and their related tweets must set fairly strict sociotechnical parameters. Because hashtags and online content generally capture real-time developments of an often-massive amount of content, this step is crucial. That is, asking a question about the text is one thing, but making sure you are capturing what you set out to find is another. One must think through the benefits and hindrances of at least the following: hashtag word choice, time period, platform, audience, and engagement. I will briefly discuss each before demonstrating how to set these parameters in the next section.

The word choice of a hashtag can be as simple as thinking through the differences between upper and lowercase or singular and plural (e.g., #Karen vs. #Karens). Choosing one or another hashtag would return different tweets and produce different results. Thinking through the differences between the words #Karen and #Karens might result in expanding one's hashtag analysis to include both, to return results of users who are engaging in this text in multiple ways. Or a researcher might solely focus on the singular version, hoping to capture individual white women who seek to police Black bodies in public. In many ways, these word choices are not unsimilar to established practices of textual analysis.[12] What is important here is that the researcher acknowledges that word choice opens and forecloses points of analyses in an online textual analysis.

Considering the parameter of time period also ensures that a particular text is appropriately engaging with the political, social, and economic inflections that the researcher is analyzing. For example, the time period of a spoken utterance such as a speech is fixed at a particular date and time. However, choosing a hashtag for analysis can result in texts across various time periods and even different conversations. Returning to the #Karen example, analyzing that hashtag in 2020 would produce temporally significant results around the COVID-19 pandemic and racial justice protests in a different way than, say, #Karen at the height of the "call your manager" memes in 2016.

The platform must also be considered when setting up textual analysis online. Because hashtags span multiple platforms and each platform has a different affordance, ethos, and discursive practice, the researcher must decide which platform(s) fits their research question and intervention. Although hashtags were popularized on Twitter, their subsequent ubiquity across almost every social media platform and mainstream media outlet, as well as the everyday lexicon, is truly remarkable. The cultural understandings of each site will influence the kinds of results we might expect to find in a textual analysis. For example, the ease and primacy of video creation on TikTok affords a certain culture on that platform (such as affective publics) differently than Twitter, which might impact the hashtag under analysis.[13] Thus, while platforms indeed bend the boundaries of space and place, there are limitations inherent in any one site, a concept media scholars have termed "media specificity."[14] These limitations and possibilities must be properly fleshed out and justified, ideally connecting back to one's research question and aims.

While audience research most commonly involves interviews and focus groups, textual analysis can reveal a great deal about the audience of a hashtag or tweet under study. Most notably, hashtags are rooted in language. Take #ThanksgivingClapback, for example, which many Black Americans engage in every year around Thanksgiving to connect around food, family, and culture.[15] This hashtag signals, through the "clapback," a long tradition of linguistic jousting that many African Americans have come to master.[16] Studying the hashtag as text, then, opens up possibilities for uncovering an audience linguistically and historically. Moreover, hashtags are often intertextual and even visual.[17] The references that audiences make to other media through hashtags create possibilities for the researcher to focus on audience complexities through intertextual media.[18] Textual analysis offers interesting potentials here as the researcher can tap into rich discursive practices behind a given hashtag to make an argument with and about the audience under study.

Lastly, one must consider the reception or engagement of a hashtag. That is, the researcher must make decisions—and be careful in doing so—about the extent of engagement that they deem important in their study. For example, some studies simply include hashtags with an arbitrarily high engagement (e.g., number of likes or retweets), while others include hashtags that are found in the trending topics page of a platform. While high engagement metrics such as likes or reshares signal significance to some, one must be careful not to equate high visibility online with necessary significance. Doing so might miss important conversations and movements online that are not visible for the same reason of erasure that the researcher might be interested in. The same goes for legitimizing online hashtags that appear in mainstream news outlets. It is tempting to cite, as justification for studying a hashtag, that *The New York Times* has reported on said hashtag, and doing so is not necessarily wrong. But students and researchers must be vigilant in our attempts not to reproduce harm, as issues of commodification and exploitation abound, particularly given the virality of online content.[19]

Part II: A Textual Analysis of #RIPTwitter

In October 2022, after a tumultuous few months, Elon Musk acquired Twitter for $44 billion. In the months before the deal became final, the Tesla CEO blasted Twitter over concerns of bot accounts, joined then left the board of the company, controversially declared that he would reinstate Donald Trump on the platform, and was sued by Twitter shareholders.[20] Along the way, actual Twitter users were watching their engagement and activity online being negotiated most publicly. For example, in reference to the famous line in *Titanic*, one user tweeted on November 17, "Gentlemen, it's been a privilege tweeting with you tonight #RIPTwitter."[21]

While many were in disbelief and disapproval over the future of Twitter, Black users had a unique vantage point to the "passing" of the platform, given many years of their making Twitter a cultural conduit for hilarious, trending, activist-related discussions.[22] Moreover, the hashtag #RIPTwitter revealed a long-worn truth: media platforms, though useful, do not always hold dear the best interests of their users, particularly their most marginalized ones. As online creator Mylissa "Mikki" Veal wrote in an article for *Essence*, "It felt like the beginning of the end of our little communal space."[23] She continued, "In true Black fashion, I felt it right to give the platform a proper goodbye." My analysis focuses on the hashtag #RIPTwitter with an explicit lens toward the Black historical tradition of the homegoing.

With roots in ancient African societies, homegoings honor the dead through practices of celebration and community. Specific homegoing rituals include the free expression of song and dance, including collective swaying, wailing, and dancing. Known as the "ring shout," this call-and-response-style singing and dancing was originally believed to embody intimacy between mourners and their ancestors.[24] The ring shout is also said to have influenced later African American blues and jazz music. In these early African traditions, a homegoing included practices of "body removal," such as carrying the body through a hole in the wall and taking a zigzag path to the burial site to ensure that the deceased would not return to haunt the living.[25] In the US, the homegoing tradition took on additional important meanings. For enslaved Black Americans, who were buried in unmarked graves with little to no expectation of remembrance, the homegoing was a way to preserve community, sanctity, and the promise of a better future ahead.[26] Since then, the themes of pain and joy in the homegoing have been particularly important for Black Americans, who have historically had shorter life spans than their white counterparts.[27] Contemporary rituals of the homegoing include elaborate dress of both the living and the deceased (e.g., funeral attendees donning big church hats and immaculate hair and makeup), "ring shout" led by church organs, and a customary postfuneral "repast" wherein food is shared among the bereaved. Through #RIPTwitter, Black users tapped into this long tradition of the homegoing by "mourning" Twitter, conjoining the sacred with the elaborate and the serious with the humorous, while, importantly, signaling a "world beyond" Twitter.

My interest in #RIPTwitter came from this seemingly paradoxical—and deeply cultural—relationship between the sacred and the irreverent online. To that end, my research question asked, How does #RIPTwitter circulate meaning about the place of social network sites, and Twitter specifically, in everyday life? What might the text reveal about the broader relationship between Black users and platforms during times of technological change? Following André Brock's formulation of CTDA, I approached both the artifact (Twitter as a service) *and* the discourse of #RIPTwitter (Black traditions of the homegoing) as text. In doing so, both Musk's actions after acquiring Twitter and the hashtag itself were understood to generate meaning. I conducted an in-depth textual analysis of #RIPTwitter to gain a deeper understanding of the ways that Black folks online use this hashtag. The patterns that emerged were twofold: #RIPTwitter demonstrates the ways that Black users, firstly, lead conversations about seismic shifts in the tech world and, secondly, reassert agency in the delicate and often-exploitative relationship between social media and its users.

To set up parameters around my object of study (#RIPTwitter), I considered the wording that would determine my search. While similar hashtags circulated around the same time, I focused solely on #RIPTwitter, given its close ties to Black users who explicitly paired the hashtag with the homegoing tradition. In the beginning of this chapter, I noted the importance of a researcher's cultural familiarity with a text. Because I am a part of "Black Twitter" (albeit the now-older, millennial side), I gleaned the cultural significance of #RIPTwitter and began collecting posts with explicit mentions of "homegoing" as well as posts signaling themes of the homegoing, such as pain and joy, elaborate dress, and humor (see figure 17.1). I focused on the time period of October to December 2022, during which Musk officially acquired Twitter and made major public changes to it, prompting a large response on the site and elsewhere.[28] While posts online might seem (and can be) ephemeral and ever-changing, many are also clearly marked by date on many sites, making such a time period consideration accessible for researchers. Because my research question focused on Twitter explicitly, I set my platform parameter to that site. I also defined the audience and engagement of #RIPTwitter as Black users who discursively engaged with the homegoing tradition. Notice here that my parameters did not look for physical markers of Blackness online or even self-identification in a tweet. That is, my research question aimed to reveal the relationship between Black users and social network sites during times of change, which I did through the discursive articulation of a homegoing. Specifically, I paid attention to tweets that referenced funerals as well as rituals within a homegoing (e.g., repast, wailing, dancing, ring shout, call and response) in order to discern which tweets fit my research question and parameters. The historical and cultural significance of homegoing here allowed me to study Black users as an audience without reducing race to physical (online) characteristics. The benefits of such an approach include not reducing race and ethnicity to biological markers (leaving the researcher to assume the race of an avatar, for instance), while the drawbacks include a longer process of discerning discursive traditions (e.g., the homegoing) on the researcher's part.

After collecting tweets under #RIPTwitter that explicitly referenced "homegoing" and/or its rituals, I grouped posts into themes using thematic analysis. What became evident from emerging themes of #RIPTwitter was that Black users tapped into the homegoing tradition to perform a "funeral" for Twitter, creating in real time the space and language for millions of users to process (and even grieve) this jarring technological and cultural shift.

One of the first major changes after Musk's acquisition was the firing of about half of Twitter's 7,500-person workforce.[29] These layoffs caused

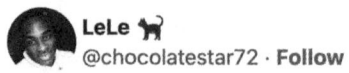

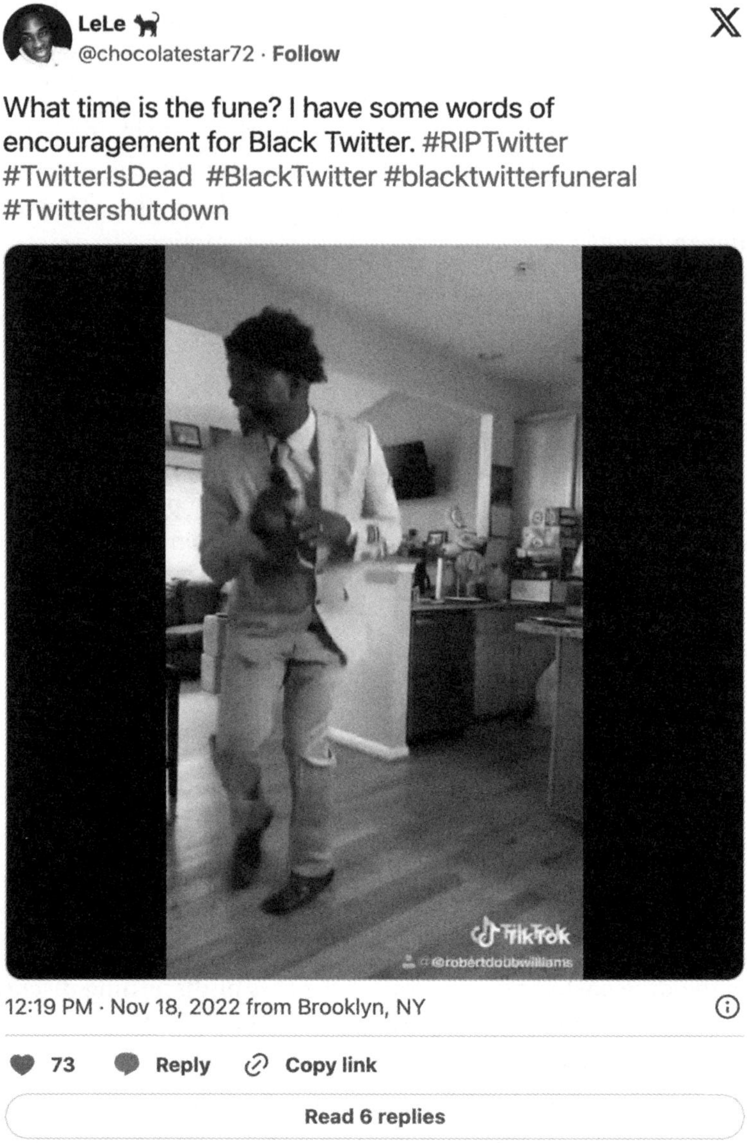
LeLe
@chocolatestar72 · Follow
What time is the fune? I have some words of encouragement for Black Twitter. #RIPTwitter #TwitterIsDead #BlackTwitter #blacktwitterfuneral #Twittershutdown
TikTok
12:19 PM · Nov 18, 2022 from Brooklyn, NY
73
Reply
Copy link
Read 6 replies

Figure 17.1: Example of homegoing-referenced post, highlighting Black cultural pain and joy, elaborate dress, and humor at the "death" of Twitter.

a firestorm as many ex-employees decried Musk's takeover with the hashtag #StopToxicTwitter, which, among other things, called for advertisers to boycott the service. Users tweeted in droves about the layoffs as rumors swirled about the legality of the firings. Other sites reported that Twitter under Musk would gut the content moderation division, opening the floodgates to hate speech and extremism online, a claim that Musk denied in a tweet.[30]

While Twitter's interface did not immediately change as drastically as did its services (e.g., the introduction of the Twitter Blue subscription service) between October and December 2022, what emerged was a circulating discourse of the role of social network sites more broadly. The change in services, from the layoffs to announcements of a subscription model, was met with intense public outcry, as evidenced by hashtags like #RIPTwitter and #StopToxicTwitter. That the outcry about Twitter's layoffs and changing services was so loud speaks to its established role in the U.S. imaginary. That is, social media users have come to expect what Safiya Noble critiques in relation to Google as technology for the public good.[31] While much has been written about the counterculture ethos of Silicon Valley and the lure of technological progress, the shift in Twitter's services to a more explicitly profit-driven model raises questions about what happens to an entire generation who have come to understand the platform as part of their everyday lives.[32] Black Twitter users, who are no strangers to conversations about exploitation and commercialism, used #RIPTwitter and the homegoing tradition to reassert agency in the relationship between social media and its users. Posts ranged from clips of Whitney Houston singing with the caption "Me at Twitter funeral with my Black Twitter family" to videos of Black pastors preaching at the imaginary funeral. So, while we might have had little control over the sale of the platform, its changing policies, or its bold allowances of hate speech, what users showed through #RIPTwitter was a recentering of themselves as the true creatives behind the platform. By framing this technological shift in terms of a homegoing, Black users made plain the significance of users' cultural situatedness—including rituals such as wailing and swaying to grieve the dead—that allowed the platform to thrive in the first place. They also signaled to a life beyond Twitter or any platform, as the homegoing tradition celebrates not only the end but a regeneration of life among the living.

Tweets around the #RIPTwitter hashtag showcased the primacy of Black culture, from the visual intricacies of mourners' attire to the feast of the repast, beyond any platform or set of affordances. #RIPTwitter laid bare the deeply held critical distance that marginalized groups have had to keep from media conglomerates, given the storied ways in which they have not held our interests. So, while Black folks thrived on Twitter for more than a decade, its demise cannot possibly signal the demise of our creativity. What #RIPTwitter ultimately demonstrates is that while users negotiate the complicated online media landscape of profits and commercialism, Black communities continue to prioritize cultural mainstays such as the homegoing tradition and Black humor to outrun the fate of any one platform at any one time. Conducting a textual analysis of hashtags allows researchers to glean real-time negotiations between communities and those in power, including the increasingly tenuous relationship between tech billionaires and politicians. Indeed, hashtag textual analyses allow researchers to access communities perhaps left out of traditional textual analysis found in television and film, giving primacy to these creatives, such as the Black online users who centralize the homegoing tradition in #RIPTwitter.

Notes

1 Liz Calvario, Anna Kaplan, and Samantha Kubota, "Man Seen Wielding Folding Chair in Montgomery Brawl Turns Himself In," *TODAY*, August 11, 2023, www.today.com/news/alabama-montgomery-riverfront-brawl-rcna98690.
2 Bambi Haggins, *Laughing Mad: The Black Comic Persona in Post-Soul America* (New Brunswick, NJ: Rutgers University Press, 2007); Glenda Carpio, *Laughing Fit to Kill: Black Humor in the Fictions of Slavery* (Oxford: Oxford University Press, 2008).
3 Ryan Stoldt, Raven Maragh-Lloyd, Tim Havens, Brian Ekdale, and Andrew C. High, "Using Racial Discourse Communities to Audit Personalization Algorithms." *Communication, Culture & Critique* 16, no. 3 (August 25, 2023): 158–65, https://doi.org/10.1093/ccc/tcad015.
4 Andre Brock, "Critical Technocultural Discourse Analysis," *New Media & Society* 20, no. 3 (2018): 1012–30, https://doi.org/10.1177/1461444816677532; Catherine Knight Steele, "Black Bloggers and Their Varied Publics: The Everyday Politics of Black Discourse Online," *Television & New Media* 19, no. 2 (February 2018): 112–27. https://doi.org/10.1177/1527476417709535.

5 Yarimar Bonilla and Jonathan Rosa, "#Ferguson: Digital Protest, Hashtag Ethnography, and the Racial Politics of Social Media in the United States," *American Ethnologist* 42, no. 1 (February 2015): 4–17, https://doi.org/10.1111/amet.12112.
6 Bonilla and Rosa, "#Ferguson," 5.
7 Brock, "Critical Technocultural Discourse Analysis."
8 Brock, "Critical Technocultural Discourse Analysis," 1024.
9 Michael Kackman and Mary Celeste Kearney, eds., *The Craft of Criticism: Critical Media Studies in Practice* (New York: Routledge, 2018).
10 For more on #cleangirlaesthetic, see www.byrdie.com/clean-girl-aesthetic-critique-6744031.
11 Raven Maragh-Lloyd, "Black Twitter as Semi-Enclave," in *Race and Media: Critical Approaches*, edited by Lori Kido Lopez (New York: New York University Press, 2020), 163–77.
12 Jonathan Bignell, *Media Semiotics: An Introduction*, 2nd ed. (Manchester: Manchester University Press, 2002).
13 Samantha Hautea, Perry Parks, Bruno Takahashi, and Jing Zeng, "Showing They Care (Or Don't): Affective Publics and Ambivalent Climate Activism on TikTok," *Social Media + Society* 7, no. 2 (April–June 2021), https://doi.org/10.1177/20563051211012344.
14 Kackman and Kearney, *The Craft of Criticism*.
15 Maragh-Lloyd, "Black Twitter as Semi-Enclave."
16 Mel Watkins, *On the Real Side: A History of African American Comedy* (Chicago: Lawrence Hill Books, 1999).
17 Bonilla and Rosa, "#Ferguson."
18 Jonathan Gray, "Intertexts and Paratexts," in *The Craft of Criticism: Critical Media Studies in Practice*, edited by Michael Kackman and Mary Celeste Kearney (New York: Routledge, 2018), 207–18.
19 Tonia Sutherland, *Resurrecting the Black Body: Race and the Digital Afterlife* (Oakland: University of California Press, 2023).
20 Max Zahn, "A Timeline of Elon Musk's Tumultuous Twitter Acquisition," ABC News, November 11, 2022, https://abcnews.go.com/Business/timeline-elon-musks-tumultuous-twitter-acquisition-attempt/story?id=86611191.
21 ¥le (@yleniaindeniah1), "Gentlemen, it's been a privilege tweeting with you tonight #RIPTwitter." Twitter, November 17, 2022, 6:41, pmhttps://x.com/yleniaindeniah1/status/1593434299348516870.
22 Meredith Clark, *We Tried to Tell Y'all: Black Twitter and the Rise of Digital Counternarratives* (Cary, NC: Oxford University Press, 2024).
23 Mylissa Veal, "Creator of 'Black Twitter Homegoing Service' Talks Sparking the Viral Trend," *Essence*, November 28, 2022, www.essence.com/culture/twitter-homegoing-service-feature/.
24 Samuel A. Floyd, "Ring Shout! Literary Studies, Historical Studies, and Black Music Inquiry," *Black Music Research Journal* 11, no. 2 (1991): 265.

25 Brittiny Moore, "In Black Communities, Homegoing Rituals Honor the Dead and the Living Through a Blend of African and Christian Traditions," *Evermore*, January 31, 2023, https://evermore.org/in-black-communities-homegoing-rituals-honor-the-dead-and-the-living-through-a-blend-of-african-and-christian-traditions/.

26 Brian Palmer, "American Homegoing: On the Richness of the Black Funeral Tradition," *Virginia Quarterly Review* 98, no. 3 (2022): 24.

27 Writing about Black death, exploitation, and the internet, Tonia Sutherland refers to the sacred act and history of the homegoing as a powerful act of community in "Making a Killing: On Race, Ritual, and (Re)Membering in Digital Culture," *Preservation, Digital Technology & Culture* 46, no. 1 (April 28, 2017): 32–40, https://doi.org/10.1515/pdtc-2017-0025.

28 Zahn, "A Timeline."

29 Zahn, "A Timeline."

30 Raquel Maria Dillon, "Twitter Layoffs Begin, Sparking a Lawsuit and Backlash," NPR, November 4, 2022, www.npr.org/2022/11/04/1134263184/twitter-layoffs-elon-musk.

31 Safiya Umoja Noble, *Algorithms of Oppression: How Search Engines Reinforce Racism* (New York: New York University Press, 2018).

32 Fred Turner, *From Counterculture to Cyberculture: Stewart Brand, the Whole Earth Network, and the Rise of Digital Utopianism* (Chicago: University of Chicago Press, 2006); Ruha Benjamin, *Race After Technology: Abolitionist Tools for the New Jim Code* (Cambridge: Polity Press, 2019).

18

The *Dateline* Formula

True Crime, Genre, and Citizenship

LAURIE OUELLETTE

Ouellette shows how genre analysis and textual analysis can inform each other greatly, as she focuses on Dateline *as an "emblematic text" that masters and hence exemplifies common formulas of, in this case, the true crime genre. She delves into its mechanics and messages to gain a better appreciation of the genre's ideological positions, framing of citizenship, and cultural and political work.*

Late at night, I often wind down with an episode of *Dateline* (NBC, 1992–). A stalwart of U.S. television with thirty-two seasons under its belt at the time of writing, *Dateline* began as an investigative news program but now presents real-life murder mysteries across broadcast, cable, and digital channels. Billed as the "original true crime," the *Dateline* franchise packages murder as a suspenseful and emotionally charged narrative. The crime is usually personal, and solving it exposes deadly secrets and betrayals among spouses, lovers, family members, friends, and acquaintances. While the details of the cases change, an impetus to unmask dangerous individuals in quotidian settings and seemingly wholesome communities flows across them. *Dateline* whodunnits revolve around the "evil" that lurks within mostly white, pastoral, middle-class America, with each episode resolving a particularly shocking crime—until the next one.

As a middle-aged white woman, I am situated within the core audience for *Dateline*, which feminizes true crime by weaving the conventions of women's culture (such as tearful testimony and sentimental victim backstories) into real crimes presented as detective fiction.[1] With predictable story arcs punctuated by cliffhangers and recaps and on-air correspondents who explain every piece of the puzzle, the episodes fold enigma into sameness and are simple to follow. While *Dateline* trades in horrific violence and suffering, its formulaic conventions and cathartic resolutions encourage easy and habitual viewing. This is not television that wins creative awards, unsettles expectations, or develops complex plots over episodes and seasons. Yet it is precisely because of its unremarkable and formulaic structure that *Dateline* serves as a powerful and valuable text, one that can be used to spotlight and interrogate the conventions of the genre.

I gravitate to *Dateline* when I'm tired or distracted, but my motivation is also more than personal. As a feminist media scholar, I'm interested in the notable proliferation of true crime in recent decades, and I want to understand how this burgeoning content informs societal assumptions of gender, whiteness, criminality, and citizenship. *Dateline*'s reinvention as a formulaic true crime show, longevity, and gendered mass appeal make it especially useful for thinking through these questions. This chapter analyzes *Dateline* as an *emblematic text* that has helped me make critical sense of the true crime boom and its societal implications. As I will show, this is an interpretive process that involves repetitive viewing, critical analysis, contextualization, and engagement with social and political theory.

Genre and Formula: *Dateline* as Emblematic True Crime

True crime is not new: tales of real-life murder and mayhem originated with nineteenth-century broadsheets and took modern shape in hard-boiled mid-twentieth-century pulp magazines.[2] Since the 1990s, true crime has become more prolific and culturally mainstream, and it now circulates across broadcast television, specialized cable channels, streaming platforms, and podcasts. This content comprises a media genre to the extent that it borrows from fiction to tell stories about the "worst kinds of crimes" and is commonly preoccupied with "safety, order, and justice."[3] Some true crime productions, such as the Netflix docuseries *Making a Murderer* (2015–18), are hailed as outliers that bring more complexity, artistry, and social relevance to the genre. To date, scholarship on the mainstreaming of true crime media has focused on these same quality programs, overlooking vast swatches of unexceptional content that have much to teach us about the cultural politics of television culture.⁴ My research homes in on this run-of-the-mill material, for it is here that we can observe cultural shifts and patterns of sensemaking pressed in media forms.

In this chapter, I outline an approach to media analysis focused on *emblematic texts* that are seldom complex or prestigious but play an outsized role in media, culture, and society. Taking *Dateline* as a case, I situate emblematic texts as programs that catalyze mainstream cultural sensibilities, inform other texts, and circulate broadly within the mediated public sphere as recognizable approaches to topics and problems. Emblematic texts are quotidian, formulaic, and aimed at mass audiences. They are cultural touchstones, or visible representatives of specific genres (such as true crime) at specific moments in time. Reading these texts critically can help media scholars unpack the cultural and political work that genres do.

Dateline is an example of an emblematic text for several reasons. Combining the TV news investigation, the fictional detective drama, and melodramatic women's culture, *Dateline*'s formulaic approach to true crime storytelling catalyzed a now-ubiquitous strand of TV programming and gave it a sense of purpose. *Dateline* also set in motion the changing preoccupations of true crime media since the 1990s, from serial killers and "stranger danger" to the intimate peril of the "ordinary, the trusted, and the prosaic."⁵ *Dateline* formularized the real-life murder mystery as an endless cycle of intimate peril for predominantly female audiences. Because *Dateline* was (and continues to be) produced by NBC's news division, it simultaneously injected the previously marginalized true crime genre with signifiers of social realism and public urgency.

Dateline is also emblematic because it circulates broadly—on repeat. According to NBC, *Dateline* is the most watched "broadcast newsmagazine" in the United States. During the 2021–22 broadcast season, more than "133 billion minutes of *Dateline* were consumed across TV and digital platforms," including the NBC network, cable and broadcast syndication, NBC's Peacock platform, and the 24/7 streaming *Dateline* channel.⁶ Episodes of *Dateline* are rerun, repackaged, and "stripped" as marathons, and its saturation and commercial success have inspired vast swatches of similar programming, including ABC's *20/20*, which followed its lead by transitioning from news to true crime, and the entire schedules of true crime–themed cable channels like Oxygen and Investigation Discovery.

Emblematic texts can be factual or fictional (or a combination of both). What matters is their centrality to broader patterns and trends. Emblematic textual analysis is a way to understand generic tendencies and sociopolitical shifts. My attempt to understand the true crime takeover led me to focus on *Dateline* as an emblematic text. For researchers with other puzzles to solve, the most useful and representative texts will necessarily be different. Identifying such emblematic texts involves preliminary research. For me, this involved tracing the history of true crime and mapping the contours of contemporary true crime content. My habitual viewing of *Dateline* begat closer analysis of its narrative formula, which also shaped my thinking about true crime as a genre.

Questions of verisimilitude (whether something is true or false) and the specific meaning of any specific episode are less important to emblematic textual analysis than the discursive mediation of the social world. Discourses are recurring patterns of thought that propose how important topics and concepts (such as crime) are to be understood. Discourses define problems and authorize solutions in repetitive ways that become taken for granted and commonsensical.[7] These frameworks become powerful when embedded in genres and the narrative formulas within them.

A formula is a "conventional system" for structuring similar cultural narratives within genres. Formulas organize texts in predictable ways that allow audience members to "vicariously participate in their patterns of suspense and resolution." Formulas are repetitive, ritualistic, and typically reassuring—in the crime drama, "the detective always solves the crime."[8] *Dateline* is formulaic at the level of the program or media brand, as each episode follows an identical narrative structure, with similar conflicts, characters, themes, representational codes, and resolutions. At the same time, the *Dateline* formula has seeped into and shaped the mainstream conventions of true crime as a whole.

Mapping discursive frameworks and their intersections with generic formulas involves engagement with a significant amount of media content. Identifying and focusing on emblematic texts helps to narrow the scope. Nonetheless, *Dateline* has produced nearly three thousand episodes, and decisions about what and how much of this material to analyze closely must be made. In the empirical social sciences, random sampling is endorsed as a mechanism to create reliable findings, but in the critical humanities, where my scholarship is situated, the process is more deliberate and involves tracing patterns of significance up to a saturation point where nothing new emerges.

My analysis is based on close viewing of around twenty episodes of *Dateline*, in addition to the countless other episodes I've watched casually over the years. I watched these episodes on live broadcast television and on-demand platforms. I looked for continuities in how situations, people, places, and problems are characterized by both *Dateline* correspondents and subjects (detectives, family members, attorneys), and I traced the discursive construction of concepts like innocence, evil, and safety across episodes.

While *Dateline* draws from journalistic techniques such as documentation, reportage, and interviews, this nonfiction material is made meaningful through representational codes (B-roll of quaint rural settings, close-ups of tears) and structured as a narrative with a predictable progression from beginning to end. While documentaries also tell stories about real life, *true crime presents real life as if it were fiction*, connecting truth claims to the pacing, conflicts, characters, settings, and chains of events found in TV crime dramas and strands of women's culture.[9] For scholars of factual entertainment, unraveling this generic assemblage to see how the components constitute the whole is not formal analysis for its own sake. The point is to see how dominant discursive frameworks take hold in hybrid genres and their formulas.[10]

To complement my analysis of *Dateline*, I also examined promotional materials to learn how the franchise is pitched to advertisers and audiences and traced references to *Dateline* in media culture, including *Saturday Night Live* (NBC, 1975–) parodies and a flurry of attention around the show's thirtieth anniversary. This intertextual research solidified my initial observations about the *Dateline* formula. For example, on the Peacock platform, archived episodes are grouped together in collections like "Summer Mysteries," "Tainted Love," "Unmasking a Killer," "Troubled Waters," "Feuds," and "Diabolical," and *Dateline* 24/7 marathons are organized according to common themes including "Romantic Rivalries," "Holiday Whodunnits," and "Killer Twist." In appearances celebrating the history of *Dateline*, correspondents referenced the lure of mystery, especially when secrets are involved, and also attributed *Dateline*'s success to its focus on places where murder isn't supposed to happen, such as small towns and leafy suburbs. In a newspaper interview, a producer confirmed that *Dateline* is as much about emotional drama as crime—the "jealousies, the disappointments, the alienation of people," and the impact on victims and relatives.[11] The popular (nonaffiliated) podcast *A Date with Dateline*, which makes light of the same conventions and discourses that drew my attention, irreverently explains that its female hosts watch *Dateline* to learn how to prevent their husbands from murdering them for the life insurance money and to know what to say when (correspondent) Keith Morrison interviews them about each other's murder.

Popular media texts circulate within economic and sociopolitical contexts that shape their conventions, assumptions, and priorities. The purpose of emblematic textual analysis is to make these complex connections visible. To read *Dateline* critically and contextualize its reinvention as formulaic true crime, I revisited media industry developments in the 1980s and 1990s, including the transformation of TV news as public interest mandates dissolved into corporate profit margins, prompting experimentation with factual entertainment like *America's Most Wanted* (Fox, 1988–2011; Lifetime, 2011–12; Fox, 2021–) and *Cops* (Fox, 1989–2013; Paramount Network 2013–2020; Fox Nation, 2021–).[12] I also considered true crime's relationship to neoliberalism, or the free market approach to the organization of institutions and social life that has dominated capitalist societies in recent decades. Neoliberalism has brought about the privatization of public institutions and culture, the expansion of law enforcement and mass incarceration, and the intensification of risk assessment and surveillance—what scholars call a logic of detection—as everyday strategies.[13] My aim was to situate the rise of true crime, and meanings constructed by *Dateline*, within the forces and discourses at work in our historical conjuncture.

Reading media critically is a way to denaturalize repetitive ways of imagining and ordering the world and to create space for alternative possibilities. In this sense, textual analysis is always an imaginative endeavor. To place true crime within our contemporary conjuncture requires conceptual tools, including theories. Critical theories are explanations for cultural patterns and uneven power dynamics at the abstract level. My conceptual toolbox includes feminist and critical race theory, poststructuralist theories, and interdisciplinary theorizations of neoliberalism, affect, and citizenship. These critical perspectives inform my understanding of true crime, and my reading of *Dateline* brings something new to my understanding of theory. To engage with theory is not to impose a critical framework onto a text, but to dwell in the generative space between theoretical explanations and specific observations. Moving from the abstract to the concrete and back again allows media critics to interpret texts from critical angles, test assumptions, and contribute to collective processes of cultural theorization.

Intimate Citizenship and the Dystopia of Detection

On Superbowl Sunday, I was working on this chapter when a promotion for *Dateline* caught my attention. For viewers like me who are uninterested in football, NBC was counterprogramming "When Evil Paid a Visit," a two-hour episode about intimate betrayal in a leafy Connecticut suburb with not-to-be-missed plot twists. Despite the hype, the episode was merely the latest installment of the repetitive *Dateline* plot. *Dateline* presents "news" of crime as a melodramatic detective story and formularizes situations, settings, people, and resolutions across all episodes. In so doing, *Dateline* stitches feminized cultural pleasures into a narrow problematization of crime and recasts public life as an indeterminate cycle of interpersonal risk and wounded citizenship.

The standard *Dateline* episode unfolds as follows: NBC evening news anchor and *Dateline* host Lester Holt introduces the crime, alluding to interpersonal drama and dramatic twists and turns that entice viewers to want to know more. This setup also conveys to viewers that what they are about to see is important and true. Next up is a short synopsis of the episode that includes 1) testimony from a grieving relative or friend who becomes emotional recalling the shocking revelations to follow; 2) scenes from the picture-perfect community where the crime occurred; 3) the introduction of a beloved victim whose life was tragically cut short by a person they trusted, often a spouse, family member, or friend; and 4) interviews with police detectives who weigh in on the shocking nature of the case and the process of solving it.

The *Dateline* correspondent doubles as on-screen investigator and off-screen narrator. Their voiceover overlays the episode with dramatic flourish, utilizing literary clichés and ominous inflection to craft a coherent and compelling story. The episodes combine crime scene footage; 911 calls; family photographs and home videos; the testimonies of siblings, partners, children, friends, and others close to the victim; police interrogation videos; interviews with members of law enforcement and attorneys; and B-roll footage (detectives at work, footage of the home where the victim lived). These elements are assembled into a chain of events overlaid with representational codes (sad music, close-ups on tears) to cue emotions and connect the dots. While *Dateline* knows the outcome of the criminal investigations it covers, multiple suspects are always considered and red herrings are woven into the narrative for dramatic purposes.

To manufacture and maintain suspense up until the final reveal, *Dateline* deploys conventions such as blurring the background of potential perpetrators to conceal whether they are already imprisoned. The correspondent/narrator guides viewers in a process of detection and moral judgment anchored in the discursive and formulaic universe of the *Dateline* episode. On-screen graphics that break the fourth wall solicit opinions about the situations and people in the stories as if they are unmediated and direct responses to *Dateline*'s social media sites. In this respect, *Dateline* predated the tendency of much of contemporary true crime to persuade viewers to "make judgements based on strong emotional reactions and responses generated within the texts themselves."[14]

The mystery to be solved before the end of the episode is not only whodunnit, but why and to what effect. On *Dateline*, interpersonal relationships gone wrong are presumed to be causal to the crime at hand and investigated retrospectively for signs of deception, immorality, greed, and wickedness. Friends and relatives, as well as detectives, testify to the discovery of financial problems, extramarital affairs, and toxic behaviors below the surface of happy marriages, perfect families, and peaceful communities. The *Dateline* correspondent narrates the discord, weaving the deadly drama of daily life into the narrative arc of crime solving. Virtually every *Dateline* episode also emphasizes the emotional pain and trauma of losing mothers, siblings, partners, and cherished friends to murderers who acted in plain sight and were close to their victims.

Dateline's victim-centered approach remedies prior manifestations of true crime that focused on (and sometimes glorified) killers and heroized law enforcement. Police are an integral part of the *Dateline* formula and are regularly presented in a favorable light, excepting a few cases in which crime investigations are bungled. However, the narrative is built around righting the wrongs of tragic circumstances that impact innocent victims and grieving families. *Dateline*'s impetus to solve the crime (even through it has often already been solved and tried in court) is to bring emotional resolution in the form of carceral "justice" to real-life victims and their loved ones. While these are actual people with real feelings, they are also cast as stock characters in *Dateline*'s formula, and the uses to which they are put are not inherently progressive. *Dateline*'s victim-centered mysteries construct a hierarchy of innocent victimhood, as its cathartic resolution hinges on punishing individuals—with little attention to power dynamics or societal contexts.

Dateline's mystery of the week exaggerates the problem of murder (which has declined significantly in the United States in recent decades) and distorts its circumstances by disproportionately focusing on white middle-class victims, particularly women. This is the case with the majority of true crime and much news reporting as well—so much so that critics coined the phrase "Missing and Murdered White Woman Syndrome" to describe the problem and protest the comparative lack of attention to poor, Black, and brown victims. As media scholar Rebecca Wanzo argues, victims who generate the most attention are consistently characterized as "innocent" and therefore particularly worthy of public concern and sympathy. The discourse of innocence, she points out, does not apply to all, but correlates with the performance of idealized white femininity and upper-middle-class family status.[15] Female and male victims who experience systemic poverty, racialized oppression and violence, and state surveillance are excluded from the category of innocence and are rarely featured in true crime—including *Dateline*.

Dateline takes the Missing and Murdered White Woman Syndrome further than news reporting by incorporating elements of melodramatic women's culture into its formulaic construction and resolution of violent crime. Melodrama is a cultural sensibility that flows across genres historically associated with female audiences, including soap operas, daytime talk shows, and film and television dramas that emphasize interpersonal conflicts and emotions within the privatized sphere of everyday life (called "weepies" by early film critics). *Dateline*'s victim-centered approach to suspenseful true crime reproduces the cultural logic of melodrama, including a bifurcation of good and evil, sentimentality, and a focus on the private lives of white middle-class women.[16] This melodramatic frame delimits the nature and consequences of crime to individual characters and emotional registers.

Dateline centers an idealized version of Middle America "where crime isn't supposed to happen" and wholesome communities are "torn apart" by evil individuals concealed within them. This version of "America" is simultaneously feminized as a space of intimate danger, victimhood, and suffering.[17] While not all *Dateline* episodes focus on white female victims, the majority of them do. More importantly, the *Dateline* formula places the problem of violent crime as a whole within a melodramatic framework that centers individuals, whiteness, femininity, the nuclear family, emotion, domesticity, and private life. This aids and abets the narrativization of shocking and tragic crimes against some people as interpersonal drama, and the diminishment of a preponderance of violence that impacts other people and occurs elsewhere.

Dateline's murder mysteries are rarely set in urban areas, never in large cities like Chicago, New York, or Los Angeles. They unfold in pastoral settings such as "quaint" small towns and leafy suburban enclaves, typically in the Midwest, but also in the nonindustrial expanses of coastal and Southern states. These settings are coded as nostalgic, family-centered spaces where residents know each other, children can play outside from dawn to dusk, and murder is an extremely unusual and disorienting event. Signified through rolling scenes of lovely, old-fashioned downtowns and stately homes with manicured lawns, as well as local testimony and voiceover narration, this framing bestows innocence on geographical spaces and communities steeped in taken-for-granted associations of whiteness, middle-classness, and family-centeredness.

The single-family home and its surroundings similarly occupy a central place in the majority of *Dateline* episodes. Fatal crimes deemed on brand for *Dateline* (poisonings, deadly falls, stabbings, shootings) often occur in the domestic space of the comfortable familial home; the victims, perpetrators, and grieving survivors are usually family members. The tension between the idealized small town or suburban family and the horrific acts of repetitive violence presented by *Dateline* does not lead to a critical reassessment of the nuclear family or an exploration of social problems such as domestic violence, which impacts women and families of all kinds.

Rather, this tension is mobilized for melodramatic purposes, namely the expression of strong feelings about "evil" individuals, the monsters who threaten pastoral spaces and perfect families from within. On *Dateline*, violent crime is the result of pure evil embodied by lone individuals.

The pre-Enlightenment religious discourse utilized by *Dateline* disavows the sociopolitical contexts of repetitive violence (such as patriarchy) and shuts down any possibility of rehabilitation or social change. In typical melodramatic form, moral binaries of good and evil prompt empathy for innocent victims and judgment of those who are— and might be—perpetrators. Determining who is evil and who is not requires a process of endless, everyday detection that *Dateline* facilitates. By narrativizing true crimes as detective fiction and connecting suspense to the sensibilities of melodrama, *Dateline* displaces violent crime prevention onto emotional registers and an endless cycle of detection.

By locating evil individuals within idealized spaces, communities, and families, *Dateline* avoids racial stereotypes associated with urban violence and random crime. However, it nonetheless supports carceral logics and practices. In "Evil Pays a Visit," *Dateline*'s promise to expose the identity of a "wolf in sheep's clothing" who has committed a terrible crime casts an investigative spotlight on family members, colleagues, close friends, and acquaintances. According to the *Dateline* formula, anyone and everyone is a suspect until proven otherwise. This hermeneutic of suspicion may create good drama, but the presupposition that evil lurks unrecognized until it strikes supports a presumed need for aggressive policing that disproportionately impacts Black, brown, and poor communities. *Dateline* simultaneously conveys the neoliberal idea that risk management is a personal affair. To avoid being victimized by the people in our interpersonal orbit, we must all become our own private detectives, endlessly investigating everyone and everything, including the people we love and trust.

Conclusion

Because *Dateline* incorporates the iconography of TV journalism and operates under the banner of NBC News, its discursive construction of crime, innocence, victimhood, evil, and justice enters the public sphere as a matter of fact. Unlike fictional detective programs and emotionally wrought melodramas, *Dateline* circulates as a mediated pathway to citizenship and engagement with the public sphere, which makes its repetitive narration of interpersonal betrayal and emotionally driven justice all the more powerful. Unlike factual genres that address matters of public life, however, *Dateline* constructs and repeats a dystopian version of the social world in which "problems . . . are insoluble, because they are rooted within the individual and have no apparent roots in social conditions."[18] This dystopian vision of social life requires caution and endless management on the part of law enforcement as there is no plan or possibility for change in sight.

Dateline connects the suspicious, risky, security-oriented sensibilities of the neoliberal era to feminized forms of citizenship based on feeling and suffering. Addressing its gendered audience as an "intimate public," in the words of cultural theorist Lauren Berlant, *Dateline* renders the act of citizenship private and personal. Shaped through melodramatic women's culture, intimate publics foster a sense of collective membership and belonging based on emotion and trauma, but these feelings do not lead to public action, Berlant argues. As the mediated public sphere dissolves into mediated intimate publics like the one constituted by *Dateline*, intimate citizenship has emerged as a dominant structure for thinking about and solving problems—not just for women but for everyone.[19]

Dateline mainstreamed true crime by transforming it from a marginalized genre focused on serial crime and masculinized law enforcement to the cultural sphere of intimate citizenship. In his studies of earlier manifestations of true crime, media scholar Mark Seltzer suggested that tales of stranger violence conjoin citizens in a "pathological public sphere." True crime, he asserts, assembles publics around collective fascination with and anxieties about unresolvable violence "out there" in the social world, much as spectators gather at the scene of a deadly accident.[20] What has changed in recent decades is that vast amounts of true crime now situate violence within ordinary domestic spaces and direct public fascination inward to the intimate sphere of personal action and emotion. The public wound culture Selzer identified has become regularized, formularized, and privatized. *Dateline* and the countless true crime programs it spawned make violent crime seem both unbelievably shocking and utterly mundane.

Notes

1. Mark Seltzer, *Serial Killers: Death and Life in America's Wound Culture* (New York: Routledge, 1998).
2. Jean Murley, *The Rise of True Crime: Twentieth Century Murder and American Popular Culture* (Westport, CT: Prager, 2008).
3. Murley, *The Rise of True Crime*, 2.
4. Other examples include the podcast *Serial* and original docuseries presented on prestige streaming platforms such as Netflix and HBO. For more on how mundane and quality true crime are differentiated, see Elizabeth Walters, "Netflix Originals: The Evolution of True Crime Television," *The Velvet Light Trap* 88 (Fall 2021): 25–37.
5. Murley, *The Rise of True Crime*, 159.
6. NBC News, "Dateline is the #1 Most-Watched Newsmagazine for the 2021–2022 Broadcast Season," September 20, 2022, https://press.nbcnews.com/2022/09/20/dateline-is-the-1-most-watched-newsmagazine-for-the-2021-2022-broadcast-season-with-over-127-million-total-viewers-across-all-of-tv/.
7. Michel Foucault, *The Archaeology of Knowledge* (New York: Harper and Row, 1969); Stuart Hall, "The Work of Representation," in *Representation*, 2nd ed., edited by Stuart Hall, Jessica Evans, and Sean Nixon (Los Angeles: Sage, 2013), 1–47.
8. John Cawelti, "The Concept of Formula in the Study of Popular Literature," *Bulletin of the Midwest Modern Language Association* 5, no. 2 (1972): 119, 121–123.
9. Seltzer, *Serial Killers*.
10. Richard Campbell, *60 Minutes and the News: A Mythology for Middle America* (Champaign: University of Illinois Press, 1991).
11. Bill Carter, "A Prime-Time True-Crime Spree." *New York Times*, August 19, 2021, www.nytimes.com/2011/08/21/arts/television/true-crime-tv-on-shows-like-dateline.html.
12. Chad Raphael, "The Political-Economic Origins of Reali-TV," in *Reality TV: Remaking Television Culture*, edited by Susan Murray and Laurie Ouellette (New York: New York University Press, 2009), 123–40.
13. Wendy Brown, *Undoing the Demos: Neoliberalism's Stealth Revolution* (Princeton, NJ: Princeton University Press, 2015).
14. Tanya Horeck, *Justice on Demand: True Crime in the Digital Streaming Era* (Detroit: Wayne State Press, 2019), 10.
15. Rebecca Wanzo, "The Era of (Lost) White Girls: On Body and Event," *differences* 19, no. 2 (2008): 99–126.
16. Lauren Berlant, *The Queen of America Goes to Washington City* (Durham, NC: Duke University Press, 1997); Ben Singer, *Melodrama and Modernity* (New York: Columbia University Press, 1991); Christine Gledhill and Linda Williams, *Melodrama Unbound: Across History, Media, and National Cultures* (New York: Columbia University Press, 2018).

17 Laura Browder argues that true crime allows its predominantly white female audiences to vicariously process everyday sexism and male intimate partner violence and, in that sense, serves as a dystopian version of the romance genre. My analysis of *Dateline* addresses the extent to which the dystopian dimensions of true crime have expanded to personal relationships beyond heterosexual coupledom and emphasizes how its hybridized cultural form and melodramatic sensibilities displace public solutions onto private, intimate forms of citizenship. See Laura Browder, "Dystopian Romance: True Crime and the Female Reader," *Journal of Popular Culture* 39, no. 6 (2006): 928–53.
18 Browder, "Dystopian Romance," 932.
19 Berlant, *Queen of America*.
20 Mark Seltzer, "Wound Culture: The Pathological Public Sphere," *October* 89 (Spring 1997): 3–26.

19

Playing with Patterns

An Approach to Analyzing Children's Television Texts

KYRA HUNTING

Hunting turns to children's television, a genre often derided, seen as holding too little depth of meaning, and often discussed only when causing a moral panic, and she offers an approach based around exploring "patterns." The pattern she analyzes as an example is that of art education programs, considering what these say about art and creativity to children.

Think of a children's television show. What comes to mind? If you grew up in the early 2000s, *Avatar: The Last Airbender* (Nickelodeon, 2005–08) or *SpongeBob SquarePants* (Nickelodeon, 1999–) might have sprung to mind. Millennials might think of *Batman: The Animated Series* (Fox Kids, 1992–95) or *Care Bears* (syndication, 1985); someone from Generation X might remember *Scooby Doo* (CBS, 1969–78) and *She-Ra: Princess of Power* (syndication, 1985–87); and for baby boomers, it could be *Captain Kangaroo* (CBS, 1955–84) or *Sesame Street* (NET, 1969–70; PBS 1970–). A child today, however, might happily name *Sesame Street*, *SpongeBob*, *Scooby-Doo*, and *Care Bears* together with *Octonauts* (CBeebies, 2010–2021) and *Waffles + Mochi* (Netflix, 2021), series you may have never heard of. This exercise illustrates some of the fundamental challenges faced in including children's media in textual analysis scholarship. For many people, including media scholars, children's television tends to be frozen in time: perpetually defined by either the shows that they (often fuzzily) recall from their own childhood or from when their children, if they had them, were young. By contrast, for child viewers, children's television is infinitely flexible; kids are often, particularly at preschool ages, agnostic when it comes to time, geography, and original platform. An afternoon of viewing can easily take a four-year-old from the nearly twenty-year-old *Mickey Mouse Clubhouse* (Disney Channel, 2006–16) to the Russian *Masha and the Bear* (syndication, 2009–) to the Peabody award–winning *City of Ghosts* (Netflix, 2021), with a chaser of shorts made for social media. The contrast here is telling. While adults often consider children's media as either an undifferentiated mass ("Saturday morning cartoons" or "educational programming") or a single remembered exception, children are experiencing media in a rich, shifting, and diverse context. This dynamic contributes to a problematic lack of textual analysis of children's media, with many people content to collapse a wide variety of series with many genres, purposes, and audiences into indistinguishable "kids' stuff," barely worth differentiating except for the rare "exceptional case" like *Bluey* (ABC Kids, 2018–) that attained an adult fandom and, as a consequence, received significant press coverage.

This undifferentiated and dismissive view of children's media leads to a paradox in which children's media as a whole is treated as crucially important, the subject of anxiety around screen time and congressional hearings about violent or sexual content, but rarely as an aesthetic or cultural artifact worth attention in its individual instances. There have been short periods of excellent textual analyses of children's television by scholars like Heather Hendershot, Marsha Kinder, and Ellen Seiter, but even this work has frequently been embedded in industry or regulation studies.[1] While some similar work continues to individually appear, there has not been a consistent extended effort to analyze children's media texts (particularly television) as aesthetic and cultural objects. However, it is essential to examine children's media through the lens of textual analysis to better understand not only the cultural and aesthetic worlds of children but also these texts' relationship to larger media phenomena.

Children's media texts, in part because of their relative lack of scrutiny by critics, have a tendency to be playful and carnivalesque, experimenting with new looks and genres and breaking their own rules. They also are not infrequently the testing ground for new approaches to technology before they're taken up by more "serious" texts; by the time *Black Mirror* (Channel 4, 2011–14; Netflix, 2016–) had its much-lauded interactive episode "Bandersnatch," Netflix had already tried interactive episodes with children's texts like *The Adventures of Puss in Boots* (2015–18) and *Stretch Armstrong and the Flex Fighters* (2017–18). Looking at children's shows and films can provide a new way to think about established questions in textual analysis about intertextuality, temporality, and genre, as these series often experiment with genre or have expansive intertextual webs.

Despite the richness of the untapped world of children's media texts, they are infrequently chosen for textual analysis for, I believe, several reasons. It is unclear at times which texts should be "elevated" to analysis, texts that are important to children and that will also be perceived as important by readers. Rarely do critics or scholars provide significant attention to a children's show unless it garners a large adult audience. But thoughtful evaluators of children's media texts should not prioritize children's shows for analysis based solely on their appeal to adults, but instead adjust their aesthetic and narrative expectations to the goals of the programs and the target audience. Adults don't extensively watch and "discover" these programs. It requires concerted effort. Yet it is a concerted effort that we need to make; otherwise, our understanding of children's media will be dominated by social scientific content analysis that collapses texts together without sufficient consideration to aesthetic or contextual nuances. Further, with the rise of YouTube facilitating a rise in children's content designed to be released cheaply and frequently to promote engagement or toy tie-ins, it becomes even more important that we take the time to look closely at what children's television *can* be, what we *want* it to be, and how it has evolved. If we treat children's media as an amorphous whole whose individual texts are of minimal aesthetic or cultural consequence, then it can become easy to allow cheap, lower-quality, or homogenous texts to replace innovative, educational, or culturally meaningful ones. We can see the real consequences of this in multiple media contexts. Australia removed quotas on children's content and saw an 84 percent drop in locally made content, while HBO Max removed original, critically acclaimed children's content while adding cheap YouTube programs from kidfluencers.[2] If we don't take both the artists that create children's content and the content itself seriously, we can expect little else.

So how then do we approach the textual analysis of children's media effectively? Of course, nearly every textual analysis approach can be applied, but many of these approaches tend to consider only minimal "exemplary texts" often decontextualized from children's media in general. Instead, I argue that a wider range of children's media can be effectively studied through textual analysis that looks at patterns and relationships across programs and contexts. This approach draws from genre studies—an approach that focuses on the ways in which looking at media texts with shared attributes can help elucidate their characteristics, meanings, and artistic approaches. Children's media texts can be profitably understood by analyzing texts in clusters of media with shared attributes. Sometimes these may be explicitly networked texts such as franchises, or texts with clear and specific intertextual relationships. Parody and intertextuality are very common in children's media, with series such as *Phineas and Ferb* (Disney Channel, 2007–15, 2025–) reworking genres, classic literature, and famous films including *Star Wars* (dir. George Lucas, 1977). But children's media often also has looser relationships that are meaningful for children and families, including programs with similar types of characters, such as superheroes or talking animals; episodes tackling similar topics, such as the first day of school or Black hair care; or even programs sharing aesthetic attributes, such as the presence of musical sequences. Looking at children's media by first considering relationships and patterns using a cluster-based analysis allows us to better engage the world of children's media texts while avoiding the pitfalls discussed above.

An Approach to Accounting for Children's Media Patterns and Systems

This approach to analysis can avoid the problem of finding the perfect "representative" text or the sufficiently "significant" text. The first step in a cluster-based textual analysis is to immerse yourself in a number of children's media texts that you think may have connections or shared attributes to identify patterns and "hot spots." You should be creative and flexible in this approach, allowing for the possibility of discovery. You might explore posted episodes from a variety of shows on a children's television channel's website or suggested related series on a streamer, or you could take a more targeted approach by looking for series with a shared theme or overlapping creative teams. This open process of discovery is facilitated by two factors in children's media. First, many episodes are short—twelve minutes or even less—and second, most children's series are relatively episodic, able to be entered and understood at nearly any point. As you watch, keep an open mind and look either for patterns between texts, or for a topic or technique for which you want to find additional instances. This is a useful first step in identifying key texts, periods, or elements in children's media that are worthwhile for closer textual analysis. This broad viewing sets a foundation for the selection of a smaller number of exemplar texts or episodes that will be the focus of your textual analysis.

The quantity of exemplar texts should be manageable, but they should be sufficiently varied to make an argument. If you are comparing series or films as a whole, I find that three to five texts make a good-sized cluster for analysis. However, you may instead choose to look at individual episodes that share some attributes and, in these cases, more exemplars are typically useful, depending on the depth you wish to go into. Exemplar texts (or episodes) should share key characteristics or themes to support your central analysis but also have some key differences that make the consideration of multiple texts worthwhile. Topics for analysis can have a wide range, and many researchers will draw from other approaches or information gleaned from the industry. For example, you may choose to look at texts that share an interesting area of representation (such as films or series that include depictions of disability or video game culture), a specific context (such as a channel's brand refresh), or a goal, as in math-based educational programs. Because we often fail to think of children's media as artistic objects, contrary to how we often think of adult film and television, it can be particularly useful to choose exemplars because they share some aesthetic or structural elements. For example, you might choose to look at television episodes that tell the same story multiple times or use multiple perspectives or children's films and specials that combine animation techniques. It is not necessary that exemplars approach the attribute you choose the same way; in fact, it can be particularly interesting to analyze groups of texts that treat a topic or an aesthetic technique in varied ways.

After your exemplars have been selected, you should view the chosen texts multiple times. While you watch, you should take open-ended notes. Begin with general notes on the first viewing. Think about emerging patterns, moments you want to go back to, or questions you have. On subsequent viewings, your notes should become more detailed and targeted. Avoid writing down everything you see. At first, your notes should be just enough to help jog your memory and help you identify the patterns and themes that will make up your eventual argument. As you go on, your notes should focus on only the attributes of the text that you think may be relevant to your topic and argument as it emerges. After you feel you have a good handle on your exemplars, you should review your notes and begin making connections to help you form your argument. I usually like to do a mind map of my key observations and examples to organize my ideas and help me see patterns and connections that I missed in more linear experiences of the media I watched. Whatever way you choose, the key here is to find a way to move beyond description of the exemplars to an argument about them and to avoid getting caught up in too many details that may not fit together. Before you begin outlining or writing your textual analysis, it is key to first organize your thoughts into an argument with clear connections and observations. During this phase, you may also want to look for external information about the texts to help contextualize what you are seeing, such as production information you find in the trade press or information about events that occurred around the same period as your exemplars, influencing their content.

Once you are ready to outline or write, it is important to keep a few things in mind: don't apply the same lens you would to an adult text; instead, think about the text's audience and purpose—for example, what group of children is meant to be viewing this, what is their developmental stage, and how does this impact what you are seeing or how the text attempts to meet, for instance, an educational or representational goal? You also need to make sure you give each exemplar sufficient consideration and provide detailed examples. While this approach is designed to help tackle texts that are not necessarily considered "important" or "quality" by critics and the public, when you are writing you must treat them as important and highlight their significant qualities. How does this work in practice? I deploy this approach for a group of preschool series from different European contexts below.

Playful Patterns—Art Education Programs

A pair of cats examining the work of great Dutch masters, a one-eyed girl comparing a sunset to the work of Vincent Van Gogh, and a mischievous bright blue drop of paint climbing into a surrealist Joan Miró painting: these scenes come from European preschool programs celebrating art and music. Featured in the 2022 Prix Jeunesse International festival, *Pim & Pom at the Museum* (NPO Zappelin, 2021–22; hereafter *Pim & Pom*) depicts two cats who explore the works of famous Dutch artists as they follow their owner, "The Lady," to the museum where she learns about famous works and then emulates them. This same festival included *Jasmine & Jambo* (SX3, 2021–22), a Catalan-language Spanish series centering on two friends who play and celebrate music in the surreal "Soundland." It was at the Prix that I first discovered this cluster of programs: series for young children that center the arts and feature stylized animation drawing on iconic art and illustration styles used in playful "nonrealistic" ways. My interest in this kind of children's series expanded when I encountered *Mironins* (Clan, 2021) at the 2022 Chicago International Children's Film Festival. Like *Pim & Pom*, this Spanish series is set in a museum and follows three paint drops (blue, yellow, and red) who've escaped from a painting as they explore different Joan Miró paintings. While these series intermix references to artists and technical terms to varied degrees, they all share a relationship as fine arts educational programs that center art as something playful and changeable, a realm for imagination. This stands in stark contrast with American arts-based preschool series like *Little Einsteins* (Playhouse Disney, 2005–09), which are more didactic.

These three series' episodes are five to seven minutes long and engage with art and music as expansive living things. When the cats Pim and Pom and the paint drop Mironins enter art, they see activities and parts of the world that go beyond the canvas. They make art appear accessible by emphasizing its constructedness through familiar aesthetic features. In *Pim & Pom*, the cats observe the art as it appears in photographs, true to life, reflecting the varied artists' styles. But then the pair of cats enters the paintings, or imagines they do, and the paintings' worlds retain some of their distinctive features and brushstrokes but also take on distinctive, episode-specific features. The features of human and animal characters are simplified with heavy black outlines that draw attention to their facial features. The look is similar to the UPA style, a visual look popularized by animation from the United Productions of America studio that included flat graphic characters, often with abstract art influences,

Figure 19.1: The animated residents of various Miró paintings waiting to visit a carnival painting in the Mironins episode "Ro, artista de circo." www.rtve.es/infantil/serie/mironins/video/ro-artista-circo/6261318/.

although less clean in places. In contrast with most contemporary animation, these choices draw attention to the characters as illustrated, *constructed* art in and of themselves. While the museum itself is visually realistic, using photos in backgrounds, the human characters, like The Lady, share these distinctive animated features. *Mironins* similarly draws on the primary colors of Joan Miró and shows a featured painting as it would appear in a museum, but it also brings out specific elements of the art and reworks them into playful, more easily recognizable versions (see figure 19.1). The elements they often pick—dogs, ladders, or clowns—are elements familiar to children's worlds.

Jasmine & Jambo shares with these series bright colors, simple shapes, and playful elements—like living music notes called tra-la-las—but its focus is primarily on music. Music-oriented series in the US like *Little Einstein* or *Beat Bugs* (Netflix, 2016–18) tend to focus on music appreciation with accurate performances of famous pieces. *Jasmine & Jambo*, by contrast, depicts the process of making music and features elements that are familiar for children. For instance, Jasmine's beautiful but sad songs in "Festival in a Minor Key" are played on a xylophone, a common early instrument or toy, while in "Bang Bang Bang" she uses pots for her percussive protest. The series employs these basic instruments in elaborate and creative ways. Similarly, *Pim & Pom* and *Mironins* present the art as both expansive—able to stretch with children's imaginations—and accessible. When the cats or Mironin paint drops enter a painting, they see more of its world: the rest of a forest, the yard outside a window, or the varied potential of a single flexible line on a canvas. The world of a painting or sculpture becomes a sort of story or playground for the characters and is associated more with the emotional or imaginary world of children than with the historical context of the paintings. The characters solve problems like helping a chained-up bird go out and play with their friends, helping a friend out of a hole they've fallen into (a common trope in children's animation), having fun in a surrealist circus, or swimming in the sea.

All three series use simple shapes in innovative ways to construct their world. *Pim & Pom* features mod rectangular blocks in the background of both The Lady's home and the various places the cats visit inside the painting. *Jasmine & Jambo*'s home of Soundland is constructed by layering simplified solid color shapes in a modernist style reminiscent of Mary Blair (see figure 19.2). The surrealism in *Mironins* is much less pronounced than in the work of the series' namesake artist, but the style is still firmly rooted in modern art with cubist as well as surrealist influences. These elements draw explicitly and implicitly on the work of modern artists but also evoke children's toys like Colorforms or blocks. The possibility of play implied here is particularly clear in

Figure 19.2: The sun and landscape look down in frustration in the *Jasmine & Jambo* episode "AaaaaaRHG!" *https://www.youtube.com/watch?v=NZE26v8AIDE&ab_channel =SX3*.

Figure 19.3: Pim and Pom ride a rocket ship they made out of shapes in the episode "What Is This?"

episodes or scenes in which the shapes are broken down and recombined in new ways. In the episode "What Is This?," Pim and Pom try to figure out what the painting *Suprematist Composition 1915* by Kazimir Malevich—a collection of layered black, red, blue, green, and yellow rectangles, trapezoids, and squares—represents. When they enter the painting, they immediately begin to rearrange its shapes, with one cat trying to put the colors together in order and another turning them into a "colorful trampoline." As they try to decipher the work they remake, they turn the shapes into a variety of objects, like a staircase and a windmill, before settling on it being a rocket ship they ride through space (see figure 19.3). At the end of the episode, the shapes in the painting are mimicked in similar paper cutouts the cats play with on the floor, concretizing the playful potential of the abstract painting. This episode uses two principles, transformation and movement, that underline the imaginative possibilities of art. They also serve a pedagogical purpose, showing child viewers how the basic elements of a work of art—colors and shapes—can be manipulated into something new.

The idea that art is there to be reworked and played with flows throughout these series. The Lady in *Pim & Pom* ends most episodes by showing her own reworked version of the famous artwork featured in the episode. Often, she makes significant changes to the piece, making it more cheerful or painting her cats into the scene. She frequently provides upbeat critiques of her own work, thematically communicating that art doesn't need to be perfect and that the enjoyment and voice of the creator matter. Transformation is modeled in The Lady's reworked masterpieces and in *Mironins*, where features of Miró's paintings are recombined as the mischievous paint drops take objects from one painting to another. But re-creation is most literal in *Jasmine & Jambo*. Large and cheerful Jambo can transform his body into anything he can imagine. At one point in "Evening Blues," he becomes a train and carries Jasmine across lines from sheet music. Like transformation, movement functions as an invitation to play with art as objects come to life. A line in a Joan Miró painting creeps around smiling and inviting the Mironins to follow it, or the shafts of wheat in a Van Gogh painting shuffle in the breeze, providing a hiding place for the playful Pim and Pom. These moments of movement not only facilitate storytelling across the series, but also help viewers see the action captured and conveyed in art, even the most abstract. This is exemplified in the *Pim & Pom* episode "The Big City," featuring the Piet Mondrian painting *Victory Boogie Woogie* (1944). The abstract modernist painting is explained by the teacher in the museum as a cityscape, and Pom begins pointing out the taxis and buildings in the collection of colorful squares and rectangles. Pim and Pom enter the piece, and the small colorful shapes launch into motion, accompanied by a jazz soundtrack bringing the city to life. The moving rectangles become cars with the help of honking horns. Pim and Pom zip along a winding subway route and steadily rise in a rectangle elevator. Like the reconfiguring shapes in the "What Is It?" episode, the movement in "The Big City" makes abstract art appealing and accessible by using motion to help children see the art as decipherable and playful.

The use of simple shapes in a way that utilizes movement and transformation to connect fine art to the world of childhood goes to the core educational proposition of these series. While I have noted that they are not didactic, they *are* pedagogic, with clear educational dimensions beyond simply exposure to fine art. Instead of focusing on facts or terminology, which are present but minimal, these series focus on modeling ways to *look at*, and listen to, art. This is particularly clear in *Pim & Pom*, where the cats point out small, but important, details to one another. Often these details are about the story conveyed in the painting: noting a person peeking through a window, the expression on someone's face, or a strange combination of animals. By showing the characters discussing these small, often easily overlooked, attributes and pairing these conversations with close-ups of the noted elements, these series show children how to look at art to make their own discoveries instead of instructing them on what they should find important. The mostly nonverbal series *Mironins* mirrors this approach in a playful way. Each episode ends with a teacher addressing a group of bored children standing in front of a work of art with a droned "Blah, blah, blah." The children look miserable but then burst into laughter when one of the Mironins pops out of the featured painting and shows the children the work of art in a new way, climbing down the frame as an outline silhouette, for example, or spraying the adult with a burst of water.

While I identify these series as art appreciation education, they meet this goal in a way that centers play. These series break down the notion that fine art is sacred or historical and allow it to burst from the confines of its frames. It's notable that the museum space in *Pim & Pom* is photorealistic and in *Mironins* the museum is dull black, white, and gray, highlighting the colorful paintings by contrast. It is the art, unconfined or disciplined, that is made welcoming. These series introduce students to difficult and lauded pieces of art and complex music, but they do so as an invitation to play, creating worlds out of art and sound that are bursting with color, movement, and transformation. I have begun by arguing for the importance of employing textual analysis in helping us understand and elevate children's programming, an essential goal in itself. I now want to end with these observations, which demonstrate how doing textual analysis can also help us see the effects that things like media policy and export norms have on what children see in the first place. As of this writing, while these series are available for English-speaking audiences in the UK and Canada, none have been exported to the US. These productions also garnered investments from government incentives or cultural organizations, and I venture that some of the aesthetic risk-taking involved in these programs reflects their creation in countries that invest in cultural or educational programming. This context suggests that these wonderfully creative and culturally celebratory programs not only share narrative and aesthetic attributes but also represent both a European sensibility and a specific kind of investment in children's programming rarely seen in the United States.

Through this case study, we can see that textual analysis can not only draw our attention to key attributes in children's programming but also elucidate an approach to teaching children about art. And this textual analysis opens up larger questions for scholars interested in processes such as global media export culture or in different financing models. Talking about texts allows us to do many things. We can observe not only the ways in which children's shows deploy playful aesthetic elements to support their educational goals, but also the relationship between the contexts that shape children's media and the content that emerges. Most essentially, this method encourages us to grow our understanding and appreciation of children's media texts as aesthetic and narratively rich. This form of analysis allows us to fully appreciate and understand children's media texts not as a monolith or a set of "good" or "bad" objects but as diverse, complex, and meaningful works of art and culture.

Notes

1 Heather Hendershot, *Saturday Morning Censors: Television Regulation Before the V-Chip* (Durham, NC: Duke University Press, 1998); Marsha Kinder, *Playing with Power in Movies, Television and Video Games: From Muppet Babies to Teenage Mutant Ninja Turtles* (Berkeley: University of California Press, 1991); Ellen Seiter, *Sold Separately: Parents and Children in Consumer Culture* (New Brunswick, NJ: Rutgers University Press, 1995).
2 Burke, Kelly, "Australian-Made Children's TV Content Found to Have Collapsed Between 2019 and 2022," *The Guardian*, August 1, 2023, www.theguardian.com/culture/2023/aug/01/australian-made-childrens-tv-content-found-to-have-collapsed-between-2019-and-2022.

20

A New Situation

Textual Analysis Across TV Texts

DAPHNE GERSHON

Gershon showcases how we can effectively work across texts by looking at smaller narrative units, such as recurring situations that appear across genres and texts. Through a variety of brief examples followed by an extensive example of "Can't get it up" jokes about erectile dysfunction, Gershon explains how to trace and utilize this analytical category of a "situation," and how it can uncover important, yet overlooked, representational patterns.

Over the last two decades, television scholars have had to contend with an overwhelming volume of television content. While several recent articles have noted that the era of "peak TV" may be over, with the rapid expansion of television shows declining somewhat, hundreds of new scripted television series are still being released every year, leading to a highly scattered and dispersed media landscape.[1] In addition, the continued proliferation of viewing platforms and modes of distribution, and the rise of "nonlinear" viewing, have profoundly altered our understanding of television as a mass medium that revolves around audiences receiving the same content at the same time. Whereas previously, scholars were able to explain the necessity and significance of studying a specific television show due to its wide-ranging exposure and ability to speak to entire nations, it has now become increasingly challenging to argue that any single program and its ideological meanings can have a significant and far-reaching societal impact. Therefore, to adapt to the vastness of contemporary TV and ensuing audience fragmentation, I argue that today's television analysts could consider working across texts, incorporating more extensive collections of television programs.

Yet, if we are to pursue this approach, the question then becomes, How do we analyze numerous different television texts without diluting the richness and depth that characterize the close readings of individual shows? I propose that one way to accomplish this is through an analysis of smaller narrative units that I term "situations." These recurring events, plot conventions, conditions, and narrative tropes, which do not span an entire series or even an entire episode, make the analysis of a larger number of texts and the articulation of their shared patterns more manageable.

In this chapter, I explain how we can shift our focus from entire series or characters to situations. I demonstrate how to utilize existing resources and databases to search for specific narrative themes across various television texts, and how to identify and deconstruct their recurring patterns. In addition, I show the benefits of this mode of analysis, pointing to how it can provide new perspectives that in part uncover long-overlooked representational structures by spotlighting the interactions between characters. In the first part of the chapter, I illustrate the expansiveness and flexibility of this analytical category by using a wide variety of brief examples of what might constitute a situation. In the second part of the chapter, I offer a more in-depth step-by-step guide through a single case study that draws from my research on the portrayals of erectile dysfunction in television comedy, detailing how I analyzed the appearance of this situation in forty episodes from thirty television shows.

Defining and Finding the Situation

According to Lauren Berlant, "A situation is a state of things in which *something* that will perhaps matter is unfolding amid the usual activity of life. It is a state of animated and animating suspension that forces itself on consciousness, that produces a sense of the emergence of something in the present that may become an event."[2] Thus, a situation involves some sort of evolving and temporary disruption or change in the course of events. While some situations are framed as transformational moments, such as virginity loss or coming-out narratives, which, especially when experienced by a main character, can shape the narrative of the series beyond a single episode or scene, many other situations are almost exclusively confined to one episode and are not referenced subsequently. While the same situation can often appear across different genres, its temporary state also makes it akin to what Bob Rehak and Elizabeth Ellcessor each refer to as a "microgenre," which involves small shifts or moments of representation that occupy "a middle ground somewhere between individual shot and full-length movie."[3]

Consequently, although the analysis of situations benefits from an understanding of the texts' broader plot, characters, genre conventions, and industrial profile, centering the analysis mainly on these kinds of briefer moments allows scholars to include multiple TV texts rather than just selecting one or two shows, a pattern that has often led to the overrepresentation of certain programs within TV scholarship over others. Take, for example, the series *Buffy the Vampire Slayer* (WB, 1997–2001; UPN, 2001–03), which has been the subject of hundreds of academic articles and anthologies and is known for being especially beloved by academics. This pattern has inevitably led to a select number of texts shaping our understanding of certain fields or areas of representation. *Buffy* is often the go-to series when referencing representations of teen girlhood, postfeminism, and the supernatural television genre, for instance. Yet, looking across texts through the prism of situations, we might ask, What additional or different perspectives can we gain on these very same subjects if we were to expand our view? Furthermore, in examining a situation, researchers might gravitate to a particular text not because it has considerable social resonance and significance, but simply because it frequently features this situation, perhaps even incorporating the situation in its premise. For example, to examine depictions of giving birth, some scholars have chosen to focus on TLC's *A Baby Story* (1998–2007) or Channel 4's *One Born Every Minute* (2010–18).[4] While these individual texts contain many representations of giving birth, they are not quite able to speak to the wider media discourse about this experience that has commonly been featured in a variety of different television texts.

Although some scholars may argue, as does Roberta Pearson, that the brief situations featured in television episodes "cannot be considered in isolation from the broader series into which they accumulate," and that we must examine a television series in its entirety to understand its representations and ideological messages, we must also be conscious that this all-consuming pattern of consumption does not reflect how most viewers watch television and how they come to be influenced by its messages.[5] This is perhaps especially true in the digital era, in which moments from television episodes and their meanings have frequently developed an independent existence outside of the larger texts they are part of, transforming into memes, GIFs, and brief clips that circulate widely on social media platforms such as Facebook, X (formerly known as Twitter), and TikTok. As a result, the mode of analysis that examines situations across texts is possibly especially well suited for this contemporary fragmented media landscape in which television content is bracketed and partitioned, challenging our conceptualization of television as operating mainly as a "long-form narrative."[6]

In order to identify and select certain situations as objects of analysis, there are several aspects to consider. It is important to identify events that are common enough to appear in numerous texts, but specific and narrow enough that the number of examples is not overwhelming. For instance, students attending class, especially in teen dramas, is likely too common, uneventful, and broad of a situation. By contrast, a school shooting (or attempted school shooting) is a more distinct and unique situation, which, due to its social relevance and significance, has appeared in multiple teen shows, including *One Tree Hill* (WB, 2003–06; CW, 2006–12), *Degrassi: The Next Generation* (CTV, 2001–09; MuchMusic, 2010–13; MTV Canada, 2013–15), *Glee* (FOX, 2009–15), *My So-Called Life* (ABC, 1994–95), *Veronica Mars* (UPN, 2004–06; CW, 2006–07), *13 Reasons Why* (Netflix, 2017–20), *Buffy the Vampire Slayer*, and *Grand Army* (Netflix, 2020). This balance allows researchers to include all the episodes they can find that feature a particular situation rather than having to engage in random sampling of episodes, which can often lead to misleading findings. In constructing an analysis that works across texts, the goal is often to identify common themes. To accomplish this, the situation should also be cohesive and formulaic or structured enough to contain specific "narrative beats and representational choices" that reappear in different texts.[7] For example, in her analysis of "disability dates," an episodic arc of 1990s sitcoms in which a lead character and a disabled person have a brief romance, Elizabeth Ellcessor describes how different episodes follow the same pattern, cohering into an identifiable narrative trope or "microgenre."[8] She details how in these episodes the "nondisabled lead characters often appear uncomfortable or surprised by the revelation of disability," yet despite their initial missteps they develop a sense of acceptance through conversation with the disabled character or with other regular characters, only at the end to encounter a "reversed rejection," "with the nondisabled lead dumped or the disabled suitor revealed as otherwise unsuitable."[9] It is through this repetition that we are able to make a stronger argument about the ways in which disability is represented and understood within television texts.

While some recurring situations or events in television episodes, such as weddings, are also frequent in real life, others might only be a common occurrence in media texts, such as being left at the altar, a narrative trope that has appeared in multiple television comedies such as *Happy Endings* (ABC, 2011–13), *Cheers* (NBC, 1982–93), *A Different World* (NBC, 1987–93), *How I Met Your Mother* (CBS, 2005–14), *Frasier* (NBC, 1993–2004), and *Friends* (NBC, 1994–2004), as well as a number of television dramas such as *Pan Am* (ABC, 2011–12), *Grey's Anatomy* (ABC, 2005–), *Downton Abbey* (ITV, 2010–15), and *Charmed* (WB, 1998–2006). Such media conventions have long been spotlighted and mocked by various parodic and satirical media; however, in recent years the subject of media tropes has gained even more visibility, with the advent of YouTube channels such as WatchMojo and The Take, *Buzzfeed* listicles, and sites such as TV Tropes dedicated to defining various tropes and identifying their presence in different kinds of popular media.[10] Although some tropes refer only to types of characters (e.g., The Manic Pixie Dream Girl) or narrative arcs (e.g., enemies turned to lovers), much attention has also been given to types of situations. For example, many articles in the popular press have commented on and listed various instances of the "meet-cute," a term that refers to a repetitive scene and structural device commonly found in romantic comedies in which the two protagonists meet for the first time, usually in a humorous, unexpected, or surprising way that sparks a romance between the two.[11]

This growing commentary on narrative patterns across media texts not only illustrates the cultural relevancy of examining situations, but also points to some useful ways of finding relevant examples. Tracing instances of a specific situation can often be more challenging and less straightforward compared to other modes of analysis that examine a collection of texts, such as the study of a genre, the works of a particular artist or director, shows from a particular era, or series that center on a specific social identity. While the design of research methods has much to do with how we choose to analyze data, it is also about the ways in which we try to find and collect data, a task that is certainly more challenging when analyzing a brief narrative trope, which might not be easily defined. Unfortunately, even when scholars do focus on narrative tropes or situations, they do not always disclose how they found their media examples. Therefore, I maintain that we must offer more transparency about existing resources and databases and how to utilize them. In addition to popular websites, and the aforementioned site TV Tropes, which contains a detailed index of countless media tropes, there are also databases of TV show transcripts and synopses of episodes such as IMDb, the Paley Archive Database, SnapStream, and Pop Mystic, which can be used to trace specific narrative themes across various television texts.[12] In addition, there have also been researchers who have built their own databases for the study of a specific situation. For example, Gretchen Sisson, Steph Herold, and Katrina Kimport have developed the Advancing New Standards in Reproductive Health's (ANSIRH) Abortion Onscreen Database, which is "a listing of all film and television depictions available to viewers in the United States in which a character obtains an abortion, or discloses having one in the past."[13] Different databases hold different features and advantages, and thus, the best results often come from combining and using multiple resources and databases.

After we have found a satisfactory or substantial collection of examples, there are several questions to consider to reach important insights and identify valuable links between texts, such as:

- What are the causes or motivating factors that led to the situation?
- How is the emergence of this situation signaled?
- Which characters are involved in this situation? What are their roles and their responses?
- Is the situation depicted as a problem? If so, what solutions are suggested? How is the situation ultimately resolved, if at all?
- What are the consequences of this situation and for whom? Is there a return to the status quo or is there lasting change and transformation?
- What is the duration of the situation: a scene, an act, an episode, or multiple episodes and seasons?

- In what kinds of television texts does this situation usually appear: for example, is it associated with a particular genre or era of television? How might the portrayal of this situation, its stages, and conventions be shaped by era, genre, contexts of production, and authorship?

In answering these questions, the purpose is not just to identify and organize patterns in representation through numeric data, as is common in social sciences and mass communication approaches, but to probe and explore these patterns further, to flesh them out through rich detail and description, and to interrogate their connections to broader social and cultural meanings.

As Michael Newman asserts, the power of representation and its connection to larger systems of power often come from repetition, and thus there is much value in tracing commonalities across depictions of a situation.[14] At the same time, however, interesting realizations can come from finding differences, such as tracing the ways in which the depiction of the same situation changes over time. For example, Lisa Cuklanz, in her study of TV depictions of rape, contends that while earlier depictions in the 1970s typically included formulaic depictions of violent stranger rape, in later decades, depictions became more complex and tended to focus more on date or acquaintance rape.[15] In addition to the time period, one can also explore variations based on identity. For example, if we were to examine the situation of a character being pulled over by the police, we would likely notice that this scenario contains distinctly different narrative patterns based on the character's race. When white characters are pulled over, as in shows such as *Friends*, *How I Met Your Mother*, and *Seinfeld* (NBC, 1989–98), this exchange with the police typically revolves around the character's (in)ability to flirt or charm their way out of a ticket. Conversely, in shows such as *The Fresh Prince of Bel-Air* (NBC, 1990–96), *Family Matters* (ABC, 1989–97; CBS, 1997–98), and *Brooklyn Nine-Nine* (FOX, 2013–18; NBC, 2019–21) that feature Black characters being pulled over, the interaction revolves around racial discrimination and police brutality. Similarly, Alfred Martin Jr. points to how "coming out" narratives have a meaningful and ostensible relationship to race. He maintains that in the 1990s and early 2000s, while white- and multicultural-cast sitcoms had moved beyond the sole situation of coming out, incorporating gay characters in a variety of story arcs and motifs, the same did not hold true for Black-cast sitcoms and their representation of Black gayness.[16]

In the aforementioned examples, although these situations can be defined as mainly occurring to or performed by an individual character, fundamentally, they rely on the notion of interaction, forming as a result of the presence and reaction of multiple characters. Consequently, the focus on situations allows us to spotlight the relational aspects of representation and to highlight the significance of characters' interactions. Much of TV scholarship on representation, as well as work done by media advocacy groups such as the Gay and Lesbian Alliance Against Defamation (GLAAD), the National Association for the Advancement of Colored People (NAACP), and the National Hispanic Media Coalition, has focused on the depiction of characters, examining the visibility and image of a particular social group or identity. Although this kind of research has certainly been valuable to media studies, as Lori Kido Lopez points out in chapter 3 in this volume, it has also too often led to rehashed and reductive analyses that center simply on whether members of a particular social group exhibit negative or positive, stereotypical or nonstereotypical, attributes. The study of situations helps us to approach representation through new perspectives and to uncover long-overlooked mechanisms that shape representational structures. For example, Elizabeth Ellcessor, in focusing on the disability "date" rather than simply on disabled characters, is able to address the dynamic that is created between disabled and nondisabled characters, a dynamic that establishes a neoliberal view of disability and elucidates the ways in which disabled people contend with being perceived as undesirable and nonsexual.[17] In addition, the focus on experiences can help better direct us to when media depictions are able to evoke a sense of cultural specificity. According to Kristen Warner, the current popular discourse on representation, which focuses primarily on visibility, the need and value of seeing people who look like you on screen, fails to account for the ways in which representation provides meaning through the sensation of resonance and recognition, which necessitates, in part, cultural specificity. The focus on situations might be a way to help us better articulate the kinds of representations that evoke resonance versus those that, as Warner terms, are considered "plastic."[18]

Lastly, the focus on situations can remind us that representation studies can go far beyond the examination of social identity, focusing on actions and habits such as substance abuse and alcohol consumption. One can look, for example, at the recent media course offered at the University of Notre Dame titled "Drunk on Film" on the popular depictions of drinking, especially at college or high school parties.[19] While we can learn a great deal about dominant social values from the repeated portrayal of the situation or event of a college kegger, this subject remains largely underexplored outside of the fields of health communications and media effect studies. Consequently, the study of situations is an approach to textual analysis that not only is particularly well suited for the new industrial reality of television, but can encourage new avenues of research in the field of critical television studies.

Case Study: Portrayals of Erectile Dysfunction in Television Comedy

In this section, I demonstrate how to put this approach into action through a case study from my published work on sexual depictions and the social norms they privilege. A particular sexual situation I was interested in exploring was the depiction of erectile dysfunction, since it is so closely tied to notions of loss of masculinity and is frequently meant to induce anxiety among characters precisely because of its disruption of expected gendered norms. In my analysis, I centered on the appearance of this situation in television comedy because of the genre's tendency to expose sexual taboos and anxieties, which have made instances of erectile dysfunction a more common trope in comparison to other media texts, appearing in numerous television comedies going back to the 1970s.[20]

The first step to examining depictions of this stigmatized subject that has regulated gender roles and sexual interactions was to find examples. As a trope that relates to sex, the occurrence of erectile dysfunction, especially in television comedies, is often described in episodes through euphemisms, double entendres, and visual cues rather than explicit language. Therefore, trying to find examples only by searching through episode transcripts that contained relevant keywords would have likely not been very effective. Fortunately, I was able to find a large collection of examples using the website TV Tropes, which has a webpage titled "The Loins Sleep Tonight" that specifically addresses the subject of impotence.[21] The list of examples does not mention episode names, but contains sufficient detail that allowed me, for the most part, to find the episodes through Google searches. To increase the collection of episodes, I also looked at Nielsen ratings to find top-rated shows from the last five decades and cross-searched the name of each show with the terms "impotence" and "erectile dysfunction."[22] In addition, once I realized that the sample consisted exclusively of white straight males, I used the same procedure of cross-searching these terms with comedies that feature leading or recurring gay characters and racially diverse casts. Yet, only two shows were discovered during this process, *The Jeffersons* (CBS, 1975–85), a Black-cast sitcom, and *It's All Relative*, which features a male gay couple as part of its core cast (ABC, 2003–04), leading to a final sample of forty episodes from thirty television programs. Although I attempted to be as methodical as possible, the episodes I found are by no means a complete tally of all episodes in American and British television to feature this situation. Nevertheless, these episodes represent a sufficiently expansive selection of key texts that together have much value in helping us understand how television comedies talk about erectile dysfunction and how they utilize this trope in ways that shape gender and sexual norms. Furthermore, this collection includes texts that have rarely been discussed in relation to sex and television, as opposed to television comedies that are more critically acclaimed and in which sex is a more frequent and prominent feature such as *Sex and the City* (HBO, 1998–2004) or *Girls* (HBO, 2012–17).

In attempting to find dominant themes across episodes, prior to viewing, I had several research questions in mind, such as, What is the context in which erectile dysfunction occurs? What are the common causes for it? What are the reactions of different characters, and what solutions do they offer? In addition, given that I was focusing on the genre of television comedy, I wanted to know how humor was cued in these narratives. In addition, there were also several patterns and questions that came up inductively through the process of viewing and taking notes, such as the overexuberance and relief expressed by the male character once the issue of his inability to have an erection was "fixed." Although this collection of texts included over thirty different instances or storylines about erectile dysfunction, the task of analysis proved manageable, in part given the uniformity across episodes. There were a number of dominant themes that appeared across different decades and forms of comedy, in network shows, cable programing, and Netflix originals, and were featured in both female-centric and male-centric series, showcasing the pervasiveness and endurance of these themes throughout the televisual landscape. In addition, most examples were confined only to episodic arcs or plotlines. This tendency to quickly resolve the issue is likely the result of sitcom tradition, which is characterized by the constant return to the status quo.[23] Nevertheless, this pattern also appeared in several programs that are more serialized and less aligned with the classic sitcom such as *The Office* (NBC, 2005–13), *How I Met Your Mother*, *The Inbetweeners* (E4, 2008–10), *BoJack Horseman* (Netflix, 2014–20), and *Fleabag* (BBC, 2016–19), highlighting that the study of brief situations should not be limited just to TV genres that are episodic. Furthermore, the duration and recurrence of a narrative trope are also important parts to include in the analysis itself. Therefore, in my analysis, I discussed how the quick resolution of erectile dysfunction storylines not only fails to acknowledge that it can often be a chronic issue but also limits the depiction of its possible causes, treatments, and solutions, focusing mainly on psychological rather than physical causes, such as the "dangers" of men having emotion in relation to sex.

The most consistent theme, found in thirty-nine out of the forty episodes, was that following the male character's inability to achieve or maintain an erection, sexual activity comes to a complete halt, and the characters do not attempt alternate ways to provide or receive sexual pleasure. In fact, it is this pause and animated suspension of sexuality that transforms the occurrence into a situation. This moment of discontinuation served as a jumping-off point through which I showed how this pause is tied to male anxiety and the social linkages that are made between erectile performance and masculinity. In addition, I explored how this response relies on the coital imperative, the primacy of penile-vaginal intercourse as the standard for "normal" and pleasurable sex, promoting an androcentric view of sexuality that is not necessarily reflective of how most women achieve sexual gratification.

To interrogate this pattern more fully, I used not only the commonalities among episodes, but their exceptions as well. Out of all of the episodes, there is one, *Californication*'s (Showtime, 2007–14) season 7 episode "Levon," in which a male character attempts to provide sexual pleasure in alternate ways in response to his erectile "inadequacies." Yet, this attempt is depicted as unpleasant and undesirable, only further affirming the notion that not having penetrative sex is a form of failure. In the episode, Charlie begs his wife to let him "go down" on her after multiple unsuccessful attempts to achieve an erection. During this attempt, Charlie, overwhelmed by his depression, begins to cry while his wife Marcy exhibits feelings of frustration, annoyance, and, finally, apathy.

As the description above illustrates, although sexual dysfunction may appear to be a condition occurring only within the male character's body, the inability to have an erection gains meaning and becomes an issue or situation within the context of sex, a relational activity and shared experience between and among individuals. In the series I examined, these interactions are almost exclusively between a male and a female character. As a result, there is much significance to the reactions of female characters. In examining the responses of female sexual partners, I found that they are repeatedly placed in a supportive and attentive role to contain the volatility of the scene, promoting the traditional social norm that women must alter their behavior and desires to tend to the male ego. These women offer words of encouragement, reassure the male character there is nothing to be concerned about, calmly tolerate his outlandish behavior, attempt to cater to his desires to make him feel better, and show much dedication and patience to finding a solution, while hiding their own fears and frustrations. Due to my previous viewing of these series and familiarity with their characters, I was able to further strengthen this claim by noting how the anxiety associated with erectile dysfunction and the blow to the male ego are seen as so significant that some female characters become uncharacteristically sympathetic and kind. For example, Marie in *Everybody Loves Raymond* (CBS, 1996–2005), whose behavior toward her husband is typically truculent and belligerent, is surprisingly warm and loving once she finds out he has been struggling to perform sexually, while Marcy in *Married . . . with Children* (FOX, 1987–97), who is typically assertive and domineering, becomes uncharacteristically doting and subservient. This added detail shows that though a deep examination of the series in its entirety is likely not necessary in order to analyze its depiction of this kind of specific situation, a basic understanding of the series' premise, characters, and genre is beneficial and encouraged.

By deconstructing this sexual situation, analyzing its causes, its ramifications, its resolution, and the kinds of interactions and dialogue it creates among characters, I was able to illustrate how this overlooked comedic trope about male sexual performance serves as a valuable and revealing mechanism through which we can uncover what media texts are saying about gender and sexuality. In examining the performances and roles each character thinks they, and their sexual partner, are meant to play, it is clear that women do not have equal standing to men in shaping their sexual experiences according to their own desires, needs, and free will, while men continually face the expectation to provide a successful sexual performance and risk their masculinity with each sexual engagement. Thus, by alerting our attention to situations, we are able to tie together numerous shows and trace the ideological work these texts perform, offering new paths that illustrate the continued relevancy and importance of textual analysis within television studies, even in an age of audience fragmentation and seemingly boundless amounts of television content. Furthermore, beyond television, we can consider how this approach might enrich our textual analysis of other media as well, such as films, video games, and comics, which similarly feature recurring situations that play an important role in how these media texts construct meaning.

Notes

1 Tyler Aquilina, "The Death of Peak TV: A Special Report," *Variety*, March 4, 2024, https://variety.com/vip-special-reports/the-death-of-peak-tv-special-report-1235921131/; Brad Adgate, "Why Peak TV May Have Reached Its End—After a Decade of Success," *Forbes*, January 23, 2024, www.forbes.com/sites/bradadgate/2024/01/23/why-peak-tv-may-have-reached-its-end-after-a-decade-of-success/?sh=22214f805f5e.
2 Lauren Berlant, *Cruel Optimism* (Durham, NC: Duke University Press, 2020), 4.
3 Elizabeth Ellcessor, "Disability Dates as Microgenre: 1990s Sitcoms and Backlash to the Americans with Disabilities Act," *Television & New Media* 25, no. 2 (2024): 168–84; Bob Rehak, "The Migration of Forms: Bullet Time as Microgenre," *Film Criticism* 32, no. 1 (2007): 26–48; quotation at 43. Rehak defines microgenres as "instances of genre on a compressed and accelerated scale" (29). While Rehak associates the term with stylistic and formal features, addressing the slow-motion visual effect of "bullet time," Ellcessor applies the term to issues of narrative and representation. In using the term, both emphasize the importance of utilizing an intertextual lens that works across texts; however, unlike the approach I forward here, they view their unit of analysis primarily as an expression of genre.

4 Emily Winderman, "Times for Birth: Chronic and Kairotic Mediated Temporalities in TLC's *A Baby Story*," *Feminist Media Studies* 17, no. 3 (2017): 347–61; Sara De Benedictis, Catherine Johnson, Julie Roberts, and Helen Spiby, "Quantitative Insights into Televised Birth: A Content Analysis of *One Born Every Minute*," *Critical Studies in Media Communication* 36, no. 1 (2019): 1–17.
5 Roberta Pearson, "Star Trek: Serialized Ideology," in *How to Watch Television*, edited by Ethan Thompson and Jason Mittell (New York: New York University Press, 2013), 214.
6 Jonathan Gray and Amanda D. Lotz, *Television Studies* (London: Polity, 2019), 80.
7 Ellcessor, "Disability," 173.
8 Ellcessor, "Disability," 168–84.
9 Ellcessor, "Disability," 175, 178.
10 WatchMojo, www.youtube.com/channel/UCaWd5_7JhbQBe4dknZhsHJg; The Take, www.youtube.com/channel/UCVjsbqKtxkLt7bal4NWRjJQ; www.buzzfeed.com/in/tag/lists; https://tvtropes.org/.
11 Cady Lang, "20 of the Sweetest, Funniest, and Most Outrageous Meet-Cutes in Rom-Com History," *Time*, September 23, 2022, https://time.com/6215146/best-rom-coms-meet-cutes/.
12 www.imdb.com/search/title/; www.paleycenter.org/collection-2/; www.snapstream.com/ (this database is primarily suited for news media rather than entertainment media); https://popmystic.com/.
13 "Abortion Onscreen Database," accessed April 20, 2025, www.ansirh.org/research/abortion/pop-culture#:~:text=ANSIRH's%20Abortion%20Onscreen%20Database%20is,Let%20us%20know.
14 Michael Z. Newman, *The Media Studies Toolkit* (New York: Routledge, 2022), 98.
15 Lisa M. Cuklanz, *Rape on Prime Time: Television, Masculinity, and Sexual Violence* (Philadelphia: University of Pennsylvania Press, 2000).
16 Alfred L. Martin Jr., *The Generic Closet: Black Gayness and the Black-Cast Sitcom* (Bloomington: Indiana University Press, 2021).
17 Ellcessor, "Disability," 168–84.
18 Kristen J. Warner, "In the Time of Plastic Representation," *Film Quarterly* 71, no. 2 (2017): 32–37.
19 PBS NewsHour, "College Course Examines Depiction of Drinking in Film and its Social Consequences," May 17, 2024, YouTube, 7 min., 14 sec., https://youtu.be/8k_jITPWLoU.
20 Daphne Gershon, "Maybe It Is a Big Deal? Portrayals of Erectile Dysfunction in Television Comedy," *Feminist Media Studies* 22, no. 3 (2022): 732–46.
21 "The Loins Sleep Tonight," accessed April 20, 2025, https://tvtropes.org/pmwiki/pmwiki.php/Main/TheLoinsSleepTonight.
22 Tim Brooks and Earle F. Marsh, *The Complete Directory to Prime Time Network and Cable TV Shows, 1946–Present* (New York: Ballantine Books, 2009).
23 David Marc, *Comic Visions: Television Comedy and American Culture*, 2nd ed. (Malden, MA: Blackwell, 1997).

21

Transmedia Tarantino

Reading the Many Texts of Once Upon a Time in Hollywood

HENRY JENKINS

Jenkins considers an especially challenging form of textual multiplicity, namely transmedia and the authoring of meaning across texts and paratexts. Jenkins's ensuing focus on the various transmedia fragments of and surrounding Quentin Tarantino's Once Upon a Time in Hollywood *models how analysts can collate meaning across texts and paratexts, how we might textually analyze authorship across texts, and indeed how to collate various approaches to textual analysis (for Jenkins, author-, paratext-, genre-, and intertext-centered) while doing so.*

On May 19, 2023, the news media announced the death of a fictional character, Rick Dalton, the protagonist in Quentin Tarantino's 2019 film *Once Upon a Time in Hollywood*. The *Video Archives* podcast, hosted by Tarantino, his sometimes collaborator Roger Avary, and Avary's daughter Gala, dedicated two episodes to exploring the imaginary career of this midlevel Hollywood actor and the contexts in which he worked (television, Hollywood, Italy and the Philippines, and straight-to-DVD exploitation movies).[1]

Should we read this project as a "publicity stunt"? It certainly was that, but publicity for what? The film (and its afterlife as a novelization or on streaming or DVD) had played out several years before; Tarantino had not yet begun work on what he has claimed will be his final (tenth) film. We might best understand the podcast as a transmedia extension of the *Once Upon a Time* story-world designed to answer unresolved questions about Dalton and his stunt double, Cliff Booth. I want to argue here for Tarantino as a transmedia auteur, considering the many different ways he works across media. This will necessarily be a sketch more than a fully developed analysis, but I model what a particular kind of analysis might look like.

We can trace the concept of "transmedia" to Marsha Kinder's *Playing with Power in Movies, Television, and Video Games*. Kinder wrote about children's entertainment franchises as "an ever-expanding supersystem of entertainment, one marked by transmedia intertextuality."[2] Kinder wrote primarily about characters who appeared across diverse media platforms (television cartoons, films, children's books, toys, coloring books, etc.), which she primarily understood as a marketing strategy. I would later apply "transmedia" to describe a mode of storytelling: "Transmedia storytelling represents a process where integral elements of a fiction get dispersed systematically across multiple delivery channels for the purpose of creating a unified and coordinated entertainment experience. Ideally, each medium makes its own unique contribution to the unfolding of the story."[3] My original example was *The Matrix* and its two (now three) sequels, and the associated anime, comics, and games. I explored the Wachowskis' distributed yet coordinated authorship—working with comics and anime creators who had their own cult followings and allowing them to expand the story-world in whatever way they wished, showcasing other creative collaborators on the film's homepage, encouraging a very active interpretive community, and so forth.[4]

Since then, I have suggested that transmedia may best be understood as a modifier, attached to some practice or logic: transmedia storytelling takes its place alongside transmedia marketing, performance, play, learning, documentary, journalism, or activism, to cite some common examples, and the same work might serve multiple logics.[5] If they expand the story, they are part of the storytelling process, whatever marketing or other functions they perform.

Here, I explore whether authorship might constitute a transmedia logic that functions through discursive practices alongside and in relation to transmedia storytelling. And if so, where would we look, how would we construct arguments, if we wanted to do textual analysis of a work by an author who is drawn toward a range of citational, intertextual, paratextual, and transtextual processes? Provisionally, we can define transmedia authorship as a logic whereby the reader is invited to construct a mental model of the author from information and performances spread across the media landscape that shapes how she reads and responds to any particular text. Some authors, Tarantino among them, work hard to call attention to their fingerprints as an author, whereas others seek to erase all signs of their existence, counting on critics or fans to signal what they define as marks of authorship, if at all.

Authorial Discourse

Michel Foucault's "What Is an Author?" encouraged a move from conceptualizing authors as human agents in favor of understanding authorship as a discursive practice: "An author's name ... serves as a means of classification. A name can group together a number of texts and thus differentiate them from others. ... The name of the author remains at the contours of texts—separating one from the other, defining their form, and characterizing their mode of existence."[6] Our concept of the author determines particular reading practices. For the auteurist critics (e.g., Andrew Sarris, *Cahiers du Cinéma*), understanding a film auteur required locating distinctive themes, stylistic elements, casting, motifs, and genre preferences by seeing as many films by this creator as possible. Today, we have access to more authorial discourse than ever before, as filmmakers perform as authors across a range of media. They participate in interviews or provide DVD commentary; they speak on podcasts, blog, or make public appearances, promoting their work, shaping how we interpret it, and citing other texts. Among contemporary filmmakers, Tarantino may be one of the most aware of his authorial legacy. If Roland Barthes declared the "death" of the author, Tarantino loves to pop his head up and proclaim, "Not dead yet!"[7]

Writing about James Bond as "popular hero," Tony Bennett (the cultural scholar, not the singer) debated the value of classifying texts through authorship: "It will be necessary to question the assumption that texts can be thus grouped into stabilised sets—whether with reference to an author, a genre or whatever principle of classification might be proposed—if the full range and variability of their signifying functioning, their operation in history, are to be adequately understood. 'The Bond phenomenon', I shall argue, can best be conceptualised as a phenomenon located within the intertextual relations which have been constructed by (and have comprised the theatre for the operation of) the signifier 'James Bond.'"[8] Bond interested Bennett because the character had passed through so many different authors, activated by different secondary texts. Bennett mapped "the shifting orders of intertextuality within which they have been culturally active during different moments of 'the Bond phenomenon.'"[9] Similar models have been applied to other such figures, such as William Uricchio and Roberta Pearson's account of "the many lives of the Batman" or Will Brooker's of *Alice in Wonderland*.[10] We might try to understand Rick Dalton in terms of a similar analytic frame, except that so far, most of the Dalton texts have been produced by Tarantino. Sure, he collaborates with others in producing those works, but Tarantino as the screenwriter, director, producer, and sometimes actor exerts a stronger presence than any other creative force.

We might start our analysis with a deceptively simple question: What constitutes the text of *Once Upon a Time in Hollywood*? Is it simply the Tarantino film of that name, or might we extend it to include direct by-products, such as soundtrack records and DVD extras, missing scenes, and director commentary? Do we add various texts consciously developed by Tarantino as extensions of the "mother ship," such as Tarantino's novelization or the *Video Archives* podcasts? Interviews where Tarantino speaks about possibilities he imagined in making *Once Upon a Time*? Do we include various other texts Tarantino references as influences? Where and when does the text end, given the porous nature of the world Tarantino has constructed, and the various ways he has returned to add new information and encourage fan engagement?

Once Upon a Time is built from both fictional and nonfictional media, though often Tarantino combines the two: the insertion of film history and criticism in the novel, the use of a conversational podcast to construct the career of a fictional character. Some media—the film for example—are expensive to produce, while others—say, the podcast or the novel—cost much less and thus allow a more expansive experience. Some are enduring—the film will be watched for years to come—and some are more disposable—the podcast may already have disappeared from memory, given how many podcasts are released each day.

The Author as Host

Those of a certain generation will recall hosts on television in the 1950s and 1960s—Rod Serling with *The Twilight Zone* (CBS, 1959–64), Alfred

Hitchcock with *Alfred Hitchcock Presents* (CBS and NBC, 1955–65), and Walt Disney with *The Wonderful World of Disney* (ABC, 1954–61). Our responses to the stories were shaped by the personalities, physicalities, and voices of these authorial personas. They introduced the shows, constructing themselves as authors, even though they had varying degrees of control. Tarantino has sometimes played a curatorial function—directing attention to the works of others he admires when he oversaw the American releases of films such as Wong Kar-wai's *Chungking Express* (1994), Takeshi Kitano's *Sonatine* (1993), and Zhang Yimou's *Hero* (2003), which gained greater visibility in the United States as a result of his imprimatur.

But it does not end there. Tarantino purchased the New Beverly Cinema in Los Angeles in 2010 and began to play a more active role in its programing starting in 2014, regularly showing his own films, sharing prints from his own collection, commenting on movies through the theater's blog and podcast, and otherwise calling attention to neglected works. Before *Once Upon a Time* was released, Tarantino curated two months of related film programming, including a month focused on 1960s actors as Dalton inspirations, and appeared on an almost two-hour-long podcast episode mapping what he called his "curriculum" for understanding the film.

Paratexts

Often, Tarantino is less a transmedia author and more of a paratextual one. Building on French theorist Gérard Genette, Jonathan Gray offers this account of the work performed by paratexts: "Paratexts are not simply add-ons, spinoffs, and also-rans: they create texts, they manage them, and they fill them with many of the meanings that we associate with them.... Paratexts often take a tangible form, as with posters, videogames, podcasts, reviews, or merchandise.... However,... intangible entities can at times work in paratextual fashion. Thus, for instance, while a genre is not a paratext it can work paratextually to frame a text."[11] Tarantino, thus, functions across paratextual practices designed to instruct readers how to appreciate his films.

We might look at *Once Upon a Time*'s making-of video as a classic example of a paratext. Here, two key themes surface: first, the film as "a love letter to Los Angeles, our industry, and the people who came before us" (Brad Pitt), including ideas about a transitional moment in Hollywood's history: "It's fascinating that he chose 1969 because it was really the year of transition between the old Hollywood and the birth of the new Hollywood (actor Nicholas Hammond)." "1969 was a year to be reckoned with. And you feel that in this movie. You are touched by all of the things that are going on (executive producer Georgia Kacandes)." If the statements complement each other, it is because the speakers are delivering essentially scripted talking points developed by the marketing team.

The second strand of discourse locates this film as Tarantino's "most personal" work: "In a way he is looking back on his influences, the movies he loved, the period he was growing up in, and what helped shape him, what forms him as a person, what informs his work" (producer David Heyman). And then, Tarantino explains, "I am just in a lucky situation to be able to remember the city—what it was like when I was six and seven in a town as big as Hollywood and a town as iconic as Hollywood. I was able to actually recreate it and turn it into what it was." The video links the public history of Hollywood and Tarantino's backstory, understanding *Once Upon a Time* as springing from its author's memories.

Genre

Paul J. Rabinowitz suggests that we understand genre not as a property of the work but as a reading hypothesis that cues us as to how to configure and interpret the text, how to speculate about what might happen next and evaluate its merits.[12] The same film might be read as operating within multiple genres—*Once Upon a Time* fits into the same genre as *The Bad and the Beautiful* (dir. Vincente Minelli, 1954), *Sunset Boulevard* (dir. Billy Wilder, 1950), *The Day of the Locust* (dir. John Schlesinger, 1975), *The Last Tycoon* (dir. Elia Kazan, 1976), and the many different versions of *A Star is Born* (dir. William Wellman, 1937; George Cukor, 1954; Frank Pierson, 1976; Bradley Cooper, 2018), melodramas about what it is like to live and work in Hollywood, but there are moments where it taps the iconography and conventions of the Western, and the Manson subplot pulls it toward a true crime saga. The paratexts identify the filmmaker's preferred genre placement, whereas intertexts—such as the scene where Sharon Tate watches herself in *The Wrecking Crew* (dir. Phil Karlson, 1968)—situate *Once Upon a Time* in relation to other media products.

Across his nine films to date, Tarantino has systematically explored diverse genres, including the heist film (*Reservoir Dogs*, 1992), the gangster film (*Pulp Fiction*, 1994), blaxploitation/film noir (*Jackie Brown*, 1997), the martial arts film (*Kill Bill 1 and 2*, 2003 and 2004), the horror film (*From Dusk to Dawn*, dir. Richard Rodriguez, 1996) and the Western (*Django Unchained*, 2012; *The Hateful Eight*, 2015). The film's title links it to Sergio Leone's films *Once Upon a Time in the West* (1968) and *Once Upon a Time in America* (1984). Often, Tarantino's interviews identify the films he believes should be understood in relation to his works. One interview with a Japanese fanzine promised, "Quentin Tarantino Reveals Almost Everything that Inspired *Kill Bill*," as the author and his fan geeked out on Asian cult classics.[13] Not long before the *Video Archives* podcast, Tarantino released a book of critical essays, *Cinema Speculation*, where he discussed films of the late 1960s and 1970s, classics of New American Cinema and grindhouse films alike.

Often, paratexts construct Tarantino as a self-taught connoisseur of lowbrow cinema, working as a clerk at the Video Archive rental store, as an underaged usher at an adult movie theater, and as a flaneur moving between different cinematic worlds. Gerald Peary characterizes Tarantino as "that t-shirted guy or gal, embarrassingly overqualified, who didn't let a seven-dollar-an-hour salary curb an energetic discourse about film, film, film, whether European auteurist masterpieces, Hollywood genre works, or Hong Kong kung-fu."[14] Tarantino cannot stop talking about movies; he is as good a critic and historian as he is a filmmaker.

Intertexts

The intertext points outward from the work and the paratext points inward. The intertext refers to a reference inside the work that places one film in conversation with another. Tarantino's scripts construct moments where, for instance, the characters pontificate about the meaning of Madonna's "Like a Virgin" in *Reservoir Dogs*. Many of his casting choices—Pam Greer and Robert Forster in *Jackie Brown*, John Travolta in *Pulp Fiction*, and so forth—are also citational. Or think about the way he plays Samuel L. Jackson against type in *Django Unchained*, inviting us to read his performance as a treacherous Uncle Tom in relation to tough guy and rebel roles he played elsewhere. In one interview, Tarantino references Pauline Kael's review of Jean-Luc Godard's *Band of Outsiders* (1964): "It's as if a couple of movie-crazy young Frenchmen were in a coffee house and they've taken a banal American crime novel and they're making a movie out of it based not on the novel but on the poetry that they read between the lines." Tarantino adds, "And when I read that I said, 'That's my aesthetic! That's what I want to do! That's what I want to achieve!'"[15]

Across both paratexts and intertexts, Tarantino has developed a counterhistory of global cinema, which includes all of Tarantino's favorite films and the people who made them. And around this canon circles a wealth of "Hollywood Lore," which surfaces often in *Once Upon a Time*, the making-of videos, the novelization, and the podcasts. Much of the film's representation of Sharon Tate feels like it comes directly from the popular *You Must Remember This* podcast, which dedicated a full season to the Manson murders. Tarantino includes excerpts from the era's local radio DJs or depicts local theaters (the Vista, the Cinerama Dome) and eateries (Musso and Franks). The Hollywood location justifies cameo appearances by other celebrities from Roman Polanski to Bruce Lee. Tarantino also pastiches popular film and television genres, including the television Western, the war film, and the spaghetti Western, as we watch Dalton's rise and fall.

Asked if he expected his millennial and postmillennial fans to understand his references, Tarantino explained, "Whenever I give my film writing to, like, a millennial to read, they can never get through it because they want to Google every name I mention. . . . Every film book I ever read, I expected the guy to know more than me. And I'm Mr. Look Up Things, constantly, as I'm watching stuff."[16]

Tarantino is not the only filmmaker to encourage viewers to watch other films to understand his own. Martin Scorsese's films draw heavily on Westerns, gangster films, and film noirs from the 1940s and 1950s; he maps a canon of such works in the 1995 British documentary *A Personal Journey with Martin Scorsese through American Cinema*; he programs for Turner Classic Movies. As a NYU graduate, Scorsese's knowledge of film history comes from formal training; he systematically maps genre traditions and respects the classical canon. Tarantino's curriculum is more haphazard and eclectic, as would be the case of someone who is self-taught through working at a video rental store where there was always some movie playing in the background.

Transmedia Authorship

One model for analyzing Tarantino's works would be to trace these intertexts, working through what he is referencing and why. Each citation is there for a purpose. His films are not simply a postmodern collection of quotes; rather they cohere into distinctive worlds, such as Hollywood as depicted in *Once Upon a Time*, which become environments of fantasy, speculation, and identification for his fans. Tarantino's world-building pulls him toward transmedia storytelling practices.

As the paratexts and intertexts suggest, Tarantino uses his storyworld to explore a series of transitions. On the *Pure Cinema* podcast, he situated Dalton within dramatic changes shaping Hollywood in the late 1960s:

> Rick Dalton is made up from a bunch of these guys. He's a bit like George Maharis. He's a bit like Ed Burns. . . . a bit like Tab Hunter. . . . Fabian. . . . Vince Edwards. These are all guys that were handsome, kind of he-men. . . . Most of them were kind of rugged. They spent their careers running pocket combs through their pompadours. Then, all of sudden, boom, the culture changes within two years. . . . Now the leading men are these long shaggy haired androgynous types. . . . And if Rick is going to get a part, he's probably going to be the cop who is busting them.[17]

This shift in Hollywood style is tied to larger changes in the construction of masculinity off-screen and to a shift in American society, perhaps best represented by Cliff's encounter with a barefoot hippie girl who takes him back to the ranch where she lives with the Manson family. The Manson reference hints at something else—the "summer of love" gives way to the brutality of the Manson killings. Yet, there's an irony here in the fact that Rick and Cliff are working on Westerns, a genre itself depicting a transition between wilderness and civilization, where the lone wanderer uses his violent skills to pave the way for the homesteaders. Dalton is thus a man out of time playing another man out of time. Booth is a man of the past confronting a totally different reality as he visits a ranch once used to film Westerns and now used to prepare for "Helter Skelter," which Manson imagined would be the triggering event for an all-out race war.

One of Tarantino's more controversial insertions of himself as an author comes when he rewrites the history of the Manson murders. On the night Sharon Tate was originally killed, three Manson associates confront Cliff and Rick in Dalton's home, one with a flamethrower. Tarantino had already reversed history twice in his earlier films—allowing Jewish GIs to kill Hitler in *Inglourious Basterds* (2009) and slaves to overcome their masters in *Django Unchained*. Here, we see the older generation get out their aggressions on hippies.

In his foreword to Tarantino's novelization, literary critic Walter Kirn writes: "In *Once Upon a Time in Hollywood*, which exists now as a twice-told fairy tale, written both in light and ink, Dalton and Booth are flawed, imperfect men who strive to rise above temptation. . . . In the movie, we see their struggles from the outside, against a golden, nostalgic backdrop that's beginning to darken at the edges. In the book, we track their struggles from the inside."[18] Tarantino uses this capacity of novels to take us into the characters' heads—for example, sharing Sharon's thoughts about her performance in *The Wrecking Crew*. Reading the book encourages us to spend more time with the characters. The film makes us feel, the book makes us think, and together they create a fuller picture of the story-world.

Kirn illustrates what it means to do a close reading of a transmedia text. Key questions are, Which media does the story deploy, what are the affordances and potentials of that medium, and how does the author exploit those potentials to add something—to extend—the original texts and thus deepen our experience of the story?

We might consider another transmedia example. Tarantino created a series of featurettes—commercials, trailers, even an extended black-and-white television episode—which were shown as a preshow at the New Beverly and released as DVD extras. In another segment, we see Dalton, uncomfortably, doing a guest appearance on *Hullabaloo* (NBC, 1965–66), an actual 1960s variety show whose look and feel Tarantino recreates. The potential variety of these materials is infinite and that's part of the point. They tell us very little about the plot, a bit more about the character (especially the stiffness Dalton brought to some appearances), and more about the mediascape surrounding him.

The *Video Archives* Podcast

All of this brings us back to the *Video Archives* podcast and the announcement of Dalton's death. Video Archives was the name of a rental store that Tarantino and his boyhood friend, Roger Avery, used to run on Manhattan Beach, California. As Tarantino explains in a trailer for the first episode, "We had this cool store. We watched movies all day.... Customers came in just to talk to us." They kept many of the actual VHS tapes they rented to customers and rewatched them to inform podcast episodes.

When the podcast launched, it was understood as part of the framing of Tarantino as a video store–generation auteur and as an opportunity to display his knowledge of films from the 1980s and 1990s. But retrospectively, one wonders to what degree the extensive conversations about American Giallo films, *Star 80* (dir. Bob Fosse, 1983), *Women in Cages* (dir. Gerardo de León, 1971), *The One Armed Executioner* (dir. Bobby Suarez, 1981), and *Piranha* (dir. Joe Dante, 1978), set up the discussion of Dalton's late vehicles, *Operation Nam, Blastfighter,* and *Jungle Raiders*.

Just as Tarantino uses pastiches of a 1960s variety show number in *Once Upon a Time* to illustrate the places a star like Dalton might appear, on the podcast he uses a pastiche of film discussion programs to explain what happened to the character after the film's fire-spurting climax. Avery confesses that he only watched a few syndicated reruns of Dalton's fictional television series, *Bounty Law*, but he was assigned to reedit an episode when he was in Pasadena College of Design. Roger mentions a *Cinefantastique* interview with Rick that discusses how Booth became the director of the second and subsequent films in the *Fireman* franchise (inspired by news stories about his deployment of the flamethrower). Avery and Tarantino discuss the various companies (many of them real, some fictional) where his films were produced, the circumstances under which they were produced, and even the box designs and the quality of the video reproductions.

Tarantino taps the film's closing events to explain the origins of a fictional franchise: "There is something attractive about the star of *Bounty Law* killing a bunch of hippies that broke into his house . . . so he got invited to the Republican convention. He's a lifelong Democrat but he went. . . . They put him on Johnny Carson after that. . . . Because of his notoriety, he started to get better TV shows. He went from *Land of the Giants* and *Green Hornet* to doing *Mission Impossible*." We are expected to know what each of those shows meant in the hierarchy of television history. In the first podcast episode, the hosts detail imaginary episodes of actual television series, such as *Cade's Country* (CBS, 1971–72) and *The Quest* (NBC, 1976), and in the second, his final films as Hollywood's interest in him dried up completely. Tarantino fancasts the imaginary works with popular performers, including Kurt Russell, whose films are often featured at the New Beverly. The hosts describe specific plot points and rank performances much as they had done for actual movies on prior installments. All of this rewards the expertise the most hardcore Tarantino fans have acquired through listening to him and watching recommended titles through the years. The informality and seeming spontaneity of the podcast only adds greater credibility to the fictions being constructed.

Tarantino reads excerpts from a "previously unpublished interview" with Rick Dalton recorded at the Hawaii International Film Festival, filling in gaps in our understanding of the early phases of Rick Dalton's career. Dalton is having none of Tarantino's intellectualization of his B movies and shoots him down repeatedly. Tarantino spoofs his own nerdy preoccupations. Rick grumbles about his male co-stars and claims to have slept with his female ones, suggesting how Dalton related to the other (actual) performers of his generation. And intertwined across the two podcast episodes were passages from another fabricated text—a popular star biography detailing the new visibility Rick achieved after the flamethrower incident:

> Soon Dalton could be seen sitting behind a desk surrounded by Wally Cox, Paul Lynde, and Charlie Weaver on the *Hollywood Squares*, playing guessing games on *Password* and the *100,000 Dollar Pyramid*, bowling spares on *Celebrity Bowling*, horsing around and filling in blanks with Richard

Dawson, Brett Summers, and Charles Nelson Reilly on *Match Game*, and acting cute with the other Hollywood couples on Burt Convy's *Tattle Tales*, where Francisca with her ditzy Italian schtick was a big hit. . . . Rick [was] enjoying his Hollywood career as he had never done before.

Each reference to popular shows and performers makes the fiction seem more real until a baby boom–generation listener may misremember watching Dalton do these things.

The podcast creates a context where Tarantino can expand his protagonist's backstory and detail his world through informal data dumps. I have tried to model here some of the ways we might do textual analysis of such a work—tracing and drawing comparisons to the related texts signaled by the intertext, considering how the paratexts prepare us for certain experiences, and identifying the additive comprehension achieved through the transtexts. Each suggests that the text is incomplete and porous, best understood in a more expanded fashion rather than read as self-contained and autonomous. Tarantino's transmedia strategies construct him as a particular kind of author, one who speaks across all media and who is knowledgeable about his place in film history. Tarantino makes himself the point of intelligibility through which various discourses within or about the film flow. And, as Foucault might have predicted, Tarantino's relations to these various texts make him the basis of classifying them as part of or an influence upon *Once Upon a Time in Hollywood*.

Notes

1 Quentin Tarantino, Roger Avary, and Gail Avary, hosts, *Video Archives*, podcast, "Day of the Dalton Part One: The Marshal of Madrid, Manhunter," May 22, 2023, https://podcasts.apple.com/us/podcast/123-day-of-the-dalton-pt-1-the-marshal-of-madrid-manhunter/id1627069896?i=1000614091041; and "Day of the Dalton Part 2: Operation Nam/Blastfighter.Jungle Raiders," June 6, 2023, rhttps://podcasts.apple.com/us/podcast/124-day-of-the-dalton-pt-2-operation-nam/id1627069896?i=1000615807702.

2 Marsha Kinder, *Playing with Power in Movies, Television, and Video Games* (Berkeley: University of California Press, 1993), 1.

3 Henry Jenkins, "Transmedia Storytelling 101," *Pop Junctions* (blog), March 21, 2007, http://henryjenkins.org/blog/2007/03/transmedia_storytelling_101.html.

4   Henry Jenkins, *Convergence Culture: Where Old and New Media Collide* (New York: NYU Press, 2006).
5   Henry Jenkins, "Transmedia Logics and Locations," in *The Rise of the Transtexts: Challenges and Opportunities*, edited by W. L. Benjamin, Derhy Kurtz, and Mélanie Bourdaa (New York: Routledge, 2016), 288–313.
6   Michel Foucault, "What Is an Author?," in *Aesthetics, Methods, and Epistemology*, edited by James D. Faubion (New York: The New Press, 2003), 304–5.
7   Roland Barthes, "The Death of the Author," in *Image/Music/Text*, translated by Stephen Heath (Glasgow: Fontana-Collins, 1977), 142–48.
8   Tony Bennett, "The Bond Phenomenon: Theorising a Popular Hero—A Retrospective," *The International Journal of Bond Studies* 1, no. 1 (Spring 2017), https://jamesbondstudies.ac.uk/articles/10.24877/jbs.4.
9   Bennett, "The Bond Phenomenon," 2.
10 Roberta E. Pearson and William Uricchio, eds., *The Many Lives of the Batman: Critical Approaches to a Superhero and His Media* (London: BFI, 1991); Will Brooker, *Alice's Adventures: Lewis Carroll in Popular Culture* (London: Bloomsbury, 2005).
11 Jonathan Gray, *Show Sold Separately: Promos, Spoilers, and Other Media* (New York: New York University Press, 2010), 6.
12 Paul J. Rabinowitz, "The Turn of the Glass Key: Popular Fiction as Reading Strategy," *Critical Inquiry* 11, no. 3 (March 1985): 418–31.
13 Tomohiro Machiyama, "Quentin Tarantino Reveals Almost Everything That Inspired *Kill Bill* (2003)," in *Quentin Tarantino: Interviews*, edited by Gerald Peary (Jackson: University of Mississippi Press, 2013).
14 Gerald Peary, "Introduction," in Peary, *Quentin Tarantino: Interviews*, ix.
15 The Upcoming, "Quentin Tarantino on Godard: What She Said: The Art of Pauline Kael new clip official from Berlinale," February 12, 2019, YouTube, 1 min., 52 sec., www.youtube.com/watch?v=vb70UEVjFj0.
16 Stephanie Zacherek, "'Nothing Lasts Forever': Quentin Tarantino on Sharon Tate, *Once Upon a Time . . . in Hollywood* and Retirement," *Time*, July 22, 2019.
17 Eric Kane and Brian Saur, hosts, *Pure Cinema Podcast*, "New Beverly Calendar: July, 2019 (with Quentin Tarantino)," July 3, 2019, https://purecinemapodcast.libsyn.com/new-beverly-calendar-july-2019-with-quentin-tarantino.
18 Walter Kirn, "Foreword," in Quentin Tarantino, *Once Upon a Time in Hollywood* (New York: Harper Perennial, 2022).

PART V

Combining Textual Analysis with Other Methods

Introduction

A danger with books that explore a particular method is that in demarcating that method, they artificially isolate it from others, encouraging a solipsistic, even chauvinist approach. We do not wish this book to do so, for our vision of a rich and vibrant media, communication, and cultural studies is one in which textual analysis works in tandem with other methods. This section, therefore, offers several chapters that connect textual analysis to other methods and to larger discussions and projects.

The first three chapters each consider how textual analysis can be integrated with another method, namely historical and technological analysis for Michele Hilmes, industrial and production studies for Amanda D. Lotz, and audience research for Joke Hermes. Each outlines and illustrates how textual analysis can both benefit from and contribute to other methodological approaches.

The final two chapters look not to other methods of analysis, but to other methods of how we *present* our analyses. Jason Mittell discusses the video essay, moving beyond the long-assumed requirement that our analyses be written, to instead explore the vitality and affordances, especially for audiovisual media, of using an audiovisual format for discussion, analysis, and interpretation. Then Eric Deggans reflects on a career as a television critic who writes for and speaks to the public, not "just" academics, thereby offering a reminder that textual analysis is always open to use outside the academy, in our everyday lives as media consumers and as citizens.

Collectively, the chapters challenge readers to think about the many projects that could benefit from rigorous, thoughtful textual analysis, and indeed about the many ways in which textual analysis can be practiced.

22

Exploring Soundwork

Texts, Technologies, and Cultural Form

MICHELE HILMES

Hilmes models how a textual analyst might consider the affordances of various technologies, and might also contextualize their analysis within an awareness of media history. As an example, Hilmes considers the OG of true crime podcasts, Serial, *drawing both from Raymond Williams's theoretical examination of television flow and from consideration of the radio documentary program* The March of Time *to make better sense of a podcast that many others have seen as lightning out of a clear sky, but that Hilmes connects to sound culture history.*

Introduction

When we talk about media, we are nearly always talking about communication through some kind of *technology*: machines and instruments that take an existing form of human expression and turn it into something new and powerful. The printing press, which transformed the written and spoken word into newspapers and mass-market books; the phonograph, which captured and multiplied staged performance on discs and tape; movies, which mobilized photography and sound recording to create rich new audiovisual narratives; broadcasting, which sent radio and later television flying invisibly across the airwaves, reaching millions in their homes; and our current digital universe, which has gobbled up all the above and created its own new mediated world: all these textual forms were born from an emerging set of available technologies that not only made new kinds of narratives possible but also changed the way that people experienced and understood the world around them. In this chapter, I focus on the intersection of technology and textual forms in *soundwork*, the universe of sound-based media texts, by comparing the sound documentary as it was produced during radio's live broadcast era with the groundbreaking podcast *Serial* (NPR, 2014–18).

One point of doing this is to highlight the role that changing technology played in inventing exciting new sound-based texts and narrative forms, like *Serial*. Another is to emphasize the way that soundwork, though a critical part of global media production and consumption over the last one hundred years or so, is also its most neglected and forgotten art form. As radio comedian Fred Allen once quipped, "Radio is the only medium that died before it was born." Partly because radio was quickly eclipsed by television in the 1950s but also because of the limitations of audio recording and broadcasting technologies during radio's prime, the lively and inventive world of twentieth-century radio programs, particularly radio documentaries, is largely lost to current popular memory and has only recently begun to be recognized and revived by scholars.

From Radio to Soundwork

No single audio work made a more powerful impression on the emerging field of podcasting than did *Serial* when it hit the airwaves in October 2014. Backed by the team behind U.S. public radio's long-running weekly program *This American Life*, producer Sarah Koenig and her crew delved into the story of Adnan Syed, a Maryland high school student convicted in 1999 of murdering his girlfriend, Hae Min Lee. "To say it was addictive is an understatement. . . . Suddenly, investigative journalism became our hobby, our passion. People were talking about it everywhere you went. It was a true cultural phenomenon," wrote Ewan McGregor in his nomination of Koenig as one of *Time* magazine's "100 Most Influential People" of 2015.[1] That same year, *Serial* became the first podcast to win a Peabody Award.[2] The show's quirky, conversational style, its deep dive into details of a crime that most people had never heard of, its integral website that not only collected episodes of the show for relistening and sharing but encouraged listeners to participate in the process, posting comments and questions: this was a brand new kind of narrative form, in sound.[3] *Serial* was radio—with millions of on-air listeners at its regular broadcast time over public radio stations—but it was also more than radio: it was a powerfully different kind of sound-based experience. And, along with other shows in the rapidly developing podcast field, it revolutionized the sound documentary form itself, along with the way we understand, appreciate, and use sound as a medium in today's digital environment.

To analyze this phenomenon and its role in the soundwork revolution, I draw on the theories of renowned British cultural theorist Raymond Williams. His 1974 book *Television: Technology and Cultural Form* has been called "a, if not *the*, foundational work of television studies," due to its emphasis on the ways that emergent technologies shape new texts and ways of experiencing them.[4] In particular, Williams's linked concepts of television's "mobile privatization" and "flow" seem particularly relevant to understanding how podcasting, and digital media more generally, both drew on and irrevocably exploded the broadcast model, particularly in the documentary, podcasting's most popular genre. To make this argument, I compare *Serial* with the once-popular radio documentary program *The March of Time* (CBS, 1931–37; Blue, 1937–42; NBC, 1942–44; ABC, 1944–45).

Theoretical Framework

Raymond Williams was writing at a time when television broadcasting was relatively new and its practices and social impact still emerging. His previous works had explored how twentieth-century literature, theater, and cinema had invented new forms of communication and entertainment that reshaped society. In *Television: Technology and Cultural Form*, he took on the task of explaining how television differed from these earlier modes of communication, how its unique technology affected the types of entertainment and information piped into people's homes, and how that experience itself influenced the way viewers came to understand the world around them.

One thing about television that struck Williams powerfully was its deepening of something radio broadcasting had innovated, a phenomenon he called "mobile privatization." Unlike earlier forms of culture and communication that brought people together in shared *public* spaces—theaters, arenas, town squares, lecture halls—twentieth-century media enabled people to experience events occurring all around the world from the privacy of their own homes; viewers could roam the world with their eyes and ears (mobility) while not budging from their individual living rooms (privatization). The printing press had begun this process, as books, magazines, and newspapers became privately consumed mass media; broadcasting intensified it, allowing events occurring hundreds or thousands of miles away to be experienced not only privately but *simultaneously*, as they occurred ("live" broadcasting). The trade-off, however, was a narrowing of the cultural pipeline: since both radio and television were complex technologies that required the allocation of scarce spectrum space, broadcasters around the world were limited in number and heavily regulated by governments. By the 1970s, in most countries, a small number of powerful networks had acquired unprecedented access to millions of people in their homes. "Thus within the broadcasting model there was this deep contradiction, of centralized transmission and privatized reception," as Williams puts it, a largely unanticipated side effect of the process of mobile privatization.[5]

Another aspect of broadcast technology radically different from any previous medium of communication was its continuous *flow* of programs into private homes from the centralized broadcasters: persistent, unalterable, available at the flick of a switch. "This phenomenon, of planned flow, is then perhaps the defining characteristic of broadcasting, simultaneously as a technology and as a cultural form," Williams wrote.[6] He identified three different kinds of flow: "First, there is the flow . . . within a particular evening's programmes. . . . Second, there is the more evident flow of the actual succession of items within and between the published sequence of units. . . . Third, there is the really detailed flow within this general movement: the actual succession of words and images."[7] By the first, he means the TV schedule, the sequence of planned programs on each channel on any given day; by the second, he refers to the way television's flow intersperses ads, promotions, news bulletins, and so on, alongside and within the programs themselves; and the third is simply the flow of images and sounds as a child might see them, just one thing after another, creating a new kind of experience all its own. On each level, the flow is remote and unstoppable; we might switch channels to access a different flow, or turn the TV off completely, but, until the introduction of the VCR in the 1970s, the flow of television could not be captured, reversed, repeated, or altered in any way by the viewer at home. You could take it—or leave it.

The March of Time: Flow, Mobile Privatization, and the Radio Documentary

The phenomena of flow and mobile privatization were characteristic of broadcast radio as well; indeed, as Williams argues, radio invented both. Broadcast radio, like television, ran on a strict, limited schedule under conditions of scarcity. In the US, into the 1950s, though hundreds of radio stations spread out across the country, there were only three major networks whose continuous, all-day flow of programs could be heard pervasively nearly everywhere. Local stations filled in limited allotted bits of the schedule with local materials. In Britain and many other countries, an official national broadcaster, often with two or three separate feeds, provided the equivalent setup. Under these conditions, the flow of radio programs was limited, unalterable, and directed to a general audience, its texts and genres taking only mainstream tastes and interests into account.

However, while network *distribution* sent programs flowing widely into homes everywhere, radio *production* was still very much trapped inside the studio until the 1950s, primarily due to the lack of lightweight, durable recording devices that could get out of the studio and onto the scene to record actuality sound.[8] This meant, as media historian Lawrence Lichty notes, "Documentary programs did not play a large role in the history of American radio broadcasting," a phenomenon prevalent around the world.[9] Radio in its early decades did provide a growing amount of headline news, public affairs commentary, and live talk shows—but all from the inside of a studio. This meant that very rarely were the voices of ordinary people heard over the air, and very rarely could radio audiences hear for themselves what the world actually sounded like outside the studio.

One of the first attempts to address this limitation was *Time* magazine's innovative program *The March of Time*, debuting on CBS in 1931. It launched the "dramatized documentary" style of radio program (sometimes called a "radio feature"), a form that would be taken up widely during World War II, when getting informational and morale-building broadcasts out to the public became a priority. *The March of Time* was unique, however, in its use of actors to imitate the voices of real-life newsmakers, from President Roosevelt (who eventually objected, for reasons of security) to police detectives to movie stars to ordinary everyday people who just happened to become newsworthy. The show's enormous stable of actors re-created items from the news, reciting scripted lines sometimes taken from actual speeches and news coverage but often enacting a dramatization imagined entirely by the show's scriptwriters.

For example, the program of August 29, 1935, opened with a story on the upcoming 1936 presidential election, with bits of speeches by candidates Huey P. Long, Upton Sinclair, and William Randolph Hearst. Long's words were excerpts from an actual recording, but the others were performed by actors reading from print news coverage, imitating Sinclair's and Hearst's voices. The second story dramatized the recent discovery of a potential vaccine against polio in a scripted conversation between actors playing a doctor and a reporter, followed by a completely fictional scene set in a hospital, with the doctor reassuring children about to receive the vaccine. Next up were political events in Moscow, combining an English translation of a snippet of a Russian radio speech with a fictional dialogue between actors playing an American reporter and his editor discussing recent crackdowns on free speech in Russia. And so it went. Music and sound effects and a fast, staccato pace were vital elements of *The March of Time*'s appeal, helping to establish both setting and mood in this nonvisual but evocative medium. Conforming to the time constraints of radio's rapid flow, each program could cover only a small handful of the news topics of the day, and it had to appeal to the broadest possible audience, in the most simplistic terms, through a brief skim of the news, rather than the "deep dive" that podcasting would enable. And though the program was based in reality, its heavily dramatized performance and uninterruptible flow left listeners very little room for their own interpretations or interventions.

The show was hugely popular, remaining on the air until 1945—by which time, as Lichty writes, it had begun to mix in more "live, on the spot news reports" until, by its final season, "listeners were hearing the actual voices of newsmakers" on *The March of Time* as well as on a growing number of other news programs.[10] We can see by this account that innovative radio producers had increasingly begun to experiment with ways to extend "mobile privatization" to the *production* side of radio, allowing different kinds of texts to be produced that focused on individual voices and experiences captured outside the studio, in their actual environments, using a variety of emergent technologies—long-playing transcription discs, steel wire recorders, coated film stock, and eventually the magnetic reel-to-reel tape technology that was invented in Germany and appropriated by Americans after the war—and that could be recorded on location and edited into news programs and documentaries.[11] Such recorded productions began to disrupt radio's mandatory "flow" as well, since recordings could be repeated, preserved, and archived, though it would take the invention of the cassette tape and easily portable player/recorders in the 1960s to release soundwork from its inhibiting studio environment and make radio production and reproduction much more accessible to all.

Digital Disruption: *Serial*

Many historians of radio have argued that the dramatized documentaries of the 1940s and '50s, though limited by existing technology, produced a level of sonic artistry rarely achieved since. Renowned producers like Norman Corwin in the US and Geoffrey Bridson and Olive Shapely in the UK combined creative mixtures of music, storytelling, and performance with a dogged determination to find ways to get the voices of ordinary working-class people onto the airwaves, despite all technological difficulties.[12] As more easily portable and editable recording technology emerged, a brief "golden age" of the radio documentary flourished in the 1950s and early 1960s, until the increased influence of television, and radio's turn to music formats, made the radio documentary increasingly rare. This began to change in the 1990s, led by National Public Radio (NPR), public radio's oldest production organization. Shows like *This American Life* (1995–) took radio documentary in creative new directions, so it is not surprising that when digital media began to emerge in the 1990s, its potential was immediately recognized by radio producers—and listeners—everywhere. The advent of podcasting in the early 2000s launched radio into the digital age; public radio in particular was quick to see the advantages in expanding its outreach beyond the radio dial.

Raymond Williams's concepts of "flow" and "mobile privatization" applied to a consideration of *Serial* help to illuminate the way that digital media has revolutionized both the art of sound and contemporary media culture. First, though we use the word "streaming" to characterize digital media—which certainly sounds similar to "flow"—in fact it is radically different, in the way podcasts are both produced and received. Unlike broadcast radio's unstoppable flow, digital sound can be paused, downloaded, reversed to hear again, preserved, and archived, not just by producers but by listeners as well. This function has allowed for the in-depth study of sound media of all kinds, past and present, in a way that broadcast radio's unstoppable flow made nearly impossible. In many cases, such as *Serial*'s, their easy accessibility on a website not only enables repeat listening but provides a home for materials relevant to the podcast, as well as allowing listeners to exchange information, post comments and suggestions, and provide input; likewise, producers can continue to communicate with their listeners even after the podcast itself has ended. Digital audio streaming effectively shattered the narrow, restrictive flow of broadcast media: though the podcast field is certainly dominated by a growing number of large-scale distributors, anyone can make or post a podcast for anyone to access, no matter how obscure or specialized the topic—almost completely unregulated by governments or large institutions and available around the world. With the disruption of broadcasting's flow, Williams's "deep contradiction" between conditions of production and reception has become a thing of the past, particularly in the field of sound.[13]

Second, podcasting takes "mobile privatization" to new heights, and new places, in a way that broadcast radio never could, and that Williams could never have dreamed of. As its iPod inspiration indicates, digital sound's portable devices make listening far more private and mobile than it had ever been before: not only freed from public tastes and schedules, but individual, selectable, intimate, often delivered directly into the ear via earphones or buds, able to be taken wherever the listener goes, inaudible to anyone else. It also privatizes production: virtually anyone can make a podcast on any subject, including those that would have been too specialized, controversial, narrow, or X-rated to ever be heard on broadcast radio. It has shattered the walls of the studio: digital technology enables recording, editing, and distribution to be done at home, on the street, or indeed anywhere. And it provides a kind of privacy that allows a range of voices and experiences to be heard, yet not required to conform to mainstream tastes and interests: why not knitting, sexual advice, Morris dancing?

Communities of nonmainstream interests can be formed and protected through the kind of intimate privacy that podcasting provides.

So, what was it about *Serial* that mobilized all these capabilities so decisively, provoking worldwide attention and launching a true-crime podcast tsunami? Radio listeners who discovered *Serial* quickly realized that they could go back and relisten to each complicated episode online, thanks to the website that accompanied the show from its start. There they could also post questions and comments and enjoy ancillary materials such as maps, timelines, and actual trial materials, including letters, interview transcripts, and cell phone records. These interactive capacities, combining the power of broadcast radio with the affordances of digital privatization, effectively hitched radio's flow to digital media's deep dive in a way that not only made the podcast a global sensation but also had a real-world impact, though it took a while: Adnan Syed's release from prison in 2022.

To give a brief indication of how the program worked, I'll focus on "Episode 1: The Alibi." It begins, as all future episodes would, with a trademark rhythmic plinking of piano chords, along with the automated voice of a telephone operator saying, "This is a global telelink prepaid call from ("Adnan Syed," in his voice), an inmate at the Maryland Correctional Facility," surely chosen to remind us what the real-life stakes were, and are, in this story: the murder of a young woman, and a man held behind bars since he was seventeen. It is followed by producer Sarah Koenig's voice over a continuing soft piano bed, announcing "From *This American Life* and WBEZ Chicago, it's *Serial*, one story told week by week." The last phrase is important, since few previous radio documentary programs had operated as a unified set of episodes of a single story continued over weeks and months—hence the name, and hence the need for explanation. Koenig opens by saying, "For the last year, I've spent every working day trying to figure out where a high school kid was for an hour after school one day in 1999." She continues in the first person, drawing out her doubts and difficulties in tracking down events that happened fourteen years before, exploring how people's memory fades and how difficult it is generally to recover evidence from the days before digital media. Her tone is speculative, more concerned with thinking things through than with firing a barrage of facts at the listener as *The March of Time* and its ilk did.

The episode then introduces the main actors in the story: the victim, Hae Min Lee, a talented and charismatic high school senior; Adnan Syed, also a high school senior and Lee's ex-boyfriend, who at the time of the podcast had served fourteen years of a life sentence as her convicted killer; Jay Wilds, Syed's friend, whose ever-changing, contradictory account of circumstances surrounding the murder and its coverup provided the sole evidence linking Syed to the crime; and Rabia Chaudry, a lawyer and friend of Syed's family, whose own investigation had found key evidence never introduced in the trial and who persuaded Koenig to take on the project of clearing his name. From there, the account unreels in its own complex, intricate, at times funny, at times heartbreaking way, foreshadowing elements that she will address in future episodes, digging into cell phone records and drive times, trying to elicit memories of what exactly happened on that crucial day fourteen years before, raising more questions than answers.

In contrast to *The March of Time*'s fast-paced urgency, Koenig's tone is casual, engaging, at times poetic, and she intersperses her narrative with candid clips from those she interviewed. A light instrumental motif often enters to smooth a transition or mark an especially troubling turn of events, adding an emotional subtext. Unlike typical documentaries, which tend to maintain a stance of objectivity and stick closely to "just the facts," Koenig speaks emotionally about what she *doesn't* know, addressing the listener as "you," bringing in a variety of voices that as frequently undermine her points as support them, foregrounding her thoughts and speculations as well as hard facts. It is clear that this is a story still in progress, with no answers to be had: she doesn't know where the narrative will end up any more than her listeners do. Unlike *The March of Time*'s tightly scripted intensity mandated by broadcasting's frenetic flow, what *Serial* listeners get is a persistent circling around a set of "facts" that become less convincingly factual with each weekly installment. We listeners will be drawn into the investigation week by week as it happens, rather than presented with a closed narrative.

Subsequent episodes focus on specific aspects of the case: Hae and Adnan's relationship ("The Breakup"), the discovery of Hae's body and how it got there ("Leakin Park"), an overview of contradictory stories and evidence ("Inconsistencies"), a retracing of the route supposedly taken by Jay and Adnan on that fateful day ("Route Talk"), and an exploration of the many omissions and flaws in the case presented to the jury ("The Best Defense is a Good Defense"). But other episodes, as the series continues, focus primarily on what is *not* known: why was Jay's testimony full of so many contradictions, yet accepted in court ("The Deal with Jay")? What if Adnan wasn't the nice guy he appeared to be ("Rumors")? The final episode, "What We Know," attempts to summarize but ends with Koenig's own frustrated words: "Just tell me the facts, ma'am—because we didn't have them fifteen years ago, and we still don't have them now." In the end, what we are left with is not certainty but questions—questions that were powerful enough to lead to reconsideration of the whole case, resulting in Adnan's release from jail in 2022, though at the time of this writing his release is again under appeal.[14]

Conclusion

I've argued here that *Serial* provides not only a landmark in the evolution of the true-crime podcast—still by far the most popular genre in the podcast field today—but an excellent example of the way that streaming digital technology, as it emerged in the early twenty-first century, broke open the textual forms of radio as theorized by Raymond Williams, diversifying broadcasting's flow and dramatically increasing, and deepening, mobile privatization.[15] It has unleashed thousands of new voices, innovated a range of new textual practices, and invented new narrative techniques, structures, and participatory possibilities. It has also unlocked radio's vast, unheard archive, opening the door to recovery of the lost history of radio's creativity and cultural impact over more than a century. Digitally enabled critical attention to soundwork seems poised to bring us not only a far more intimate and interactive relationship to sound-based media but also perhaps astounding revelations, as the long-forgotten role of soundwork in the history of world culture can finally be given the attention it deserves.

Notes

1 Ewan McGregor, "The Investigator in Your Ear," *Time*, April 16, 2015, https://time.com/collection-post/3823276/sarah-koenig-2015-time-100/.
2 Peabody Awards, "*Serial*," https://peabodyawards.com/award-profile/serial/.

3   The website is still up and functioning at https://serialpodcast.org/. For a definition of soundwork, see Michele Hilmes, "Sound," in *Keywords for Media Studies*, edited by Jonathan Gray and Laurie Ouellette (New York: New York University Press, 2017), 180–181.
4   Dana Polan, "Raymond Williams on Film," *Cinema Journal* 52, no. 3 (Spring 2013): 2.
5   Raymond Williams, *Television: Technology and Cultural Form* (New York: Routledge, 2010), 24.
6   Williams, *Television*, 86.
7   Williams, *Television*, 97.
8   For more on early radio documentary production, see Paddy Scannell, "'The Stuff of Radio': Developments in Radio Features and Documentaries before the War," in *Documentary and the Mass Media*, edited by John Corner (London: Arnold, 1986), 1–26; Michele Hilmes, "Reality in Sound: Problem Solved?" in *Saving New Sounds: Podcast Preservation and Historiography*, edited by Jeremy Wade Morris and Eric Hoyt (Ann Arbor: University of Michigan Press, 2021), 71–81; and Alan Gevinson, "'What the Neighbors Say': The Radio Research Project of the Library of Congress," edited by Iris Newsom (Washington, DC: Library of Congress, 2002).
9   Lawrence W. Lichty, "Documentary Programs on U.S. Radio," in *The Encyclopedia of Radio*, edited by Christopher H. Sterling and Michael C. Keith (New York: Fitzroy Dearborn, 2004), 474.
10 Lichty, "Documentary Programs," 899.
11 For more on early radio recording technologies and uses, see Michele Hilmes, "The New Materiality of Radio: Sound on Screens," in *Radio's New Wave*, edited by Michele Hilmes and Jason Loviglio (New York: Routledge, 2013), 43–61.
12 Scannell, "'The Stuff of Radio,'" Matthew C. Ehrlich, *Radio Utopia: Postwar Audio Documentary in the Public Interest* (Urbana: University of Illinois Press, 2011).
13 See Andrew Bottomley, *Sound Streams: A Cultural History of Radio-Internet Convergence* (Ann Arbor: University of Michigan Press, 2020); and Siobhan McHugh, "How Podcasting Is Changing the Audio Storytelling Genre," *The Radio Journal: International Studies in Broadcast & Audio Media* 14, no. 1 (2016): 65–82.
14 *The New York Times* posted a timeline of the case on October 5, 2023: "Timeline: The Adnan Syed Case," www.nytimes.com/article/adnan-syed-serial-timeline-serial.html.
15 True crime comprises about 24 percent of all podcasts, according to a 2023 Pew Report: www.pewresearch.org/journalism/2023/06/15/a-profile-of-the-top-ranked-podcasts-in-the-u-s/.

23

Patterns and Categories

Connecting Textual Features and Industrial Conditions

AMANDA D. LOTZ

Lotz discusses her own attempts to use production and industry studies to ask questions about texts and vice versa, thereby delineating the stakes for how each method informs the other. She focuses on the growing scope and possibility for gendered depictions in the postnetwork, cable television era, then on how industrial practices and norms have again changed business as usual for television storytellers in the streaming era.

I have studied the changing business of television for twenty-five years, although I began my career doing research that centered the study of texts. When I trained in the late 1990s, most research about the institutions that made media, commonly identified as political economy, paid little attention to texts, or to entertainment media for that matter. But a first wave of mostly historical study had just emerged that incorporated cultural studies' call to integrate the study of texts, audiences, and industry. Books by Christopher Anderson, William Boddy, and Michael Curtin drew connections among textual features and strategies of U.S. television in the 1950s and 1960s related to industrial conditions and aims.[1] Justin Wyatt identified how the rise of "high-concept" films that were integrated with marketing and extensions—largely what are categorized as Hollywood blockbusters now—was tied to shifts in exhibition, such as the rise of the multiplex, and to broader cultural changes affecting the role of cinemagoing.[2] Julie D'Acci and John Caldwell looked at more recent moments, with D'Acci bringing together textual analysis, industrial analysis, and viewer response to investigate the challenges facing series about working women and Caldwell examining "televisuality," which derived from changes in production technologies and enabled an increase in attention to style and varieties of televisual and cinematic visual styles in 1980s U.S. television.[3]

These scholars, and others, led me to the specific question I've been chasing for more than two decades: How does changing or expanding the *modes of industrial practice*—the features of economics, technology, and regulation that guide how commercial media businesses operate—change the textual features of what can be or is likely to be produced? In this chapter, I explain how I've found textual and industrial analysis to inform each other and what the benefits are of keeping the textual and industrial in conversation—even if only in the background of a project.

I spent much of my life in the US and grew up in an age when TV was regarded as a bad object with simple characters and formulaic plots. In graduate school, at the end of the 1990s, I came to understand that the reason for that reputation was tied to the mode of industrial practice that dominated U.S. television throughout the twentieth century. The mode was set up to efficiently produce a high quantity of ongoing series that would satisfy a wide range of viewers, often watching together as families or couples on television sets that were limited in their technological capabilities. Rather than inherently characteristic of "television," the pervasive simple characters and formulaic plots were an outcome of a particular mode of industrial practice. In order for the U.S. system to consistently produce anything else, the mode of industrial practice had to change or expand.

My research examining changes in business practices and technology—work generally recognized as "media industry study"—has been driven by my interest in how adjustments to industrial norms change the texts or, in my language, stories, that can be produced and shared in a commercial system.[4] Answering my research questions requires both industrial and textual evidence. My publications rarely include extensive textual analysis, but examination of texts is often a precursor to my investigations. It is through the process of watching and considering what I see that I first become aware of possible patterns or textual trends that, after further textual interrogation, form the basis of research questions. Many of my projects have begun by observing a "textual phenomenon" and then investigating whether it is anomalous or can be identified as part of a larger pattern. When a pattern emerges, my inquiry shifts to exploring its likely industrial cause. Textual analysis is often a big part of my prewriting and research process. When my publications incorporate textual analysis, they typically aim to connect industrial practices with textual phenomena to make an argument about how the textual change may have implications for culture.

Finding Patterns

Sometimes this work explains changes in textual norms by investigating their industrial roots. My earliest research grew out of feeling that there was something different about the stories about being a woman that emerged in late-1990s U.S. television. At first, the project was restricted to three case studies, *Sex and the City*, *Ally McBeal*, and *Any Day Now*. But the years between when I proposed and completed my dissertation introduced an extraordinary number of female-centered dramas to U.S. screens—more than twenty such series had aired over multiple seasons by 2000. Any book I would develop from this project would need to expand from the original three cases. The textual phenomenon in this case was an unprecedented proliferation of commercially successful female-centered dramas. The book's (*Redesigning Women: Television after the Network Era*) research questions investigated what had changed to enable such storytelling about women (an industrial/historical question) and what could be claimed about the stories told in this array of series—particularly relative to feminist politics (a textual question).

My interest in tying industrial practices to textual phenomena means that I am usually investigating a fairly expansive number of series. Bringing order to such a range requires sorting and classifying, so the first step of the process is usually to make lists, followed by step two, to look for patterns. In the case of *Redesigning Women*, it was clear from the outset that there was not a single "feminist politics" across the series. There is rarely consistency and coherence across scores of texts. The task of looking for patterns aims to develop subcategories that allow more detailed and consistent claims about the subgroup. I found that most of the female-centered dramas could be sorted into one of four narrative types: action dramas (*Buffy the Vampire Slayer* [WB, 1997–2001; UPN 2001–03], *Xena: Warrior Princess* [Syndication, 1995–2001]), comedic dramas (*Ally McBeal* [Fox, 1997–2002], *Sex and the City* [HBO, 1998–2004]), protagonist-centered family dramas (*Judging Amy* [CBS,

1999–2005], *Providence* [NBC, 1999–2002]), and workplace dramas (*Strong Medicine* [Lifetime, 2000–06], *The Division* [Lifetime, 2001–04]).

The organization of the book relies on these narrative types to trace the features of stories being told about women and their lives on U.S. television at the turn of the century and how they were expanding from their quite limited roles and stories in the past. The chapters analyze each narrative type relative to its typical features, deviations between contemporary versions and past cases, and the contributions and limitations of each narrative type to presenting stories about female characters, as well as stories imbued with a feminist politics. It was useful, for instance, to look at *Sex and the City* and *Ally McBeal*, with their multiplicity of female characters, to investigate how they did or didn't address intersectionality or use the differences among their multiple lead characters to debate how the expectations of "new" women might vary for women with different access to social privilege. Their stories could be compared to a lineage of other similarly structured series such as *The Golden Girls* (NBC, 1985–92) and *Designing Women* (CBS, 1986–93) that likewise offered different female archetypes, and they could be studied for their notable differences from single-protagonist series that inherently struggled more with representational politics such as *The Mary Tyler Moore Show* (CBS, 1970–77), *That Girl* (ABC, 1966–71), and *Julia* (NBC, 1968–71). Industrial analysis in the form of evidence of changing business pressures and priorities explained why so many of these female-centered series had come to exist at this time.

My approach to the book *Cable Guys: Television and Masculinities in the Twenty-First Century* was similar.[5] Again, the project started from texts. In the general course of watching television series that were interesting to me in the early 2000s, I began noticing that "something seemed different" in the male characters and stories about them on offer. Again, I made lists of titles and looked for patterns in themes, characters' features and attributes, the creative teams, and the channels commissioning the series. The book did not begin as one focused on series commissioned by cable channels; rather, that emerged as a defining attribute as I listed and searched for patterns. Again, a score of series could be organized into a smaller set, though in this case I'd describe the organization more by narrative components: male-centered series investigated in terms of broad commonalities, and then subsets of series with protagonists who turn to illegal means, ones that use jocularity in a homosocial space for policing the boundaries of masculinity, and those that present deep friendships between men.

My most recent work (*After Mass Media: Storytelling for Microaudiences in the Twenty-First Century*) also engages both industrial and textual analysis in the same pages with the aim of tying changes in business models and distribution technologies to an expansion in the range of series perceived as commercially viable by U.S. commissioners. The work began from a sense that the array of stories on offer had expanded; the next step was to sort out why, in what ways, and to what extent. The first clues appeared in the late 1990s when HBO, a purely subscriber-funded channel, commissioned notably distinctive series such as *The Sopranos* (1999–2007), *Six Feet Under* (2001–05), and *Sex and the City* to considerable public notice. I understood that this was possible because HBO's mode of industrial practice differed from what was widely regarded as "normal" for U.S. television. HBO didn't sell advertising, so it wasn't first and foremost concerned with attracting the most attention to its channel every hour of the day. Instead, it relied on people paying to access it, a deviation in the economics of the dominant mode. Compelling people to pay requires offering something better or at least different from what they can get for "free." Although HBO might have loved to have 80 percent of U.S. households paying to receive it, developing a service that would be distinctive in the way 80 percent of households desired was likely unattainable. Instead, HBO provided a service with distinction, likely desirable to people who liked to watch recent movies and people who wanted programs that pushed the boundaries of what broadcasters offered. In some cases, those boundaries were about bringing greater character and narrative complexity to series, but another significant part of HBO's edgy offerings was its range of softcore erotic programs. It also offered nonmainstream sports coverage and documentaries to serve yet other interests in ways absent or underserved by existing ad-supported services.

To make sense of the change in television stories that developed from the late 1990s into the early 2020s, I began by identifying titles that my awareness of broadcast norms and strategies suggested would have been unlikely to be made within the industrial-grade mode that dominated twentieth-century television production in the US. It wasn't that all series had changed, not at all. In the first decades of the twenty-first century, there was a clear increase in U.S. series production (at least in terms of number of titles, the so-called Peak TV), but it wasn't just more of the same old thing. The old thing persisted, but there were also series different from those that had been typical.

Ultimately, I identified at least three categories that differed from previous norms, although some of these differences could overlap (series could be "different" in more than one way). The first are what I termed "international series," or series that are designed foremost for multiterritory audiences. Of course, series had long circulated across national borders, but in the early twenty-first century there was a clear increase in series that were originally designed for transnational reach, which is different from the domestic-first logic that had been the norm. The aim of international series expanded well beyond that of "international" coproductions that designed series for two (or a few) markets to instead develop series that imagined a global audience, more similar to that guiding Hollywood film production by the late twentieth century.

The imagined global audience for international series requires developing stories that do not require particular cultural knowledge. Many of these series rely on unreal worlds—whether as science fiction or premodern times (*Game of Thrones* [HBO, 2011–19], *Snowpiercer* [TNT, 2020–22; AMC 2024], *Vikings* [History Channel, 2013–20; Amazon Prime, 2020], *Rome* [HBO, BBC Two, and Rai 2, 2005–07]). Others feature globetrotting narratives about spies and intrigue that are similarly accessible to viewers in many places because of their disconnection from typical life (adaptations of John le Carré and Tom Clancy novels, *Homeland* [Showtime, 2011–20], *Sense8* [Netflix, 2015–18]). These series are expensive to produce, but the expectation is that their broad reach will enable licensing into or viewership in many markets. Although international series have grown increasingly common in the last decade, the idea of creating series *foremost* for a multiterritory audience is quite different from the logics that supported twentieth-century series production.

A second category of series encompasses those I've called "spectacular" series. These series are the "blockbusters" of television. In other words, they are titles that commissioners strategically develop and support with the aim of drawing exceptional attention—think *House of the Dragon* (HBO, 2022–) or *The Rings of Power* (Amazon Prime, 2022–).

Spectacular series typically have extraordinary production budgets as well as extraordinary promotional budgets. Those budgets are used to cast the best-known talent (*The Morning Show* [Apple TV+, 2019–]), pay for exceptional effects and sets (*House of the Dragon*), or acquire the rights to high-profile intellectual property (*The Rings of Power*). Many in society are likely familiar with spectacular series because they receive much more promotion—paid and unpaid—than other kinds of series. Even with that promotion, they apparently are not much more widely viewed than other shows, which hints at the peculiarity of this mode of industrial practice. Spectacular series can't possibly recoup their costs in the way expected in other modes of series production. This indicates they accrue value in other ways—likely in the buzz that is generated about them; and this ties to a notable feature: streaming services are overwhelmingly the commissioners of such series. This, too, is evidence that they operate with different goals than traditional networks. An aim of these series is not just to compel people to watch them but also to promote the service they are on and add to consumers' perception that the service offers valuable titles.

The third type of series is nearly the opposite of spectacular series. I've called shows such as *Atlanta* (FX, 2016–22), *Better Things* (FX, 2016–22), and *Somebody Somewhere* (HBO, 2022–) "character study" series to highlight a category of series that would have been most uncommon in U.S. industrial-grade norms because they aren't really driven by typical features of plot and instead offer deep examinations of often-banal features of the characters and their lives. Notably, many of the character series are also about characters whose stories haven't been told often on screen. There is little about character study series that would suggest they reach a broad audience, and these aren't titles that are hailed because many people watch them. The mode of industrial practice for these stories likely relies on them being comparatively low budget. They lack special effects and fancy sets, and attract talent because they offer interesting and uncommon roles—which has long explained the mode of independent and art film production. These series can also enhance the reputation of the services offering them through awards nominations, and they can encourage creative talent to want to work with these commissioners because they establish a reputation of taking risks on creatively uncommon concepts.

I also noticed an uncommon textual form—by U.S. standards—that can be found across these three series types. A key attribute of the industrial-grade mode of practice that organized most U.S. series production in the twentieth century was the efficiency that derived from long-running series built around narrative premises that could allow for twenty episodes a year and extend over decades of production (e.g., *Law & Order* [NBC, 1990–]; *CSI* [CBS, 2000–15]; *Grey's Anatomy* [ABC, 2005–]; *The Simpsons* [Fox, 1989–]; *Big Bang Theory* [CBS, 2007–19]; and *Modern Family* [ABC, 2009–20]). But many of the international, spectacular, and character study series featured short, often closed-ended seasons (that had a complete narrative before beginning production) or were designed as limited series (stories told over four to ten hour-long episodes without expectation of returning), as with, for example, *True Detective* (HBO, 2014–), *Unbelievable* (Netflix, 2019), and *The Honourable Woman* (BBC Two and SundanceTV, 2014). To be clear, this is not a new form. U.S. television mostly forgot about this form, once called a miniseries, for thirty years. The multi-episode, closed-ended form, such as *Roots* (ABC, 1977), *The Winds of War* (ABC, 1983), and *North and South* (ABC, 1985), largely disappeared from U.S. screens in the late 1980s, although this remained an abundant, if not the dominant, form of drama in many other countries. Their disappearance in the US can be traced to industrial causes of competition, costs, and audience fragmentation. Similarly, their return in the early 2010s was tied to the emergence of additional commercial modes of industrial practice.

Here, too, a basis for textual change existed in the shifting industrial conditions. The observed textual phenomenon was an increasing number of limited series being commissioned by U.S. channels and services. Most of these series were commissioned by subscriber-funded HBO and streaming services such as Netflix, both of which operated with different industrial priorities, and sought to offer distinctive content that compelled payment. By the 2010s, both could also deliver content on demand. Unlike the industrial-grade logics of "filling a schedule," these services sought buzzy titles they could promote and make available for audiences to view with greater time flexibility. The emergence of services with different industrial logics from those of commercial broadcasters helped expand the range of stories in the marketplace.

Tracking Change: Textual, Industrial, Social

Notably, the "textual analysis" in the research I've mentioned may look quite different from the analysis in a lot of the other cases described and presented in the chapters here. This ties to some differences in the types of arguments made in different kinds of scholarship and thus differences in the evidence needed to support it.

A commonality across textual analysis is a reliance on the text for evidence. Many different kinds of arguments can be made about the features of a piece of media. When textual analysis and industrial analysis are blended, both textual and industrial evidence come into play. For example, the key to what I'm doing at a textual level is identifying a type of series prevalent enough to be a type or identifiable phenomenon—not a single or quite rare case. That requires looking broadly at the features of many, many series, and this is not work typically included in my publications. In my work, the textual analysis is the identification of these patterned phenomena and, thus, it happens before writing and shapes the argument and aim. In most cases, I can explain the patterns, categories, and titles that comprise the phenomena in just a few pages. Readers familiar with the titles don't require much convincing about this general sorting; if I've done my work well, the legitimacy of my categories should be pretty obvious. Notably, *the categorizing isn't the primary analytic project of the work.* The categorizing is what explains or justifies the scope or provides me with the ability to talk about a set of texts as a coherent "phenomenon."

Of course, many additional textual questions remain to be explored beyond the categorizing. In the books centered on gender, I've then asked deeper questions about the nature or implications of the groups of texts I establish. Much of the analysis in *Redesigning Women* focuses on assessing the feminist politics of the dominant themes or features of different types of series and in advancing arguments about how the series produced at the turn of the twenty-first century were different from those produced previously.[6] It wasn't possible to support an argument so broad as claiming U.S. television was now feminist, or even just more feminist. Even by that pre-streaming moment, audiences had fractured across so many channels that many viewers could easily continue to watch hours and hours of television weekly without ever encountering a female-centered drama.

In *Cable Guys*, the deeper textual analysis explored how the masculinity constructed within different narrative components deviated from what had been the hegemonic construction of masculinity on U.S. television historically. Here, too, it was impossible to claim that the series featured in the book represented U.S. television as a whole. But I could amass evidence of a textual phenomenon that defied many features of the construction of hegemonic masculinity that was historically pervasive and still plentiful on several other channels available alongside the series I explored. Textual change need not be so extreme as the replacement of one norm with another. Change in cultural forms often takes quite a long time and is so gradual that it can be difficult to pinpoint precisely when a discourse or representation shifts from being dominant to residual, or from emergent to dominant, in a framework offered by Raymond Williams.[7] For instance, at some point in the last forty years, the humor in many of the teen movies that I regarded as "normal" or "just how things are" in the late 1980s became cringey and, in some cases, offensively unwatchable. That shift didn't happen overnight but over decades, during which different kinds of teen stories that might have at first seemed exceptional and uncommon coexisted with the past norm and gradually shifted from being emergent to dominant.

After Mass Media's exploration of the expansion in the modes of industrial practice that enabled international, spectacular, and character study series focuses on applying information about industrial changes and building a case for how developments such as decreased reliance on advertiser funding and the different business model available to multiterritory streaming services such as Netflix supported alternative commercial modes. The book doesn't examine the texts in much detail; at this stage, it has mainly been a work of categorization to enable more sophisticated general conversations.

What are other textual questions? The aim of my book is a rather sweeping account of broad trends over a thirty-year time frame. Such scope is needed to trace out an expansive frame of industrial change, but there are many cases where more detailed analysis can enrich understanding. Part of the thinking that led me to connect different modes of industrial practice that produced series with particular textual features was a sense that previous mechanisms for categorizing texts were decreasingly effective. It was well known that the number of series being produced annually had increased, and the widespread use of streaming services made many titles, including many produced decades previously, available at any time. But conversations about "television" grew difficult as viewers' attention fragmented across many shows, without the enforced shared temporality that had long been common. That there were more shows was empirically obvious, and it wasn't difficult to sense some greater variation, but it wasn't clear what could be said about "television" or "series" as streamers also became major commissioners and moved from limited to mainstream use. In the early twenty-first century, series produced for U.S. cable tended to have distinctive features from series produced for broadcast networks in a way that enabled distribution technology to be a reliable category for organizing titles (e.g., "cable series are like X"). But it quickly became clear that series commissioned by streaming services had too much variation for distribution technology to be a reliable category.

Another scholar might take those patterned phenomena and ask further textual questions of them. For example, they might explore differences in the character and narrative construction of limited series, or do a systematic analysis of the international series and posit arguments about their ideological significance, which would be more purely textual analysis projects. Rather, my interest is in explaining how or why those patterned phenomena can be explained by new modes of industrial practice. Closer textual analysis might identify differences among international titles developed by multiterritory streamers from those developed by other commissioners. It might explore whether there are clear differences between those series produced by U.S. production companies and those from other countries or regions, or how gender is portrayed in different types of series or in different distribution technologies.

In one way or another, scholarship blending industrial and textual analysis answers the question, "Why does television look this way/tell these stories/feature these characters?" by appreciating the underlying industrial conditions that shape textual possibilities. Components such as the economic features tied to financing or the ways viewers pay for content, the available technology, and regulation do not strictly determine textual features, but they do structure the boundaries of what is more or less likely. When systematic and patterned changes in texts develop, there is often an industrial reason, just as relative stasis in industry conditions at other times leads to uniformity.

Notes

1. Christopher Anderson, *Hollywood TV: The Studio System In The Fifties* (Austin: University of Texas Press, 1994); William Boddy, "Building the World's Largest Advertising Medium: CBS and Television, 1940–60," in *Hollywood in the Age of Television*, edited by Tino Balio (London: Routledge, 1990), 63–89; Michael Curtin, *Redeeming the Wasteland: Television Documentary and Cold War Politics* (New Brunswick, NJ: Rutgers University Press, 1995).
2. Justin Wyatt, *High Concept: Movies and Marketing in Hollywood* (Austin: University of Texas Press, 1994).
3. Julie D'Acci, *Defining Women: Television and the Case of Cagney and Lacey* (Chapel Hill: University of North Carolina Press, 1994); John Thornton Caldwell, *Televisuality: Style, Crisis, And Authority in American Television* (New Brunswick, NJ: Rutgers University Press, 1995).
4. See, for example, Timothy Havens and Amanda D. Lotz, *Understanding Media Industries* (Oxford: Oxford University Press, 2016); and Daniel Herbert, Amanda D. Lotz, and Aswin Punathambekar, *Media Industry Studies* (Cambridge: Polity Press, 2020).
5. Amanda D. Lotz, *Cable Guys: Television and Masculinities in the Twenty-First Century* (New York: New York University Press, 2014).
6. Amanda D. Lotz, *Redesigning Women: Television after the Network Era* (Champaign: University of Illinois Press, 2006).
7. Raymond Williams, *Marxism and Literature* (Oxford: Oxford Paperbacks, 1977).

24

Audience-Led Textual Analysis

The Case of Bridgerton's *Daphne Raping the Duke*

JOKE HERMES

Hermes makes a strong case for how well audience research can inform textual analysis, as analysts can follow audiences' leads on precisely what to study, and can challenge themselves to consider which parts of a text matter, how, and why. After offering step-by-step instructions on how to find relevant audience discussion online, and how best to use it, she then offers a case study from the first season of Netflix's Bridgerton.

The one thing that is clear about audience research, or so we are told, is that it is not textual analysis. Neither, from such a perspective, can textual analysis take the shape of audience research. Textual analysis, after all, focuses on careful consideration of a television series, a novel, a comic book, a game, or so forth—that is to say, *not* on what people think of these or do with them. However helpful generalizations can be, neither of these is very true. Audience researchers do a fair amount of textual analysis when they work with transcripts of interviews or use online discussions of media texts. Textual analysis, in turn, can benefit from audience research and the reflections of audience members. This chapter will focus on how. As a case study, it offers an example of how audience discussion of the first season of *Bridgerton* (Netflix, 2020–) allowed for unexpected and valuable insight.

Bridgerton is a Shondaland production for Netflix. Its first season, released in 2020, was watched, according to Netflix itself, by a whopping 82 million households worldwide.[1] Those viewers used various social media platforms to discuss the series. On what was then still called Twitter (now X), disgruntled viewers complained about how the music they heard sounded authentic to the period and place depicted (nineteenth-century London) but was actually an Ariana Grande song played by an orchestra. They also complained that the producers seemed to think that the British nobility in the so-called Regency period was a mixed-race group. Even the simple use of such observations can help a researcher approach a television text. In fact, as researchers, we are often aware of such discussions and may even be inspired by them. We tend to leave this inspiration out of our research publications, though, where we focus on what came after we became intrigued by, for instance, a series such as *Bridgerton*.

The first part of this chapter will explain how to go about using audience materials in order to study a media text and the merits of such an approach. The second part will turn in more detail to the first season of *Bridgerton* and a key scene that unexpectedly started discussion, initially in YouTube reaction videos and comments and then much more broadly. This is a scene in which Daphne Bridgerton, the heroine, has sex with Simon Basset, the Duke of Hastings, against his wishes. This scene is not a substantial part of the text itself. It does not comprise a dominant or repetitive theme in the storyline. In addition, it is not mentioned subsequently. Yet, for many, it became one of the most impactful moments of the series and was viewed as the moment most worthy of discussion and attention. As such, it shows the power the audience has to reshape a text and change our understanding of which aspects of the text "matter."

Part I: Audience-Led Textual Analysis as a Method to Approach Media Texts

Audience-led research profitably starts from an open question a researcher has. An example would be, "Something irritates me about this series: why does it not 'work'"? In itself, that is not a good research question. It is vague. It depends on intuition without providing any grounding or support for what is assumed, implicitly or explicitly, to be going "wrong." Intuitions can, however, trigger looking for what others have noted. Whether those others' reactions are more positive or more negative is not really that important; they are useful in nudging you into coming to a more formal question. For researchers schooled in anthropological and ethnographic methods, this would be a common route to take. In the humanities and in many other social sciences, such a strategy is not a formal part of a research project. In papers and in publications, authors prefer to offer arguments based on existing research and/or validated news sources to justify their project. In fact, using such sources, rather than what people are talking about, is also a perfectly good way to introduce audience-led textual analysis should you not be in a media and cultural studies field in which a more personal and open approach to research is credited.

Regardless, the next step when using audience-led textual research is to formalize findings by coding and analyzing comments. In the case of *Bridgerton*, there would be the reasons people gave for being upset and confused. You would then check which of the elements mentioned apparently do not conform to the historical period that is depicted: for instance, the setting, the dress code, the music. This, in turn, would need a brief set of principles to check the confusion, questions, and critique against. These textual analytical principles are usually referenced as generic or "genre" rules. For historical drama, such rules pertain to, for example, setting, dress code, and speech and dialogue. The television text suggests to us what interpretative context we should apply, but it does not always do so to the satisfaction of viewers.

> I.1: Check initial comments against representational codes in the text, and include genre-specific representational rules (for example, in the case of satire, other rules apply than in documentary or historical drama).

In its classical definition, genre is a contract between makers and viewers in which viewers need both to get what they expect to find and to be given something extra to keep them interested. Even in formulaic genres that stick very closely to a given set of rules and conventions, there needs to be this extra element. Ultimately, no two television series (or, for that matter, no two pop songs, crime novels, games, etc.) are exactly the same. This can charm audiences but also present openings for them to voice objections, confusion, and critique.

You might want to delve further into such audience discussion, as there might be more that could help you understand the meanings or pleasures offered by a particular text. You then need to devise a plan to extend your search. A useful way to do so is to chart where your text of interest is discussed and pay attention to what the media industry calls "engagement" (are there high numbers of reactions?), to the "temperature" of the comments (are reactions especially heated?), and, if there a great deal of disagreement, to what we might call "polarization."

> I.2: Check where there is discussion of the text you are interested in. Social media platforms are an easy option. It is also possible to simply "ask around" and conduct short interviews, or to watch an episode of a series or play a game with others. This is called "participant observation." When using available online materials, check for engagement, temperature, and polarization. You are now doing "virtual" or "online" ethnography. These are research forms that observe cultural phenomena and meaning-making in everyday life.

Delving further, you will have collected (or, as it is called, "gathered") data. How, where, and what need to be recorded carefully. If you want to use material you have found in the future, you need to be able to give its exact location. With online materials, that is not always easy. There are issues of privacy (these days, often neither names nor handles are named in publications or reports). Sometimes users remove comments. Saving screenshots at a safe online server—for example, in a university environment—is considered to be a good way to archive your material.

Possibly, you will want to extend your data collection and use so-called scraper tools. These are software tools that are used to roam a platform for comments that contain specific keywords, hashtags, or names. Such tools report what they found in formats that can be translated into spreadsheets, in which your material can be usefully sorted. They also allow for leaving out (or even deleting) identifiable characteristics. Nonetheless, such results need to be stored in safe online (or offline) environments. Although a bit scary to use for those who do not feel technologically gifted, scraper tools have two enormous advantages: they offer all the material that can be found on the platforms they can search (which are, admittedly, a small number), and they offer easy ways to limit which of the data you will want to use. Those could be key periods, content from key users, or content defined by a combination of keywords or hashtags. They allow, in short, for playing around with the audience data. The one thing they do not do is save time. You still have to actually read the material that has been gathered. Also, all advanced forms of sorting and coding rely on human work, be it up front in selecting material as a check on what the machine has done or in teaching the machine how to do it right.

> I.3: You have used a scraper tool (or you have manually copied and pasted comments around a specific search term) and your data are now in a spreadsheet. Now play around! Maybe include more columns that allow you to sort the material according to what feels as if it is more relevant versus less relevant, to what is intriguing versus boring or hateful versus loving, or to the possible gender or other identity markers of the person who posted the material. With longer comments, you can also "code" the comments and pull apart the different ways in which your series or performer apparently can be talked about. This is to move to the level of cultural meaning-making. Rather than focus on individuals and their attitudes or ideas, you start looking for shared cultural logics. Since such logics also ultimately inform how people feel they can act in the world (or refrain from acting), these logics form an important part of cultural critique.

The last step of this trajectory is to translate what you find into engaging with the text as text. It is to return to the representational codes, the genre characteristics, the narrative, or perhaps the characters. You now have the benefit of seeing all of these through the eyes of a community of readers who, together, in a way have scripted how the text can be understood. The nice thing is that you do not have to agree with these comments to work with them.

> I.4: Inspired by the discussion, find out more, defend, turn around, critique the reception of your text. Compare what you have found to your own initial interest and intuitions to get started on this fourth step. Based on what spoke to you most in your findings, connect these findings with a narratological, semiotic, genre-analytic, or ideology-critical analysis. Carefully report on

the findings from your dive into audience reactions and how you interpret them. Use the report to come to a strong research question for your project. Now write it up as audience-led textual analysis and answer that research question!

Part II: The First Season of the TV Series *Bridgerton* as a Case Study

This case study is based on collective work with a colleague and three student co-researchers.[2] Here's a first tip that comes with this particular method: do use your own and your friends' audience experiences to get started! All of us had watched *Bridgerton*'s first season and noticed our very different ways of engaging with the text. One of us was a reader of Regency romance, the book genre that the television series is based on. For her, the series was considerably flatter and felt a bit like a parody; one of the others had fallen in love with the hero, the Duke of Hastings (played by Regé-Jean Page); a third preferred the more realistic historical romance series *Outlander* (Starz, 2014–). We were all greatly amused by the incensed reactions of viewers on Twitter.

Several lines of inquiry suggested themselves. We could look at how the novels had been adapted for television. We could compare *Bridgerton* to other examples of historical drama. We could try to assess what qualities the formerly scorned genre of the romance novel could be found to have (despite the backlash against the TV series). As we were discussing this, *Bridgerton* became a television hit.

We decided to scout for online reactions and do an audience-led study of the text. The four steps unfolded as follows:

II.1: What representational practice was to be found in *Bridgerton* at first glance? Settings, costumes, the weather, the music?
II.2: Where were people discussing *Bridgerton* online? And where did we have access to that discussion?
II.3: Scraping YouTube for comments underneath response videos, what pattern(s) or themes emerged?
II.4: In combining the patterns in online discussion with a textual analysis of *Bridgerton*, what ideological critique suggests itself?

First Check of Impression of Comments Against Representational Practice

As this is an exploratory exercise, a check at first glance of what might be the case, we compared comments against our own viewing. That seemed to make clear that the series is not historical drama but plays with the genre. It might matter whether one is aware of two significant aspects to its production process. First, the original text is part of the romance genre. While popular culture in many ways has emancipated, this remains a lowly regarded, if very well-selling, genre of women's fiction. Second, the Shondaland production company has earned credit for shifting the television landscape. Its founder, Shonda Rhimes, has developed several unique series with diverse casts that managed the near-impossible challenge of making diversity ordinary as well as often an issue. To be of color, or to identify as gay (or any other way of defining who you are as a human being), matters to individuals, but how and when it matters will depend on context. Nondominant identities are far too often translated into "problems" in media production, which reinforces discriminatory practice. Rhimes allows diversity to just "be" while also deftly finding ways to thematize mechanisms of exclusion and discrimination.

Unsurprisingly, therefore, *Bridgerton*'s characters are a diverse bunch. There are people of color and different body shapes and sizes. Key character Penelope Featherington is played by actor Nicola Coughlan, who is well rounded and proud to be so. In the books, Penelope is described as "plump" and "round," although she loses her "baby fat" in later novels. In terms of their sexual identities, a vast majority of the characters appear to be heterosexual in their orientation. There are gay characters, though, in addition to what looks like a polyamorous arrangement. Sex workers are portrayed as carefully as the "ton," the upper layer of British nobility at the time.

This is a light approach to the serious issue of fair representation, which clearly was not noticed by some commenters. Neither apparently could they appreciate the "tongue-in-cheek"-ness of the series. The ridiculously good weather, and the oversaturated colors of what are suggested to be outdoor settings, are more reminiscent of Teletubbyland than what we imagine nineteenth-century London looked like. Décor selections are more stage settings than actual, existing places. All in all, our recce set us up to defend *Bridgerton*, the series. Had we chosen to pursue a solely textual approach, we would have missed how *Bridgerton*'s first season ended up setting in motion valuable discussion that provided a very different entry point to understand the layered meanings of the text.

Where Was Bridgerton *Discussed?*

Online comments had started us wondering about *Bridgerton*, so that is where we went to get a better of idea of what people were saying exactly and where. Here, initial interest shifted to a more strategic approach to find useful data to work with. Using a scraper tool, we searched both Twitter and YouTube for comments. By hand, we checked Facebook and Reddit. The scraper tool pointed us to YouTube response videos and the large volume of comments beneath them. We decided to go with that one platform and see how the three layers of analysis now in play had their own stories to tell. The layers were the response videos, the comments beneath them, and our own analysis of *Bridgerton*.

And How Was Bridgerton *Discussed?*

Given the sizable number of comments, we needed criteria to select and reduce the data. We decided to take a closer look at the most watched, best-subscribed, and most commented-on YouTube channels. Surprisingly, these were all made by men! They reviewed games, the television series, and books. One was a comedian who congratulated the *Bridgerton* viewers for their "labial fortitude," given the extreme sexiness of the duke.[3] A group of gamers were taken aback by the heroine's quest for true love and her disdain for a priceless necklace given to her by a prince (not her true love, clearly).[4] The most subscribed, viewed, and commented-on response video offered literary criticism. Rather than reacting to the television series itself, this YouTuber said the poor quality of the writing of the book series—the many adjectives, the bad construction of sentences, and more—made him puke.[5] The most interesting one was by a lone gamer, asked by his faithful following to take a look at this intriguing series. A man of color, he was the first creator, as far as we have been able to tell, to spot that the duke is raped by none other than his wife.[6]

Mapping the comments, we see a combination of lay analysis focused on clever commenting and humorous observations. For all of these YouTubers, it worked well to take the series seriously enough either to watch it or to read the books and use snippets of content to discuss themes close to their hearts. Two young fans of popular television and romance novels were extremely taken with an older character, the duke's aunt and also a woman of color, whom they called "their spirit animal," pointing to how we might discuss a television series through its characters.[7] Likewise, the comments about the priceless necklace point to the importance of a narratological approach when the storytelling comes to crucial turns.

Generally, the comments showed close-knit communities enjoying sharing their impressions. Mostly, the YouTubers used humorous pedagogics, allowing their audiences to be both critical and reassured about their own assessments. The intended meaning of the text was discussed, along with their thoughts about whether they felt that had been successfully conveyed.

In short, the advantage of audience-led textual analysis is in making good use of the "wisdom of crowds." In the example from *Bridgerton* discussed in this chapter, a YouTuber noted how sex was had without consent by both partners. Romance fiction was not his usual fare, which helped him not take generic rules for granted. More generally, viewers help broaden the perspective that can be brought to bear on a television series or another text, less invested as they are in analytical rules compared to scholars. Not only do viewers bring a "fresh" viewpoint to a text, but they are also not hindered by implicit professional rules. Whether as fans or as activists, they can significantly shift how popular texts become meaningful and what, as cultural critics, we might want to attend to.

Bridgerton *as Text: Where Did Our Audience Survey Take Us?*

Watching the response videos and reading the comments underneath them, we started to wonder whether *Bridgerton*, the television series, was involved in what might be called a generic sleight of hand. Genre analysis usefully looks at the contract between producers and readers or viewers by identifying key rules the text should never break—or, rather, at how breaking a rule needs to pay off, which in most cases it can only do when it strictly adheres to all other conventions. In a romance novel, we need a strong heroine who is not aware of how attractive she is. We need a hero who is attractive and has social status (although that may not initially appear to be the case). Often, heroes have had bad experiences and need to learn that not all women are manipulative. The heroines quite often take a strong dislike to the hero. Both hurdles need to be overcome.

The subgenre of the Regency romance is typically a novel rather than a television series or a movie, although this might change, now that *Bridgerton* has been a success in terms of viewing figures, as is *Outlander*, a somewhat different, more realistically and less romantically styled series. *Outlander* is also based on a series of novels, dubbed romances by fans but not by its author, Diana Gabaldon, who prefers to call them "historical novels." Sexual attraction and descriptions of the main characters having sex (whether more or less explicit) are a key part of the genre. No reader will have been surprised to see Daphne and the duke in bed. As viewers, they will not be surprised either when Daphne takes matters into her own hands and stops the duke from withdrawing in order not to impregnate her. His issues include not wanting children. Readers of the books recognize a moment of victory for the heroine, who never had any sexual education.[8] The game reviewer, though, was shocked and saw marital rape. True, the duke did not consent. The popular-culture enthusiasts retracted their earlier favorable discussion of the episode. Comments turned into serious discussion of consent. Intriguingly, the one case of nonconsensual sex in *Bridgerton*, rape according to some, is of a man and not of a woman, which is what almost all other rape scenes in television drama series confront us with.[9]

Looking up *Bridgerton* on Wikipedia today, the rape scene is almost the first thing you come across. How the discussion spread and whether it started with "our" YouTuber are impossible to say. There is a good chance, though, that it started with "lay critics." Today's audiences, after all, are also media makers as they post views and exchange ideas on social media.

Audience-led textual analysis in the case of *Bridgerton* and the rape of the duke thus turns into ideological criticism. Using such resources as adaptation studies or narrative analysis, studying YouTube reaction videos and their viewer comments leads us to how a popular cultural text helps people discuss and gain insight into what "consent" actually means. As the issue seems part of historical reality, it becomes easier to talk about. Does it matter what power women and men can wield socially, what their rights are? In the Regency period, married women had no bank accounts (if, of course, they were of a social background to have a need for those) or the possibility to own property. Education was not only for the privileged but for men only. Is Daphne's initial ignorance of human reproduction any excuse to deny her husband his reproductive rights when he is drunk?

Without looking further into audience reactions, it is likely that a combination of narrative and semiotic analysis of *Bridgerton* would have foregrounded the satirical touch deftly employed by the makers to alert viewers to how they privilege whiteness while, for instance, Dutch seventeenth-century paintings show many a nonwhite face. Even the merest suggestion that the British nobility might not have been lily-white is to use television to intervene in a political debate. As this is also popular culture with its stringent rules for popular drama, the makers of *Bridgerton* needed to underline that it was not a political treatise: hence the oversaturated colors and scenery and the Ariana Grande song set to a score for an orchestra.

As it turns out, the no-consent sex scene also shows something else. In the novels the television series is based on, the scene evokes a sense of triumph for the heroine to literally have taken matters in her own hands. The genre contract for readers was a different one than that for viewers—which takes us from audience-led textual analysis to how textual analysis will benefit audience research. But that is a topic for another book.

Notes

1. Rey Mashayehki, "Netflix CEO Reveals Streaming Giant's Most-Watched Series and Films," *Fortune*, September 27, 2021, https://fortune.com/2021/09/27/netflix-most-watched-series-films-bridgerton/.
2. Many thanks to Clair Richards, Linda Kopitz, and Zofia Pacewicz for discussing and researching *Bridgerton* reactions. For the *Bridgerton* case study in detail, see Joke Hermes, Linda Kopitz, and Clair Richards, "Data Analysis in Practice. Data-Scraping Meets the Regency Era: *Bridgerton* Commentary on YouTube," in *The Pocketbook of Audience Research* (London: Routledge, 2024), 121–32.

3 Josh Pray, "Bridgerton on Netflix has redefined how I want to be loved," January 12, 2021, YouTube, 2 min., 9 sec., https://www.youtube.com/watch?v=-abULrZQtT0.
4 Blind Wave, "Bridgerton 1x1 REACTION!! 'Diamond of the First Water,'" April 5, 2021, YouTube, 34 min., 33 sec., https://www.youtube.com/watch?v=XDkkOobjQG8&list=PL6nVTBxW49HkAPv-IcoKD4e-bOIHN7pLK.
5 Jack Edwards, "i read the 'bridgerton' book and it's . . . problematic (racism, sexism, consent, and bad writing)," January 26, 2021, YouTube, 15 min., 28 sec., https://www.youtube.com/watch?v=--ELuZ5z3X0&t=24s.
6 Sean Thompson, "Watching Bridgerton Out of context *Ep1&4*," February 11, 2021, YouTube, 25 min., 42 sec., https://www.youtube.com/watch?v=yFP75eh-n84&t=541s.
7 The Pink Popcast, "we loved BRIDGERTON *SEASON ONE REACTIONS* (reupload)," March 6, 2022, YouTube, 2 hours, 8 min., 59 sec., https://www.youtube.com/watch?v=o-Yo5pab7lc.
8 For the more usual depiction of sexuality in period drama, see Katherine Byrne and Jullie Anne Taddeo, *Rape in Period Drama Television: Consent, Myth, and Fantasy* (London: Rowman & Littlefield, 2022).
9 See Lisa Cuklanz, *Rape on Prime Time: Television, Masculinity, and Sexual Violence* (Philadelphia: University of Pennsylvania Press, 2000).

25

Analyzing Texts Using Sounds and Images

Making Video Essays as Critical Practice

JASON MITTELL

Mittell challenges textual analysis's usual practice as written criticism, instead arguing for the added valence and utility of videographic criticism. He helpfully surveys several prominent models and exemplars of the video essay format, charting various genres and possibilities within the form, while also discussing his own use of the format to study a pair of secondary characters from Breaking Bad.

Nearly every work of textual analysis of media involves translation. Whether the object of analysis is a film or a board game, a pop song or an advertisement, a key part of textual analysis involves describing the work in written language. Across the other chapters of this book, you've read detailed descriptions of theme park experiences, podcasts, video games, and TikTok videos, translating sounds, images, motions, and physical experiences into words on a page. But let me pose a question: How would textual analysis work without that specific transformation between media and language, presented in the "inherent form" of the media object itself?

We do have a prototype of such critical work in one of the most well-established modes of textual analysis, literary criticism. Most analyses of novels, poetry, and other forms of literature are written in the same basic modality as the original work, presented as words on a page. Certainly, an analysis of poetry still describes the poem, both in its static published form and in how it comes alive when one reads or speaks the text, but literary criticism features a core device that is less common in media analysis: the direct quotation. Literary critics will quote the precise phrasing of a poem or novel to discuss its meanings and style, allowing the reader to experience an excerpt of the original alongside its critical analysis. For critics of visual, sonic, and experiential media, quotation has not been feasible within written criticism except in partial forms, such as quoting the dialogue of a film, the transcript of a podcast, or the lyrics to a song, but leaving out the sensory dimensions of sounds and images.

Until recently, that is. With the rise of digital publication and media creation in the twenty-first century, critics have started presenting textual analysis that quotes images and sounds directly. This can involve embedding audio and video clips within a digital publication of written criticism, functioning much like selective quotations within a piece of literary criticism—this expands on a long-standing tradition of written film criticism reprinting still images from a movie, which offers a visual reference but removes both sound and motion. More recently, a more thorough and transformative approach has emerged called *videographic criticism*, creating textual analysis via the raw materials of sounds and moving images themselves. Commonly known as "video essays," such works offer a broad new set of possibilities to the practices of textual analysis, particularly for the criticism of films, television, and other moving-image media.

The term "videographic" evokes the concept of writing, as the suffix *-graph* refers to a mode of writing or expression, as in telegraph or autograph. "Videographic" is itself a bit of a misnomer, as this mode can best be defined as "writing with sounds and moving images"; hence, a more accurate but clunkier term would be "audiovideographic." In practice, videographic criticism produces critical work that remixes clips from the source materials being analyzed and recontextualizes them into a video essay that makes an argument and conveys ideas and experiences. Thus, instead of just serving as illustrations, the sounds and images from the film directly perform much of the critical work—the texts function as tools of their own analysis.

As with conventional written textual analysis, there are a wide range of approaches to videographic criticism, as it can be applied to nearly any object of analysis using any critical method; additionally, critics adopt an array of videographic styles and techniques to analyze media. Some video essays are hugely popular, racking up millions of views on YouTube by appealing to mainstream audiences, while others are much more esoteric in exploring niche topics, explaining highly academic concepts, or using techniques more typical of experimental filmmakers. Many other forms of video practice engage with footage from other media, ranging from fan videos to TikTok memes to response videos on YouTube; videographic criticism distinctly foregrounds its analytic goals, making it more akin to the various approaches to textual analysis detailed in this book. No single chapter could capture the entirety of the video essay landscape, so for my purposes here I will focus on works that analyze film, television, and related moving-image media in particular, and that ask similar questions about form, representation, and cultural impact that are explored throughout this book. Unlike other authors in this book, I cannot offer a case study of this videographic approach directly within this chapter; thus, I will first lead a tour of various exemplary videos (all which are available to view online) before turning to my own videographic work for some self-directed textual analysis.

A Brief Tour of Videographic Criticism

One of the most common types of videographic criticism is formal analysis, analyzing texts to understand how they function to tell stories, convey meaning, and generate emotional responses. In conventional written criticism, formal textual analysis requires lengthy descriptions of sounds and images to evoke a mental picture for readers seeking to understand the detailed operations of textual elements like camera movement or sound effects; clearly, videographic criticism can take advantage of the cliché "A picture is worth a thousand words," using (moving) pictures and sounds to avoid detailed description. A good example comes from Patrick Keating, who exemplifies formal analysis in chapter 4 of this book through an account of storytelling techniques. His video essay "Music and Point of View in *Harry Potter and the Prisoner of Azkaban*" (dir. Alfonso Cuarón, 2004) explores the film's formal techniques used to align viewers with Harry's perspective, including camera angles, editing patterns, and musical motifs.[1] In each instance, Keating presents quotations from the film to directly convey the relevant techniques more efficiently and effectively than possible via the written word, framing the clips with his voiceover narration, visual juxtapositions, and on-screen text; the effect is a thorough and convincing account of the film's formal design presented in less than eleven minutes of videographic criticism.

Certainly, video essays excel at making such formal techniques clear and compelling, but the format is also apt for many other types of textual analysis. A burgeoning area of media criticism is cultural analysis of historical practices and representations; videographic criticism can thrive by bringing otherwise unseen and obscured texts to light, allowing us to see material that has previously been hidden from view. A notable example of such work is Liz Greene's video essay "Spencer Bell, Nobody Knows My Name," which examines the performance of Black actor Spencer Bell as the Lion in the first film version of *Wizard of Oz* (dir. Larry Semon, 1925).[2] The essay uses a straightforward videographic style, editing all of the clips from the silent film in which Bell appears together, but playing them in reverse; this approach makes the footage seem odd and unfamiliar, as well as renarrating the character's arc to lead up to the film's most racist representations, which occur toward the beginning of the film (and thus later in the video essay). Greene's calm voiceover provides the history of Bell's performance and analyzes the representations, creating a striking piece of criticism around an obscure version of a very familiar story; this piece of criticism is greatly enhanced by our ability to directly witness and experience previously unseen footage.

Within these two broad realms of analyzing form and content, video essays offer a huge range of approaches to their subject matter. The format allows for a much wider range of tones and styles than are typically found in written textual analysis. Most academic writing embraces a formal, serious, and detached tone, rarely venturing into the realms of self-examination or emotional provocation; while criticism written for a wider audience can be more casual and personal, even these analytical essays rarely achieve a memorable emotional impact. Since videos are using clips from media that are typically quite emotionally charged, whether evoking fear or sadness, laughs or tears, videographic criticism has the ability to leverage that footage to convey emotional and aesthetic responses in a way that written criticism rarely can. Thus, in Jessica McGoff's "My Mulholland," a personal video essay about trying to make sense of *Mulholland Drive* (dir. David Lynch, 2001) as a hyper-online teenager, the clips from the strange and powerful film capture the uneasy sensations that she describes via on-screen text, as we follow her journey to process her own experiences.[3] An equivalent written essay would probably read more as personal memoir than textual analysis, but the inclusion of film clips amid her recounted journey invites analytical reflections on their function and power that deepen the insights of McGoff's emotionally moving video essay.

Videographic criticism that evokes emotions need not be harrowing and uncanny, as one of the most enjoyable modes of video essay embraces playful humor alongside legitimate textual analysis. Academics, generally not known for humorous writing, have been more reluctant to embrace comedic forms than the nonacademic critics who make up the bulk of YouTube's video essay community. While YouTube's algorithm-driven environment incentivizes entertaining videos, encouraging creators to employ high-energy voiceovers and flashy graphics, that style still allows for compelling and insightful textual analysis. One of the most successful examples of a playful YouTuber who still produces compelling analytic videos in conversation with academic work is Grace Lee. As an example, Lee's video on how the film *Jaws* (dir. Steven Spielberg, 1975) might belong to the horror genre launches from the aesthetic theory of philosopher Noël Carroll to explore the nature of the film's shark as a monstrous figure, the role of visibility in the film, and its comparative values to director Steven Spielberg's other hit monster film *Jurassic Park* (1993).[4] Along the way, Lee uses overtly humorous narration and graphics, as when she compiles clips of horror films that "take things that people are already afraid of and [say], 'Yeah, but what if it was really big?,'" illustrating the point with spiders, rats, and women; Lee's cheeky tone doesn't undermine her critical insights, but makes her thoughtful textual analysis more entertaining and accessible for everyday viewers.

While many video essayists strive to analyze media using entertaining and playful styles, some are more inspired by the work of experimental and alternative filmmakers to create more aesthetically challenging and off-putting videos. Such work still aims to perform textual analysis, but it is presented with less of an explanatory tone. In one of the first and most influential critical writings on videographic work, Christian Keathley proposed that most video essays belong on a continuum between two poles: an "explanatory mode" driven by analytic language and a "poetical register" foregrounding manipulated images and sounds.[5] A strong example of a poetical video is Eva Hageman's "shiplap," which analyzes the comparatively mundane and conventional HGTV reality series *Fixer Upper* (2013–18) to explore the racial politics of housing and history in

Waco, Texas.[6] Rather than presenting a straightforward analysis of the material, Hageman uses unusual juxtapositions between the series and historical documents, repeats and manipulates images, and intersperses a fragmented whispered voiceover, all to evoke feelings of temporal disorientation and uncanny haunting by historical resonances buried beneath the surface of the home improvement series (and the houses themselves). Even though it lacks much straightforward explanation and allows for more ambiguity than a conventional written textual analysis, the video essay still creates a distinct "knowledge effect" (in Keathley's words) that is much more resonant and affective than could be created through conventional writing.

In surveying these various approaches to videographic criticism, it might appear that its distinctiveness is as a mode of presentation—any type of textual analysis or media criticism could be presented as a video essay. While this is probably true, it overlooks a key benefit of the approach: the process of making videographic criticism itself functions as a distinctive research method.[7] Certainly, many video essays present ideas that could have just as easily been generated through writing, and some videos do effectively translate a critic's written work into videographic form; however, there are some ideas and analyses that uniquely emerge from videographic work. For instance, Kevin B. Lee has pioneered the format of "desktop documentary," recording his computer screen to convey how he explores and connects various ideas. In his video essay "Viewing Between the Lines," Lee analyzes the narrative construction of Hong Sang-soo's film *The Day He Arrives* (2011) by capturing the images of his video editing software as he manipulates and arranges the film's sixty-five distinct shots to demonstrate how it uses repetition and temporal patterns.[8] His videographic approach allows Lee to access the film's distinctive construction in a way that not only effectively conveys it to viewers, but also reveals patterns that would be hard to perceive without breaking the film down into its component shots.

One of the most prolific and influential videographic critics, Catherine Grant, has discussed her own videographic practices as a distinctive form of "material thinking," in which she arrives at new insights into her objects of analysis through manipulating and working with footage in her digital editing platform. One detailed example is her video "Dissolves of Passion," which compiles all of the dissolve transitions in the David

Lean film *Brief Encounter* (1945); Grant writes of her own process of discovery about the film through her hands-on processes of both selecting the material and manipulating its color, timing, and accompanying soundtrack. While the resulting video might not strike viewers as textual analysis per se, as it has almost no explanatory material or contextualization within the video itself (with Grant's written commentary providing that analytical layer), she argues that it is still "a work of material thinking, one that brought to the surface of its production new knowledge both about Lean's film and about this method of re-handling it."[9] Across the continuum from Kevin Lee's novel explanatory analysis to Grant's poetic exploration, videographic criticism allows for a mode of hands-on textual analysis that reveals new insights through the material thinking of the manipulation, juxtaposition, and recontextualization of the sounds and images that comprise both our objects of criticism and the building blocks for creating video essays.

An exceptional video essay that embraces nearly all of the tendencies and possibilities discussed above is "Watching *The Pain of Others*" by Lého Galibert-Laîné.[10] The video is an analysis of a found-footage documentary film, *The Pain of Others* (2018), whose director, Penny Lane, compiles YouTube vlogs of women who claim to have a mysterious disease that the medical establishment does not recognize. Galibert-Laîné explores the film via a desktop documentary chronicling their research process around the film as well as their own personal experiences that emerged through that exploration, centered around female-presenting vloggers and filmmakers.[11] The video essay is clearly a textual analysis of the original film as well as its YouTube sources, with explanatory rhetoric considering their form and content, as well as research that contextualizes the material. However, it is much more than that, as Galibert-Laîné mirrors the vlog form to narrate their own experiences as presented with ambiguous reliability, framing the entire essay as a reflection on issues of gendered authenticity and authority within online videos and documentary filmmaking; along the way, the video evokes a range of emotional responses from fascination to amusement to horror. After watching "Watching *The Pain of Others*," it is clear not only that its analytic ideas are dependent on the videographic form as a mode of presentation, but that those ideas could have only emerged through the material processes of making the video essay itself.

"Focusing on Hank (and Marie)"

My own videographic practices embrace many of the styles and formats discussed above, as all of the critics I have cited are inspirations for my work; however, my focus is somewhat different. Most academic video essays analyze films, often focusing on a single film as source material—the scope of a feature-length movie is both manageable and sufficient to create a video of ten to fifteen minutes, which characterizes most of the videos referenced above. However, my research is primarily on American television series, especially long-form serialized narratives of the twenty-first century, in which a given series has dozens of episodes that cannot easily be analyzed outside its whole serial context. Videographic criticism of television has been less prominent than for film, largely because managing so much footage can be challenging, and it can be difficult to pare it down into fairly brief video essays. But television is as worthy an object for videographic analysis as film, allowing exploration of all of the formal and content facets typical of film-based video essays, as well as medium-specific concerns such as seriality, temporality, ongoing fan engagement, and the industrial contexts of television. Thus, to offer a more wide-ranging videographic view of a television series, I have taken a different approach.

In 2024, I published a "videographic book," an online-only open access book that presents more than twenty videos alongside written contextualization, all focused on a single media text: the acclaimed television series *Breaking Bad* (AMC, 2008–13).[12] The videos embrace a wide range of videographic styles and tones, from explanatory to poetical, playful to scholarly to experimental, and examine many different facets of the series, all through the lens of character analysis; some chapters cover the arc of the entire series, while others focus on specific episodes, characters, or plot lines. Taken as a whole, they strive to catalog a wide range of approaches that videographic criticism might use to analyze television texts.

To look more closely at an example of videographic textual analysis, I will zoom in on one of the book chapters, a video essay called "Focusing on Hank (and Marie)." This video has the narrowest scope among the chapters (and thus is the easiest to discuss in this context), providing a detailed close analysis of a single scene that occurs near the midpoint of the entire series, centering on a pair of *Breaking Bad*'s secondary characters, Hank and Marie Schraeder (Dean Norris and Betsy Brandt, respectively). Unlike many scenes throughout the series and even in this episode, "One Minute," this scene is not action packed or tension filled, nor does it feature highly stylized and flashy visuals; instead, it is a low-key dialogue scene with subtle acting and deeply felt emotions between the characters. And yet the scene is pivotal to Hank and Marie's relationship and arcs, providing a window into larger storytelling techniques used throughout *Breaking Bad*.

I begin the video with voiceover narration contextualizing the episode as one of my favorites, particularly as it concerns Hank's character arc, interspersed with a succession of clips from the episode that offer contrasting images and contextual material about Hank's situation. I introduce the primary scene at the video's two-minute mark by saying, "When I think of 'One Minute,' I don't focus on the epic climactic standoff between Hank and the cousins. Instead, I remember one of Hank's most underplayed and emotionally vulnerable scenes, running just over four minutes with virtually no action." The scene takes place in the Schraeders' bedroom as Hank dresses for a meeting where he will be questioned by his superiors at the Drug Enforcement Agency about his violent outburst we witnessed earlier in the episode, as he beat defenseless Jesse Pinkman (Aaron Paul) badly enough to put him in the hospital. In a conventional written analysis, I would describe the scene in detail, quoting dialogue and describing elements of the visual framing and performances; in my video essay, I play the four-minute scene in its entirety. This is atypical of most video essays (including every other chapter in my book), which depend on editing and juxtapositions between shorter clips, but in this case I want to focus viewers' attention on the slowly paced scene and invite them to experience it in full before diving into close analysis through edited fragments—showing an object of criticism before analyzing it is a powerful possibility of videographic criticism, which is unavailable in most other forms of textual analysis.

After the scene concludes, the image reappears with the last moments of the scene playing in high-speed reverse, as my voiceover highlights the analytical approach: "What I find most remarkable about this scene is its use of focus." I signal the video's manipulation to viewers by slightly reducing the size of the image to appear within a black border, with a caption reading "«5x»." I am aiming to evoke the experience of a media studies classroom, where a teacher plays a clip, then rewinds and replays segments to call students' attention to particular moments. I intersperse repeated dialogue from the scene with my narration—for instance, repeating Hank's key line, "I'm just not the man I thought I was," four times—as well as playing some moments in slow motion, creating a continual immersive experience in the scene, even as my explanatory voiceover operates at a critical distance. Through this approach of presenting the scene while studying it, the analysis becomes accessible to people who have not seen the original series—while *Breaking Bad* fans certainly would understand aspects of the analysis that a novice viewer would not, being able to watch and replay the scene within the essay provides a level of accessibility that conventional written textual analysis rarely can.

The bulk of the analysis focuses on visual composition and staging, walking viewers through the scene to show how visual techniques help shape the viewing experience and resulting meaning. The voiceover invites viewers to notice visual subtleties, such as the use of a mirror shot and choices of which character is in focus, arguing that these compositional elements are central to our understanding of Hank's emotional state and his decision to step away from his job to deal with his trauma. Importantly, I argue that the use of shallow focus that makes Marie more visible than Hank works to present his monologue from Marie's empathetic perspective, aligning viewers with her in reacting to his realization. The videographic form guides viewers' understanding of the scene, but it was also crucial to my own research—I only recognized some of these visual techniques through the close analysis made possible by breaking the scene into its component shots within an editing platform, highlighting how videographic criticism functions as a research method.

Hopefully this brief textual analysis of a video essay highlights how this critical mode can provide its own analytical insights via an accessible and engaging form. While the ability to present ideas via moving images and sounds is quite powerful for both critical possibilities and engaging viewers, we shouldn't pretend that videographic criticism is not ideal for all purposes. Undoubtedly, more complex theoretical ideas and specialized terminology can be harder to understand via the temporal flow of a video, rather than through the self-paced reading (and rereading) process. Additionally, some analyses are less conducive to being presented via visuals and sounds, like detailed production and reception histories or the inclusion of written primary sources. But videographic criticism offers so many possibilities for creating and consuming textual analyses that allow for distinctive, captivating intellectual and affective experiences, ideal for disseminating critical media studies to a broader audience than academic writing; thus, I hope that we see the form continue to proliferate into a mode that is equally valid and widespread as more traditional written work.

Notes

1 Patrick Keating, "Music and Point of View in *Harry Potter and the Prisoner of Azkaban*," *Movie: A Journal of Film Criticism*, no. 9 (2020): 52–53, https://warwick.ac.uk/fac/arts/scapvc/film/movie/contents/movie_issue9_azkaban.pdf.
2 Liz Greene, "Spencer Bell, Nobody Knows My Name," *Open Screens* 5, no. 1 (July 31, 2022): 1–5, https://doi.org/10.16995/OS.8160.
3 Jessica McGoff, "My Mulholland," *The Cine-Files*, no. 15 (Fall 2020), www.thecine-files.com/on-mulholland-drive/.
4 Grace Lee, "*Jaws*: When Seeing Isn't Believing," October 30, 2020, YouTube, 15 min., 46 sec., www.youtube.com/watch?v=tWnLq4UOxuE.
5 Christian Keathley, "La Caméra-Stylo: Notes on Video Criticism and Cinephilia," in *The Language and Style of Film Criticism*, edited by Alex Clayton and Andrew Klevan (London: Routledge, 2011), 176–91.
6 Eva Hageman, "shiplap," *[in]Transition* 9, no. 2 (2022), https://doi.org/10.16995/intransition.11351.
7 See Jason Mittell, "Videographic Criticism as a Digital Humanities Method," in *Debates in the Digital Humanities 2019*, edited by Matthew Gold and Lauren Klein (Minneapolis: University of Minnesota Press, 2019), 224–42.
8 Kevin B. Lee, "Viewing Between the Lines: Hong Sang-soo's *The Day He Arrives*," September 26, 2012, Vimeo, 11 min., 22 sec., https://vimeo.com/50379364.
9 Catherine Grant, "Dissolves of Passion: Materially Thinking through Editing in Videographic Compilation," in *The Videographic Essay: Practice and Pedagogy*, edited by Christian Keathley, Jason Mittell, and Catherine Grant, 2019, http://videographicessay.org.
10 Lého Galibert-Laîné, "Watching *The Pain of Others*," *[in]Transition* 6, no. 3 (2019), https://doi.org/10.16995/intransition.11428.
11 Galibert-Laîné identifies as nonbinary and uses they/them pronouns; however, within this video, they present themself as female, which is relevant to the ideas explored in the video essay.
12 Jason Mittell, *The Chemistry of Character in* Breaking Bad: *A Videographic Book* (Ann Arbor: Lever Press, 2024), https://doi.org/10.3998/mpub.14330227.

26

Getting Critical

How NPR's TV Critic Analyzes Media for a Mass Audience

ERIC DEGGANS

NPR television critic Eric Deggans discusses what textual analysis of media looks like outside academia, and when presented—as with his own work—to a more popular audience. We asked him to reflect on what a popular critic and analyst of media is, and on how he got to be one.

When thinking about how arts criticism for a general audience works, I often recall a conversation with one of the best film critics in the business: my colleague at National Public Radio, Bob Mondello. I told him once that I enjoyed interviewing performers, producers, and writers because I wanted to learn what they really meant when they put together a given film or project for television. "My dear boy," he said, with the patience of a veteran schooling a clueless newbie, "it's up to us to tell them what they mean."

At first, that sounded a little arrogant—though Bob is hardly that. We critics didn't spend months or years developing, shooting, and editing a script into something that might reasonably be called an entertainment experience. We don't know for sure whether Tony Soprano was killed in the final episode of *The Sopranos* (HBO, 1999–2007)—I'll have more on that infamous ending later in this chapter—or if the visions various characters have in *True Detective: Night Country* (HBO, 2024) are manifestations of mental illness or emissaries from the spirit realm. Ideally, conversations with the people who actually wrote this stuff might help solve those mysteries.

But after a few years letting his words roll around my head, I've become convinced Bob was absolutely right. Often, even the people who make this stuff don't necessarily know exactly what it means to an audience—until someone with experience, taste, and a perceptive eye truly breaks it all down.

That's what I, as an arts critic writing for a wide audience, generally aim to do: give everybody a compelling, plausible story explaining what a given TV, film, or artistic experience is really saying. In the process, I hope to expose a bit of truth about humanity itself.

Yeah, I know. That *really* sounds arrogant.

Turns out, especially in the television industry, people who spend all day making TV shows don't have time to actually watch them. So, they may not have the same perspective on the history of police procedural shows or why American TV audiences were ready for an authentic, epic remake of James Clavell's *Shōgun* with most of its dialogue delivered in Japanese (FX's *Shōgun*, 2024–).

And, as one big-name TV showrunner told me once, it doesn't really matter what producers, directors, actors, or writers *intended* to say. What really matters is what most people in the audience *believe* they said. A good critic finds a great way to offer a distilled version of that story, with a sharp eye trained on all the audiences who will consume it, making sure they understand what the critic is trying to say as well.

All of that analysis is based on sifting through the actual text of the work, examining what is said and shown. Who does the camera spend time with and who does it marginalize? Which figures are supported by the story, and which are buried by it?

Critics know the long history of how different kinds of shows have evolved, through success and failure, into their modern forms. We've watched as the passions of different generations of artists have affected their work, which then goes on to influence others and continue a wonderful, ever-evolving cycle. Listening to *Barry* (HBO, 2018–23) creator and star Bill Hader describe in great detail why he loves Ridley Scott's choices as a director in the first *Alien* (1979) film, for example, provides a unique window into why Hader's HBO series takes the chances it does in the way that it has.[1]

In this chapter, I'll attempt to describe how a modern TV critic goes about dissecting the form for a general audience. As is obvious if you've read this far, I'm not going to be using the often-impenetrable language of academia to tell this particular story. Instead, I'm going to try serving as a bridge between the worlds of layman and expert, joining the land of academia with the pop culture universe by using language that can hopefully straddle both sensibilities and remain effective.

And we'll start with the question I get asked most often: How do you know what to write about?

Picking Topics

As any journalist will tell you, more than half the battle in assembling a great news story is finding the right idea. Figuring out what you want to talk about and how you will assemble all the elements needed is like developing a battle plan—and the sharpest battle plans usually bring the biggest victories.

Stories are a wonderful delivery system for ideas. And the best critical reviews use stories to communicate what it's like to experience a particular work, why the work matters, whether it is entertaining, and what the work is saying—or is *trying* to say—to those who consume it.

A critic's work can do a lot of other things, too: debunk hype and hypocrisy, push storytellers to answer questions that weren't handled well in the work itself, expose the emotional pressure points and social values storytellers leverage to produce audience reaction, and outline how the work fits into the long history of TV and film or the history of issues explored in the work.

Ultimately, the story of why most TV and film projects work or don't is a tale about how humanity works or doesn't. As I said once in an interview published right after I started as NPR's first full-time TV critic back in 2013, my critical analysis explores "what we value and don't, what we find frightening and funny, what we desire and find repulsive, and much more. So the story of our relationship to television and what's on the various TV-producing devices we all own is really the story of us. And telling THAT story is my real job."[2]

So, deciding what to write about means deciding what critical analyses best tell the story of us.

First, of course, I look at programs that are popular, both because my audiences are already interested in these shows and because learning why they are popular can tell important lessons about what viewers value and why. When *Godzilla x Kong: The New Empire* (dir. Adam Wingard, 2024) hit movie theaters, most consumers just wanted to know if the film was entertaining or an empty effects spectacle. But a look at the enduring popularity of the sitcom *Friends* (NBC, 1994–2004)—which tells how a batch of appealing young people created a found family in a magical city just after graduating college—can explore how its framework depicts an eternally replicating, aspirational tale, something every generation experiences in its own way.

Second, I also look at projects that are in the news or are likely to make news when they debut. Watching episodes of the Investigation Discovery docuseries *Quiet on Set: The Dark Side of Kids TV* (2024) more than a week before they would air, I knew its procession of performers and crew members facing the camera to tell stories of toxic behavior and abuse while working on popular Nickelodeon kids' shows in the late 1990s and early 2000s would likely make headlines. While many of the stories had been detailed in news reports years earlier—and one of the reporters who broke those stories was a key contributor to the TV series—there is something more impactful about seeing a succession of people face a television camera to relate their experiences personally.

I had already covered a similar attention explosion when Lifetime's *Surviving R. Kelly* (2019) featured several women detailing abuse allegations against the R&B star; it was obvious *Quiet on Set* would produce a similar reaction—particularly after former Nickelodeon star Drake Bell agreed to speak publicly for the first time, revealing he had been abused by a dialogue coach working for the network about twenty years previously.

This is more than true crime sensationalism. Recent docuseries have made a mini-industry of pushing audiences to reconsider questionable pop culture content from the past, urging viewers to apply modern sensibilities about sexism, harassment, abuse, and toxic behavior. Twenty years ago, Nickelodeon viewers snickered at sexually suggestive scenes showing a young Ariana Grande lying on a bed and dousing herself with water or yanking on a potato, convinced she could produce juice. In contemporary times, after the influence of the #MeToo movement and a drive to curb sexual harassment in the industry, those old scenes take on a different tenor, demonstrating how changing social mores can allow us to perceive toxic behavior more clearly.

A third consideration is whether a critical review offers the opportunity to explore concepts about how society works or what it values. This is where so much of my effort examining diversity, race, prejudice, and stereotypes lives. Close attention to who gets to be heroic, who is the villain, where stories are set, and how they play out ultimately delivers bracing lessons on who society values or admires and why.

There are other ideas that are important to keep in mind. TV shows and films set in the past are never about the time they are depicting; they are a different way of talking about issues in the times they are made. No matter how despicable or dysfunctional a character is, if the camera spends lots of time with them, they will be humanized. And humanizing a character isn't the same as glorifying or celebrating them, though it can surely feel like that sometimes.

In the end, I tell my students, most arts reviews start by answering basic questions: Did this work move me (or not)? And why?

Quite regularly, for this middle-aged Black man raised in Gary, Indiana, what moves me most are stories focused on race, identity, and culture—evoking, too often, the original sin of American life.

Exploring Society's Race and Racism by Dissecting TV

When I first began covering television in 1997, I started traveling to Los Angeles for a gathering of TV critics from across the nation, held twice a year, featuring all the big players in television presenting press conferences with stars, producers, and executives to preview their next six months of programming.

I quickly discovered there weren't many nonwhite people involved in covering the industry as journalists or critics. Because of that, few people were challenging the flood of troubling messages about race, identity, and culture embedded in scores of television programs. This mostly white audience of industry professionals—like most white people—had been trained not to see their own racial culture and to be oblivious to the many ways in which that culture was elevated in film, TV, and media—not to mention how nonwhite cultures were suppressed and maligned in many works.

For me, questions piled up. What did it mean that Emmy-winning police drama *NYPD Blue* (ABC, 1993–2005) made an awkward hero of a volatile, middle-aged white detective who slung around the n-word and made a habit of beating confessions out of suspects, many of whom were not white? Why would a long string of popular comedies such as *Friends, Mad About You* (NBC, 1992–99), *Seinfeld* (NBC, 1989–98), and *Sex and the City* (HBO, 1998–2004) be set in an idealized vision of New York City—where there also seemed to be astonishingly few people of color?

How could TV executives not realize casting just two or three Black people on early seasons of competitive reality TV shows such as *Survivor* (CBS, 2000–), *Big Brother* (CBS, 2000–), and *The Apprentice* (NBC, 2004–17) virtually guaranteed the white contestants would band together, eventually stereotyping, marginalizing, and ejecting those non-white players—who faced a mountain of challenges rooted in racism in addition to the same obstacles as every other player? And why would reality show producers, eager to develop successful contestants into stars with followings who could move to other programs, minimize the racism of those white players, instead depicting contestants of color as overly sensitive and racially paranoid?

As I would later note in my own media classes, television and film often teach us how to dream—how to see not only what is possible for ourselves and people like us but also what we might expect from types of people we have never met before. I don't think it's a coincidence that Barack Obama was elected the nation's first Black president a few years after the film *Deep Impact* (dir. Mimi Leder, 1998) and the TV show *24* (FOX, 2001–10) featured popular, competent, heroic Black presidents in high-stakes fictional settings. But negative depictions can swing society's pendulum in the opposite direction.

I eventually developed a process for judging how TV series handled race and culture, distilled down to a few questions that made sifting through the messaging much easier.

First, are the characters in the work seemingly defined by their race, or is their identity treated more as a part of who they are? Watching Matthew Moy's character Han Lee in the CBS sitcom *2 Broke Girls* (2011–17) or Sofia Vergara's Gloria in early seasons of ABC's *Modern Family* (2009–20), you wonder how much viewers would know about the characters if there were no jokes about their accent or cultural heritage allowed.

Other questions can help parse how race is handled. Do nonwhite characters sacrifice their own comfort, well-being, or family for a white character? Do nonwhite characters act out stereotypical pathologies—violence, overt sexuality, laziness—for no real reasons? Are the characters of color isolated, with no friends, family, or significant others who are nonwhite? Is there just one nonwhite character who is "special"—smart, talented, or physically gifted enough to stand equally alongside white characters—while most other nonwhite characters are subservient or substandard in some way? (I also call this "*Django Unchained* Syndrome," after the 2012 Quentin Tarantino film.)

Of course, there are character types rooted in stereotypes to watch out for—from wide-eyed, simple-minded coon-like figures, such as J. J. Evans in the classic comedy *Good Times* (CBS, 1974–79), to overweight, maternal "mammy" figures such as Eloise "Mama" Curtis, the matriarch in the 1970s-era sitcom *That's My Mamma* (ABC, 1974–75). Time and again, we see characters of color with great power and ability relegated to "magical negro"-type figures whose primary goal seems to be helping the white people at the center of the story, as occurs in films such as *The Green Mile* (dir. Frank Darabont, 1999), *Bruce Almighty* (dir. Tom Shadyac, 2003), *The Legend of Bagger Vance* (dir. Robert Redford, 2000), and *The Shining* (dir. Stanley Kubrick, 1980). Novelist Stephen King is a brilliant storyteller, but he particularly loves these kinds of helpful, supernaturally incisive Black characters, featuring them in book, TV, and film adaptations of *The Green Mile* (novel: 1996), *The Shining* (novel: 1997; miniseries: ABC, 1997), *The Stand* (novel: 1978; miniseries: ABC, 1994 and Paramount+, 2020; comic books: Marvel Comics, 2008–12), and *The Talisman* (novel: Stephen King and Peter Straub, 1984; short film: Mathieu Ratthe, 2008; comic books: Del Rey, 2009–10).

As much as general-interest readers want to believe modern media is beyond such simple stereotypes, my work involves reminding them that racism, prejudice, and sexism often operate like a terrible virus—just when you think you've found a way to expose and eliminate the problem, it morphs into a different form and you're fighting a slightly different foe with the same damaging effects.

Such analyses also help introduce a general audience to terms and concepts from academia, which can name and frame issues when they surface in pop culture. After podcaster Joe Rogan stepped forward to apologize for several instances on his immensely popular podcast (*The Joe Rogan Experience*, 2009–) in which he used racist language and cracked racist jokes, I wrote a column about a dynamic I have labeled "bigotry denial syndrome"—the false sense among many that, because they don't personally consider themselves bigots, they cannot act in ways that substantially advance prejudice, stereotypes, or racism.[3]

This syndrome is really just a racialized version of moral self-licensing, in which subjects believe it is acceptable to indulge in immoral behavior because they see themselves as people whose good works outweigh any negative actions.[4] It's a dynamic that emerges often in so-called reality TV competitions, where contestants try to explain away terrible behavior—especially when it is racist or sexist—by insisting they are not racist or sexist, so whatever they've done can't be that terrible. White contestants on *Big Brother* who are exposed saying terribly racist things to nonwhite competitors—and this has happened often in the history of the show—regularly use this reasoning as a defense if they are ever confronted for their behavior.

And beyond the Black/white dynamic, I am always wary of whitewashing or white centering—where white actors or characters are placed in situations you would expect to be occupied by a nonwhite person, because the industry is more comfortable with projects centered on whiteness. It can surface in different ways—from Scarlett Johansson cast to play a Japanese character in the movie *The Ghost in the Shell* (dir. Rupert Sanders, 2017), to the way Marvel's *Doctor Strange* (dir. Scott Derrickson, 2016) film turns the Asian comic book character The Ancient One, who originates from a fictional Himalayan town, into a Celtic woman played by Tilda Swinton (the Swinton casting was an attempt to avoid recreating a horrifically stereotypical figure from the comic books, but instead Marvel Studios appropriated Asian culture to serve a character who wasn't Asian). Much as I love *The Matrix* (dir. Lana and Lilly Wachowski, 1999), much of the film's style is stolen from Hong Kong action films and Asian culture, appropriating their fighting moves and fashion while not actually casting many Asian people or characters.

All these different pitfalls in the handling of race and treatment of nonwhite characters speak to issues society also struggles with in real life. Sometimes, when discussed in the context of a TV or film review, it is easier to show consumers how structural racism works—highlighting the messaging across a myriad of projects in ways that are otherwise difficult to perceive in real life.

What can make such analyses even trickier is when a TV series evolves its approach over the course of several seasons, accessing issues and portrayals in a different way at the end of its life than it did when the series began.

Critiquing a TV Series over Its Lifetime

Watch how *Game of Thrones* (HBO, 2011–19) handled sexualized violence over the beginning of its run—with explicit scenes of rape and assault—compared to its more subdued approach in later seasons, as protests and fan anger grew. Or consider how some TV series such as CBS's *S.W.A.T.* (2017–) began to more frequently tackle questions of how police handle crimes involving people of color, following the murder of George Floyd by police in Minneapolis and subsequent civil rights protests across the world.

These are examples of the kind of changes long-running TV series can manage over the long span of their lifetimes, giving TV critics a unique opportunity to analyze how their text and messaging may evolve along with the times.

Unfortunately, many successful programs don't change radically over the course of their episodes, except to get worse (staying entertaining while not changing much is, in fact, often why they endure). So the crime and punishment series *Law & Order* (NBC, 1990–), which began as an attempt to add some grit and realism to a pretty rigid police procedural formula—half of a typical episode features New York police detectives investigating a crime and the other half features prosecutors trying the case in court—has become, over twenty-three seasons, a predictable showcase for stories copied from current headlines.

But the way a long-running series ends can provide punctuation that affects how its storytelling over its entire run is later perceived. Funny as 1990s-era sitcom *Seinfeld* was in its heyday, a disappointing final season and last episode that were focused on despicably self-centered characters took some luster off the series itself, pushing the audience to reconsider why they liked these terrible people in the first place.

A different groundbreaking HBO show, *The Sopranos*, offered another lesson. As the show progressed and its fanbase grew, I could sense creator/showrunner David Chase growing impatient with the expectations of the public and the pressure to keep up the series' boundary-breaking quality. So, the finale episode of the series—which some fans, admittedly, found to be brilliant—avoided expectations by not ending but stopping, cutting to a black screen so quickly that some viewers thought their cable service had somehow gone out.

Chase has since said the protagonist, mobster Tony Soprano, was killed by an unseen assassin. A co-star from the show, Lorraine Bracco, told me she thought that idea was nonsense—the mob wouldn't slaughter a whole family in public just to get to one boss. I think Chase, who didn't want to end the series in any way someone could predict or judge, just stopped telling the story—a bit of a cop-out from an otherwise masterful storyteller.

Most high-quality TV shows depict a journey. And at some point, if the show is to retain its quality, that journey must end. How it ends can affect the program's legacy and its final impact on viewers in ways critics are best positioned to dissect and judge.

Even the show that I consider the best drama ever on TV, HBO's *The Wire* (2002–08), was redefined slightly by its finale. The show spent five seasons exploring all the different ways systems have failed to protect and serve major American cities, subverting the typical police drama narrative. In too many average series, a virtuous cop—or a team of officers—can overcome widespread systemic dysfunction to bring justice.

Not so in the world of *The Wire*, which began focused on how dysfunction in the Baltimore police department allowed a single drug gang to take control of several public housing developments in Baltimore's poor Black neighborhoods, dominating local commerce and employment in the same way mining companies once overshadowed the life of small towns.

By the fifth season, the series had exposed how the city's schools were warehousing kids crippled by poverty and a lack of opportunity, labor unions in decline were dependent on collaboration with organized crime to survive, politicians made an industry of trading favors for cash donations, and the news media was too lacking in resources and focused on winning big journalism prizes to discover any of it.

But *The Wire*'s magic had also faded, producing in its fifth season a collection of episodes that fell short of the high standard set in the show's heyday. Over its run, the series captured precisely how the systems created to run and safeguard modern cities were failing them; along the way, its own creative engine ran out of steam like a high-performance automobile that had been run for a bit too long and a bit too far. It became another example of a failing system.

Pointing that out to the public was a painful duty for this critic. But it could also help explain why *The Wire*'s conclusion felt less like a bombastic climax and more like seeing a Lamborghini race car run out of gas just before crossing the finish line.

Writing the First Draft of TV History

"Who made you the God of TV?"

"Why does your opinion matter so much?"

"Where do you get off, saying something I disagree with?"

Usually, when someone responds to me with one of these phrases, or something else designed basically to ask, *Why do YOU get to interpret what TV means to the world?*, I provide a simple answer: because I convinced a major media outlet to pay me to do it. (Yes, I regularly crow in speeches about how I basically get paid to watch TV.)

But the real truth is a bit more boring: I decided a long time ago, probably during my freshman year in high school, that I wanted to be an arts critic with a national voice. And I began working toward that goal as a student and young journalist through high school, college, and my early jobs in newspapers.

Learning how to convert the emotional reaction from an artistic experience into a story that communicates that impact alongside a critical evaluation isn't easy. It's a skill that takes lots of practice and study. My path included writing concert reviews for newspapers on deadline at 1 a.m. over several years, reading the work of people who are already skilled at such analyses for important lessons, visiting places where the work happens, and interviewing practitioners to see why the art turns out the way it does.

To become a critic, I climbed a ladder to success that doesn't exist anymore. In 1990, when I got my first professional job in a newspaper, midsize regional newspapers had features departments stacked with critics. The *Pittsburgh Press*, where I started my career, had critics for TV, film, pop music, and more, writing every day for an audience of thousands. I was a news reporter at the *Press* but wrote lots of reviews and feature stories on the side, developing my skill and writing enough samples to nab a job as pop music critic for the *Asbury Park Press* in New Jersey and, later, the *St. Petersburg Times/Tampa Bay Times* in Florida.

As I write this chapter, due to industry contractions, layoffs, and shrinking revenues, very few newspapers at that level employ arts critics in such numbers anymore. Instead, aspiring critics hone their craft working for online platforms that can sometimes feel more like fan publications than news outlets, making it tougher for modern critics to develop the journalism skills and independence needed for quality work.

By the time I began freelancing TV reviews for National Public Radio in 2011, I already had more than twenty years' experience as a critic in various venues. When I became NPR's first full-time TV critic two years later, I had written a book, taught at the college level, and hosted a media analysis show on CNN.

All of this backstory is the real answer to those questions asked above. It's also the answer to a different query: what's a TV critic's role in an era when so many people are posting their thoughts about pop culture and entertainment on every social media platform available?

In an odd way, it's the same answer you'd probably hear if you asked that question of a professional comedian or professional musician. Just because everyone has thoughts about TV and can post them publicly, doesn't mean they can do this work the way professionals can. Anyone can post a joke on TikTok; very few people can tell that joke as well as someone who regularly gets paid to be funny.

Over the course of my career, I've hung out backstage with Bruce Springsteen and Jon Bon Jovi. I've stood on the sets of TV shows such as *Sex and the City, The West Wing* (NBC, 1999–2006), and *Saturday Night Live* (NBC, 1975–). I've interviewed everyone from Oprah Winfrey to Prince, Norman Lear to Jon Stewart. And I've produced reviews for newspapers, TV, radio, books, podcasts, classrooms, and public presentations. It all comes together: experience, professionalism, ideas, insight.

Modern TV and film criticism can feel a bit like a combination of journalism and large-scale therapy. You're trying to identify the themes and messaging inside a piece of entertainment that has likely cost millions to build and launch; understanding why and how one story receives this attention over others and whether or how it might resonate with a larger audience provides loads of lessons on the state of society.

But pulling that analysis together can require a combination of reporting, research, savvy analysis, and careful guessing—trying to pinpoint the impact of any given work and what that result might say about the audience who consumed it.

It remains a fascinating and elusive task: trying to explain the world to itself by digging through the bones of what entertains us all.

Notes

1 Eli Roth, host, *Eli Roth's History of Horror: Uncut*, podcast, season 2, episode 1, "Bill Hader," September 28, 2020, 57:24, https://open.spotify.com/show/4djlRs068esSVcyStrapQK; "Monsters," *Eli Roth's History of Horror*, season 2, episode 2, directed by Kurt Sayenga (AMC, October 17, 2020), www.imdb.com/title/tt13240336/.
2 Eric Deggans, "TV Critic ProFile: 'Television [Is] a Window into How American Society Works,'" NPR, November 8, 2013, www.npr.org/sections/npr-extra/2013/11/08/242949617/tv-critic-profile-television-is-a-window-into-how-american-society-works.
3 Eric Deggans, "I Have a Name for What Fueled Joe Rogan's New Scandal: Bigotry Denial Syndrome," NPR, February 9, 2022, www.npr.org/2022/02/09/1079271255/joe-rogan-spotify-racism-controversy.
4 Anna C. Merritt, Daniel A. Effron, and Benoît Monin, "Moral Self-Licensing: When Being Good Frees Us to Be Bad," *Social and Personality Psychology Compass* 4, no. 5 (2010): 344–57, https://doi.org/10.1111/j.1751-9004.2010.00263.x.

ABOUT THE CONTRIBUTORS

ANIRBAN K. BAISHYA is Assistant Professor of Communication Arts at the University of Wisconsin–Madison. His research interests include new media and digital cultures, media aesthetics and politics, and global media. His work has been published in journals such as *International Journal of Communication, Communication, Culture & Critique, Communication and Critical/Cultural Studies, Text and Performance Quarterly*, and *Media, Culture & Society*.

LILLIAN BOXMAN-SHABTAI is Assistant Professor of Communication and Journalism at the Hebrew University of Jerusalem. Her research examines interpretation, meaning multiplicity, and methodological innovation in qualitative and mixed methods of analysis. Her published work has applied these interests to investigations of cultural production and political expression on social media including humor and parody, protest and inequality, and wartime communication.

COLIN BURNETT is Associate Professor of Film and Media Studies at Washington University in St. Louis and Associate Editor of *JCMS: Journal of Cinema and Media Studies*. He is the author of *The Invention of Robert Bresson: The Auteur and His Market* and is currently completing a new book, titled *Serial Bonds: The Shape of 007 Media*.

DIANE CARR lives in London and is Professor of Media and Cultural Studies at University College London, based in the IOE. Carr teaches game studies and research design courses. Carr's current research involves game studies, technology and academic practice, intersectional disability, and the use of game studies concepts to explore the lived experience of discrimination.

ERIC DEGGANS is NPR's TV critic, media analyst, and guest host. He is an adjunct instructor at Duke University and Indiana University, as well as guest instructor and National Advisory Board member at the Poynter Institute for Media Studies. In April 2024, he was inducted into the Indiana Journalism Hall of Fame. He is also author of *Race-Baiter: How the Media Wields Dangerous Words to Divide a Nation*.

SUSAN J. DOUGLAS is the Catharine Neafie Kellogg Professor of Communication and Media at the University of Michigan. Her books include *In Our Prime: How Older Women Are Reinventing the Road Ahead*, *Celebrity: A History of Fame* (with Andrea McDonnell), *The Mommy Myth*, *Listening In: Radio and the American Imagination*, *Where the Girls Are: Growing Up Female with the Mass Media*, and *Inventing American Broadcasting*.

PAUL FROSH holds the Karl and Matilda Newhouse Chair in Communications at the Hebrew University of Jerusalem. His research spans visual culture, photography theory, media aesthetics, cultural memory, and media witnessing. His books include *The Image Factory: Consumer Culture, Photography and the Visual Content Industry* and *The Poetics of Digital Media*.

DAPHNE GERSHON is Lecturer at Gonzaga University. Her research center around media discourses about masculinity, transnational feminism, and portrayals of sexual dysfunction. Her work has been published in *Feminist Media Studies*, *Journal of Cinema and Media Studies*, and the *International Journal of Cultural Studies*. She has also served as the editorial assistant for the *International Journal of Cultural Studies*.

JONATHAN GRAY is Hamel Family Distinguished Chair in Communication Arts at the University of Wisconsin–Madison. He is the author or co-editor of multiple books, including *Dislike-Minded: Media, Audiences, and the Dynamics of Taste*, *Television Goes to the Movies* (with Derek Johnson), *Show Sold Separately: Promos, Spoilers, and Other Media Paratexts*, *Television Studies* (with Amanda D. Lotz), *Watching with The Simpsons: Television, Parody, and Intertextuality*, and *Keywords for Media Studies* (with Laurie Ouellette).

JOKE HERMES is Professor of Inclusion and the Creative Industries at the Creative Business Research Center of Inholland University of Applied Sciences and is affiliated with the Media Studies Department of the University of Amsterdam. Her work is in qualitative audience research. It focuses on inclusion, diversity, representation, and media literacy. Her most recent books are *Cultural Citizenship and Popular Culture* and *the Pocketbook of Audience Research* (with Linda Kopitz).

MICHELE HILMES is Professor Emerita of Media and Cultural Studies at the University of Wisconsin–Madison. Her research centers on media history, with an emphasis on radio and sound studies and on transnational media flows. Her books include *Hollywood and Broadcasting: From Radio to Cable*, *Radio Voices: American Broadcasting 1922–1952*, *Network Nations: A Transnational History of British and American Broadcasting*, and *Only Connect: A Cultural History of Broadcasting in the United States*.

KYRA HUNTING is Associate Professor of Media Arts and Studies at the University of Kentucky. Her research focuses primarily on children's entertainment film and television with a particular interest in gender, transmedia, and audiences. Her work has appeared in journals and edited anthologies, which include *Popular Communication, Journal of Fandom Studies, Feminist Media Studies, Mass Communication and Society*, and *Critical Studies in Media Communication*.

MEHITA IQANI holds the South African Research Chair in Science Communication at Stellenbosch University, South Africa. She is the author and editor of several books on media, consumer culture, luxury, waste, and the Global South, including *African Luxury Branding, Garbage in Popular Culture*, and *Consumption, Media and the Global South*.

HENRY JENKINS, the Provost's Professor of Communication, Journalism, Cinematic Art, Education, and East Asian Languages and Cultures at the University of Southern California, is the author or editor of twenty-one books, including *Convergence Culture: Where Old and New Media Collide, Comics and Stuff*, and the forthcoming *Where the Wild Things*

Were: American Boyhood and Permissive Parenting in Postwar America. He is the cohost of the *How Do You Like It So Far?* podcast.

PATRICK KEATING is Professor of Communication at Trinity University, where he teaches courses in film studies and video production. He is the author of several books on the history of cinematography, including *Film Noir and the Arts of Lighting* (forthcoming), *The Dynamic Frame: Camera Movement in Classical Hollywood Cinema*, and *Hollywood Lighting from the Silent Era to Film Noir*. His audiovisual essays can be found on Vimeo.

LORI KIDO LOPEZ is Professor of Communication Arts and Associate Dean for Social Sciences in the College of Letters & Science at the University of Wisconsin–Madison. She is author of *Race and Digital Media: An Introduction*, *Micro Media Industries: Hmong American Media Innovation in the Diaspora*, and *Asian American Media Activism: Fighting for Cultural Citizenship*, and editor of *Race and Media: Critical Approaches*.

AMANDA D. LOTZ is Professor in the School of Communication and the Digital Media Research Centre at Queensland University of Technology, where she leads the Transforming Media Industries and Cultures research program. She is the author, co-author, or editor of fourteen books that explore television and media industries. She has consulted for a range of government and industry clients for more than a decade and is a Fellow of the International Communication Association.

RAVEN MARAGH-LLOYD is Associate Professor of African and African American Studies and Film and Media Studies at Washington University in St. Louis. Her work examines how digital media culture is structured in large part by Black publics and their communication histories. Her first book is *Black Networked Resistance: Strategic Rearticulations in the Digital Age*. Her work has appeared in *Information, Communication & Society* and *Communication, Culture & Critique*, among other publications.

JASON MITTELL is Professor of Film and Media Culture at Middlebury College. His books include *Complex Television: The Poetics of*

Contemporary Television Storytelling, *The Videographic Essay: Practice and Pedagogy* (with Christian Keathley and Catherine Grant, videographicessay.org), *Narrative Theory and Adaptation*, *How to Watch Television* (co-edited with Ethan Thompson), and *The Chemistry of Character in* Breaking Bad: *A Videographic Book*. He is also project manager for *[in]Transition: Journal of Videographic Film & Moving Image Studies*, and series editor for Videographic Books at Lever Press.

SOUVIK MUKHERJEE is Assistant Professor in Cultural Studies in the Centre for Studies in Social Sciences, Calcutta, in Kolkata, India. A pioneering researcher on video games in South Asia, he is the author of *Videogames and Storytelling: Reading Games and Playing Books*, *Videogames and Postcolonialism: Empire Plays Back*, and *Videogames in the Indian Subcontinent*. He was named a DiGRA Distinguished Scholar in 2019. He also researches ancient Indian board games and (the) digital humanities.

SORAYA MURRAY is Associate Professor of Film + Digital Media at the University of California, Santa Cruz. Murray's first book, *On Video Games: The Visual Politics of Race, Gender and Space*, considers video games from a visual studies perspective. Murray's next book considers American anxieties around technological innovation as revealed in technothriller films from the 1970s to the present.

TED NANNICELLI teaches in the School of Communication and Arts at the University of Queensland, Australia. His most recent book is *A Companion to Motion Pictures and Public Value*, co-edited with Mette Hjort, and he is editor of *Projections: The Journal for Movies and Mind*.

LAURIE OUELLETTE is Professor of Media and Cultural Studies at the University of Minnesota. She researches nonfiction media, gender and feminism, and television culture and is the author or editor of multiple books, including *Lifestyle TV*. She has published in a wide range of journals, including *Cultural Studies* and *Journal of Cinema and Media Studies*, and is the editor in chief of *Television & New Media* and a columnist for *Film Quarterly*. She is currently writing a book on white feminism, women, and true crime.

SIMPHIWE RENS is Associate Professor of Communication Science at the University of South Africa (UNISA). He teaches media studies and supervises postgraduate research projects in media and cultural studies. Simphiwe's research interests cut across cultural studies, gender studies, popular culture, celebrity culture, communication and culture, audience studies, and media consumption studies in the Global South.

MEG L. THOMAS is a PhD candidate at the University of Queensland. Her work is interdisciplinary in nature, branching across digital media research, film and television studies, and philosophy of art. In her dissertation titled "The Platformization of Film and Television Aesthetics" she explores how media platforms (including streaming, social media, and generative AI platforms) are changing the aesthetics of contemporary film and television. Her work has been published in journals such as *Film and Philosophy*.

JULIE TURNOCK is Professor of Media and Cinema Studies at the University of Illinois, Urbana-Champaign, and was awarded an NEH fellowship in 2024. She is the author of *Plastic Reality: Special Effects, Technology, and the Emergence of 1970s Blockbuster Aesthetics* and *The Empire of Effects: Industrial Light and Magic and the Rendering of Realism*. She has published on special effects, spectacle, and technology of the silent and studio era, the 1970s, and recent digital cinema.

ESZTER ZIMANYI is Research Director at the Center for Advanced Research in Global Communication at the University of Pennsylvania. She holds a PhD in Cinema and Media Studies from the University of Southern California and specializes in global media cultures, migration and refugee studies, and documentaries. Her writing on topics such as refugee selfies, humanitarian immersive media, migrant documentaries, and antimigrant government propaganda is published in *Journal of Cinema and Media Studies*, *Feminist Media Studies*, and *Transnational Screens*, among other publications.

INDEX

ability, 88, 90, 91, 92
Advancing New Standards in Reproductive Health's Abortion Onscreen Database, 291
advertising, 26–27, 30, 68–69, 73–79, 101–6, 224n4, 234, 321, 336
aesthetics, 9, 14, 102, 138, 175, 178, 274–75, 277, 284, 285
affect, 139–40, 148, 175, 181, 250, 265
Afrikan Tähti, 127, 129
Afrobeats, 111–12
After Mass Media: Storytelling for Microaudiences in the Twenty-First Century, 334–37
Alaqad, Plestia, 207
algorithms, 124, 129, 130, 133, 200–201, 207, 210, 358
Alsultany, Evelyn, 42
Amer, 205–6
amusement parks, 184–98
anchorage, 34, 234, 239
Appadurai, Arjun, 126, 172
art, 14, 27, 29, 96–100, 107, 139, 141, 175–81, 278–85, 365–66, 375; education programs, 278–85
Atonement, 59
audience, 10, 15, 28, 34, 79, 253, 261, 270, 275, 338, 342–52, 366; research, 10–11, 16, 30, 201–2, 250, 342–52
Austen, Jane, 9, 126
author, 8, 61, 154–55, 180, 235, 301–6, 308–9, 312
autotheory, 139–48
Avary, Roger, 300
Avatar, 185–98

Awkwafina Is Nora from Queens, 41
Azaiza, Motaz, 207

Bakhtin, Mikhail, 6
Barry, Peter, 125–26
Barthes, Roland, 34, 72–73, 82–83, 86, 88, 92, 124, 169, 234, 235, 302
Batman, 11
Beat the Clock, 28
Bell, Spencer, 357
Bennett, Tony, 302–3
Berlant, Lauren, 270, 287
bigotry denial syndrome, 372
blackface, 43
Black humor, 246, 251–56
Black Twitter, 246–56
Black women, 39–40
Blitzer, Wolf, 220
Blum-Kulka, Shoshana, Blondheim, Menahem, and Hacohen, Gonen, 155
board games, 15, 123–34
bodies, 82, 87–93, 111–12, 116–17, 120–21, 140, 141, 174–75, 246, 297
Bogost, Ian, 124
Bonilla, Yarimar and Rosa, Jonathan, 247
Bonjour Tristesse, 58
Booth, Paul, 124
Bordwell, David, 13–14, 66n4, 67n9, 96–99, 107–8n1, 108n11, 109n21
Bornstedt, Pawel, 124
Breakfast at Tiffany's, 45
Breaking Bad, 361–63
Bridgerton, 342–43, 344, 347–52
Brock, André, 247, 252

Brunsdon, Charlotte, 36, 46
Buffy the Vampire Slayer, 288

Cable Guys: Television and Masculinities in the Twenty-First Century, 333–34, 339
Californication, 296–97
"Calm Down," 115–21
Carmody, Teresa, 138
cartography, 128–29
Cawelti, John, 32–33
Centre for Contemporary Cultural Studies at the University of Birmingham, 31, 34
Charulata, 59
Citizenship Amendment Act (CAA), 242
codes, 82–83, 86, 88, 89, 116–18, 152, 160, 263, 266, 344, 346
collaborative disputation, 152–64
colonization, 40, 125, 132
Colonization, 129
comedy, 41, 101, 287, 290, 294–98, 358, 370
comic books, 8, 24, 30, 60, 62, 63, 65, 234, 301
consumerism, 171–75, 178
content analysis, 7, 21n8, 23, 69, 82, 113, 116–18, 152, 154, 160, 275
Cooppan, Vilashini, 142
Creeber, Glen, 17
critical technocultural discourse analysis (CTDA), 247, 252
Cruise, Tom, 213, 216–22
Cuarón, Alfonso, 223
Cuklanz, Lisa, 292
cultural studies, 3, 13–16, 31, 34, 46, 114–15, 127, 330

Dalton, Rick, 300, 303–4, 307, 308–12
Dateline, 259–70
Dawkins, Richard, 232
Dead Space, 91
decoloniality, 132
de Saussure, Ferdinand, 69, 70
detective shows, 24, 29, 33, 261
Deus Ex: Human Revolution, 87–88
Dixit, Priya, 132

Doge meme, 236–43
Dora, 84, 86–87
Doyle, Jennifer, 139–40
DVD, 15, 29, 216, 300, 302, 303, 309

Eco, Umberto, 10
effects program, 215, 223–24
Ellcessor, Elizabeth, 288, 289–90, 293, 298n3
enframing, 158
Entertainment Weekly, 77
erectile dysfunction, 294–98
Eurogames, 125, 127, 128, 134n6
Europa Universalis, 133
Everybody Loves Raymond, 297

Faidutti, Bruno, 125, 126
fans, 5, 7, 303, 307, 311, 350, 363, 373; fan edit, 104, 106; fan studies, 16
Fast and Furious franchise, 216
femininity, 41, 45, 141, 267, 268
feminism, 34, 46, 47, 83, 111–12, 116, 121, 141, 332–33, 338
film, 55–66, 96–99, 101, 213–24, 277, 300–312, 330, 360; studies, 13–14, 16–17, 96
First Nations of Catan, 133
Fish, Stanley, 7, 10
Flanagan, Mary and Jakobsson, Mikael, 127
Flow, 321–25, 327, 328
Foasberg, Nancy, 128
Ford, Dom, 127
formalism, 13, 14, 55, 97, 98, 99, 100, 184, 188, 200, 263, 298n3, 356–57
formula, 32, 33, 35, 145, 260–70
Fortugno, Nick, 147
Foucault, Michel, 302
Fournier, Lauren, 140–41
fragments, 82–83, 85, 86–92
franchise, 8, 276, 301
Friedman, Hershey H., 155
Frosh, Paul, 3

Galibert-Laîné, Lého, 360
Game of Thrones, 373

Game on the European Colonization of Africa, 129
Garland Thomson, Rosemarie, 91
gender, 29, 71–72, 110–21, 141, 270, 294–98, 332–34, 338–39, 360
Genette, Gérard, 8–9, 68, 214, 304
genre, 29, 32, 33, 75, 76, 187, 235, 260–65, 274–76, 288, 292, 302, 304, 305–6, 344, 346, 348, 350; conventions, 32, 60–61, 83, 85, 88, 98, 99, 210, 260, 262, 264, 266, 287, 290, 305, 344, 351, 358; microgenre, 288, 289, 298n3
Gerbner, George, 24, 31, 32
Gill, Rosalind, 17
Global South, 123, 127, 173
Godfather, Part II, The, 58
Grant, Catherine, 359–60
Gray, Jonathan, 9, 235, 304
Greene, Liz, 357
Gutter Pop, 176–80

Hader, Bill, 366
Hageman, Eva, 358–59
Hall, Stuart, 6, 7, 10, 24, 27–32, 34–35, 42
Harrer, Sabine and Lahti, Outi, 129
hashtag, 203, 205, 229, 246–56, 345
Hevruta, 152–3, 154–58, 160, 163–64, 166n10
Hill Collins, Patricia, 40
historical analysis, 126, 141, 234, 242, 247, 318–28, 330–40
historical poetics, 96–107
Hoggart, Richard, 24–27, 29–31
homegoing, 248, 251–56
horror, 75–76, 78, 90, 91, 239, 240, 242, 358
Huggan, Graham, 128

ideology, 13–14, 27, 31, 32, 34–35, 43–44, 73, 110–11, 121, 137, 242, 288, 340, 351
Imagineers, 186–90, 191
Indigenous people, 40, 127, 131
Instagram, 200, 201, 205, 207, 210
intercoder reliability, 152, 160

interpretive communities, 10, 157, 301
intertextuality, 6, 11, 156, 200, 229, 234–35, 237, 239, 241, 242, 247, 250, 275, 276, 301–3, 306–8
intimate citizenship, 265–69, 270
Israel-Hamas War of 2021, 158–64
Israel-Hamas War of 2023, 161, 207–8

Jaipur, 127
Jasmine & Jambo, 279, 280–81, 283
Jayanth, Meghna, 129–30
Jeanne Dielman, 23 Commerce Quay, 1080 Brussels, 57
journalism, 34–35, 199–200, 204–5, 207, 250, 261, 263, 267, 269, 322–24, 367–69, 376
Juden Raus, 127
Jurassic Park, 217–18, 226n15

Keathley, Christian, 358, 359
Keating, Patrick, 356
Kinder, Marsha, 301
King Kong, 223
Kristeva, Julia, 6
Kurdi, Aylan, 204

Last of Us, The (game), 91
Law & Order, 373
Leavis, F. R., 25
Lee, Grace, 358
Lee, Kevin B., 359, 360
Lesage, Julie, 83
Leurs, Koen and Prabhakar, Madhuri, 203
literature, 4, 10, 26, 125, 154, 354
Lord of the Rings, The films, 216
Loring-Albright, Greg, 125, 131–32
Lotz, Amanda, 15
Lukow, Gregory and Ricci, Steven, 235
lyrics, 100, 111, 120, 121

magazines, 24, 26, 29, 30, 31–32, 77, 260, 321
Main Street, USA, 188–89
male gaze, 111, 116–18

March of Time, The, 322–24
Marling, Karal Ann, 188
Marlowe, Philip, 56
Married . . . with Children, 297
Marvel Cinematic Universe (MCU), 8, 372
masculinity, 33, 45, 76, 78, 270, 294, 296, 298, 308, 333–34, 339
mass culture/media, 15, 24–28, 31, 274, 286
materiality, 171, 175, 177, 180, 181
McGoff, Jessica, 357–58
Mean Girls TikTok account, 101–7
meaning, 4–9, 10–11, 14, 25, 29, 34–35, 47, 68–71, 77, 79, 83–85, 115, 138, 144, 160, 171–73, 174, 181, 231, 233–36, 240, 243, 252, 262, 286, 289, 293, 346, 350
media literacy, 4, 28, 30
memes, 103, 104, 204, 207, 231–43, 249, 289; pool, 236; memetic relay, 235, 237, 239
Mignolo, Walter, 126, 132
migrant-authored media, 200–210
Milner, Ryan, 233, 240
Mir, Rebecca and Owens, Trevor, 129
Mironins, 279–84
misreadings, 10, 94n9
Missing and Murdered White Woman Syndrome, 267
Mission: Impossible films, 213–14, 217–23
mobile privatization, 320–24, 325
Molina-Guzmán, Isabel, 41
Mondello, Bob, 365
Monopoly, 127, 129
#MontgomeryBrawl, 246
Morra, Joanne, 139
Moulthrop, Stuart and Grigar, Dene, 138
multimodal discourse analysis, 113–21
music, 5, 28, 29, 110–21, 126, 207, 251, 279, 280, 323, 324, 342–43, 356; music video, 110–21
Musk, Elon, 247, 251, 252, 253, 255
Muslims / Arabs, 42, 159, 242

narratology, 55–66, 184–98, 350
neoliberalism, 264, 265, 269, 270, 293

neutrosemy, 7
Newcomb, Horace, 33–34
Newman, Michael Z., 14, 292
Nishime, LeiLani, 47–48
Norcia, Megan A., 129
NYPD Blue, 369

objectification of women, 29, 111–18, 121
Once Upon a Time in Hollywood, 300–312
Orientalism, 125–26, 127, 129
Other, the, 131–32, 152, 156
Owda, Bisan, 207

Pandora: The Valley of Mo'ara, 185–98
Paranormal Activity, 240
Parasite, 223
paratextuality, 8–9, 68–69, 73–79, 214–23, 304–5, 306, 312
Parks and Recreation, 41
participant observation, 345
patterns, 38, 40, 42, 107, 113, 119, 184, 185–86, 190, 192–93, 262, 264, 276–85, 288–92, 332–37, 340, 347, 359
Pearson, Roberta, 288
photography, 34, 224n3, 318
Phruksachart, Melissa, 45
Pim & Pom at the Museum, 279–84
plastic, 171–81
platformization, 101
play, 81–93, 123–34, 137–48, 187, 193, 243, 279, 281–84; repairing, 133
plot, 55–66, 118–19, 184–98, 265; twists, 55–66, 265
podcasting, 15, 264, 300, 302, 303, 304, 307, 308, 310–12, 319–20, 324–28, 371
poetics, 96–100, 107
point-of-view, 58
Poirier-Poulin, Samuel, 132
polysemy, 7, 152, 160
Ponzanesi, Sandra & Leurs, Koen, 203
postcolonialism, 123, 125, 126–29, 133, 134
posters, 68, 70, 73–79
Pratt, Mary Louise, 125–26

production, 48, 100–101, 107, 216–17, 278, 322–25, 329n8, 330–40, 348
prospection, 59

Quiet on Set: The Dark Side of Kids TV, 368
Quijano, Anibal, 132

racism, 25, 38–48, 129, 357, 369–72
radio, 23, 24, 26, 318–24, 325, 326, 328
Ramirez Berg, Charles, 41
reader, 7, 35, 61, 68, 79, 99, 140, 153–54, 156, 214, 235, 301, 346, 350, 352, 356
re-cognition, 59
Redesigning Women: Television after the Network Era, 332–33, 338
refugee-authored media, 200–210
Rema, 111–12, 116, 119–21
representation, 38–48, 292; of Asian Americans, 41, 45, 46, 47–48, 372; of Black people, 39–40, 43, 292–93, 370; of disability, 88, 90–92, 277, 289–90, 293; of gay people, 25, 292–93, 295; of Latinas, 41; of men, 33, 45, 71–72, 76, 116–18, 294–98, 333–34, 339; of migrants and refugees, 199–210; of whiteness, 33, 39, 41, 43, 45, 267; of women, 30, 33, 35, 41, 45, 46, 48, 71–72, 112–18, 199, 290, 294–98, 332–33
Resident Evil 4, 90–91
retrospection, 59, 64
#RIPTwitter, 247–48, 251–56
Rise of the Tomb Raider, 88–89
Risk, 128
Robinson, William, 125, 128
Rogan, Joe, 371–72
Roma, 223
Rosenberg, Bernard, 24
rubbish, 171–81
Run Lola Run, 57–58

Said, Edward, 126
Sandvoss, Cornel, 7
Sato, Atsuko, 236

Scannell, Paddy, 25
Scorsese, Martin, 307
scraping, 202, 203, 347
Seinfeld, 292, 370, and 373
semiotics, 34, 69–79, 247
Serial, 319–20, 324–28
Settlers of Catan, 123–34
Shadow of the Colossus, 143–48
Shah, Amit, 241–42
Shehada, Nisreen, 201, 207–10
Shifman, Limor, 233
Shining, The, 239
Shyamalan, M. Night, 63, 65
signs, 69–79, 233–34, 238, 241–42
situations, 286–98
Snapchat, 201, 202
social media, 100–107, 200–210, 236–43, 246–56, 345–46, 348–50
Sopranos, The, 78, 334, 365, 373–74
sound, 16–17, 102–3, 104, 106, 109n19, 115, 156, 190, 232, 236, 318–28, 355, 356
special effects, 186, 190, 213–24, 224n3–4, 225n6, 226n16, 323, 336, 367–68
spectacle, 215, 217–18, 225n7
Spirit Island, 133
Star Wars, 10, 276; *Episode VII—The Force Awakens*, 216
stereotypes, 36n5, 39–48, 111, 269, 293, 369–72; counterstereotypes, 41–42, 44
Sternberg, Meir, 59
story, 55–66, 184–86, 193, 194–95, 197, 198, 215, 283, 301, 308, 309, 362, 366, 367, 371
streaming, 15, 69, 261, 300, 325, 328, 336–40
stunts, 213, 216, 218–22
subaltern, 126, 128, 131, 133
superhero genre, 60–66, 276
Suttner, Nick, 144
S.W.A.T., 373
Swift, Taylor, 5

Talmudic study, 155–58, 159, 164
Tarantino, Quentin, 300, 302–12
techné, 100

technology, 90–91, 109n18, 202, 214–20, 223, 226n13, 247, 255, 274, 318, 320–21, 324–25, 329n11, 331, 340
television, 15, 24, 26, 28, 33, 73–79, 99, 101, 259–70, 273–85, 286–98, 303, 320–21, 324, 330–41, 342–52, 361–63, 365–77; cable, 15, 259, 260, 261, 333–34, 340; character study series, 336–37; children's, 273–85; international series, 335, 340; "peak TV," 286, 335; reality, 370, 372; spectacular series, 335–36
Terminator 2: Judgment Day, 223
terra nullius, 128, 132
Teuber, Klaus, 123
text: definition of, 5–9; emblematic, 261–62, 264; exemplary, 275, 277, 278; layers of a text, 5, 115–16, 121
textual analysis: audience-led, 342–52; autotheory, 139–48; collaborative disputation, 152–64; current attitudes towards, 12–18; definition, 9–12; ethics of, 200, 202–3; formal analysis, 13–14, 55–66, 96, 98–99, 184–98, 356–58; historical poetics, 96–107; narratology, 55–66; solitary paradigm of, 151–52, 153–54, 164; stereotype analysis, 39–48; as ur-method, 13
textual articulation, 163
#ThanksgivingClapback, 250
theme parks, 184–98
This American Life, 319
Thompson, Kristin, 13–14, 66n4, 67n9, 108n14
TikTok, 100–107, 159–64, 200, 201, 207, 210, 250
Top Gun: Maverick, 216
Trammell, Aaron, 133
transmedia, 186, 194, 197, 300–301, 312; authorship, 301–2, 304, 308–10
trash, 171–81
trope, 35, 40, 45, 120, 129, 145, 200, 220–21, 281, 287, 289, 290–91, 294, 296
true crime, 259–70, 271n4, 272n17, 326–28
TV Tropes, 290–91

Unbreakable, 55–56, 60–66
Ussing, Jonas, 216

Veal, Mylissa "Mikki," 251
Video Archives podcast, 300, 310–12
video essays, 354–64
video games, 81–93, 127–28, 129–30, 132, 137–48
videographic criticism, 354–64
von Reisswitz, Georg Leopold, 130
Vossgätter, Elize, 176–80
Voyage of Discovery, 127

Wagner, Paula, 218
Walking Dead, The (game), 91
Walking Dead, The (television show), 73–79
Wanzo, Rebecca, 267
war games, 130
waste, 171–81
Westerns, 29, 32–33, 75–76, 78, 305, 307, 308–9
Whannel, Paddy, 24, 28–30
whiteness, 25, 33, 38, 39, 41, 42–43, 45, 130, 249, 259, 267–68, 292, 352, 369–70, 372
whitewashing, 372
Williams, Raymond, 24, 25, 29, 320–22, 324–25, 339
Wire, The, 374–75
working classes, 25, 26, 27, 154, 324
wow, 215, 217
Wyatt, Justin, 330

X (formerly Twitter), 201, 248–55

Younger, David, 189
YouTube, 112, 275, 343, 347, 349–51, 355, 358

Zhang, Cat, 104
zombies, 75–76, 90–91
Zuo, Mila, 48
Zwartjes, Arianne, 140, 149n10